ANALYZE WEST

A Psychiatrist Takes Western Civilization on a Journey of Transformation

DR NICHOLAS BEECROFT

Analyze West:
A Psychiatrist Takes Western Civilization on a Journey of Transformation

Copyright © 2014 Dr Nicholas Beecroft

Analyze West Oil Painting by Melanie Mortiboys Copyright © 2014

ISBN-13: 978-1500496371
ISBN-10: 1500496375

Book design by Maureen Cutajar
www.gopublished.com

ACKNOWLEDGE~

Melanie Mortiboys has been fundamental t~
incubation, birth and delivery. She has been the~
ment, challenge, support, wisdom and good judge~.
the cover picture. When Melanie interviewed me at the ~
series, she asked, 'If you imagine Western Civilization bein~
your PA says on the phone, 'Excuse me, Dr Beecroft, we have an~
It's Mr or Mrs Western Civilization,' what would you say the state o~ ~on's
mind, body, and soul is right now?' That concept enabled the book to fl~ ~e with
ease through improvisation, acting all the parts myself.

Very special thanks to my friend Matthew McGuinness for his literary wisdom and encouragement. Matthew generously shared his professional skills as Chief Editor, proofreader and literary consultant.

My mum was the first person to read the first draft of the book as it was written. Her enthusiasm and encouragement helped draw it out of me. Thanks to Howard Donenfeld who patiently coaxed me into action.

The early drafts of **ANALYZE WEST** were edited on four continents by Matthew McGuinness, Linda Beecroft, Nisaar Dawood, Howard Donenfeld, Soleira Green, Fareed Haddad, Samuel Humphreys, Jane MacAllister, Melanie Mortiboys, Chris Parish, Matthew Wall and Dick Werling.

ANALYZE WEST is the product of 30 years work so there are a vast number of people who have helped and inspired me. For example, Mr Fairman taught me to explore history from every perspective. Dr Peter Salmon taught me the Philosophy of Science. Dr Stott taught me to examine a patient with intention. Thanks to the patients, doctors and nurses who taught me the art and science of medicine, psychotherapy and psychiatry.

Thanks to my dad for inspiring me to be a curious, questioning explorer and to debate. He taught me that each person has their own world view and perceptions. Thirty years later, Dr Don Beck trained me in *Spiral Dynamics Integral* which is built upon the Emergent, Cyclical, Double Helix Model of Adult Biopsychosocial Development of Professor Clare Graves. In Graves's words, 'What I am proposing is that the psychology of the mature human being is an unfolding, emergent, oscillating, spiralling process, marked by progressive subordination of older, lower-order behaviour systems to newer, higher-order systems as man's existential

...rehensive, powerful and elegant theory of human ...seen. Don has been a selfless role model and source of ...agement. More information at www.spiraldynamics.net

...ed *Eye Movement Desensitisation and Reprocessing Therapy* on some of West's core emotional wounds. Francine Shapiro discovered and developed EMDR which is by far the most powerful psychological technique I've used or experienced. These EMDR sessions were created live, playing both parts myself. The results may seem strange or far-fetched to those not familiar with the therapy, but I can assure you that they're authentic. If you'd like to know more about EMDR, visit www.emdr.com

Voice Dialogue Technique gives voice to West's many different subparts and peers. *Voice Dialogue* was invented by Hal and Sidra Stone. I was introduced to it by Mark Josephs-Serra and Samuel Humphreys. For more information, see www.voicedialogueinternational.com

ANALYZE WEST frequently refers to the *Victim Triangle* and *The Empowerment Dynamic*. They are the work of Drs Eric Berne, Stephen Karpman and David Emerald. For further information, visit http://powerofted.com

This book sits on the shoulders of a vast number of people from the first caveman through to Socrates and on to current day thinkers and researchers. A comprehensive list of acknowledgements would be hundreds of thousands of pages long. Thanks to all of them.

Thank you to Ambassadors Peter Ford and Sami Khiyami, Scilla Elworthy, Adela Gooch, Wilton Park, the Defence Academy and the British Council for opening up the world of International Relations. Thanks to the London Business School, McKinsey & Co. and many others for introducing me to the business world. I learned Energetics with Soleira Green, Jane MacAllister and Santari Green. Jewels Wingfield introduced me to Tantra. The Mankind Project and the Culture of Honouring taught me much about the path of inner leadership. Thanks to Charmaine Lane for facilitating me in Equine Facilitated Learning. To learn more, visit www.charmainelane.com

Josh Archer and Peter Ford were the first to suggest that I should have a go at writing. I'd also like to thank Martin Rutte, Cherie Beck, Dorothy West, Robin Wood, Neil Doncaster, Andrew Booth, Alasdair Honeyman, Michelle Moreau, Chris Collins, Mike Baxter, Chris Manning, Russ Volckmann, Andrew Campbell and Jan Mattsson for their support and encouragement.

Thank you to all those who took part in the **FUTURE OF WESTERN CIVILIZATION** interviews: Melanie Mortiboys, Joseph McCormick, Martin Rutte, Dr Mary Gentile, Professor Jim Garrison, Dr Elisabet Sahtouris, Traci Fenton, Howard Bloom, Andrew Cohen, Dr Robin Wood, Chris Parish, Dr Don Beck, Herb Meyer, Neil Howe, Lynne McTaggart, Peggy Holman,

ACKNOWLEDGEMENTS

Richard Barrett, Bishop Michael Nazir-Ali, Adrian Wagner, Joshua Gorman, Dr Robin Youngson, Jordan MacLeod, Mark Walsh, Soleira Green, Jim Rough, Joshua Gorman, Peter Merry, Helen Titchen Beeth, Nkata Masembe, Barnaby Flynn, Danny Lambert, John Bunzl, Jon Freeman, Phil Neisser, Jacob Hess, Georgeanne Lamont, Peter Smith, Angeline Ruredzo, Steve Boley and Masana De Souza.

WARNINGS

Do not use the simplified descriptions in this book to attempt EMDR without training. EMDR is an extremely powerful technique and can have harmful side effects, especially in untrained hands. If you want to try it, consult an accredited practitioner.

ANALYZE WEST contains a diverse range of voices and opinions. It's inevitable that you won't agree with all of them. Some are voices which are suppressed or taboo in polite, politically correct society. Some may be offensive to you. If you are not comfortable with that, then please give away your book to someone who will appreciate it.

If you would like to know the author's personal opinions, read the final chapter, The 21st Century Magna Carta or read his next book *The New Magna Carta: A Psychiatrist's Prescription for Western Civilization.*

http://newmagnacarta.org

CONTENTS

MEETING WEST

I quietly placed my knife and fork on the plate, not wanting to wake the nurse who was sleeping at the next table. I had only slept two hours myself, having been woken during the night and called into the hospital. Right now, after enjoying a plateful of bacon and eggs together with a cup of coffee in the canteen, I was feeling satisfied and relaxed. The hospital canteen had few windows, looking like a 1970s airport departure lounge. It functioned twenty-four hours a day, and at any hour of day or night the staff gave off the same resentful vibe. I looked around at the women slowly wiping tables, dishing up food and taking money at the check out. Something about the way they moved made me feel positively guilty, although I had no idea why.

'Paedo's Rights' ran the headline of the *Daily Mail*. I read on. A foreign paedophile had successfully avoided deportation – something to do with his right to family life. A woman had agreed to a sham marriage with him in exchange for £5000, circumventing the immigration system. The headline of *The Guardian* didn't do much to raise my spirits: 'Climate Catastrophe!' Apparently if we didn't act soon, hundreds of millions of us would be displaced by floods and extreme weather events, provoking war and revolution worldwide.

My phone buzzed to announce a text message and interrupted my reading: 'Hi James,' the message said. 'Please call Suki in the ED xn 2378.' I tiptoed past the sleeping nurse to the internal phone by the door.

'Hi, it's James,' I said, picturing Suki as I spoke – her loving eyes and seductive smile.

'Thanks for calling so quickly,' she said. 'Sorry to interrupt your breakfast.'

'No problem. No problem at all. Anytime.'

She laughed and a blush prickled my cheeks. 'I'll hold you to that,' she said.

'What can I do for you?' I said, doing my best to sound business-like.

'We have a Mr Jones here. Abdominal pain. Fifty-six years old. Married. An accountant. The surgeons say there's nothing physically wrong with him. He's had gastrointestinal symptoms for years. Would you mind seeing him?'

Two minutes later I was in the Emergency Department. Suki was looking particularly sexy in her blue hospital scrubs, attending a patient in bed. I had previously guessed that she must be about 35 or 36 – 7 or 8 years younger than me. She was a dark brunette with deep brown eyes. I didn't know the first thing about her background, but she looked part Chinese and part European. As I was using the hand wash by the Emergency Room door I couldn't help but look over in her direction. Jane, a nurse loitering nearby, caught my eye and winked, making my cheeks burn again – I've always been prone to blushing.

1

Suki turned around, smiling broadly as I approached. 'Hi James. Mr Jones is over there in bed 7. It's his fifth visit this year. We're pretty sure it's nothing serious but we can't explain his symptoms.' Her voice was distractingly attractive, with an upbeat Australian accent. She showed me through the patient's notes, and as she was leaving I felt her hand lightly brush my elbow, then she was gone, hurrying off to her next case.

For goodness sake! What was I thinking, fawning over female colleagues like a lovesick adolescent? I resolved to pull myself together and flicked through the medical notes again before crossing the room to bed number 7.

'Good morning Mr Jones,' I said. 'I'm Dr James Hill. Consultant Psychiatrist.'

'A counsellor? I thought I was going to see a doctor.'

I chuckled, well used to this kind of reaction. 'Don't worry, I *am* a doctor. A senior doctor. How can I help?'

'I come here time and time again with bloating, tummy pain and diarrhoea and they can't get to the bottom of it!'

While we were talking I noticed, out of the corner of my eye, that the man in the next bed was listening intently. He was tall, with dark brown hair, and his spare tyre made a hump in the bedclothes. Eventually I became so distracted that I just had to look at the man directly. His face was reddish, and beads of sweat could be seen on his forehead. He met my gaze calmly and I had to look away.

Mr Jones finally finished describing his symptoms and I set about explaining the mind-body-spirit connection to him. He was sceptical, but, nevertheless, allowed me to teach him abdominal massage and even managed to focus long enough to be guided through an abdominal meditation. As he was running his attention run through his gut, he suddenly reddened and tensed, his eyes welling up with tears.

'I cheated on my wife,' whispered Mr Jones. He started to sob. 'She's a lovely women, so kind and caring but after we had children we stopped having sex. At first she didn't feel like it, then we grew apart, becoming more like friends than lovers. One day, I met Lucy.' He cried, breathing deeply, holding his abdomen. 'Lucy is the love of my life. She used to be my tennis partner.' He found it hard to speak, trying to hold back the tears. 'Five years ago, at the Christmas party, we drank too much and one thing led to another. Ever since, I've felt sick every morning when I wake up.'

Suki had returned to see to the patient in the bed next door. 'Mr West,' I could hear her saying. 'Your electrocardiogram is fine. Quite normal. And your blood tests are all clear. I'd like you to see the psychiatrist.'

I tried to focus on the patient in front of me. 'Mr Jones, place your attention on that guilty, nauseated sensation and make it as intense as you can. Picture your wife at home, so loyal and kind, unaware of your transgression.'

His face reddened again, tears flowing.

'Let go of the images and notice on the sensations in your stomach, your gut. Allow your memory to float back to the earliest time you experienced that feeling.'

Mr Jones concentrated patiently for a while, then his eyes lit up. 'When I was 7, I got into trouble with my teacher. Some money had gone missing from her purse in the classroom at lunchtime. I didn't take it but she wouldn't believe me. She told my dad. He slapped me round the face and sent me to bed without dinner. I was so upset. I haven't thought about that for years.' I arranged to see him in clinic the following week.

Suki's voice called out when I was almost at the door. 'James. I was wondering if you would you mind seeing Mr West in bed six before you go. I've checked him out and I'm pretty sure he's having panic attacks.'

'Actually I'm a bit busy just now,' I said, doing my best to look casual. 'Just call Jean and book him in for a routine appointment.'

As I began to make my escape, a deep male voice called out: 'Doctor, can I have a word?' It was Mr West in bed. He was 45, a little overweight although he carried it well on his broad frame. He was sitting up in bed with sticky electrodes attached to his chest for an electrocardiogram. In addition to a blue hospital pyjama top, he was wearing pinstripe suit trousers, which had a black belt fastened rather too tightly. His shiny black brogues were resting on the hospital blanket. The main feature of his face was a strong jawline. There were bags under his eyes and his features generally looked a little puffy. I could smell the residual alcohol on his breath.

'May I have a few moments of your time?' he said. There was a compelling quality in his voice, which I found hard to resist.

'Hello there,' I replied, walking towards his bed. 'I'm Dr James Hill, Consultant Psychiatrist.'

'West,' he said. 'Doctor, I'd really rather see you today, if you don't mind.' His blue eyes scanned for my reaction. They were dull and looked yellowish where they should have been white.

What was it about that voice? A moment later I found myself calling, Jean to make an appointment on West's behalf.

'I've got a free slot at 14.30,' I told him. Walk across the hospital gardens to the second floor in the Psychiatry Outpatients Department.'

And so it began.

———◆———

Just before my afternoon clinic, I went to check on my inpatients on the Bernie Rosen Unit, named after my most inspiring teacher. Bernie was an eclectic pragmatist, a holistic psychiatrist who understood the limitations of science and the value of the art of medicine. Built in the 1980s the unit was like a lot of rabbit hutches stacked on top of one another. The windows were small and the rooms stuffy and claustrophobic. It could feel like a prison with all the locking doors and cheap plastic chairs. I wouldn't want to be treated there myself. We like to think we're modern and advanced, but the Victorians had a lot more common sense. They built beautiful spacious asylums with large windows, usually set in peaceful parkland. Those were sold off in the 80s and 90s to developers who converted them into upmarket apartments. The patients were discharged to live alone or in small homes. It was called care in the community, a good idea – in theory.

The nurses' office was behind a glass screen from where they could observe the patients in the lounge. Phil let me in. He was a very experienced no nonsense kind of nurse with 30 years' experience – very friendly, but you just knew he wasn't to be messed with.

'Afternoon James. Did you bring me some lunch?' Phil's broad face opened up with a smile.

'I got you Beef Wellington with a bottle of 1998 St Emilion but unfortunately it was confiscated by the Health and Safety Officer.'

'Would you mind sticking your head into the meeting room? There's a case conference about Harriet Meyer. Ayesha wants top cover on the suicide risk assessment.'

'Should I be worried?' I asked.

'No,' he replied, swatting the question out of the air with his big hand. 'She's butt covering of course – reverse engineering the coroner's paperwork just in case something goes wrong. Everyone plays it safe around here now. They haven't forgotten the witch hunt after the last suicide.'

I diverted to the meeting room, and, after half an hour of circular discussion, emerged with fifty percent less energy. Phil gave me a knowing smile as I passed his station. He put two fingers together and stuck them in his mouth, miming the action of blowing his brains out. Dark humour is a tonic that helps us through.

I took the stairs up to the second floor, heading for my office. Jean, my PA was at her desk reading Hello magazine.

'Hey! I've warned you about reading that. It rots the brain.'

She looked up and gave me one of her looks. 'Not as fast as that red wine you guzzle, my love,' she said.

Women like Jean used to run the world before management went all corporate. She was 55 with changeable hair colour and a kind face that put people immediately at their ease. However, under that friendly and deferential exterior there was a powerful woman who knew everyone and everything. If she wanted something to happen it did. If she didn't, it didn't. In the past, doctors thought they ran the show, but really it was the army of Jeans.

'Casualty phoned up with a new patient for you at 14:30. Mr West. I can't find him on the system. Did you get his date of birth and address?'

'No, sorry. It didn't occur to me.'

Jean's voice followed me around the corner. 'Dr Sugden asked if you could do your stats for this month.'

I pulled a face and pretended I hadn't heard.

'You must meet your targets or you'll have to report to the Meadows for a spanking,' called Jean a little louder.

In the safety of my office, I slumped down in one of my brown leather armchairs and closed my eyes.

I awoke with a jolt. I could taste stomach acid in my throat. The clock said 14:47.

'Mr West called to say that he'd had second thoughts,' said Jean as I sheepishly emerged from the office. 'He decided he didn't really need to see you, so I let you sleep. Shall I call him to rearrange?'

'No need Jean,' I said. 'If he changes his mind again, I'd be happy to see him another time. I'm going to escape while the coast is clear.'

———— ◆ ————

My journey home through the West London traffic was slow. The nights were drawing in. As I opened my front door, Nga, my part-time pet cat dashed in and up the stairs. Two years earlier, when I was sitting in the back garden, she had launched herself over my neighbours' fence and introduced herself with a loud 'Ngaaaaaaa!' Since then, she had visited often.

I put the heating on full blast. Sometimes, on coming home, I wished there could be a family waiting for me, but mostly I was happy to enjoy my own company. I'd had a lot of girlfriends but had never settled down. The fridge was bare apart from a block of cheddar cheese and a ready-made shepherd's pie – forty-five minutes on full power. I poured myself a gin and tonic. The TV remote control was under the sofa, along with the dust, dried crisps and Nga's tortoiseshell hair. I recovered it and clicked the on button. The screen came to life with the BBC News Channel.

Before I could work out what the news report was all about, my pager went off. 'Hi James, it's Suki. Please call.' My heart pumped faster. I took a deep breath and stood up.

'Hello, Dr Chen,' she said in her melodic Australian accent.

'Hi Suki, it's James.'

'How did you get on with Mr West this afternoon?'

'He didn't turn up.'

'Oh, that's a shame,' said Suki.

'I had a snooze instead.'

'Lucky you. I wish I could have done that too. I've only just got home.'

The thought of Suki lying on the sofa with me was irresistible. I briefly thought about asking her out but pushed the thought away. I was her senior. If I misjudged the situation, the authorities would have me up for abusing my authority. I let the chat go on, and soon the moment had passed.

———— ◆ ————

Next morning, coming in late after a home visit, I had to drive around the staff car park four times before finding a space. As I walked to my office, the golden autumn leaves strewn across my path almost made up for it.

Jean looked distressed. 'James, I'm sorry. I couldn't stop him,' she said quietly, pointing to my office door.

'Stop who?'

'Mr West. He turned up without an appointment. He's already in your office. He said he had to see you immediately. I can't find him on the computer. I don't think he has a General Practitioner.'

'Is it an emergency?' I asked.

'It doesn't look like it, he was determined to see you straight away. Your 2 o'clock patient cancelled so you have an hour.'

'Thanks Jean. I'll see him.'

I went into the staff WC, flushed the toilet and took a long look at myself in the mirror, checking for any new grey hairs. I found my first last year, aged 43. I had been horrified. I leant forward to check the red patch on my nose. Probably rosacea, but you never know.

I opened my office door. There was Mr West wearing a blue chalk pinstripe suit, sitting with his back to me, apparently staring at the wall.

'Hello there.' I said

He stood up quickly to shake my hand. 'Hello Doctor.' His eyes were clearer than when I had last seen him. He seemed to scrutinise my face momentarily – uncertain. It gave me an impression of some distress under that confident, smart exterior. 'Thanks for seeing me. I know it's rude to barge in like this but I can't use normal channels.'

'Oh? Why's that?'

'I'm an unusual case. I'd like it to be off the record.'

West turned to face the wall, pointing to my oil paintings. 'What marvellous pictures you have! Are they yours?'

'Yes they are. Thanks for noticing.'

'Very bright and colourful. Part of me loves that expressionistic style. Part of me thinks they're awful, utter nonsense, childish.'

I laughed and West seemed to realise what he had said. He gave a snort of laughter and smoothed his hair. 'Sorry. I often get in trouble for blurting out every thought that runs through my head.'

'Oh don't worry. I've had much worse comments than that. Would you like a drink?'

'I could murder a gin and tonic. Ice and lemon, please.' We chuckled and I poured us both a glass of water.

West sat in one of my two leather armchairs. They were always angled at 270°, mine facing the window, just as I had been taught in medical school. It was good advice, as I learned early on in my career – being able to look over a patient's shoulder at the trees and sky helps keep you stay grounded.

West's belly was spilling over his belt. He let out a deep sigh. 'Sorry I cancelled yesterday. I've been putting this off for years.'

'That's all right. People come when they're ready or when nature gives them no choice. But look, it sounds a bit too formal calling you West. What's your first name?'

'You'll laugh. Actually it's Western Civilization.'

I must have looked surprised.

'I know, I know,' he said. 'It's a terrible mouthful. Most people just call me the West.'

Was this some kind of practical joke? Maybe Jean was about to burst in with a TV crew. I maintained my poker face. 'How about "Mr West"?' I suggested.

'Well, I'm not sure about mister,' he said. 'I'm part masculine and part feminine. Some people say I'm more masculine than feminine, but they don't know me very well. Just call me West, Doctor.'

'As you wish.'

'One more thing,' said West. 'Can we keep this between the two of us? I don't want this all over the media. That would be quite embarrassing for me, to say the least.'

'Everything you say here is confidential.' I reassured him, 'Unless you tell me that you plan to kill someone or harm yourself.'

'Well, it has been known,' he laughed. But on seeing my raised eyebrows he quickly moved to explain himself. 'Oh, don't worry. This body that you see in front of you is quite harmless – just a convenience.'

Five minutes into the first session and this was already one of the strangest cases I'd ever seen.

'Think of it as a vessel,' he continued. 'How can I explain it? I've distilled my essence – you could call it the spirit of Western Civilization – and poured it into a human form so that we can have this conversation.'

I looked out over West's shoulder at the trees and sky for a moment. 'Let's backtrack a little,' I said. You believe yourself to be Western Civilization …'

'No, no. It's not a question of belief Doctor. I'm not mad. I really am the group consciousness of The West – Western Civilization. Listen to your heart. You know it's true. After all, I am present everywhere, even in you.'

I made a note and moved on.

'I want to set some ground rules,' I said.

'Yes, yes, I know about all that. Confidentiality, respect, professional ethics. Now can we please get on with it?'

'You're pretty bossy aren't you? Used to being in charge.'

'Quite. I've ruled the roost for 300 years.'

'Well, firstly, I like to record my sessions so that I have a record of them for medico-legal reasons and so that we can refer back to them at a later date. Sometimes people find it useful to listen to the consultations to see how much they have progressed,' I said.

'No. I can't risk that falling into the hands of the media or my competitors. They'd discover my weaknesses. I'd never live it down.'

'The digital recorder encrypts the recordings with a password,' I said. I showed him the recorder.

'All right. Fair enough. What's the password?'

'You choose,' I suggested.

'Rejuvenation2014.'
I set up the recorder, configured the password, and the session began.

James: West session one. Initial Assessment.

James: How old are you?

West: I don't know exactly. About 3000 years old.

James: Where do you live?

West: Most of me lives in Europe, the United States, Canada, Australia, New Zealand and South Africa, although there are little bits of me everywhere these days. I'm spread all across South America, Africa and Asia. I live in the minds of people. I live in the culture and the institutions, the habits and the behaviours.

James: What do you do?

West: I'm a conscious being, the group mind of the modern world.

James: How long have you been having panic attacks?

West: On and off since I was young. More frequently since 2008.

James: Any idea what triggered that?

West: I think it was a few years ago. I found myself a matter of days away from economic meltdown. If I'd let that happen, very soon the oil and petrol would have been scarce. There would have been food riots, anarchy and chaos. My enemies would have dismembered me.

James: I remember that. It was bad. We've lost a lot of staff here and we've all taken a pay cut.

West: Be careful, you'll set me off again.

James: Do you have any other worries?

West: How can I put this? Basically, I've lost my mojo. For a long time I was top dog but now the others are catching up. I fight myself all the time. The First World War, Second World War and Cold War – they were all disastrous. I've seen endless battles between liberals and conservatives, postmodernists and traditionalists, black and white, men and women, children and their parents. In all that, I lost my way. I don't know where I'm going. What's the point of it all? Sometimes I wish I were dead. Financially, I've been depressed. I'm creative but others steal my ideas. I'm strong but the Chinese, Arabs, Indians, Pakistanis, Iranians and the North Koreans are becoming much stronger. I feel dreadfully insecure most of the time.

James: Carry on.

West: I used to be able to count on my own dominance in the minds of Europeans at least. Superior technology, organisation and economics gave me a free run of the world. Things were looking good. India embraced democracy, science and capitalism. China learned from my success in Hong Kong and scaled it up 100 times over. Globally, I'm flowing through everyone now, although mixed up with their local cultures, so I've lost a bit of clarity. These other countries have become successful and it's all through adopting my ideas. But the thing is, they don't acknowledge my influence, and worse than that, they see me as a competitor. It reminds me of the days before the First World War.

James: Very unsettling.

West: I'm not sure who I am anymore. I've experienced mass immigration into Europe, Canada, Australia, New Zealand and America. I think that's a sign of my success, but some of the newcomers don't fully believe in me. They enjoy the economy, education, law, healthcare, security and government but some remain loyal to foreign religions and identities. Part of me wants to change the social rules – it's what some people call political correctness – but other parts of me resist that tendency pretty vigorously. Christianity has lost its shine. I've lost my connection with God, spirit, nature, right and wrong, truth.

James: Were you ever really at ease with yourself?

West: Yes. For a long time things were quiet. Travel and communications were much slower and harder. I did my own thing until someone like Genghis Khan turned up with an army. There were turbulent times for sure – during the Crusades for example, when I tried to take back my Holy Lands and my old Eastern Roman Empire, the Byzantine Empire.

James: It sounds like your relationships weren't exactly ideal.

West: Actually it was a long time before I came into contact with other civilizations at all. I didn't know the Americas until the Spanish and Portuguese took me there in the 17th Century. I didn't know the Aborigines or Maoris until recently. I knew the Chinese and Indians were advanced and that Arabs were good at trading and conquest. I had some contact with Africa though we mainly kept ourselves to ourselves.

West lets out a huge yawn. James too.

West: Let me see. I think it was around 1500 that I began to open my mind. I challenged my beliefs, looked at the world differently and started experimenting. I found better ways to grow food. I built ships that sailed long distances and outgunned my competitors. I became ever more creative. The European population boomed and travelled all around the world.

West yawns again.

West: I have to admit I did start to throw my weight around a bit. The Spanish and Portuguese really became powerful all around the world, initially in Africa, then out to the Americas and finally Asia. I was having a great time, expanding, trading and learning a great deal. It was intoxicating – I became the best fighter, no doubt about that. I had great technology, good institutions and excellent finances. All that gave me huge self-confidence.

West looks at the ceiling, caressing his stubbly chin, unconsciously self-soothing like a baby in distress.

West: OK, so then the French, British and Dutch took over the world. They had this tremendous confidence and a warrior spirit. I totally immersed myself in science, and it blew my mind. I loved all those inventions. I was getting around the world more now too, finding myself in more countries, entering more systems and structures. I felt fantastic. Who wouldn't? All those new ways of organising things, huge advances in knowledge, new methods of manufacture, and...

West is stopped mid-sentence by a gigantic yawn.

James: You know we don't need to get all this done in one go.

West: Sure, sure. I'm fine. What was I saying?

James: About science and manufacturing.

West: Actually, there's something else I want to say. I made a mistake.

James: Oh?

West: Yes. It was to do with race. I had this idea. I thought I only belonged to white people. You have to remember, it was normal back then to attribute successes and failures to race, gender or ethnicity.

West pauses and looks up to the ceiling. His eyes are oscillating side to side.

West: I'm tired.

James: I can tell. You've been carrying a lot of weight. Maybe you're trying too hard. Are you running out of resources? Energy?

West sits up straight, his expression suddenly energetic.

West: You know, I have more people, wealth and knowledge than ever. I'm not down and out yet Doc.

James: Sure.

West: Do you know what I think my problem is?

James: Tell me.

West: My problem is basically a loss of self-confidence, low self-esteem. I have these nightmares. I see it all clearly – a Chinese Empire or some form of religious fundamentalism takes over. That's my main anxiety, that the others have nearly caught up and I've lost my way. In the nightmares I get old, sick and disabled, and that's happening for real of course. To make matters worse I have a vast appetite for oil and gas. I know it's going to run out eventually and it's getting more expensive. That's a real limit on my growth. Part of me wants to solve the problem by inventing a new solution, maybe harness the sun, the wind and waves. Other parts don't see the point. Competitors are fighting harder and harder for access to the oil and gas. It would be a disaster if we got into a war over that. The thing is, I'm already carrying wounds from the last three World Wars. I couldn't face another. I just don't know how it came to this. I used to believe in God and Jesus and all that. I thought it was my destiny to make the world a better place, but now look at it.

Another face-splitting yawn from West.

West: Excuse me. I think that's probably enough for today.

James: I think you're right. Let's finish there. It's been a pleasure to meet you. Before you go, would you mind if I run off some blood tests?

West: No, please do.

James hands over a form. West gets up to leave the office. With his hand on the door handle, he pauses and turns.

West: I'll see you tomorrow, 10AM. Good luck with Dr Chen.

West grins broadly and winks before slamming the door behind him.

I slumped in my chair. What an unusual patient. So immersed in the delusion that he was the spirit of Western Civilization. I spent the next hour recording notes on my Dictaphone until I was interrupted by a knock at the door. It was Jean.

'Doctor, your next patient is waiting.'

'Thanks. I'll be through in a moment.'

———◆———

In my dream someone was knocking at the door and I woke up with a jolt. I looked at the alarm clock beside my bed. It was 4:30AM. Collecting my senses, I realised that someone really was banging at the front door. I rushed downstairs expecting to find a neighbour in trouble on my doorstep, but peering round the living room curtain I saw a strange man in a hoodie, jeans and running shoes. I quickly pulled back from the window, my heart pumping faster. Who could it be? Should I call the police? Slowly and carefully I eased back the curtain, and there in front of me, immediately on the other side of the window, was a face. I flinched back with a yelp, before I realised it was the face of West. He was waving at me.

Well, at least it wasn't a burglar. However, a great many questions were running through my sleepy mind all at the same time. What on earth could he want? Was he dangerously unstable? It didn't occur to me to question how he had found my home address. I hesitated a moment behind the curtain, decided against calling the police and went to open the door. West stepped over the threshold. His hair was a mess.

'Yo James!' He bellowed at me as he held out his hand. I winced, already regretting my decision.

James: Morning West. Very early morning in fact.

West gives a very firm handshake — overcompensating. His sweatshirt has a large peace symbol on it.

West: I want to see you.

James wipes the sleep from his eyes.

James: Yes, certainly, of course, when?

West: Now, of course, now. I want to put right the nonsense he told you yesterday. It's important you get the story straight and do the job properly.

James: Who is 'he?' Wasn't that you I spoke to yesterday?

West pushes past James and immediately makes his way upstairs.

West: Show me the kitchen, man. I'll make the coffee while you get yourself dressed.

West walks with a swagger today, like a 1968-vintage street-fighting man. He looks at the paintings on the wall with contempt.

West: What terrible bourgeois pastiche. Just what I would expect from a psychiatrist.

James: It's 4:30AM. I'm happy to see you but I do need to set boundaries.

West: Boundaries? You people are all about boundaries, so long as you're in control. You're like him, a bully and control-freak. Chill man. Go take a shower. I'll help myself to breakfast.

James: No, West. This is my private space.

West: Property is theft.

James: Oh right. In that case, give me the keys to the nearest bank and I'll help myself. That's OK is it?

West grins broadly.

West: Yeah, cool. We can break in there and return the wealth to the people.

James: West, I'm not going to see you now and not here. I'll see you at the coffee shop on the corner at 7 o'clock.

West frowns and looks James deep in the eyes.

West: Dude, you're a real tight ass. But you've got a kind soul underneath all that doctor bullshit. OK. I'll see you in the coffee shop at seven.

He seemed deflated as he walked off down the path, but regained a spring in his step when he reached the street. I closed the door, took a deep breath and made my way back to bed. It was 5 o'clock. While setting the alarm on my phone I saw there was a text message, received at 01:26. 'Hi James. Fancy lunch today? Suki x.'

———◆———

I made a point of enjoying the fresh November morning sunshine – not much more of that left, with winter closing in. The leaves were half fallen from the birch trees in my street, crisp underfoot. I could smell the coffee at Zack's Café from twenty yards away, drawing me in. The windows were steamy but I could make out West, slouching on a huge sofa, his feet up on the table.

'Yo James,' said West, a little too loudly, as I approached. 'I got an Americano for you. Hot milk there. Help yourself to a pain au chocolat. I sat in the armchair next to him. He had a cappuccino moustache and crumbs on his sweatshirt.

'That's very thoughtful,' I said. 'How did you pass the time?'

'Tai Chi in the park. How about you? Thinking about Doctor Chen in the shower maybe?' The women at the next table began to fidget and cast glances.

'West,' I said, fixing his gaze, 'from now on, I'm only going to see you in my office by appointment. If you intrude in my private space again, I'll call the police and discharge you as a case.'

'OK, man, chill.'

I noticed West was looking at my website on his iPad.

'How do I measure up?' I asked, genuinely curious.

'I don't know. I'm non-judgmental, unlike most doctors.'

I took a sip of coffee, using the moment to refocus my thoughts.

West beat me to it: 'James, I have to set you straight on that bullshit you were told yesterday. That old story about how he brought democracy and freedom, science and the rule of law. I expect he tried to tell you capitalism has raised more people out of poverty than socialism too, didn't he? I bet he didn't tell you about the bad stuff though – the genocides, the destruction of the planet, the exploitation of women and the poor.

I had seen multiple personality cases before, but this was something special. The different parts are usually not aware of one another. This West clearly knew all about the other one.

West: He didn't tell you that we plundered the world, did he? Didn't mention that we colonised and exploited, or that men have dominated women for 5000 years since the invention of agriculture. He probably skipped over the Holocaust, slavery and the desecration of the world by corporations. Science and capitalism have devalued compassion, intuition and love. We factory farm old people. The 1% exploit the 99%. We die from diseases that our hunter gathering ancestors never knew. Corporations get doctors to pump us full of their drugs whose main effect is to enrich the shareholders. We used to live in harmony with nature, now we drive round in cars, insulated from reality. The media keeps us distracted and brainwashed.

James: You seem very angry West.

West: Of course! It's all very well for you, Mr white middle class male doctor. What would you know about victimhood?

James: I thought you said you were non-judgmental.

West: Those clothes were probably made in a Bangladeshi factory by a child working 18 hours a day in dangerous conditions. Why should they have a lower standard of living because they live in a different place? We've got military bases in over a 100 countries. It's a ravenous empire. I hope you sort West out. The world would be better off without him.

James: Aren't you part of West? Do you hate yourself that much?

> *West looks James straight in the eye, then leans forward with his head in his hands and sobs loudly. The other customers and the staff are staring. After a few moments West sits up and takes a sip of coffee with reddened eyes. He looks at James as if for the first time.*

West: I hate myself. I'm ashamed of my past, my privileges, the victims. I feel suicidal sometimes you know. I'd do anything just to get away from the pain.

> *He finishes his cappuccino in silence.*

James: West, it seems to me you have different parts to your personality that you show in different circumstances. That's normal. We're all a bit like that. I use a technique called Voice Dialogue to express and integrate these different parts.

West: I'm up for anything Doc. Anything that works.

> *James retrieves a notebook from his jacket pocket and flips through several pages.*

James: OK, so, let me check that I understand you. You're called West and you're the consciousness or spirit of Western Civilization. You live in the minds of billions of people around the world. Europeans took you around the world by colonisation and trade. You have deep roots in America, Canada, Australia, New Zealand and South Africa, but in fact you've left your traces just about everywhere. Is that right?

West: Yes, although you forgot to mention South and Central America. I'm big there too. It's just that I got mixed up with the local indigenous cultures. There are quite a lot of places where I'm present in a hybrid form, mingling with the local culture: Japan, Turkey and Russia for example. You know, you can even find me in Tehran and Beijing. Robert Mugabe comes to London to do his shopping. Kim Jong-un loves my technology, films and basketball. There's hardly anyone on the face of the earth that I haven't touched.

James flips over some more pages.

James: And I gather you're suffering from a loss of self-confidence, inner conflict, feelings of self-hatred. Part of you has a strong impulse towards self-harm or suicide. You lack clarity about who you are and where you're going. You're struggling to pay the bills. You feel threatened and insecure. You used to have a clear idea of right and wrong, what's true and false, but you've lost your way, lost your inner compass. You lost your connection to God, the sacred and the divine. Part of you thinks that was all rubbish anyway. You're proud of your successes but there have been numerous costs, mistakes and sacrifices. You've harmed your environment. Your way of life is stressful. You feel especially guilty about the Holocaust, slavery and imperialism. You're concerned about equality, fairness and justice. You're not sure how to integrate new migrants. Is that it?

West nods.

James: Right. Now I'm going to ask some quick fire questions, and I want you to answer without thinking too much. OK?

West: Fire away.

James: What's your purpose?

West: To fulfil the maximum potential of human beings.

James: What's your ethnicity?

West: I used to think I was Caucasian, but after mass migration and globalisation I'm multiracial, global, human.

James: Do you have a partner?

West: No. I have masculine and feminine parts. I live in humans, male and female. Individually and collectively I have relationships with other civilizations and cultures.

James: Do you have any children?

West: No.

James: Tell me about your family.

West: Most of my ancestors were hunter-gatherers, stretching right back to the first humans in Africa. When agriculture was invented in the Middle East, cities emerged, connected by trading routes. Consciousness became more complex. Technology spread across Asia and Europe. Different areas developed distinct civilizations. The Greeks, Romans and pagans are on my paternal side and Judaism and Christianity on my maternal side. Over centuries, they merged to form me.

James: Tell me about your childhood.

West: Repressive and conservative. It went on for about 2500 years. Often hungry. Always fighting. The plague was terrible. I nearly died. I became more confident after that, started thinking differently and challenging my old ideas. The people loosened up their old hierarchies, sharing power and resources more. I started to think more clearly. My mum taught me the Christian story in a strict and literal way. Parts of me secretly doubted it. Others were zealous and puritanical. Gradually, I loosened up and I began to think rationally and scientifically.

James: What do you mean by that?

West: I became conscious of my reasoning, judgement and tested out my assumptions. I experimented with new ways of thinking. I came up with new ideas, new theories, new ways of looking at things. I found it useful to break things down into small parts and perceive them as separate objects.

James: How did you perceive things before that?

West: My ancestors lived by their instinct, integrated with nature. I broke with tradition by perceiving things as separate, observing and measuring them. I noticed objects had properties and searched for the laws of nature through trial and error, experimenting to test out my theories. It was exciting but rather frightening because I was challenging the foundations of my way of life. My religious and traditional parts often resisted change.

James: Tell me about your education.

West: The Greeks gave me a foundation in philosophy. The Romans were more practical. Until 500 years ago, the Chinese, Arabs and Indians were more advanced than me.

We didn't communicate much. I traded and communicated with my Arab neighbours in the Mediterranean. They learned a lot from Greek science and philosophy, which I then promptly forgot. Fortunately the Arabs saved all that knowledge, which I relearned from them in the Middle Ages. They gave me the letters of the alphabet. They were good at maths, astronomy, architecture and trading.

James: How did you get ahead?

West: Clear scientific thinking. The rule of law. Good organisation. A strong moral and social foundation in Christianity. Trading. Warfare. Fierce competition between my Kingdoms. There's nothing like competition to spur on creativity.

James is staring out of the window and sucking his pen.

West: Doctor, are you listening?

James: Sorry, my mind wandered for a moment.

West: Would you like more coffee?

West attracts the attention of the waitress.

James: What did you do with all that new knowledge?

West: Gradually, I improved agriculture and justice, built better ships, expanded my universities, grew my economy. The Portuguese and Spanish were courageous and adventurous. They conquered the Americas. Gradually, they lost their dynamism and became rigid. Holland, France and England allowed people to think freely, speak their minds, debate and challenge authority. They made it safe for people to trade and own property. They learnt how to use capitalism to liberate human potential. They gave asylum to dissidents. The people started freeing themselves up from old hierarchies and, slowly, they developed what we now call democracy.

James: How did that feel?

West: Exciting. Scientists and inventors were buzzing. People created new kinds of literature, art and music. Take Mozart and Beethoven – 200 years later, they're still amazing. There's nothing like it in other cultures. I feel embarrassed to say that now.

James: We'll explore that embarrassment another time.

West: If you look at what's happened in China over the last 30 years, that started in

England with the Industrial Revolution 250 years ago, powered by freedom, capitalism and democracy. Great Britain became the workshop of the world. In competition with the French, they extended their influence around the globe. The British connected countries and continents through trade, conquest, language and naval supremacy. They established my beliefs and institutions around the world. Throughout the 19th and 20th centuries Europeans and the Americans took me to most parts of the world.

James: Was it all plain sailing?

West: Everyone was forced to submit to me. In America or Australia, I simply crushed the natives and ruled. I didn't mean to destroy their cultures, but it happened as a result of disease and then they lost their spirit and self-confidence. In India and the Far East, Europeans dominated the local hierarchies, introducing laws, trade, education, health and technology. The Japanese excluded me for a long time but the Americans and the British forced them to open up, and then they knew they had to embrace me, at least in part, or they would become a colony too. The Chinese resisted me but were forced to open up by the British. I made a huge success of Hong Kong and as a result it became clear that success wasn't down to race or ethnicity but rather science, capitalism and the rule of law. Not necessarily democracy, though.

James has stopped taking notes and sits back with his arms crossed.

West: Did I say something wrong?

James: Oh, no, not at all. I'm sorry to put you off your stride. But I do have another question. You said something interesting this morning. You said that I shouldn't take what I heard in my office yesterday at face value.

West: Exactly. That's what I'm trying to do here. I'm trying to show you that there's another way of looking at me and my achievements.

James: Sure, and I'd like to thank you for being so thorough. It's certainly a very inspiring story – the triumph of Western Civilization. But just for a moment I'd like to challenge you a little. Obviously, I'm a psychiatrist, and not a historian, but it does seem to me that your account of yourself is no more complete than the one I heard yesterday in the office.

West: But don't you see, that's my point exactly. There are always contrary forces and alternatives pulling this way and that inside me, and none of them is more important than the others. In fact it's precisely this tumult that has contributed to my success – my people are always challenging authority, always questioning things, and that keeps me fit. The English-speaking world fondly remembers the Magna Carta of 1215, when

English nobles and clergy forced King John to sign the 'Great Charter' to enshrine their freedoms and rights. The Jews and the Greeks wove doubt and debate into the fabric of their everyday life. I've always had strong parts of me that resist hierarchical authority and campaign for fairness and justice for the masses. It comes in different forms and Marxism was one of those.

James: You had a long run of success and self-confidence. What brought that to an end?

West: Knowledge spreads quickly. The Germans and Americans overtook the British economically. My competitors, the Russians and Japanese were fast learners. The rivalry led to two world wars. Nearly a 100 million died. My people were physically and emotionally wounded. Europe was bankrupt, although America came out of it very well. Europe lost confidence in me. I thought, 'How can I hurt myself like this? How could I be so stupid?' I lost faith in Christianity. Women demanded equality. People lost respect for old hierarchies. Europeans lost their belief in their right to rule their empires. In the colonies, the locals took seriously my ideas about freedom, democracy, justice and human rights and they learned from my science and technology. So they got richer and better organised. Everyone's expectations of life rose.

James: That sounds like a success, but you're describing it as if it were a failure or problem.

West: It used to be a simple them-and-us situation, but when the non-Europeans started taking on my consciousness and mixing it with their own consciousness and cultures, my identity got blurred.

James: Are you feeling guilty?

West: Yes. It felt like the party came to an end. I woke up with a hangover and felt deep remorse for racism, imperialism, war and the Holocaust.

James: How is your energy level?

West: Below par. The financial worries have got me down. In Europe, about a third of the young people are unemployed. The Africans, Arabs and Chinese seem way more energetic than me.

James: Are you getting enough rest and sleep?

West: I don't allow myself much downtime. I've got a short attention span. I lost contact with my roots. I used to live with the rhythms of nature and no one had a timetable. Now I'm always clock-watching, rushing to the next thing. I don't have time sit still, relax and let my mind go free.

James: Is there any cost to that?

West: When I rest, I become creative, discover new ideas and perspectives. I'm great at having fun with noise and stimulation. I'm putting myself at risk by not thinking ahead.

James: How's your home life?

West: Unsettled. I move around a lot. My relationships come and go. My communities have become weak. The family is still important but I'm not confident that it's in good enough shape as a foundation for difficult times ahead. The bonds are much looser.

James: How's your appetite and weight?

> *West blushes and breaks eye contact. He brushes off the bits of pastry from his sweatshirt.*

West: I'm putting on weight, feeling sluggish. Sometimes I eat healthily – organic food, lean meat, fresh vegetables – but, much of the time, I eat processed junk food. I smoke and drink too much.

James: Do you ever binge or purge?

West: I've been caught in a cycle of binging and dieting ever since the 60s. I haven't adapted to having easy access to processed food and sweets. I gorge on it and then feel guilty. No matter how much weight I lose, I always put it back on again when I feel bad or let go.

James: Do you ever worry about your body image?

West: Parts of me couldn't care less but most of me does want to look good, look attractive, young, sexy. I'm constantly making comparisons with others. The media's full of super-attractive fit bodies, but most people are nothing like that.

James: How's your sex life?

> *West leans forward, speaking quietly.*

West: To tell you the truth, I've totally lost my mojo.

James: What about your people – the one's you live in?

West: Not good. On average, young people are having lots of sex but not enough babies.

The older people don't have enough sex, particularly after they've had children. I used to be quite conservative. Then after the Second World War, I let my hair down. We started using the pill and condoms and went wild. Things have quietened down since the HIV epidemic.

James: Do you ever get suicidal?

West: Yes. I've got a self-destructive part that is so ashamed of the bad things I've done, and my shortcomings, that it doesn't think life is worth living. It thinks I should commit suicide or allow myself to be superseded by my competitors.

James: That can't be pleasant to live with.

West: No, it's horrible. I can be having a good time or feel I've got a good plan and then suddenly, in comes this highly self-critical, abusive voice telling me that everything I ever did was bad, I'm worthless, the world would be a better place if I'd never existed.

James: You told me you been living with these feelings for over a century. Is there any chance you'll act on them?

West: Sometime I have apocalyptic fantasies: death, doom, destruction and the day of judgement. When I'm dealing with hardliners in the Middle East or North Korea, I can get whipped up into an all-or-nothing state where I feel impulsive. I could press the trigger. You know, sometimes I want that.

James: What stops you?

West: Life is good and I enjoy living it, even if I do feel bad sometimes. Things usually get better in the end.

James: Tell me more about the part that wants to die.

West: I'm ashamed about racism, slavery, imperialism, the Holocaust and the other abuses I'm responsible for. I hate myself for that. I'd like to bring together people from all over the world and mix them up so that there are no white people anymore. Then I can let go of my guilt.

James: We're definitely going to need to work on all this guilt and those wounds you're carrying. What about alcohol and drugs?

West: Yes, I enjoy those – often to excess. I gamble. I'm an adrenaline junkie. Caffeine too. I'm always buzzing. It's hard to sit still.

James: Do you ever harm others?

West: Often. Recently, I invaded Iraq and Afghanistan. Historically, I've invaded almost every country. I'm very powerful, so inevitably my presence tends to have a big impact on everyone else – for better or worse. I don't intend to hurt people unless I feel threatened.

James: Tell me about your panic attacks.

West: I'm afraid of terrorism, attacks from enemies, global warming, economic collapse, climate change, destruction of the environment, pandemics. Sometimes it's a background anxiety and sometimes it bursts into a panic attack. The media whips me up into a lather very quickly. It's strange, because I used to be more resilient.

James: Do you get nightmares?

West: I sometimes wake up in the middle of the night terrified like I'm going to be overrun by aliens and violated. Then there's the one about the Earth dying. I imagine I wake up one morning and everything is like a desert because I killed it – God is punishing me by heating the Earth up to boiling point.

West fidgets in his seat, wiping his sweaty forehead.

James: Fair enough, we'll touch on them in the future when appropriate. How's your mood?

West: I'm depressed financially, but I'm not low all the time. I still enjoy things. I have ups and downs.

James: Do you have any traumatic memories?

West: Thousands. The Second World War, the First World War, the Holocaust, colonialism, slavery. Before I became strong enough to resist, the Arabs conquered and colonised the Holy Land, Syria and most of Spain. The Turks took my Byzantine Empire. They got as far as France and Austria before I managed to hold the line. The Barbary pirates from North Africa used to take my people as slaves and raid my coasts as far north as England.

James: Anything else? Anything you're normally less inclined to talk about?

West's top lip contracts and his forehead tenses.

West: Famine and disease. The Spanish flu in 1919. That was very frightening. Millions died. With all the modern communications and the much bigger population we have now, there's a risk of an even more catastrophic plague. We're developing drug resistant superbugs. One day something nasty will kill off half the population and I'll be powerless to stop it.

James: How good is your memory?

West: It used to be easy when the pace of life was slow and there wasn't that much to remember. Now there is such an explosion of information that none of us can keep up. My attention span has become very short. It's not long ago that there was widespread destitution, but now people seem to take their comfort for granted. Human beings quickly forget the lessons of history.

James: What about short term memory?

West: If I forget something, I can find out from the internet or through networks. My memory is very selective. There are so many distractions that it's hard to concentrate.

James: Do you ever get confused?

West: No

James: Irritable?

West: Sometimes.

James: Seizures?

West: Well, occasionally everything just seems to get blocked up and stuck. Like with the Y2K computer bug and 9/11.

James: Blackouts?

West: No.

James: Disinhibition?

West: If I've had a drink or I'm on holiday.

James: Change in bowel habits?

West: No

James: Chest pain?

West: No

> *West looks impatient. He starts cracking his his knuckles.*

James: Do you feel the cold?

West: No, I have central heating.

James: Waterworks?

West: Fine, thank you. Doctor, let me save you time. I'm fat and unfit, I eat and drink too much, I don't rest enough and I need to learn to relax more. Otherwise, my physical health is fine.

James: Fair enough. Are you on any medications?

West: Caffeine, alcohol, sugar. I'm dependent on oil and gas, hydrocarbons. I've made progress with solar, wind, wave and biotech energy but it's a drop in the ocean at this stage.

James: Any family history of illness?

West: I suppose so, yes. The Romans became decadent and overstretched themselves, lost their coherence, self-belief and eventually got overrun by barbarians. I fear the same is going to happen to me.

James: What happened to the Greeks?

West: Similar, I think. I don't know my family history very well. I once knew all about it, but I've forgotten.

James: What about Christianity and Judaism?

West: Christianity is on its deathbed in Europe. In Africa and China it's booming. It'll be easier the more we have in common. Judaism is remarkably resilient and adaptable.

James: Do you have a social life?

West: In the past, things were so-so with most of the world. There were conflicts. We didn't talk much then. But nowadays we meet and trade the whole time. We have fun together when we play sport, like the Olympic Games, which came from the Greeks. It makes me proud that everyone else wants to join in with us. We have creative contact through films, books and music.

James: So your communication with the rest of the world is good now?

West: I know I should learn the others' languages, to get a deeper understanding and to show respect. But I'm too busy. The Brits took English around the world and the Americans globalised it thanks to commerce, films and the Internet. Basically, that makes me lazy.

James: Do you have any social support or friends?

West: I get support from countries and people all over the world both because they share some of my consciousness and because they see their interests aligned with mine.

James: Do you have any enemies?

West: The Russian, Iranian and North Korean regimes think they're my enemies, but I don't see things that way. I see them as competitors. My elites have grown up with peace and liberal pluralism, so they can't relate to the more traditional mind sets of my competitors. This makes them naive and it's often a cause of misunderstanding. Religious fundamentalism defines itself in opposition to me. That makes life complicated because I'd rather get along well with religious people. We have a lot in common. The Chinese are both competitors and collaborators. We both benefit by working together. They've embraced science and law but I'm worried that they won't take on democracy or human rights. My worst enemies are in my own mind.

West sighs and looks at his watch.

James: I don't think you have any major mental illness but you have some issues which need specific therapy. It would be useful to introduce you to a technique which will help you gain awareness of the different parts of yourself. We'll then have a clearer idea of the work to be done. How does that sound?

West: Sure, I'll come tomorrow.

James: OK. This time make it 10AM, not 4.30.

West: I promise.

Before leaving the café I sent a text. 'Hi Suki, See you in Bellini's Sandwich Bar across the road at 1 o'clock? x'

There were some clouds in the sky now, but the sun was still hanging on. Bellini's was bustling as usual. I found a table by the window, put my coat over the back of the chair and went to the toilet. Once there, I checked in the mirror for grey hairs. Still there, over the ears. As I emerged, I saw Suki looking around for me. She was wearing dark blue jeans, rather tight, showing off her shapely legs. I waved. She gave me the most beautiful smile. I held her hand and stepped in to kiss. Although I was aiming for her cheek, the corners of our lips touched. I pulled away, a little embarrassed.

The waitress came to take our order and we chatted about this and that. I had set myself a mission to try and find out about any other men on the scene – boyfriends or baggage – but after some clumsy leading questions on my part Suki clearly decided to cut to the chase.

'Not very subtle are you James?' she observed. 'Would you like to take me on a date?' She was running rings round me. At that moment our food arrived and the moment had passed. When we settled down to eat, Suki changed the subject.

'How are things going with that patient I referred? What was his name?'

'Oh, West. Yes,' I said through a mouthful of chicken and bacon sandwich. 'I've seen him a couple of times now, and I wanted to talk to you about him. What did you think of him?'

Suki pecked daintily at her avocado salad for a moment, thinking before she answered. 'He was terrified – thought he'd had a heart attack. Once he'd calmed down he was normal enough – a bit withdrawn and formal. I don't know why, but I had the impression he might be hiding something.'

She was right. I made a mental note to follow up on that insight.

When we had finished eating, the waitress came with the bill, and before I could do anything, Suki grabbed it and paid, leaving a generous tip.

We crossed the road, back to the hospital.

'About that date,' she said when we were about to head off to our respective departments. 'Thursday night will be fine. You choose where we're going. I like to dress up.' Then she was gone.

THE WAYS WE THINK: OUR VALUE SYSTEMS

West arrived for his appointment dressed in his standard navy blue pinstripe suit. It was slightly too small for him. He made himself comfortable on one of my brown leather armchairs and I started the digital recorder.

James: Welcome back West.

West: Thank you for seeing me.

James: I'd like to introduce you to a framework of ideas, which, I hope, will enable your different parts to speak clearly. As a boy, my dad taught me that everyone you see walking down the same street is operating on a different psychological level. Each person has their own perceptions, beliefs, character, values, circumstances, behaviours, priorities, experiences, cultures, needs, desires, perspectives and different ways of thinking.

West: But hang on, Surely it's just a small step from there to making value judgements about people. I'm committed to equality and diversity.

James: If everyone is different, how can they be equal?

West: It's like this: everyone has equal value as a human being, so of course everyone should be treated equally.

James: If you treat people exactly the same, no matter how they act, surely that's showing a lack of respect for their individuality and a certain naiveté.

West: What do you propose instead?

James: Well, I was taught Spiral Dynamics Integral theory by my friend Dr Don Beck. It's based on pioneering work by Professor Clare Graves in the 60s and 70s. Graves had been challenged by his students to decide which of the many psychological theories was correct. He carried out a naturalistic study in which he invited people to say what constitutes a good life and good leadership and to give their opinions about human nature. He found there were distinct ways of thinking – structures of thought. These are the foundations on which beliefs are constructed.

West: I'm struggling a bit here. Can you give some examples?

James: Of course. He identified eight ways of thinking. Don and his colleague made the whole thing more accessible by giving each value system a colour – as a form of shorthand. Take a look at the chart.

West: BEIGE, PURPLE, RED, BLUE, ORANGE, GREEN, YELLOW, TURQUOISE. What do the colours mean?

James: Each represents a way of thinking, a world view, a value system or memes.

West: Like genes?

James: Yes. We human beings use our intellect, intuition, wisdom, sensations and social awareness to make sense of the world, to make decisions, to survive and thrive. When new challenges and opportunities arise, people activate ways of thinking which help them to adapt to their particular circumstances and challenges.

West: OK, I understand, but why are you telling me this?

James: The way we think drives our behaviour, decisions, relationships and organisation. The way a group thinks determines its culture, belief system and institutions. I think if we understand the eight styles of thought we can better understand the ways that your various parts feel they have to act.

West: So, tell me what the colours mean.

James: Right. With BEIGE thinking, the mind, body and spirit are completely focused on survival.

West: Like when someone is seriously ill?

James: Exactly. We all need food, water, shelter, health and clean air. When those are threatened, everything else is of secondary importance. When those things are secure, people can use their energy in other ways. When BEIGE thinking predominates, people act immediately in the interests of their survival. The culture, if there is one, is directly focused on whatever it takes to get food, water, shelter and bodily safety. In the modern world, the organisation might take the form of an emergency room in hospital, a mother caring for a new born baby or a disaster relief team. At the cultural level people form a clan or survival band, a small bunch of people hanging together to survive. Most of our human history was spent at that level, in the BEIGE system.

West: When survival is taken care of, what's next?

West sits forward, attentive.

James: Once basic survival was achieved, our ancestors would have been able to explore more territory, seek new resources and the population would grow. They would then come into competition and conflict with other groups of people. Security would then become the primary value in the PURPLE way of thinking. People organised into larger groups for safety.

West: Like a tribe?

James: Exactly. Individuality is subsumed into a group in return for security. Groups like that have a chief in charge with elders as guardians of wisdom and experience. The beliefs can be magical; a world of spirits, interconnection with nature, angels, fairy tales, folklore and tribal stories.

West: Like the tribe of doctors, for example.

James: Very true. The PURPLE world view manifests in the form of sports teams, social groups, communities, aristocracy, corporate tribes and tribes of professionals. Each has their own chiefs, elders, mystical stories, rites of passage and rituals.

West: Football teams carry on like a tribe, singing songs, wearing tribal clothes, retelling stories about past victories and spurring themselves on to fight the enemy.

James: People take care of each other, stick together for safety and distinguish themselves from other groups. When those primal tribal forces are unleashed, people can be exceptionally cruel and brutal because it feels like a fight to the death, a fight for survival.

West: That's what happened when Yugoslavia, Rwanda and Syria unravelled and it's beginning in Ukraine. The Nazis hijacked PURPLE thinking. They harnessed the power of deep tribal mythology and blood ties and they had a charismatic tribal chief. I'm scared that this stuff is being stirred up again by mass immigration and religious extremism.

James: Yes, that's potentially explosive stuff. PURPLE thinking is not all bad. Each of these different systems of belief arise because they have adaptive benefits. They can be taken too far and cause new problems. Each of these value systems help to solve the problems of the previous life conditions but they go on to create new ones.

West: How does PURPLE thinking show up in individuals?

James: People stick together as families for safety, they care for one another when they're sick and they emphasise rites of passage like weddings and funerals. A strong family acts like a single unit when threatened.

West: If you ask me, families can be quite oppressive and in your face. They don't allow individuals to express themselves. A lot of people try to escape their family.

James: Yes. That's what stimulates the emergence of the RED system. At the age of the terrible twos, a child starts to exert its own drives and impulses, challenging parental control. At the group level, young men, full of energy, courage and testosterone think, 'I've had enough of this, why should the Chief and those superstitious old men control my life? I'm gonna do my own thing.'

West: That sounds exciting.

James: Sure, but RED thinking drives people to act impulsively according to their drives and desires. They are courageous and take risks, exploring new territories, building bridges over wild rivers, investing in a risky business proposition, having the courage to ask someone out on a date.

West: I'm glad you mentioned that. How is Dr Chen?

They laugh.

James: The RED system gets things done, but it lacks guilt, shame and sensitivity. It can be brutal and abusive. Might is right. The powerful dominate the weak. The world of predator and prey.

West: For example, investment banking.

James: You're good at this. The RED world view is the way of the warrior, gang, brave firefighter, courageous police officer, thief, corrupt politician, conquerors, warlords, adventurers and athletes.

West: Neither good nor bad then?

James: These ways of thinking are morally neutral. They're underlying structures of thought that people need in order to adapt to their circumstances. The specific practical manifestations can take many forms. The RED system can be brave and adventurous or brutal and callous. The shadow side of the RED system is resentment, victimhood, entitlement, shame and revenge.

West: That sounds like terrorists' thinking.

James: Criminals too. A lot of violence is motivated by the wounded RED system. When people break out from PURPLE, they lose their identity and can become wild, shameless, sadistic like the West Side Boys gang in Sierra Leone or the insurgency in post-war Iraq. When the RED world view is well established with a Mafia, a dictator or a successful frontier colony, eventually, everyone tires of the endless violence and heartlessness. Even those at the top of the tree in the jungle can't sleep safely in their beds or enjoy their wealth because there's always someone trying to take their place. They yearn for control, order and justice.

West: That does sound like those children in the terrible twos needing strict discipline from their parents.

James: And love. A child develops the capacity to feel guilt at the age of 7. The BLUE system is activated. They experience shame and don't like it. They submit to their parents' and teachers' structure, discipline, rules and morality to avoid those feelings.

West: I reckon I need more shame and less guilt.

James: BLUE memes include truth, right and wrong, sacrifice now for future benefit, structure, order, discipline, charity and purpose.

West: Christianity did that for me. Later I developed the state, the law and regulation.

James: I think you're right. BLUE thinking also manifests as the rules of sport and military discipline, which harness the energy of RED warriors. But, you know, once BLUE thinking has achieved stability, order, justice and fairness, its limitations become apparent. It can become too intense and oppressive, and it stifles innovation, freedom and individuality. In excess it becomes black-and-white, absolutist, unyielding and unwilling to learn.

West: Like the Spanish Inquisition or the Puritans.

James: Yes. Too much BLUE becomes fundamentalist and ideologically inflexible. Political correctness is a modern form of BLUE thinking with rigid social rules. Anyone who disagrees or challenges it is vilified, punished and forced to change or be excluded.

West: Is BLUE thinking behind religious fundamentalism?

James: Yes, religions manifest differently within each value system. BLUE thinking religion is absolutist. The BLUE system insists that there's one right way of doing

32

things, black-and-white, right and wrong, true and false. BLUE world views tend to fight each other, marking the others out as existential enemies.

West: I've been through all that. Holy war and persecution.

James: Let's move on. When BLUE has finally managed to tame the RED system, there's greater stability and justice so people can build up the fruits of their labour, people are then freer to think new thoughts even if they haven't been allowed to express them. The conditions are right for the next value system to emerge.

West reads from the Spiral Dynamics Integral chart.

West: ORANGE. Success, science, entrepreneurship. I love it.

James: It emerged during the Enlightenment in Europe. The core code is the belief that one can control one's own destiny, a belief in progress and striving for success. This is associated with the capacity for reason, logic, science, individual rights, progress, the free market, democracy, and technology. ORANGE thinking promotes individualism, a drive to learn new skills, to acquire material possessions and to harness nature. The thinking style is strategy, business, engineering, secularism and pragmatism. ORANGE does what works.

West: The other countries are catching up fast on this one aren't they? We showed the Chinese how to get things done in Hong Kong and now they're running with it.

James: Hong Kong showed China a recipe for success that combines the BLUE system – law and order, property rights, effective bureaucracy, discipline and education – with the dynamism of the entrepreneurial ORANGE system.

West: Will they also adopt human rights and democracy?

James: Spiral Dynamics theory predicts that the ORANGE world view, having proven itself successful, will create a new set of challenges. It's heartless, doesn't care about the environment and creates winners and losers. The ORANGE system chips away at its own foundations. It loosens the PURPLE bonds of community and undermines the BLUE sense of right and wrong. This allows RED-thinking crime, corruption and exploitation to re-emerge.

West: Sounds like Margaret Thatcher and Ronald Reagan.

James: Go ahead. Explain.

West: People who could look after themselves had a ball back then. But I remember a lot of us got left behind. Crime went through the roof. Communities broke up and people became alienated. Corporate values kept appearing in places where they didn't belong, like hospitals and museums.

James: You know, it was a paradoxical time, because both Thatcher and Reagan were religious and believed in the free human spirit. But the revolutions they started crushed the human spirit through a combination of consumerism, materialism, unemployment and management by spreadsheets. Quantifying everything and insisting on experimental evidence in every situation can become a faith. Compassion, care, healing, experience, wisdom and judgement are undervalued. In hospitals, patients can feel like a lump of meat, being measured and prodded and not treated as a whole being in need of healing.

West: The baby gets thrown out with the bathwater.

James: You could put it that way. Each new value system tends to be overzealous in undermining the last one and throwing away the benefits as well as correcting mistakes.

West: You know, on reflection, this theory seems a bit patronising. You're placing people in a hierarchy from primitive to sophisticated. You're comparing cultures to children. Isn't this a slippery slope into the science of the 30s — remember how they tried to put people in racial hierarchies and justify the colonisation of primitive cultures by superior ones?

James: You've jumped ahead to GREEN thinking! Those are legitimate concerns. These world views don't represent types of people. They are value systems, ways of thinking that exist as capacities in all human beings. They can be activated when the circumstances require it. They represent a hierarchy that extends from simplicity up through increasing levels of complexity. That doesn't mean complexity is better. The differentials between racial groups and ethnicities have little or nothing to do with genetic makeup. They have everything to do with situation, values, beliefs, culture and institutions. Crime statistics vary widely according to racial groups but, as Don Beck says, the problem isn't black or white, it's RED. RED impulses get out of control without sufficient healthy PURPLE or BLUE to harness it.

West: It doesn't seem right to suggest that Christianity is like a child aged seven or that an Investment Banker acts like a two year old.

James: These ways of thinking arise in individuals long before they manifest as cultures or institutions. It's one thing to invent a new way of thinking but it takes time, effort and experience for that to manifest in a complex culture, organisation or society. There are plenty of ORANGE thinking entrepreneurs and scientists in the Congo but they don't have the BLUE foundations of security, order and justice.

West once again consults the Spiral Dynamics chart.

West: So, you think I'm showing signs of GREEN thinking. It says here that GREEN is common among students, intellectuals and liberals. Those are the people who have been involved in uprisings as part of the Arab Spring, also in Ukraine and Turkey.

James: Yes, the Arab Spring has shown the clear distinctions between the RED thinking dictators, the armies with their secular BLUE systems, RED-BLUE religion, the aspiring middle classes emerging into an ORANGE world of business and science and the young people demanding the freedom, liberty and democracy that goes with ORANGE level thinking, or even the human rights, fairness, woman's rights and diversity that goes with the GREEN system.

West: I need some clarification. What's the difference between liberal thinking and the GREEN system of thinking?

James: It depends what you mean by 'liberal.' Liberal in ORANGE thinking means individual freedom, liberty and freedom of speech, whereas in GREEN thinking it means egalitarianism, fairness, human rights and deconstructing old hierarchies like racism, sexism and class structures. GREEN pulls towards cohesion, inclusion and community whereas ORANGE pushes towards individualism and separation. GREEN values aim to correct the inequalities and dehumanisation caused by ORANGE by trying to re-humanise systems and societies, forcing capitalism to care about the environment and society through corporate social responsibility. The GREEN world view is pluralistic, sensitive, spiritual and seeks meaning. Decision making is carried out by consensus after listening to all voices, particularly the excluded underdog.

West: Spiral Dynamics theory is GREEN thinking itself, isn't it?

James: Not quite. GREEN thinking is the first to recognise that the world is complex and can be seen from multiple perspectives, but it embraces only some types of diversity. GREEN is highly intolerant of the other value systems. For example, because the GREEN world view wants to rebalance the inequalities caused by the other systems of thinking, it has a strong taboo against making judgements, observing any differences or hierarchy. This in itself creates new problems.

West: Oh yeah. I know what you're talking about. GREEN thinking likes to sit round in circles and share feelings but finds it hard to make a decision. It doesn't know how to lay down a boundary or enforce discipline. It's suspicious of science. It has contempt for the business that pays its bills. It undermines the authority of police officers, teachers and parents, the foundation of society. GREEN thinking can't tell the difference between a genuine victim and someone who's playing the system.

James: Yes, in its immature forms. The GREEN system emerged in individuals in the 19th Century when it opposed slavery, promoted workers' rights, improved the welfare system, campaigned for fairer punishments and demanded wider voting franchise. The imperialists stopped believing in their right to rule at the same time as the top tier of society in the colonies moved into the ORANGE system and asserted their right to freedom and to manage their own destiny. The GREEN system took hold in Western culture in the 60s with the sexual revolution, civil rights movement and opposition to the Vietnam war. It has embedded itself in the institutions of the public services, the arts, education and the media. It's at an early stage of development in its institutional expression. The majority of our businesses remain ORANGE and the majority of our bureaucracies are resolutely BLUE.

West: It seems to me that the ORANGE economy is in deep trouble, exploiting the environment and full of RED system exploitation and corruption. The BLUE system has lost its sense of purpose and right and wrong and is being challenged by assertive, dogmatic BLUE religion. Authority figures have lost their self-confidence. PURPLE families and communities are more fragmented than ever. Birth rates are below replacement level. We might be heading for ecological catastrophe, and when it comes to energy, frankly I'm like a train hurtling towards the end of the track.

James: The world used to seem so simple didn't it? Some people are nostalgic for the stable BLUE system of the 50s or the era of ORANGE self-confidence and progress in the 60s or the GREEN authenticity of the 70s. Suddenly, within a few decades, everything has become so complicated.

West: Everything is changing for me. Suddenly, I'm having to deal with ways of thinking that I haven't had to deal with at home for hundreds of years. It's scary. It's exciting.

James: It's not just you. It's happening the whole world over. Everyone is connected by the Internet, there's mass migration, our identities are blurred, and those processes are unleashing the most amazing human potential, creativity and new possibilities. The different parts of the world are coming together — each bringing their own strengths. Everything is in rapid evolution. It's exciting but overwhelming. All our problems and opportunities are interconnected and global now.

West: That's scarier than I thought.

James: It's daunting for sure. And none of the world views we discussed has the capacities required for us to survive, adapt and thrive in the current situation. GREEN lacks the ability to discern the differences between people and situations. It's also ineffective at decision-making and organisation. ORANGE can't do it because not everyone can be a winner. BLUE can't do it because there's no longer any uniting ideology and it would be very repressive to enforce one, something that could only emerge under very threatening conditions.

West: OK, I know you've got a solution up your sleeve. What is it?

James: Funny you should say that. Clare Graves found that there were some individuals who were beginning to reach integral consciousness which can handle high levels of complexity. The YELLOW system realises that the other ways of thinking have to run in parallel, in harmony, in adaptive manifestations for an individual, an organisation or a society to be healthy. The ORANGE and GREEN systems created the life conditions in which hyper-complexity emerged. The GREEN meme is the first value system able to see the world from many different perspectives and has the sensitivity to explore complexity. The YELLOW system is the first to be willing to take the decisions that need to be taken, to treat the system as a whole and act appropriately at the different levels of thinking, according to the needs and situation. YELLOW believes in the equality of humanity but is comfortable making distinctions between effective ideas and ineffective ones, between adaptive and maladaptive behaviours. Leaders with YELLOW integral thinking have a chameleon-like ability to speak and act out of any of the value systems so that they can do whatever is necessary in a particular situation to make things work. YELLOW is pragmatic and flexible, going with the flow of human nature, perceives the whole system and acts for the benefit of the whole.

West: Do-gooders, you mean? One of these people that goes to Africa to make themselves feel good by patronising the locals?

James: No, YELLOW thinking is compassionate but not naïve, nor is it ideological or missionary as BLUE thinking would be. It's practical. It's not driven by fear, unlike the previous systems. Unlike RED or ORANGE, YELLOW understands that, to thrive, one has to help the whole system, allowing everyone else to thrive too. Like the human body, if any part of the system is unhealthy, the whole system becomes sick. YELLOW leaders look for the supra-ordinate goals, the goals which unite everyone behind a common objective. YELLOW leaders act pragmatically, operate on all the different levels simultaneously according to what's necessary, respect the rights of people to think and live as they do and design the systems accordingly. YELLOW gets beyond treating people as victims who need to be rescued and respects their responsibility for their choices.

West: When will this YELLOW world view solve my problems?

James: YELLOW leadership already exists but tends not to announce itself with a fan-fare. It thinks and acts through the BEIGE, PURPLE, RED, BLUE, ORANGE and GREEN systems. It's new so it's finding its feet. The majority of your leaders, West, are using ORANGE or GREEN thinking, and they're not going to shift to YELLOW until they've realised that those ways of thinking don't work any more.

West: What's the evidence for this theory?

James: Spiral Dynamics Integral Theory is just one of many theories and models of human development. I personally prefer it because it is more comprehensive than the others and much richer. To me, it has very high intuitive validity, giving an excellent framework to understand culture, politics, organisations, leadership, values and group psychology. Don Beck and his colleagues have applied it to 250,000 people across many cultures including South Africa, Palestine, the Middle East, all over Europe, North America and Mexico, in business, medicine, education, the military and many other fields. When we look at some specific examples, you can make your own mind up. It is a theory that you can use to make specific prediction, so it's testable. However no one has yet done that research in a systematic way. I'm sure that will happen when enough people get interested in it.

West: I thought you said there were eight ways of thinking. Is there something beyond YELLOW?

James: Well spotted. In fact Graves did find an 8th way of thinking, the holistic TUR-QUOISE system, which sees the world, the cosmos and the whole of life as a vast interconnected, conscious living system. Have you ever sat and watched a flock of birds, a shoal of fish or a beehive?

West: Yes. It's fascinating.

James: TURQUOISE perceives it as a living thing, as a whole. Everything is intercon-nected like the electromagnetic waves passing through us. All consciousness passes through us and we can access it.

West: Wow. Have you popped a pill or something, doctor?

James laughs.

James: Not at all. TURQUOISE takes quantum physics lessons from the ORANGE system combined with GREEN introspection, intuition and consciousness. The world is made up of conscious fields that we can sense and influence. Every being, every group, every part of the living system has a field that interpenetrates with all the others. Some of the magical capacities that were last seen in the PURPLE stage of development are re-emerging, although fully integrated with all the other levels of thinking. TURQUOISE believes that we're conscious, living nature, that there's no boundary between us. TURQUOISE believes that our thoughts can change our consciousness, our behaviour, our life, our bodies and the world beyond us.

West: How do you know this isn't the old superstitious mumbo-jumbo that we left behind years ago – the PURPLE stuff? It sounds a lot like it.

James: The difference between PURPLE thinking and TURQUOISE thinking is that TURQUOISE has been through the stages of RED, BLUE, ORANGE, GREEN and YELLOW consciousness and can think and act on all those levels while still tapping into emerging consciousness capabilities.

West: If I'm honest, only a tiny part of me understands what you're saying.

James: That's only to be expected. TURQUOISE is very new and not yet well defined. Let's just take some to distil what you've learned in the session. Stand up for a moment, if you will. Take a deep breath. Stretch. Take a look out of the window at the trees over there. Now close your eyes. Relax. Tell me the key things you need to remember from this session

West pauses. He sits down.

West: I remember that human beings have many different capacities within them, enabling them to adapt and function in many circumstances. There are at least eight different value systems within us, which are activated when required by the environment.

James: Well done! The only thing I would add is that the first six ways of thinking – survival, safety, power, truth, success and humanism – act as if they are the absolute truth, whereas integral and holistic ways of thinking embrace all the others. For an individual, group, company, country or any other human enterprise to thrive, it must have all the different value systems operating in it in their healthy manifestations as adapted to the situation.

West: It's a lot to take in.

James: You've done very well. By the way, would you mind if I discuss your case with my colleagues for their advice and feedback?

West: No, please don't do that. Keep it hush hush if you would. No notes, no records. If people had the slightest inkling I was seeing a psychiatrist, confidence in me would collapse and my enemies would take advantage.

James: Not even a couple of close colleagues?

West laughs.

West: Dr Chen?

James: Yes indeed, Dr Chen. And another close colleague called Steve.

West: Steve. Yes, I trust him. OK, you can talk to both of them.

James: Thank you. So, that's it for today then. Jean will book you a follow up appointment.

———◆———

That evening I met up with Steve, an old friend from Medical School, an orthopaedic surgeon. He came over to the Rose and Crown pub on the edge of the park. I made a beeline for the seats beside the roaring fire and Steve arrived shortly after. Steve was 43 like me. Also balding, also overweight. People often took us for brothers or boyfriends. Ha! If only they knew Steve. He was a rascal through and through.

'Hi James. What would you like to drink? A bottle of red?'

'How about some claret?'

'Fine.'

Steve went to the bar.

I began staring into fire. It's something I enjoy – watching the embers and flames. I think it must appeal to some trace of our ancient past. While I was staring and thinking, it occurred to me that West had said something odd. He had quite clearly said that he trusted Steve. But I was absolutely certain I had never mentioned Steve in West's presence.

Steve himself returned from the bar clutching a bottle and two glasses.

'How's the love life?' Steve inquired as he poured.

My shoulders stiffened. 'Nothing to report.'

He laughed. 'I know that look. Spill the beans.'

'Well there's a junior doctor at work, Suki.'

'Another blonde?'

'No, brunette actually.'

'Curvy?'

I frowned and took a sip of the claret, which was excellent. Steve shrugged and put a fresh log on the fire, sending sparks flying up the chimney.

'Listen,' I said. 'Can I talk to you in the strictest confidence?'

'That sounds sinister. What on earth have you been up to?'

'Stop mucking about. It's nothing like that.'

He sighed. 'Go on.then. My lips are sealed.'

I lowered my voice. 'I've got a very unusual patient at the moment.'

I told him West's story, and when I had finished, he slapped his forehead, laughing.

'James, sometimes you are touchingly gullible. Can't you see, he's taking you for a ride. I bet he's a journalist or something like that. Just make sure he's not recording the conversations. The General Medical Council wouldn't see the funny side if he went public.'

PRESENTING COMPLAINTS

West was wearing his pinstripe suit without a tie. He sat in the brown leather chair, tapping the highly polished toecap of one shoe and staring at me with eagle eyes.

James: Welcome back, West. How are you?

West: Raring to go. I don't feel like I've told you the full story yet.

James: OK. Well, today, with your permission, I'd like to use a technique called Voice Dialogue. Now, this is going to sound a bit odd, but the idea is to speak one by one with the different parts of yourself – those ways of thinking that we talked about yesterday, ranging from BEIGE to TURQUOISE. We'll address each of in turn as a separate voice.

West laughs, rubbing his knees nervously.

West: I thought a psychiatrist was meant to stop me talking to the voices in my head.

James: Ha! Yes. Encouraging to see you're on good form this morning. As you know, we all have different parts of ourselves that pull in different directions.

West: Tell me about it Doctor. I have thousands of different voices, often arguing. Some of them refuse to speak to one another. They rarely listen to one another.

James: Of course. You were saying yesterday that you live in different types of people, all of them with distinct values and circumstances. That's good. If a person constantly thinks in one way they'll never be able to adapt to new situations.

West: Sure. But ideally I'd like them to work together.

James: You're right. It would be much better if they worked together. Right now there's a minibus full of unruly characters and they need to be taken in hand. If you can do that, it'll boost your self-confidence, clarify your values, give you a clear direction and increase your power.

West: A minibus, eh? Who's in the driving seat?

James: There's usually one or two main drivers. It might be the character we call the protector, the controller or the inner child. Once you get inside and explore, you find out that you have many different aspects of yourself. By the sounds of it you already experience some of yours as inner voices or mood states. But there are usually also parts of ourselves that we don't even know exist, either because we've never taken the time to listen to them or because we've repressed them. That can happen at a very early age, leaving no memory. But sometimes even the quiet ones can make their presence felt, directly or indirectly.

West: Like Bill Clinton with Monica Lewinsky in the Oval Office?

James: Actually that's a great example.

West: Thanks, I thought so..

James: So, the idea is to get to know your different parts and to give them a genuine opportunity to be heard and acknowledged, just like real people. When they trust you, they reveal a lot, and all the different parts are more likely to engage with one another. You get to know yourself better. Sometimes you can resolve inner conflict. It's useful to check in with all the different parts of yourself when you feel about uncomfortable but don't really know why. In general the process gives you clarity and integration.

West: Let's do it!

James: This is how it works. We're going to create a safe place and invite all the parts of yourself to step forward in turn and share their complaints. The rules are simple. Each of the different parts of yourself are going to sit back and listen – listen with respect to each of the other parts. If there's potential for a dialogue between them, I'll facilitate that until you get the hang of it.

West: Where do we start?

James: BEIGE. Stand up and plant your feet firmly on the ground. Place your attention inside yourself and find that existential, animal part which is totally focused on survival. Bring your attention to your feet on the ground. Feel your connection to the Earth. Now, your legs, the muscles holding up and feel the heat inside you. Be aware of your genitals. Imagine yourself as a new born baby, as someone in an emergency or as one of your hunter gathering ancestors.

West: That's a lot to do at once.

James: Trust your intuition. Don't censor. Let it flow.

BEIGE: There's an epidemic of heart disease, obesity, diabetes and cancer. I'm vulnerable to mutant viruses. I used to be under threat from bows and arrows but now my enemies have nuclear and biological weapons.

James: How do you feel?

BEIGE: Afraid, vulnerable.

James: Where do you feel that?

BEIGE: In my gut. That sent a chill up my spine.

James: Thank you, to have anything else to say?

He shook his head.

James: Shake your body. Release BEIGE and jump into your PURPLE consciousness. Attend to your lower back, your pelvis and lower abdomen. Think of family, community, rituals, weddings, funerals, and Christmas. Imagine yourself in the woods, as part of a tribe, music being played, dancing round the fire. See the chief, shamen and elders. Sense the spirits, the angels. You're all in this together, everyone looking out for each other, safe.

PURPLE: I'm there.

James: How do you feel?

PURPLE: My tribes have been violated. Vast numbers of immigrants have come, asserting their own ethnicity and identities. GREEN says I have to suppress my own identity, but I have to celebrate theirs. We're not having many children anymore. They're having lots. They'll become the majority and will persecute us. Why doesn't the government defend us from religious fundamentalists who are trying to force their way of life on us? They keep telling us they want peace but if anyone criticises them, they go berserk. If I were in their country I'd have to obey their rules. Why are we letting them take over?

West stands hunched over, his face distressed, fists clenched.

PURPLE: Families have fragmented. Many children grow up without a secure home, without good role models. Many families don't eat meals together. They sit in different rooms watching television or on the Internet. People don't know their neighbours. We lives separate lives, sealed in our cars. We used to stick together and look after one another.

Childhood is polluted by consumerism, television and children have got the attention span of a gnat. They sit at home texting on their mobile phones rather than going out to play with friends. We should show our elders respect, listen to their wise guidance, but instead we put them in homes. We don't value motherhood or fatherhood. Welfare has made men unnecessary, a sperm donor. Politicians are shallow and insincere. Housing is too expensive.

We've lost control over our food, water, energy, air, land and resources. It's dangerous. Every time we fill our car with petrol, we're haemorrhaging money to thugs, religious fundamentalists and corrupt regimes. They've got their fingers on my carotid.

We don't have enough children to support the old and sick. If it weren't for immigration, my population would collapse. People are too busy working, travelling the world, having casual sex and buying objects that they don't need. Those that do have children have them later in life and they only have one or two. We have a crisis in our pension system and health and social care. We can't afford them. Foreigners are buying up my companies, utilities, land and resources.

Iran is developing a nuclear weapons, North Korea already has them. It's only a matter of time before a terrorist sets one off.

James: How do you feel?

PURPLE: I'm scared. I'm angry. Why can't naive GREEN or selfish ORANGE see the danger?

James: Where do you feel that in your body?

PURPLE: It's a fluttering in my tummy. My shoulders are tense. My fists are clenched. I want to defend my people and territory.

James: What about the minorities? Sense if there are any other voices who want to speak and, if so, jump out of that one and into a new position and speak from there.

West leaps forward and takes on a different persona. He shrinks a little. Less angry, more uncertain.

PURPLE Voice 2: I enjoy the opportunity, freedom and security, but it's hard to fit in. They won't accept me. Even the GREEN ones are racist underneath. They keep telling me that I need to give up my identity and become an American, Australian or a Dane. It doesn't work that way. My identity is in my heart, connected to ancestors. I want to be left to get on with my life, I want to be accepted.

James: Thank you.

West leaps into another position. Soulful, still, downhearted.

PURPLE Voice 3: The white people came to my country and took our land, imposed this heartless, industrial system. Our spirit was broken generations ago. We got cut off from our culture and ancestors. Now the white people have done the same thing to themselves. West seems to kill off everything he touches. He should reconnect with nature.

West shakes his body and stands tall, with his legs apart like a powerful warrior.

RED: They've got me tied down – like Gulliver imprisoned Lilliputians. Other than sport and crime, there aren't many places I get to run free. Wherever I go there is bureaucracy, rules and regulations, control freaks telling me what to do. They don't take any risks. Men used to be tough and now they're wimps. Latinos, Arabs and Russians are still real men. They can take care of themselves. They assert themselves without shame, and don't let all these liberals emasculate them. Women should be women and men should be men. Now they talk about feelings and hug each other. I used to enforce honour and respect and dish out punishment. Now I'm not allowed to lift a finger. While the smug liberals live in their safe neighbourhoods, the bad guys are taking over round here. I used to inspire respect. People were in awe of me, afraid.

We form gangs and carry knives to protect ourselves. The adults, the police, they're weak. They don't protect us, so we have to protect ourselves. It's a dog eat dog world. Schools are full of drugs, bullying and crime. Our parents are too busy drinking, working, watching television or talking wishy-washy rubbish.

The state is becoming oppressive. They tell me what to think. They've always looking over my shoulder. Whether it's the politically correct thought police or the black helicopter corporate drones, I've lost my freedom.

West jumps straight out of the RED system and into the BLUE.

BLUE: I'm finding it harder to keep order. Everything is falling apart. They won't let me control the borders. GREEN wants diversity and ORANGE wants an open labour market. No one can agree what's good or bad, true or false, right or wrong. Anything goes. GREEN says its non-judgmental. ORANGE is materialistic and amoral. How am I supposed to discipline anyone if there's no morality?

James: Why does that matter?

West: Parents and teachers used to be strict and people took them seriously. People don't have respect for authority anymore. I've lost respect for myself, lost my foundations. When standards slip, you get crime, delinquency and disrespect.

I'm tied up with equality and diversity, human rights and all the stuff which gives everyone excuses to do whatever they like and play the system. I can't discipline ethnic minorities because I get HR on my back. They tell me it'll look racist so it's best to let it go. They are more worried about hurt feelings and potential compensation claims than about doing what's right.

I used to get judged on the quality of my leadership and now it's all paperwork, targets and risk assessments. No one stands for anything. The pride has gone, there's no self-respect.

The police used to maintain law and order, to protect people from criminals. Now they police your thoughts. GREEN keeps saying it's non-judgmental. If you dare to disagree with it, they threaten your livelihood, vilify you, sue you. So everyone keeps their head down. We've lost our freedom of speech.

No one is responsible or accountable. When a hospital messes up, the management blame the staff. When a business causes harm, they pay off executives who move on somewhere else. When someone commits a crime, GREEN rushes to make excuses for them. It's racism, poverty, anything but the fault of the criminal. They couldn't care less about the victims of crime.

Religious fundamentalists are on the march all over the world and especially in Europe. They know right from wrong and they are prepared to fight for it. Christianity has lost its balls. One got blown off in the First World War, then, in the 60s, all those anti-authority protesters and feminists crushed the other one. ORANGE weakened me by undermining all the morals and loosening the regulations. RED indulged in an orgy of greed and corruption that nearly brought the financial system down.

Doctors, nurses, military officers and teachers used to have vocation but now it's just a job. People are out for themselves. Everyone thinks they're entitled to something, like the world owes them a living. Many politicians have got their hand in the till.

People abuse the welfare system but whenever I try to keep it fair, GREEN helps RED to game the system, playing the victim card. GREEN should try living in a tough neighbourhood.

The media and Internet are turning our youth into airheads. They all want to be pop stars and celebrities. What happened to discipline, sacrifice and hard work?

These days it's all diversity and celebrating other cultures. What happened to being patriotic? Multiculturalism leaves us wide open to colonisation. If immigrants don't integrate into the West, all my centuries of hard work will go down the pan and we'll have inter-ethnic conflict.

The Chinese are building up their Navy, buying up resources and infrastructure all over the world. They're using economic influence and bribes to subvert democracy all over the world. It's a racist, nationalist state. That's a threat to our freedom, security and way of life. When things get tough over there, they'll start a war with their neighbours and I'll get drawn in.

The lawyers are interested in money, exploiting loopholes and technicalities. Criminals keep walking free. What happened to justice? Common sense has gone out of the window. Hospitals aren't run for the patients, they're run to protect the organisation against litigation. Children can't go on school trips anymore in case one of the parents sues the school because the child tripped over a broken paving stone. So they all stay at school and get fat and bored instead.

James: How do you feel?

BLUE: Tired, helpless, like I've got a big job to do but I'm not allowed to use the necessary tools. I'm sad at what I've lost.

James: Where is that sensation?

He points to his heart and his eyes well with years.

BLUE: West is finished.

James: Thank you. Shake off BLUE and, when you're ready, jump over there into the ORANGE system.

ORANGE: My economy is in bad shape. We've lost our confidence. We don't trust one another anymore so people are cautious. Banks are hanging on to their money. There's so much more competition for resources so the prices are going through the roof. Energy prices are a limiting factor on my economy now. We run a massive trade deficit. Since we de-industrialised, we spend all of our money on imported goods, imported energy and raw materials. We've run up a massive debt that we can never pay off. When the Chinese, the Arabs and the Russians eventually pull the rug from under the Dollar, we could be back to hyperinflation and depression.

West pauses for a moment, then shifts position and posture.

ORANGE: My education system isn't up to scratch. We had a century of increasing social mobility for the poor and minorities but now the dumbed down, victim culture, the taboo on competition, discipline and hard work has ended that. The elite gets well-trained but the masses are being failed by the education system. They're not learning the skills they need. Western people think they've got a divine right to prosperity. The rest of the world has joined the competition and we need a strategy to succeed. It won't be long before the Indians, Brazilians and others offer services better and cheaper. We need to open the borders to highly skilled migrants, compete for the best labour but PURPLE and BLUE keep complaining about immigrants. They ought to get off their backsides and improve themselves, learn the latest skills, set up businesses and take charge of their destiny before they wake up and find someone else owns everything.

James: No wonder you're in an economic recession!

ORANGE: It's expensive for me to invest in research and development when my intellectual property gets stolen, made in unregulated sweatshops and sold below cost. Our market allows easy access for the rest of the world but somehow we're stupid enough to let them keep their barriers up to us. I need to get access into the markets of the developing world, and have free trade between North America and Europe. Farm subsidies are keeping Africans poor and stopping us getting cheap food.

I'm tied down with red tape and bureaucracy. If they kill the golden goose, there won't be any eggs to feed all these unproductive bureaucrats in the bloated government.

I want the best people with the best skills and ideas. I don't care where they come from. What matters is what works and what makes money. GREEN insists I have to take quotas of people with hard-luck stories. Why can't they get on and work hard like I did? I've had enough of freeloaders.

I've invented amazing medical technologies but because we keep so many people alive for much longer, I can't afford pay for health and social care, let alone welfare.

James: Have you considered killing yourself?

ORANGE: Oh no. I'm thriving. It's just that my centre of gravity has shifted to Asia where they still know that 2 and 2 makes 4.

GREEN: ORANGE is responsible for rising inequalities between rich and poor, black and white, north and south. After years trying to eradicate it, male chauvinism and homophobia are back. Religionophobia is widespread. Minorities still suffer racism. White people don't even know that they're privileged and aren't willing to give it up. We'll never be whole until we listen to the voices of the marginalised victims.

We don't have a real democracy. A cabal of the rich and powerful choose the candidates, control the media and bribe politicians. Governments are infested with corporate spies, learning the systems, then inviting in their friends to milk it.

Capitalism is destroying the planet, depleting the world's precious resources, causing climate change, deforestation, killing off species, polluting the atmosphere, killing the oceans. Capitalism owns billions of debt slaves, forced to play by their rules. The market only values what it can measure which excludes family, community, fairness clean air or security. In Europe up to 50% of young people are unemployed. What a waste of human potential. People will complain when they turn to crime.

We are richer than ever, but people are more stressed, less happy, less fulfilled. We need to return to a natural, authentic life. Our organisations must align with human nature to harness human potential. ORANGE has crushed the human spirit. We need to re-humanise the world. Everything's materialistic, all about money, power and consumerism. Where's the meaning of life, passion and purpose? We've lost our spirituality. We need to be more conscious and stop anaesthetising ourselves with television, junk food and alcohol.

I need a huge investment in renewable energy, but vested interests buy up promising new technologies and shut them down to maintain energy scarcity, which drives profits.

The education system stifles creativity by treating pupils like robots on a production line. We have wall-to-wall porn. Women are treated like sex objects. We have amazing technology but we've lost our humanity. Medicine has become so technical that it has neglected the patient, forgotten how to heal, how to care. It's heartless, not holistic.

The industrialised food system feeds us unhealthy artificial junk pumped full of chemicals. We treat our bodies like machines to transport our brain from A to B. We must reconnect mind, body and spirit. Our systems are so heartless, so lacking in compassion. It's all logic, measurements and separation. Crime has been falling across the Western world for 20 years, but the media keep people afraid. We need to drop the fear and come from a place of love. We need to show appreciation and gratitude. We should embrace diversity.

Science has become so rigid that it can't see the nuances and complexity of the world. We've invalidated our intuition, wisdom and judgement. People aren't objects that fit into the old Newtonian system. Science is corrupted by money, ego and power.

Our foreign policy is selfish and hypocritical. We push the world around, imposing our values. Who are we to tell other people how to live? We become hysterical when a handful of people are killed by terrorists in the West but we think nothing of the thousands that get killed in Iraq or Afghanistan. What about the terrorism of poverty and malnutrition?

The security establishment keeps telling us about threats from others. Yet we keep invading other countries, violating others' rights. It's time to let the other people of the world take their place at the table, find consensus and share the resources fairly.

We exploit nature then discard it. We factory farm animals, but we hide it away so we can't see it. We used to live with the rhythms of nature. We desperately stave off death rather than trying to live the best life we can. We've forgotten to honour life.

James: Is that everything? OK. Thank you GREEN. Let's go to YELLOW.

YELLOW: You must be tired of all these complaints, Doctor.

James: Don't worry about me — worry about your effect on everyone else. It's no surprise that you've lost your self-confidence.

YELLOW: We've lost our self-confidence because we don't know who we are, where we're going, why we're here and how we should live. We're pessimistic about the future. Our society is so complex. Everything is delivered just-in-time so we're vulnerable to natural disasters, pandemics and cyber-attacks from enemies or criminals. Anyone, anywhere in the world with a grievance can travel around and has access to the weapons of the ORANGE system.

Not long ago, the British government got a shock when striking lorry drivers blockaded the country's oil refineries. Within a few days, petrol ran out. They were three days away from food riots and public services grinding to a halt. They had to call in the army.

The world's food, water and energy supplies are vulnerable because of overuse and over-centralisation. We're dependent on a few crops.

There's a spiritual deficit, a vacuum of meaning and value. We're living on past spiritual capital. Religions haven't yet adapted to our complex way of life. The secular and spiritual-but-not-religious sections of society don't bring together the community.

GREEN thinking has made it difficult to manage boundaries, make judgements, take hard decisions. In fact, it has indulged the culture of entitlement and victimhood, which is a massive barrier to human potential and empowerment.

The emergence of our global tribe is delayed by ethnocentrism, racism, historical resentments and by the naiveté of GREEN. The GREEN world view needs to stop indulging PURPLE tribalism, RED entitlement and victimhood and BLUE intolerance in minorities. GREEN must get over its guilt and shame.

Politics is so polarised. Liberals fight conservatives, left fights right, religious fights secular. We should be working together. The media focusses upon fear, threats or shallow, narcissistic materialism. If we're to shift our collective consciousness for the better, the media needs to be more responsible and mature.

We're one integrated, interdependent system, and all of its parts matter. The health of each part is vital to the health of the whole system. The pace of change is daunting for everybody. All of our systems are under strain. Fear makes people close down their perceptions, cling to what they hold dear, regress to more primitive types of thought and behaviour, disconnect from others and disconnect from love and positive vision.

Feminism gave women equal rights, but now they have to work to maintain a decent living standard. Men became more feminine but they didn't take up the old female roles of caring, family and community. Those have been neglected. Men don't know how to be a man – how to be a father.

Charity and foreign aid play the rescuer-victim game, which disempowers people and perpetuates the problems.

> *West makes a sudden shivering movement, as though a bolt of energy is going through him.*

TURQUOISE: The others have said it all really. Suffering motivates us to move on to the next stage of our journey. We're an interconnected living system, a giant being that's becoming conscious of itself and integrating all our different energies. The sacred life force flows within us. We're on the cusp of an amazing leap into a new enlightenment.

James: Right. It looks like we're done now. Thank you very much. West, can you stand in the middle of the room and make sure you're firmly back in your body. I'd like you to invite each of your parts back inside you. Imagine them walking towards you and entering you, and as they do, notice how it feels.

West sits, tired but content.

West: I never knew I was carrying around so much negativity. No wonder I've become less attractive.

James: Consider what you might need to let go of if you want to move on to something better. Let your intuition work its magic.

West: I certainly will. Can I see you next week?

James: 2pm next Thursday?

West: Perfect.

GRATITUDE & SELF-ESTEEM

West telephoned me first thing in the morning wanting to come in at short notice. I couldn't help noticing that he was wearing a particularly colourful silk tie loose around his sweaty neck.

West: Good Morning Doctor.

James: Morning West.

West: You know, I had a very strange night with very intense dreams.

James: Any particular themes?

West: There was a theme as it happens. I was being attacked by wasps — just kept finding wasps everywhere. I woke up screaming. Then there was another one about being homeless — begging on the streets.

James: Does that make any sense to you?

West: Well, I thought about that over breakfast, and my first instinct was that the wasp thing is all about immigration. I'm afraid of being overwhelmed. The other one was probably about economic collapse.

James: It's common for the mind to process a session during the night.

West: I felt low yesterday evening. My body felt heavy. I couldn't seem to shake it off. I ended up watching television, eating some cheese and crisps and I drank a bottle of wine.

James: Your trusted anaesthetics.

West nods, his forehead sweaty and cheeks red.

James: Let's get started. I want you to list all the things you're grateful for and proud of, the things about yourself that you appreciate, respect and admire.

West: And you want me to do it from the perspective of the different value systems, is that it?

James: You've got it.

West stands, pushes his chair back to give himself space and closes his eyes. After a minute or so, he speaks.

RED: I'm the strongest. I've defeated all the others militarily. The Europeans conquered the world and the Americans are now the most powerful military force in human history. We have the best technology and weapons.

GREEN: Not any more. Little Britain ruled the world for 150 years but the mighty United States can't even impose its will on rural Afghanistan!

RED: People vote with their feet. Millions risk their lives to migrate to the West. I love the right to protest, freedom to say what I like. We're the best at sport. All the sports in the world come from the West. We invented the Olympic Games.

West sits down, looking more thoughtful.

GREEN: I'm proud of our human rights. Gay rights, women's rights, anti-racism and multiculturalism. We're starting to reconnect with nature and undo centuries of damage. We're breaking down the things that divide us and becoming a global village, everyone having their fair share.

James: Anything else?

GREEN: Yes, I'm proud of our development work. Charities, aid and training. We've set up great global institutions like the UN, the WHO which are the embryonic global architecture. I'm proud of our media. We have a rich source of information if we want it.

James: Would you do something for me?

GREEN: Yes.

James: Take a deep breath, rest your fingers on your sternum, over your heart and place your attention on the sensations underneath your fingers, deep inside. Now, think of someone you love and notice the sensations that arise.

West visibly softens; a broad smile opening up. He is positively glowing.

James: That's good. Now smile back at your heart. Allow that feeling – that heart feeling – to expand. Breathe gently and imagine that you can breathe in and out of your heart. Allow all that love to flow. Invite your heart to speak, to say why it loves you.

West's eyes fill with tears.

West: Freedom. Patriotism. I love Australia, France, Germany, Canada, all my countries. I'm proud of my Armed Forces. I'm proud of this mass of thriving humanity. All the millions of people going about their business, spontaneously performing their duty and vocations. Teachers, nurses, police officers, inventors, even bankers. I'm so grateful for the....this will sound weird.

James: That's OK, let it flow, no censoring.

West: I'm grateful for the road network.

West laughs, tears now rolling down his cheeks.

West: I'm grateful for our amazing rubbish collection system! Like a liver to clean up our blood, we have a refuse and recycling system to clean up the mess. It's constantly improving.

James: Keep going.

West: Justice. The system can be slow and makes mistakes, but compared to the rest of human history, millions of people manage to live in peace and security most of the time. The rate of crime is coming down. We're more peaceful than ever. My people die of old age and diseases of excess, rarely from poverty, malnutrition or tribal warfare.

West looks peaceful. He drops his hands into his lap.

West: I'm proud of my vast, ever increasing knowledge and learning. We walk around with a phone in our pockets, the size of my ancestors' axe heads, and it enables us to speak to a couple of billion people, to send messages via satellites in the sky and to access the answer to any question that crosses our mind. We're evolving at an amazingly fast pace now. My democracy, capitalism and science have unleashed more freedom and human potential than any other civilization.

James: You seem a little self-conscious now. Stay connected with your heart and allow your consciousness to expand until it's as big as the room, as big as London, right out into space, as big as the Cosmos.

West: This is fun. I'm buzzing. I won't want to go back.

James: Look at the whole of Western Civilization. Tell me its strengths. What makes it special?

West: Its humanity. For all its faults, it's all about making life better for people, being the best we can, being as free as we can, reaching the stars, relieving suffering and having fun.

West's lips quiver and his forehead tenses.

West: I'm sorry that I've been so hard on myself. I know I'm not perfect but, it's true, I'm amazing. Even when I make mistakes, I eventually correct them. Getting involved in slavery was evil but we were the first ones ever to stop it. The Royal Navy suppressed it and we even had a Civil War to stop it. Self-criticism is only just emerging in the others.

James: Your self-criticism can be very destructive if you don't keep a sense of perspective and compassion. The fact that you keep doubting yourself, questioning everything, always trying to get to the bottom of things, trying to understand and explain, experimenting, trying new things, and, yes your intense self-criticism is one of your greatest strengths. It's the very thing which is unleashed this amazing progress, that drives your amazing unfolding of human potential.

West: Yes. Thank you. I see that.

James: I haven't heard from the PURPLE system.

PURPLE: I had a strange feeling when you asked us to expand out to the universe and look back at the Earth. I felt part of a bigger tribe, that all of us are one human tribe, and it made me wonder what it would be like to meet other tribes from outer space.

RED: Don't let your guard down. We've got a lot of enemies.

James: Hang on, RED. You've had your say, let PURPLE speak.

PURPLE: I'm finding it hard to speak.

James: Well, maybe PURPLE doesn't have much more to say. Just give yourself a bit of a shake, and feel the earth beneath your feet. Relax. Breathe. Expand out again, as far as you can go. Imagine you can hold the world in your hands.

TURQUOISE: Western Civilization was one of the prime drivers that has brought us to the cusp of this new emerging global consciousness, global civilization, this complex new world brimming with potential, like a chrysalis transforming into a butterfly.

YELLOW: That sounds beautiful but it's a challenge to manage all this complexity. This whole thing might blow up in our face, so I don't want to get carried away with all this dreamy talk.

ORANGE: I feel grateful for supermarkets. We take for granted that we can walk in there and get whatever we need. In the context of all human history, that's utterly astonishing. Behind that simplicity there must be a million components, an amazing network of people, a sourcing and delivery system, a financial system, quality control, farming, staff training. The man who fixes the brakes on the lorry that collects your bananas from the boat in the port. The packaging. The barcodes. The lighting. Supermarkets are the result of thousands of inventions, millions of people, an incredibly complex system. Yet we grumble if we have to wait in line for two minutes.

The session continued, and when it seemed there was nothing left to be said I guided him through the process of reintegrating all his parts. It's important to do that before finishing.

West seemed a different man than the sloppily dressed, tired individual who I'd greeted earlier.

'You know, this dialogue thing is really working for me,' he said. 'I feel totally different to yesterday.'

I put down my notebook and smiled at this transformed West. 'You see how much power there is in this way of choosing where to focus your attention. You have control over your mood, much more than you think. Can you to summarise the things you've learned?'

He thought for a moment. 'Self-criticism, doubt and an open mind are among my greatest strengths. Cultivating gratitude is essential to balance the tendency we have to focus upon threats, pain and fear. Gratitude engages the heart and generates peace, self-esteem and resilience. Gratitude gives us a sense of proportion and emotional stability, a strong place from which to make judgements and strategy. It's good to be confident and to have high self-esteem so long as I don't let it tip over into arrogance. I stand on the shoulders of the generations of ancestors before me. I respect all the different value systems within me and give each a fair chance to be heard. I'm leading the way into a new global civilization and need to have due respect for my past contribution to that while allowing space for something new to emerge.'

'Well done,' I said, genuinely impressed. 'That's great work. Go home and let it sink in. Let's not make an appointment. That doesn't seem to be right for you. Just let me know when you're ready to come back.'

FALSE EPIPHANY

I phoned Suki. I could feel my heart flutter in my throat. It went to voicemail. 'Hi Suki, it's James. Listen. About Thursday. Do you fancy going to the Thai Elephant?'

'Sorry,' she said, sounding a little hassled. I could hear urgent raised voices in the background too. I can't talk now. It's a bit busy here. I'll call you in a bit.'

I was more than a little deflated and decided to treat myself to some comfort food in the canteen. Having paid for my chocolate pancakes and settled down at a table I checked my phone – a message was waiting for me: 'I prefer Indian. See you at the Bombay Raj, Grosvenor St. 19.30. Suki x.' I smiled. Why had I been so worried?

When I returned to the office Jean passed me a message, 'Please call Dr Wilson regarding rota swap. xn 6423.'

'Mr West didn't make a new appointment,' she said.

'That's OK Jean. He'll call when he's ready.'

'Have you forgotten to write up your assessment and letter to his General Practitioner?' she asked. Jean loved hearing stories about all the patients. She was privy to virtually everything. She was as sharp as a scalpel.

I shut the outer door leading the lifts and stairs. Speaking quietly, I said, 'What have you noticed about West?'

'He hasn't filled in any of the forms. I don't know his address, his GP, his next of kin or anything.'

'Anything else?'

'He's good looking. Very smart and confident.'

'What about his behaviour?'

'He fidgets and keeps scratching his head. He's nervous under the surface. Sometimes I can smell alcohol on his breath. He seems to carry the weight of the world on his shoulders.'

I felt my mobile vibrate in my pocket but ignored it.

'And in terms of appearances?' I asked.

She thought for a moment. 'Well he must have been quite a catch at one time. His clothes are nice – expensive looking. Dresses a bit sloppily though, and that tummy doesn't do him any favours. He'd look better if he lost some weight. Probably feel better about himself too. All the same, there's definitely something attractive about him.'

'Interesting. Very interesting. OK, I'd better get on with this paperwork for the GP.'

I checked the phone as soon as I had closed the office door behind me. Suki had followed up with another text message: 'Wear your dancing shoes x.'

It had been a few years since I'd strutted my stuff on the dance floor, and my stomach filled with butterflies at the thought. What a woman! It really was turning out to be a roller-coaster ride – in a very good way.

———◆———

At the end of my clinic on Thursday afternoon, Jean came in to my office. 'James, I'm sorry. Have you got time to slip in one extra?' I frowned. I'd been pacing myself for a 5 o'clock get away.

'Don't worry, it'll only be five minutes,' boomed West's voice from the waiting room. 'I won't make you late for your date.' I blushed. Jean smiled like a knowing mother.

'Thank you Jean. Come in West.'

'Can I make you both a cup of tea?'

'No thanks Jean, I need to get away sharpish.'

West was glowing, smiling from ear to ear. He shook my hand firmly and vigorously. His skin looked clearer. His tie was tied today, although it looked uncomfortably tight.

'I won't stay long Doctor. I came to thank you. Please have this as a token of my appreciation of your excellent work.' He handed me a bottle of St Emilion Grand Cru Classé.

'1998. My favourite. Thank you. How did you know?'

His kind eyes seemed to have greater depth than ever – the bags seemed to have been replaced by laughter lines today.

'After that last session, I feel like a new person, refreshed and ready to face the world. I've got my confidence back. I haven't had the slightest flicker of anxiety since. Thank you.'

'I appreciate this generous gift and I'm delighted that you are feeling good, but I have to warn you, I think that this may be a false epiphany. We've got a lot more work to do.'

'I've been going strong for 3000 years, I'll be just fine.'

West gave me a final firm handshake and was gone.

I was genuinely concerned for him. Usually after a false epiphany something triggers things off again and the patient returns to the old state, or worse. Sometimes it takes a few weeks. Sometimes years.

———◆———

The traffic was flowing well and I reached home by 17:35. As my key went into the door, little Nga appeared out of nowhere. As usual she rushed straight upstairs to the kitchen and sat in front of the fridge, doing what I call the pouch dance. She stretched out her legs and spread her paws in turn. I would mimic her and she would then come forward for a stroke. She was letting me know she was ready for a pouch of meat with gravy.

59

I took a long time selecting my clothes and trying on various combinations in front of the mirror. It made me a little late and I had to run to catch the bus from the end of the street.

The two mile journey to Grosvenor Street helped to calm me down. I love watching life go by – people watching without having to think or speak. I got so relaxed, in fact, that I missed my stop. It was 19:25 so I was going to be a few minutes late. I got off at St James Place and walked briskly towards Grosvenor Street. I didn't want to arrive sweaty and out of breath so I deliberately slowed myself down. I was wearing some black Oxfords, suitable for dancing – I naturally assumed that she meant ballroom. I checked my watch: 19:37. The Bombay Raj was a modern Indian restaurant, a far cry from the red velvet chairs and garish wall paper of my student haunts.

'What name Sir?' asked the waiter.

'Dr Chen or Dr Hill.'

He checked his chart. 'Ah yes, Sir, please follow me.' He led me to a table for two in the corner. 'Can I get you a drink while you wait for your guest?'

'Yes, please. A double gin and tonic. With ice and lemon.'

19:48 now. Fashionably late. No messages from Suki.

I was comfortable with sitting alone in a restaurant. As a boy I had been shy, but six years of medical school followed by travel had knocked that out of me, or at least buried it. I watched a family enjoying their meal and tried to guess how they were related to one another. A group of students were becoming a touch too loud but the staff remained respectful – well beyond the call of duty.

I was two-thirds through the gin and tonic. It always goes straight to my head. In fact, it's the perfect alcohol-to-blood-stream delivery system, other than an intravenous line. I started thinking about the safari holiday in Botswana where I'd first got a taste for gin and tonic.

20:10. The waiter asked me if I would like to order any poppadoms to nibble. 'No thank you. She'll be here soon.' He could sense my embarrassment.

I went outside to call Suki. The phone was engaged and went to voicemail. 'Hi Suki, I'm at the Bombay Raj. Let me know what you'd like to drink and I'll get the order in.'

After 15 minutes, I asked the waiter for the bill.

Next morning, I awoke to the vibration of my phone. Suki had sent a text message: 'Sorry James. I forgot about our date. I was tired.'

Later that day, I saw Suki in the hospital corridor talking to a colleague. She looked at me but didn't smile. I felt sick. From then on she treated me as if nothing had happened between us.

In the afternoon I drove across to The Meadows. The people there lived in a world insulated from the frontline of medicine. No distressed patients. No emergency calls. No choosing between compassionate care and meeting targets. No threat of violence.

They had soft carpets, comfortable chairs and beautiful gardens. The old Victorian building used to be part of the psychiatric asylum. Now it was converted into expensive flats but the poshest part housed the hospital's Chief Executive and Directors.

I waited outside the Medical Director's office, feeling irritated to be there. Part naughty school boy, part fish out of water.

'James, James my dear friend, come in.' Doctor Sugden was always insincere. He wouldn't stab you in the back. He'd stab you in the front and tell you how much he didn't want to do it – that it was hospital policy.

'Hello Stuart,' I said, 'how's things in the ivory tower?'

'I'd swap places with you in a flash if I could James.'

Stuart was 55, tall, thin, with swept back grey hair and a big gold ring. He always smelled of cigars although I'd never seen him smoke one. He'd been responsible for bringing in one change programme after another, all counterproductive and harmful to clinical care and staff morale, but without fail enhancing his CV, smoothing the way to his next executive appointment. He so clearly had his eye on the top job. Showing deference to such people was the cost of remaining a clinician.

'Now James, there is a delicate matter to discuss.'

'Stuart, I don't believe in the Worcester Protocols.'

'No. I gave that to Dr Prasad. He's an ambitious young doctor.'

The corners of his lips were upturned. The rest of his face faked concern and seriousness.

'I've had a complaint about your conduct, James.'

My heart sank.

'It has been drawn to my attention that you have been taking an unprofessional interest in one of the junior doctors, Suki Chen.'

My face turned scarlet. I could feel his hand reaching inside me, twisting my gut, enjoying my shame like a school bully.

'James, we all get tempted to cross the line from time to time.'

And so it went on. I tuned out eventually – pretended sympathy veiling a threat.

'I'm going to leave it there for now,' he said at last. 'But I shall have to keep a close eye on you. If I were you, I'd keep things with Dr Chen on a purely formal basis from now on.'

I wanted to piss on his Persian rug. As I left the room, he winked at me.

PANIC ATTACK & ADMISSION

I picked up a KFC family bucket and a tub of ice cream on the way home. I closed the curtains, turned the heating up and put my feet on the couch, allowing Nga enough room to curl up beside me. I cracked open West's St Emilion, allowing it to breathe for two seconds before pouring myself a large glass. It had a beautiful deep burgundy colour and smelled of deep dark cellars and time. It slipped down leaving a warm, complicated aftertaste.

I surfed the live news channels., ending up at the BBC: 'Russian troops have taken over the Ukrainian Naval Headquarters in Sevastopol … President Putin received a standing ovation from the Duma today. He said it was the proudest moment since the collapse of the Soviet Union. … This is like the Nazis invading the Sudetenland in 1938. If they get away with this, they will grow hungry for more … If Russia withholds gas supplies to Europe, confidence in the Euro will collapse … The Saudis, Chinese, Indians and Russians are meeting in Qatar as we speak to discuss a new global reserve currency.'

I watched the Russian stage show in Crimea, celebrating the annexation. Maybe it was the wine, but I felt moved. Such heartfelt patriotism.

I tuned to CNN. 'Mass stabbing by Uighur separatists in Kunming. The People's Liberation Army has increased its presence on the border with Tajikistan. In Beijing, yesterday, the Chinese Central Bank suspended trading in banking shares following revelations about shadow banking. Analysts say that the Chinese economy is heading for its Lehman Brothers moment. Chinese state officials blame the rumours on imperialist forces in Japan. "We will not hesitate to punish the aggressor."'

The France 24 channel showed French troops getting out of the back of a transport plane in Bangui, capital of the Central African Republic. People of one faith were taking revenge for atrocities committed by those of another. There were menacing crowds shouting, some demanding that the French leave, others begging the French to save them. Maps of Mali, Niger and Libya, appeared on the screen, then pickup trucks with machine guns mounted on the back. According to the English voiceover she said it was make or break time for Europe. Cut to pictures of thousands of worshippers asserting their religion on the streets of Paris, Marseilles and Toulouse.

Little Nga climbed on my chest, turning round until she felt comfortable. She settled with her nose close to mine, purring. I think she could feel the sadness in my heart and was sharing her love.

Fox News showed some footage of the extreme cold spell in Canada and the US. Then there were images of the floods in southern England. A Greenpeace representative said, 'We need to drastically cut carbon dioxide emissions before we get widespread famine.'

Nga wasn't bothered about global catastrophe. She was in a trance. She loved me playing with her ears. I turned over for some light relief and found it in the form of *The Pink Panther* – the cartoon, not the film. It had good associations from my childhood – a more innocent time. I wondered if that was true. Was it really more innocent or was it just my age that made it seem so?

I heard my phone ringing on the kitchen table, but failed to reach it in time – I didn't want to startle Nga by leaping up. I checked the screen when I eventually got there: 'Missed call – Suki.' She hadn't left a voicemail.

———

The next day, passing through the Bernie Rosen Unit, Ayesha waved at me, inviting me into the nurses' station. She wore a maroon headscarf. The Christmas decorations were up.

'Good morning Doctor Hill.' She was smiling. 'There is a message for you from the Emergency Department. They'd like you to see someone who came in overnight.'

I had mixed feelings as I emerged from the lift into Minor Injuries. Sure enough, Suki was there examining a patient. She smiled at me very warmly, and pointed to a side room in which three police officers were casually chatting.

Suki followed me to the nurses' station. 'Hello James. I'm sorry,' she said quietly. 'I'm so embarrassed, it was one of my colleagues who reported you. She's jealous. She told Matron.'

I nodded. 'Tell me about the patient.'

She looked upset. 'OK. West came in overnight on a Section 136. They found him sitting on Waterloo Bridge, drunk, having taken an overdose, intending to jump into the Thames.'

'No, really?'

'He's been vomiting up cupfuls of blood. We're going to have to keep him on the Medical Assessment Unit. His ALT and AST are sky high. His heart rhythm is erratic but I it's probably due to hyperventilation from a panic attack. He's nil by mouth in case we have to take him to theatre. The surgeon suspects it's a gastric ulcer. He took a lot of analgesics with a bottle of vodka. They reckon he was moments from jumping in the river.'

'I didn't see that coming. He has suicidal impulses but last time I saw him, he felt great.'

'Would you check his suicide risk?' she said. 'And determine whether he's able to consent to treatment? We can't hold him against his will under common law. The police are waiting for you to make a decision.'

Those were her words, but her face was saying something else. It had an openness and a sadness, but also an invitation. I wasn't ready to accept.

'Can you call the Bernie Rosen Unit and tell them that I'm going to need a nurse for one-to-one observations please?'

'Sure.' She handed me his medical notes, still smiling.

The police officers described how they had talked West down from the bridge. He was in hospital pyjamas, blood and vomit down his front. Joyce, a nurse, stepped out for a break. West was pale and shaky. He was too weak to hold out his hand, but I held it. It was cold. He had had a blood transfusion. Type A+. He was on a saline drip. His heart was fast but with normal rhythm. His eyes were glazed, slightly yellow. The room stank of vodka, vomit and blood. He was only half present.

'Doctor, thanks for coming,' he croaked. He gripped my hand tightly and started to cry. He was taking around 18 breaths a minute and resting a hand on his abdomen. He blew his nose, filling the tissue, which he handed to me. He leant forward and retched. I held the sick bowl under his chin and stroked his back, but nothing came up this time. I put an extra blanket over him.

'I'm sorry. I lost control of myself.'

'I can see you're tired so I want to know the headlines and make sure you're safe.'

'Did you see the news?' he asked, coughing.

I nodded. 'Things can unravel at any time. Under the surface, there are massive tectonic shifts going on. I'm braced for the earthquake. I'm genuinely scared I won't be able to cope.' He burst into tears.

'You're safe here now. There are fantastic staff to look after you.'

'The vultures are circling. Any moment, the financial system might crash. The Dollar will lose its place as the global reserve currency. The Euro will collapse. Interest rates will go through the roof. My mountain of debt will become unsustainable and the economy will go into free fall. It'll make 2008 look like a dress rehearsal.'

He was breathing faster. His pulse rose to 128.

'Keep breathing all the way out or you'll provoke another panic attack.'

'My stomach hurts.'

'Do the best you can'

He squeezed my hand tighter then let go. Joyce returned to flush his IV line. She had come to England from Jamaica to study nursing. I always felt calm and safe in her presence. She went to the other side of the bed to take his blood pressure.

'If the Russians get a taste for it, they'll be invading the Baltic States, Kazakhstan, maybe even Poland next.' West looked terrified. 'I don't have much to stop them. Europe's forces are weak. I can't risk a nuclear war. Our economies are interconnected. If I apply sanctions it'll be like a bee sting. I'll hurt myself more. So Russia has a free hand to do what it likes. The others are watching carefully. If they see how impotent I am, all kinds of things might kick off. China's finances are ready to go bust. Their political system is sitting on a volcano of discontent. When it erupts, powerful group dynamics will be unleashed. They may use war and nationalism as a distraction. The Chinese are desperate to find an excuse to grab Taiwan and the Spratly Islands. The People's Liberation Army are just itching to take revenge on the Japanese.'

He looked at me with desperate eyes, like an old man, once powerful, now weak. It was unsettling. 'Do you know how many religious fundamentalists there are all over the West? It's not just the threat of terrorism. That's a minor side issue. My immune system has been compromised by political correctness and relativism. They are trying to take over by stealth, aided by oil money.

'You can't say that,' scolded Joyce. 'Keep your voice down. The police will hear.' I couldn't tell if she was being sarcastic or not.

West continued. 'People watch wars in the Middle East on TV, falsely imagining that they're insulated from it. It'll be happening here within 15 years. The Europeans believe in nothing other than welfare and human rights, and they don't have the strength or will to defend themselves.'

'Oh come on,' I said, trying to calm him and get his heartbeat down. 'You're getting obsessed with these disaster scenarios. Sure they're possible, but there are many other possible outcomes.'

He continued rambling, regardless of my efforts. 'We're not having enough children. I can't afford the pensions and welfare bill. I've deindustrialised to the point of being unable to defend myself. I live off a giant credit card and I've reached the limit. The bailiffs are at the door. The climate is up the spout. The 1% have concentrated all the wealth in their hands. People don't bother to vote any more. There is an epidemic of diabetes. Food prices are spiralling out of control. We're destroying the planet. I can't cope.'

West leant forward and let out the most odd sound. I couldn't tell if he was trying to be sick, coughing, laughing or crying. He was shaking. Joyce held the bowl up to his mouth. She put her arm around him and he sobbed like a baby. Joyce is the sort of woman you want with you when things get tough.

Gradually West settled. His heart rate dropped below 100.

'Are you still feeling suicidal, West?'

'Yes, I hate myself. I want to get away from the fear and pain.'

'Are you willing to stay in hospital to receive treatment?'

'Do I have any choice?'

I looked at Joyce. I wasn't sure if she was the do-it-by-the-book type or a pragmatist. She leant forward and spoke softly in his ear. 'We need to take care of you my darling. You've injured yourself. This lovely doctor needs to help you mend your broken heart. You can agree to stay now and let us help you – that's the easy way – or ...'

'OK, I get it. I'm happy to stay.'

I winked at Joyce and she returned a warm smile.

'I'm going to arrange for a psychiatric nurse to be with you 24 hours a day until you're safe.'

'Thank you doctor. I won't let you down.' I squeezed his hand.

'What's the score Doc?' asked the senior police officer.

'He's going to be all right. He's agreed to stay voluntarily. I think you saved his life. You'll never realise the difference you made.'

I filled Suki in on my assessment. She whispered, 'Please call me,' but I didn't agree to anything. I headed back to my office.

Saturday morning. A text message: 'Are you coming to your sister's for Christmas? We're there from Christmas Eve through to Boxing Day. You're welcome any time, love Mum xx.'

I replied, 'That'd be lovely. I'll call her to arrange, x.'

I always looked forward to Christmas. We weren't a religious family, but it was a very special time of year. Other than birthdays, it was the only set piece occasion that we celebrated. I looked forward to singing at Midnight Mass, sharing presents and, of course, the feast. That reminded me, it was time to do my Christmas shopping before the streets got unbearably busy.

Soon after that I had a call from Steve inviting me to go hill walking in North Wales. Just what I needed in order to put the Suki business behind me. I told Steve exactly that. We agreed the details and signed off. Things were really beginning to look up again. How wonderful, I thought, to have family and old friends there for you when you need them.

We stayed at the Pen-y-Gwryd Hotel – my favourite spot. It was a very traditional old inn at the base of Mount Snowdon, run by a family who'd had it for generations. They somehow preserved the atmosphere and culture of the 1950s. My favourite thing was to soak in the huge tin bath after a day's walk, looking forward to a seven course meal, washed down with fine wine.

Much refreshed after the weekend I drove into work on Monday. My junior doctor, Seth, was on the ball, as ever, and there was nothing much for me to do. Phil said, 'West is still on the MAU. They kept him because he bled during the endoscopy. He should be ready to transfer across later this week.'

'Thanks Phil.' I could tell he had something else to say.

'James, watch out for Sugden. I've heard he's got it in for you.'

My clinic finished early so I took the opportunity see how West was doing. I was met by Dr Prasad, the ambitious protégée of Dr Sugden.

'Hi James. Don't often see you down here. To what do I owe this pleasure?'

'Me,' West called out from a bed in the first bay. I waved.

'Sanjay, would you mind filling me in on West's progress?'

'Sure. 45 years old, single, white man. He came in late Thursday night after an overdose of analgesics and vodka. He damaged his liver but his levels are returning to normal. He had some bleeding from a gastric ulcer. Mild hypertension. Hypercholesterolaemia. Otherwise, anxiety, low self-esteem, suicidal ideas, binge drinking, longstanding panic attacks, your department.'

'Thanks Sanjay. When you think he's physically ready for discharge, we'll transfer him across.'

Ayesha was sitting with West. She came over to see me. 'Hello Doctor Hill. I think Mr West doesn't need one-to-one. He's not suicidal any more.'

'Thanks. Take a break, Ayesha. I'll be at least half an hour.'

'How are you feeling West?'

His hand was warm. The wound from his IV line had begun to heal. 'Much better thanks Doctor, though embarrassed.'

He spoke much more quietly. 'Please don't let on to anyone who I am or there'll be hell to pay.'

'No of course not. Besides, no one would believe you anyway. They'd give you anti-psychotics.'

'I think Joyce knows. I like her. Please thank her for me.'

'Will do. West, have you ever tried to kill yourself before?'

'Yes, a few times. I tried to drown myself after the collapse of the Roman Empire. Then again when I lost Jerusalem and the Holy Land. I cut myself when I lost the Byzantine Empire. I lost a lot of weight during the plague but I think that was due to bereavement. I came close again during the First World War. The Holocaust made me sick to the pit of my stomach. Part of me was ready to die then but I kept going. I was determined to put it right. Somehow, hope always shines through.'

'What gives you hope now? What is there worth living for?'

'Love. Life. Fun. Art. Music. The joy of liberating humans fulfilling their potential. The thrill of making new discoveries. Expanding my consciousness ever more. The challenge of going truly global. The desire to heal old wounds. The opportunity to discover life out in the universe. In my heart of hearts I know that, for all the problems I told you about, there are a lot of hopeful solutions.'

'Excellent.' I said. 'You adapt quickly.'

'I wouldn't have reached 3000 years old without it.'

Ayesha returned.

'Ayesha, I agree with your assessment. Mr West doesn't need one-to-one observations any more. Thank you very much for your help,' I said.

I turned to West. 'While you remain in hospital, we can make a gentle start with tackling some of your concerns. It's best if we start off with some of the less emotionally intense subjects. Since you're in hospital, shall we have a session on Healthcare and Medicine?'

'Yes, that's been on my mind since I've been seeing it up close the last few days. I also have some thoughts about science I'd like to share if there's time,' replied West.

'Excellent, I'll visit you tomorrow.'

'Thanks James.' West looked relieved.

MEDICINE, TRUTH & SCIENCE

Tuesday – a free morning. I decided to read the Lancet while lounging on the office sofa, but I quickly found myself thinking about Suki instead. Maybe I hadn't given her a fair hearing. Jean popped her head around the door. 'Joyce is on the phone from the MAU. West is insisting on being discharged.' I made my way down there.

West was wearing jeans, polo shirt, leather jacket and loafers. He looked physically well but harassed.

'James,' said West on seeing me. 'I've got to get out of here. I've had enough of hospitals. Some of the staff are very kind, like Joyce, but I just feel like a number being processed on a production line here. People come and go, stick needles in you, take measurements, talk about you then they spend ages over there on the computers.'

'Maybe so,' I said. 'But you did nearly kill yourself just a couple of days ago. You shouldn't be running away from those feelings. We need to get a grip on it now or it'll come up to bite you another time.'

'I'm, sorry, I know you're right.

'I'd like to transfer you to the Bernie Rosen Unit for a few days to make sure you're settled before you go home.'

'I'll have a think about it. I'd certainly like to get on with the therapy. Perhaps this is the best way.'

We walked out to the hospital garden. It was a cold day but there was a lovely clear blue sky.

West: You know, James, you were right, this stay in hospital really has made me think about health and medicine. On the one hand, things seem better than I remember them. The technology and science available to medicine now is obviously much better than 30 years ago, let alone 100 or a 1000 years ago. I've received some powerful treatments over the last few days, and the doctors and nurses have a vast amount of data and evidence to draw on – that's clear. People live much longer too, don't they? Twice as long as a mediaeval person. They routinely survive diseases that would have killed them years ago. I've conquered quite a few infectious diseases in my time, I can tell you.

James: But on the other hand?

West: There's high mortality in heart disease, cancer, stroke and increasing morbidity in dementia, stress, depression, anxiety, diabetes, obesity, asthma, hypertension and allergies. People eat rich, fatty, artificial food stuffed with sugar, salt and additives. And that's just the hospital food!

They laugh.

West: We anaesthetise fear, stress and pain with alcohol, sugar, drugs and caffeine. Some old diseases are creeping back, like TB, due to migration and drug resistance. Microorganisms evolve much faster than we do.

West is visibly relaxing – watching people come and go.

West: Technology breakthroughs come at a rate far beyond my ability to pay for them. Tens of millions of Americans can't afford healthcare. I spend most of my money trying to keep people alive in their last few months when, rationally, it'd be much wiser in health promotion and illness prevention.

James: You're uncomfortably close to the truth.

West: You must have seen a lot of change during your career.

James: Yes, I started medical School in 1988. Doctors and nurses were still PURPLE tribal in attitude and loyalty. ORANGE evidence-based medicine was ramping up. The organisation of medicine was heavily bureaucratic BLUE, about to be revolutionised by Margaret Thatcher's introduction of the ORANGE business culture.

West: What do you mean by tribal?

James: Traditional medicine goes right back to the days of the PURPLE witch doctor and shaman figures, deep in our history. The role of the doctor is still to heal and relive suffering, to work some magic, connect with the spirit and to say the unsayable within the sacred space of the consulting room.

West: Dr Prasad talked about me as if I were a lump of meat and a set of blood results.

James: I'm sorry about that. The idea that medicine should be based upon the best evidence and use best practice is unassailable, but the way it is implemented is far from perfect.

West: I would never want to go back to the world of mysticism, oppressive tradition and religious zealotry, but I would like to be cared for with compassion as Joyce and Suki did. Medicine seems to have prioritised technology over healing and humanity.

James: So, what constitutes science at its very best in your view?

West: Science is an open-minded, creative and serious enquiry for the truth. It puts aside tradition and prejudice in a single-minded search for the best theory to explain and predict how the world works and how to change it.

James: This is a more difficult question. What's the difference between science and what you might call philosophy and reason?

West: The difference is to do with testing hypotheses. That's what you do in science — through observation, prediction and experiment. A good theory explains a phenomena in the simplest, most elegant way, is logical, intuitively makes sense, has measurable phenomena and makes clear predictions. A good experiment is one that tests those predictions in a way that is accurate, standardised and repeatable by other scientists. That way, you no longer have to rely assertions of individuals or have to trust their integrity. You can do the experiment for yourself. Science gives us ever better models of reality, and technology puts them to practical use.

West crosses his legs, his arms animating his words.

James: Reductionist science is fantastic but, it can't explain everything. By limiting our mindset to the ORANGE system thinking, we lose out on many of our other faculties. We neglect all those things that we can't yet measure, like healing and compassion, as you said, even though they're important.

West: That's the problem. I've embraced science fully because it is so useful, but I sometimes feel I've devalued the other ways of knowing, like wisdom, experience and intuition. People still use their instinct and gut feeling but we've lost confidence in that. When someone asks 'What's the evidence base for that?' they feel they can't just say, 'It's my gut feeling,' or 'my experience tells me that' or 'I know it in my heart.' People feel the need to cite a scientific study or an evidence based protocol to justify every assertion. We give credence to numbers, graphs and the paraphernalia of science even when science doesn't yet have the answers.

James: We have an array of intelligences including intuition, instinct and wisdom which go well beyond our rational mind. You're right that reductionist science doesn't value things we can't see. If only we knew our bodies, minds and instincts the way an Amazonian tribesman knows his body and environment.

West: Why would I want to return to the level of an Amazonian tribesman? I've spent thousands of years progressing beyond that.

James: You wouldn't. Science is brilliant but it mainly operates in the rational, objective and logical realm. That's important but we shouldn't forget the other intelligences hard wired into our biology. Have you ever made a decision and then regretted it?

West thinks for a moment then nods.

West: I got involved in the West African slave trade. Part of me was dead against it but I turned a blind eye to it for a long time.

James: What made you doubt your decision, having made it?

West: I was hard hearted, telling myself that life was cruel and harsh, that it was the way of the world. Occasionally, I felt discomfort, churning in my stomach. I weighed the different arguments. I found that I could justify any case, but it didn't make me feel any better about it. So, I listened to my gut instinct. I knew that I had to ban slavery in my territories and to use my power to bring it to an end elsewhere.

James: How do you know that kind of intuition is valid? How did you reassure yourself?

West: The decision felt right. I knew. I sensed it, I feel it. My heart opened, my stomach settled and I felt comfortable again.

James: Let me give you a medical example from my life in medicine. A junior doctor, wanted the team to validate a suicide risk assessment she had made. She wanted protection in case of future litigation. She methodically presented her thorough and competent assessment. The team listened diligently. There was a feeling of infectious anxiety in the room. The team asked meticulous questions about every detail of the case. The inquiry was sensible, intelligent and everyone knew the scientific evidence about suicide risk. After 20 minutes, no one felt comfortable enough to take responsibility for saying that the doctor had made a good judgement.

West: It must be hard to make a decision like that without having met the patient yourself.

James: You've hit the nail on the head. You can only confidently make that judgement by meeting the patient, listening, feeling their emotions, observing their body language, sensing the risk directly though the subtle instrument of your body. It isn't a tick-box exercise. We're much more than rational machines.

West: What happened with the doctor's risk assessment?

James: I said to her that she had been very thorough. It sounded to me that she had made a very reasonable judgement and come to a sensible plan but, none of us in the room could know for sure whether it was right decision. Only she had met the patient. I asked her to go within herself, to put all of that information together and to read her gut reaction. She did that, closing her eyes for about three seconds. She opened her eyes, sparkling with self-confidence. Without hesitation, smiling broadly she said, 'It's fine, the suicide risk is low.' Nothing else needed to be said. Everyone instinctively knew that that was the right answer. They trusted him, her assessment, her plan and her judgement.

West: So, what took 20 minutes of intellectual debate could have taken three seconds of intuition! I haven't forgotten my instincts. I devalued them. I can give you an example from the financial industry. At the height of the bull market, two very clever investors in New England thought that they'd found the Holy Grail of how to get rich using rational, linear mathematical formulas to eliminate financial risk. That worked for several years while the embedded assumptions held true. When conditions changed, they lost billions of dollars. Their arch rival, a hugely successful investor who still relied on using his own judgement capitalised on their mistakes.

James: I remember that. They had to go cap in hand to him to bail them out. He was thrilled.

Suki walks by, smiling, running her fingers though her hair.

West: She still likes you. Take a risk, trust your instincts!

James: Can you stick to being the patient, please?

West chuckles.

James: You know, there is a fully scientific basis to our gut reactions. The gut has several layers of muscle which run all the way through it and this is coordinated and controlled by the nervous system within the gut and links via the autonomic nervous system to the brain. The 'gut brain' is about the same size as a cat's brain.

West laughs, miming stroking a cat on his belly.

James: Gut instinct is part of our biology. There's a mind-body interaction. There are 100 million neurones in the gut and only 2000 pre-ganglionic neurones in the vagus nerve running up to the brain, so, it operates mostly independently of the brain. The brain has an override switch for some things, most obviously in choosing when to open the bowels and when to eat. Peristalsis, the gastrocolic reflex, digestion and the rate of excretion are controlled locally.

West furtively checks his pulse.

James: Indian Ayurvedic medicine and traditional Chinese medicine don't make these distinctions between the mind and body. They understand that the mind, body and spirit are all the same thing, looked at from different perspectives. For example, the third chakra, an energy centre that we call the solar plexus, can be found below the rib cage at the top of the abdomen, a couple of inches inside. When it is activated, you feel the territorial, physical animal within you as a heat.

West: I have felt that in battle. I sometimes feel fear in my belly.

James: Some people describe courage as being exactly the same sensation as fear, that feeling in the solar plexus, tension, heart pumping, sweating, aroused, hackles raised and so on but with the decision to act anyway. Both traditional Indian and Chinese medicine have a sophisticated understanding of the role of the third chakra or gut energy system in our health.

West: Does Western medicine make use of Eastern knowledge?

James: Increasingly, gradually. In psychiatry, we're using Eastern techniques which are thousands of years old including mediation and yoga. They were brought to the West by explorers and pioneers and by migrants who brought them here. The techniques have been put together in a standardised package to make it amenable to scientific research. The results are so compelling that even the American Health Insurance companies are willing to pay for it because it gets patients home quicker, better, with fewer complications and less medication.

West: What's it called?

James: Mindfulness-Based Stress Reduction. It's an eight week course which teaches meditation, yoga, mindful awareness and equanimity. It yields benefits in physical health, faster healing, reduced anxiety, resolution of physical symptoms, less frequent relapse of depression, lower blood pressure, fewer heart attacks, better sex, better relationships, improved happiness, improved judgments, self-mastery and better leadership skills.

West: I'd like that.

James: You can. We run the course on the Bernie Rosen Unit. It's an example of the benefits of bringing GREEN thinking, the open minded, non-judgmental, pluralistic world view to break down the old assumptions, without compromising scientific principles.

West: Is Western Medicine incorporating the Eastern knowledge about the gut, the third chakra and energy system?

James: Not as far as I know. I did once mention it to a gastroenterologist and he looked at me as if I were a charlatan. In France, Pierre Pallardy has 30 years' experience teaching people to connect with their abdomen through meditation, massage and touch. He found that the common symptom of a bloated abdomen is associated with psychological blocks. His techniques have healed many people, alleviated their symptoms and made substantial changes in their lives. Someone like him could help many cases from the GP's and gastroenterology clinics.

West: Why isn't this being done more widely then?

James: Unfortunately, those techniques haven't yet been subject to scientific studies. We have to justify ourselves according to the evidence, and one man's case studies and testimonials are not good enough. There are hundreds of thousands of people who make all kinds of claims. Doctors have to stick reasonably close to the scientific evidence.

West: I remember, Donald Rumsfeld, the former US Defense Secretary, once said, 'There are known knowns. There are things we know that we know. There are known unknowns. That's to say, there are things that we now know we don't know. There are unknown unknowns. There are things we do not know we don't know.'

James: And I'd like to add another: unknown knowns – things which we know without knowing that we know them. Most of medicine is still an unknown. We don't even know what we don't know. That's why we must keep our minds open and listen to our instincts and experience.

West: I really don't want to go back to the PURPLE world of mysticism, witch doctors, magic potions and quack healers.

James: Neither do I, but remember that the placebo effect – in other words the belief that a pill or treatment will make you better – and the therapist effect – that's the power that a therapist has to heal someone – are together responsible for at least half the efficacy of medicine, whether an it's antidepressant or knee surgery. We don't understand how that works.

West: So a doctor is still a bit like a witch doctor.

James: Yes, science is yet to fully explain the process of healing. However, because medicine has become so technically orientated, because the ORANGE belief system has become dominant and dogmatic, we have neglected to practice the art of medicine, the healing and the care. We could probably substantially improve our results if we focussed our research, training and attention much more on the power of the placebo and therapist effects.

West: But there's no money in that for the pharmaceutical companies and it's not so sexy for the academics to do something simple that anyone could do. You say we don't understand the mechanism of the placebo effect or the therapist effect? Could it me to do with epigenetics?

James: Gosh, you've been doing your reading. The answer is maybe. Our beliefs and behaviour seem to affect the way in which our genes express themselves. It's a new area of research. We're just getting the first glimmers of what's to come.

West: I must keep an open, creative mind to be truly scientific. Science, like any other human endeavour, is vulnerable to groupthink, complacency, ego, money, power and habit.

James: West, you're doing my job for me. Keep it up. It's important to make sure that we are disciplined in sticking to the fundamentals of science. Since you're so well informed today, can you tell me the basic assumptions of science?

West: That there is a world out there beyond us. It is made up of objects, particles or waves which have properties that we can measure.

James: Keep going.

West: There are laws of nature. We can generate hypotheses about them by observation, induction and reason and test them by experiments to see if the predictions of the theories are true.

James: Carry on. I'm enjoying this. Any other assumptions that science makes?

West: I don't know what you're fishing for.

James: Well, current Western science unconsciously assumes that the universe exists as non-living, non-conscious matter and waves within a giant empty space, the cosmos, within which conscious lifeforms are an inexplicable aberration. There's no proof for that. They are assumptions. Ideas held as faith. Non-Western sciences are increasingly experimenting with their own alternative assumptions, for example that the universe is alive and conscious. That's a potentially rich source of innovation, something that the Western ORANGE system could be very excited about, embracing the pluralism of the GREEN world view as a way to increase scientific creativity and power.

West: Even I, as an outsider, can see that scientific research isn't always as squeaky clean as people imagine. Take the pharmaceutical industry. Their primary duty, I imagine, is to maximise their profits for the shareholders. If they bring relief to patients and improve the health of the population, that's a positive by-product, but the main aim is to make maximum profits.

James: You said capitalism is a driver of human progress.

West: In my view, true science is disinterested concerning the outcome of research. Business is primarily driven by the desire to make money. Academics have egos, status and positions to maintain. They need finance to fund their research and personal lives. There's a conflict of interest. Pharmaceutical companies publish data when it shows their drugs in a good light but they don't publish the negative or neutral results. Doctors don't get to see all the evidence, only what it suits others to let them see.

James: Well, governments are beginning to force pharmaceutical companies to publish all their data. That's good at least, if the BLUE system regulators are successful in defeating the RED system impulse to cheat.

West: It still isn't enough.

James: Why?

West: Because the financial interests and unscientific groupthink severely limits what research is done in the first place. There are so many potential hypotheses and phenomena that go untested because there's no money, power or status for the vested interests.

James: What can you do to make it the best it can be?

West: I need strict regulation backed up by the force of the law. Scientists should be legally bound to be honest in their scientific endeavour and to publish all the results even if it is harmful to their finances or reputation. Also, we can't rely only on the profit motive for research. Much research that is of vital importance to humanity isn't necessarily going to make money. Governments need to invest substantially in science. Many innovations come from military research, for example. Most of the innovations are serendipitous or emergent. The practical applications of technology is often not obvious at the stage of the pure science.

James pulls out an iPhone from his pocket.

James: Let me read you a quote about wisdom from Professor Jim Garrison. He said, 'Socrates said that wisdom is the disposition to live in questions rather than to live in answers. It's the opposite of religious dogma. It's distinct from science, which seeks to find the facts, explanations for measurable phenomenon which can be tested by experiment. A wise person is one who tries to see the biggest picture, understands the ebb and flow of life, tunes into the gut reactions, uses all of their senses. The wise person is one who has the courage to sit with questions, to be patient in dialogue in search of answers and not to rush the process. A wise person aims not to make the fundamental attribution error, being fully aware of the power of situation and environment to influence an individual's behaviour. A wise person shows humility, compassion and sensitivity to others while being courageous enough to define themselves and to put the truth above their own short-term interests. A wise person is aware of human frailty and fallibility. A wise person lives in the present, not the past or future, is comfortable with paradox, able to connect the dots between distant phenomena and spends time in nature, grounding oneself with time in meditation and contemplation.'

West: We could all benefit from doing more of that. I'm struggling a bit. How can I integrate all these different types of truth and knowledge?

James: You have to sit with the complexity and the paradox. You don't every have total, absolute knowledge and truth. You just do your best, integrating the best of all your faculties. Let's draw the threads together by inviting your different world views to define their understanding of the truth. Go through them in order. Take on their voices and tell us what truth is.

West stands up and turns to face James.

BEIGE: The truth is whatever is necessary to survive.

PURPLE: Whatever keeps me secure, whatever protects the tribe and maintains the honour of the elders, the wishes of the spirits and the power of the chief is what's right. I believe in tradition.

RED: Whatever the powerful say is true. The truth is whatever I have to say or do to get what I want right now.

BLUE: There's only one truth, one right way, a divine higher purpose or the infallible logic or ideology.

ORANGE: We can only know what we can measure and test. We're limited, therefore, by the structure of our brain, the assumptions which we've made, the physical biology of our senses, our ability to process information, and by a choice of concepts and language, metaphor and perception. Science is our best hope of getting close to the truth by coming up with and testing theories with experiment.

GREEN: Truth is subjective, biased by culture, dogma, money and power. People distort their perception of the truth to avoid pain, fear, risk, responsibility or shame.

Human beings are easily influenced by stories and prefer emotions over statistics and abstraction. These are hooks which wise players use to manipulate us all the time whether they're salesmen, politicians or scientists. We distort our perception of the truth and our assertion of the truth because we're lazy. We don't want to change or because we're too busy to think. We distort the truth to fit with our identity, interests and desires.

ORANGE: Don't forget cognitive distortions like groupthink, self-serving bias, omission bias and the fundamental attribution error. We seek out information to confirm our current perception of the truth and to minimise or dismiss information that challenges it.

GREEN: People align with the most powerful, attractive or persuasive people. People distort their beliefs to be popular, to avoid intimidation, to maintain power, to inspire trust and respect, to receive rewards, to gain control, to protect their interests. In some contexts, money buys the truth.

James: Can YELLOW integrate all of those?

YELLOW: I can try! That's the challenge. The truth can only be found by intelligently combining science, philosophy, intuition and faith with wisdom and experience.

James: Invite all the parts to come back within you. Allow them to integrate.

> *West sits down with head bowed and eyes closed. After a minute or so, he opens his eyes and smiles.*

James: Well done, West. How does that feel?

West: Much clearer.

James: Good. In future as you apply your new thinking to specific examples it should become even more focused. Let's call it a day there. Will you agree to come over to my ward for a few days?

West: OK, you've twisted my arm. Just a couple of days.

CARE, LEADERSHIP & HUMAN POTENTIAL

I sat in the nurses' station with Phil and Ayesha, watching the comings and goings in the patents' lounge. West was holding court, telling stories to a group of patients sitting in a circle of chairs – those horrible rubbery ones designed for the convenience of the staff, not the comfort of the patients.

Phil said, 'He's really made himself at home, hasn't he? I don't know what you think, but to me he doesn't seem depressed, as such, any more.'

Ayesha chipped in, 'He came up with some unusual paintings in art therapy. I tried to talk to him about it, but he was very prickly. He can come across as a bit on an arrogant know-it-all.'

'I think that's because his self-esteem is still a bit fragile under the surface,' replied Phil. 'He's unstable. Different parts of him fighting for control while he tries to keep up the appearance of confidence.'

I sensed there was a bit of an ego battle going on here. Ayesha turned to me for support. 'Dr Hill, do you think we should we enrol him in the Personal Mastery and Inner Leadership Course?' she asked.

'Yes, please do, Ayesha, if he's interested.'

'Who knows, it might be the last time the course happens,' said Phil. 'Dr Sugden has asked Seth to do an audit on it. He wants to see evidence that it increases patient throughput.'

'Of course it doesn't,' said Ayesha. 'It keeps them in longer. We're helping people learn skills and grow. It's better for their long term well-being.'

'Don't shoot the messenger,' replied Phil. 'They only care about spreadsheets and money. This ward's days are numbered. There's no room for holistic practice in a sea of pill-pushing, protocol driven, risk-management psychiatry.'

I decided to keep my opinions to myself. Sugden wasn't exactly my best friend, apparently, so it wouldn't be wise to make mutinous noises in public. You never really knew who you could trust. I'd recently learned that to my cost.

West tapped on the window. Ayesha opened the door. 'The doctor's busy, go back to your room.'

'Hang on Ayesha, it's all right, I have some time before my clinic. Can I use the meeting room?'

She checked the diary, 'No, it's being used by the Pilates class until 2 o'clock. You could use the Executive Suite on the ground floor. That's usually empty.'

I made my way down there with West in tow.

West: Thank you for seeing me so soon.

James: My pleasure. Do you mind if I record this?

West: No, so long as you encrypt it, as per normal.

West looks around the Executive Suite, at the comfortable furnishings and attractive decor.

West: I met a lovely nurse from Jamaica in the Emergency Department.

James: Joyce?

West: Yes. She laughed at me for being uptight. She said it was the curse of the modern lifestyle. Rushing, stressing and missing out on life altogether.

James: A nurse from Tanzania told me that he felt, in England, he was always having to watch the clock, work to deadlines. He said that in Tanzania people would turn up for their appointments whenever they felt like it and no one got very worried about that. Things took as long as they took and the doctor would meet the patient when they were ready. He said it was common for people to turn up to a dinner invitation at a different time or even on a different day.

West: If that happened here, people would consider it disorganised and rude.

James: Yes, he acknowledged that, and he said he'd had to consciously adapt in order to live here. The consequence is a feeling of tension – always worrying about the future. He's less relaxed.

West: Until 10,000 years ago my people lived freely in nature, guided by instinct. But these days things have moved on a long way. We expect to have their lives ordered, regulated, measured and assessed, from the cradle to the grave.

James: You quite like that thought, don't you? I can tell.

West: It's quite a comforting feeling having those rules and regulations around you. You could see it as a restriction, but it's also a protection. Rules and measurements make things safer and more predictable.

James: Could you see yourself integrating the discipline and organisation of modernity with that freedom, presence and instinct of our ancestors?

West: Let me throw that question back at you. Could you see yourself integrating the best of scientific medicine with the art of healing?

James: Touché.

West: It's a hypothetical question. Frankly, I'd rather be treated by a doctor who used the latest science to get me better rather than loving care from someone with imaginary magic potions and placebos.

James: I understand that. But all the same, people who in healthcare often yearn for some kind of change in the way they work. There's a big gap between medicine as we'd like to practise it and medicine as we're able to practise it. I've been asked to do psychiatric clinics with 16 patients all of whom were new to me, each with thick files, multiple pathologies, serious risks, poor previous medical care. I was allocated 15 minutes per patient. It's impossible to do the job properly, humanely or professionally like that.

West: That's why doctors dish out so many pills. It's quick and easy and gives the impression of doing something useful and effective. Patients can apparently be receiving highly technical medicine, expensive scans, drugs, tests and treatments from highly educated staff but no one has time to speak to them, no one takes a proper history, no one has time or sometimes the inclination to care for the patient. Malnutrition is common in hospitals because the food is low quality and the staff are either too busy or too proud to help patients eat the food. The staff say they don't have time to give what used to be considered basic care.

> *West's face lights up as Joyce appears at the glass panel of the door. He waves her in and embraces her. She holds him like a son.*

James: Hi Joyce. Perfect timing. We're discussing the medical system, compassionate care and…'

Joyce: Don't get me started. Sometimes, I hate it here. I'm ashamed to say that.

James: I would never guess that by the way you act, Joyce.

Joyce: Vocation is a burden when the system exploits it.

West: Why did you become a nurse?

Joyce: I wanted to care for people and wanted a job that I could combine with family life.

West: Has it turned out as expected?

Joyce: I enjoy caring for people, seeing people get better. It's a real privilege to help people through difficult times. It's a struggle to relate to my patients as people. I'm always rushing, always feeling guilty that the someone else that needs my help and knowing that the management are only interested in the paperwork and avoiding responsibility.

West: Surely patient care is the most important thing?

Joyce: You would have thought so wouldn't you? No, it's all about avoiding blame — reverse engineering from a court case in the future. Everything has to be written down like a legal document so that one day when the coroner asks you why something bad happened, you can prove that you did what's considered to be best practice, followed the guidelines, ticked all the boxes.

James: Shouldn't everyone should be following best practice and evidence-based medicine?

Joyce: James, I know you're teasing. 'Evidence-based medicine' assumes that the evidence exists and is of high quality. 'Best practice' assumes that the researchers and bureaucrats truly know what that is.

James: Most research that comes out of psychiatric ivory towers doesn't have much practical use. Guidelines and protocols are written by people who don't have to live with complexity, imperfect information, imperfect science, chaos, limited resources, imperfect colleagues, dysfunctional systems and poor relationships.

Joyce: Staff end up going through the motions, leaving humanity and common sense at the door, ticking the boxes.

West: That must be soul destroying

Joyce: I have this parallel life where, in private, I do my very best for my patients, trying to help them, heal them and, in public, I have to demonstrate compliance with the bureaucracy and practice defensive medicine.

West: Maybe there could be a box to tick to say that you've connected with the soul of the patient, seen them, heard them, shown them love and care, asked them deep incisive questions, supported your colleagues and used your wisdom and experience!

Joyce: Very funny. Don't suggest that to Dr Prasad or he'll introduce a new form and spreadsheet for it. The system is a heartless, soul-crushing machine. It's set up to absolve the people at the top of responsibility. They're 'covered' because they've made sure that, 'systems are in place and fit for purpose' even though they know that's largely for show. When my children have left school, I'm going to leave nursing and become a complimentary therapist so that I can focus on caring for people.

West: It would be a real shame for your patients to lose such a caring nurse. What support do you need for you to deliver the best service that you can?

Joyce: To get out of the way and let us get on with the job that we know how to do. To give us enough resources, time, training, support, and clinical leadership. Minimise the bureaucracy. I'd like them to be accountable for the effects of their decisions. I'd like them to support us when things go wrong rather than finding someone to use as a scapegoat. I'd like them to acknowledge that health care can't be perfect, we can't get things right the whole time and medicine has limitations.

Joyce goes quiet suddenly, shrinking in her chair. The Chief Executive's face is framed in the glass of the door.

CEO: Hello. Christine Pearson, CEO. We've got this room booked for a meeting, but you're welcome to join in.

West introduces himself as a patient from the ward. The CEO turns to West, feigning equality and chumminess.

CEO: Good to meet you Mr West. I couldn't help overhearing the interesting conversation you were having – all about healthcare and rules and so on. Fascinating.

She gives a mirthless smile.

CEO: I have a few minutes between meetings and I was wondering if I could just chip in. Would that be OK? In the interests of fairness? Just to set the record straight, as it were?

Joyce shrinks further into her seat.

James: We'd be delighted. Thank you Christine.

CEO: Thanks. OK, now, I just wanted to say that the staff here do an excellent job under very difficult circumstances. However, much as I would love to be able to leave them to act on their own judgement, healthcare is a very complex service. I manage multiple risks. Demand always exceeds supply. I have a system of continuous learning, performance management and a relentless focus on quality and accountability. I'm accountable to the stakeholders, regulators, the public and government.

West: As a patient, I want to get well, have my pain and suffering relieved. I want high-quality staff who know what they're doing, are competent and care. Anything that delivers that's fine with me.

CEO: Mr West, I had to suspend a gynaecologist yesterday. He lost his temper, 'Leave me alone. I know how to do my job,' he said. But what he really meant was 'I don't want anyone interfering with me. I've worked hard for this position, now I intend to milk it. I will work as hard as I want, when I want and how I want. The patients will get what they're given. They should be grateful to have someone like me look after them.' He was a fool to let his guard slip, but many of them think that way. I can't leave the staff to their own devices. I need tight governance and regulation.

Joyce sits up, her eyes shining with anger.

Joyce: Good medicine is holistic. It integrates the best of science, art, wisdom, compassion and humility and empowers staff to use their judgement, intuition and experience.

Dr Prasad: Joyce, that sounds lovely. No, really, it does. But what I need is statistical data – the outcomes for different clinicians so that I can performance manage them, benchmark them, make decisions, allocate resources, assess training needs, design leadership interventions and detect problems in the system where they exist. That's how we cure people.

Joyce: It isn't just about time, money and numbers. Taking a blood pressure takes two minutes. But when I do it, I try to bring a loving presence to bear, smiling, saying a few comforting words, explaining what I'm doing and asking the patient how they are. Attentiveness, kindness and gentleness.

West: That is true. Another nurse took exactly the same two minutes to take my blood pressure but he treated me as an object, treated the task as an irritating one to be done quickly before getting on with the next priority. He didn't look at me or even talk to me. I was just another task to tick off the list. Some of the night staff could be rude, disrespectful, unkind and rough.

CEO: The staff here do an excellent job under very difficult circumstances.

James coughs and fidgets in his seat.

James: Let me frame that slightly differently, West. It seems to me that personal or impersonal approaches to a simple medical procedure take more or less the same time and effort. However, one encourages the therapist effect, the other doesn't. One can generate fear or anxiety, the other can alleviate it. A touch can be healing or it can harm. Each approach influences the autonomic nervous system, staff morale and well-being and the atmosphere of the whole clinic. Imagine scaling that up to every medical interaction.

CEO: Fine. But how can I operationalise it, James?

James: Christine. It's like this. Behaviours are determined by attitude, values, culture and leadership. You need good training, resources, organisation, clear vision, effective processes and good clinical skills. Staff need to care for themselves and each other as well as for their patients. Mindfulness practices teach people to bring attention to their breath, body, gut reactions, instinct and heart, how to use their judgement, presence and the power of their thoughts and attitudes. We need to help staff reconnect with their vocation and tap into their values and we need to align the systems to help them do that to the very best.

Dr Prasad: Show me the numbers, the audits, the business case, the randomised controlled trials. Otherwise, we cannot justify spending taxpayers money on it. Am I right Christine?

James: This reminds me of a New Zealander, Dr Robin Youngson. He came from engineering and went into anaesthetics, one of the most apparently technical and rational areas of medicine. He was the most senior doctor in his hospital. He used to dislike being on call for the obstetrics department. He would have to get up in the middle of the night, already after a busy day, to drive to the hospital and give epidurals to mothers in labour. The midwives were hostile, the patient wasn't ready, the equipment wasn't prepared and he usually arrived to a chaotic and negative atmosphere. He couldn't wait to get home. He would find himself being resentful and grumpy.

Dr Prasad: No one likes having to wake up during the night.

James: Anyway, one night, on the way to the hospital, he stopped his car for a few moments. He realised what an amazing privilege it was to be present at such an important time in people's lives, at the birth of a new life and to be able to bring relief from pain and distress. He committed to bringing his full presence, awareness and intention to each interaction with the mothers and midwives. He took his time and treated them as human beings.

The CEO looks at her watch.

James: Gradually, he began to enjoy his work, rediscover his vocation. He was no longer bitter, resentful and angry. The midwives came to love him. Now, when he arrived, the patient would be ready, laid out on her side, fully prepared with all the instruments ready, the medications drawn up. The midwives told the patients how lucky they were to see the best doctor in the hospital. You can imagine the boost to the placebo and therapist effects. He was happier, the job was quicker and the patient was better, the midwives happy. The complications rate dropped. They needed less medication and fewer medical interventions.

The CEO sighs.

CEO: How can I scale that up to the size of an organisation?

Joyce: I'm sorry, but leadership and organisation aren't only about structures and processes. People have focused exclusively on external leadership, on the structures, processes and measurements and they've neglected the inner leadership – the purpose, values, ethos and so on. James, you've been to the London Business School, you must have studied all the top research. What's the one top secret of leadership?

Everyone looks at James expectantly.

James: The secret is that there isn't a single formula. I'm a big fan of Don Beck. Whenever he's asked for leadership advice, he asks, 'Who is trying to do what task in what situation, with what purpose, with whom, where and why?' If you can answer all of those questions then you can ask the 'how?' question.

West: Don't be coy James. There have to be some known principles of leadership, surely.

James: Well, first of all, let me say that we're no different than our ancestors of 10,000 years ago. We're hardwired, neurologically and genetically, to operate in groups of up to eight existing within larger groups of about 150. That's called the Dunbar number. It's the human equivalent of the optimum size for beehives – larger than that and the hive splits up. So also for humans. When the size of the group becomes too large for a face-to-face system of governance, things get uncomfortable.

West: So people split off with a new Queen bee to make a new organisation?

James: Yes, in our evolutionary history, people lived in small bands. You can see it in the development of organisations. Small family businesses or entrepreneurial startups tend to exhibit PURPLE thinking. Flat hierarchy, tribal leadership, close-knit, run by relationships. As they get bigger, it's harder to organise things face-to-face. People are stifled by the oppressive group dynamics. Individuals strike out on their own. Sometimes that's a bold RED-thinking leader like Richard Branson, sometimes it's corrupt, self-serving manipulation of the system like hiding sub-prime mortgages in credit default swaps, passing them off as low risk.

West: Wait, don't tell me. That's where the BLUE system comes in. Justice, rules, regulation and order.

James laughs, but the CEO and Prasad look mystified.

James: That's right, but the BLUE system isn't only external, it's internal. People can be self-regulating when they choose to be righteous, to avoid guilt, shame and social judgements.

West: I get the picture. Then there's the ORANGE system with their science, rationality, entrepreneurialism and then the GREEN system with its caring, compassion and equality. What about motivation and performance management? How do you get the best out of people?

James: This is very specific to the individuals concerned. You have to look at their values and needs. For example, ORANGE thinkers might want share options and new opportunities. RED wants immediate cash and status. BLUE wants stability and just reward. GREEN wants meaning and community. PURPLE wants safety and belonging.

Dr Prasad: There must be examples of good leadership in medicine.

Joyce: There's one at the Semele Barracks, Istanbul, where Florence Nightingale treated her patients in the Crimean War. Florence was away from the hospital when a new intake of nursing students arrived. She wrote a note to them. The first page, in her, old-fashioned handwriting said, 'A good nurse is a good woman. A good woman has the following characteristics: compassion, kindness, self-discipline, fortitude, resilience, honesty…'

CEO: That's sexist and paternalistic.

Joyce: Let me give you a bit more of what she says. 'A nurse's purpose is to care for the sick with love and kindness and to carry out doctor's orders.' Florence Nightingale's showed leadership has clarity of purpose. She trusted her nurses to get on with the job – empowering them, to use modern language.

West: Values first, then the task. It makes sense to me.

CEO: Nurses aren't doctors' servants these days.

Joyce: She lived in a different era with different values and people.

Prasad: It's true that a lack of authority, discipline and hierarchy in hospitals doesn't benefit patients.

The CEO give Prasad a 'look'.

CEO: It's easy to complain from the sidelines when you don't have to carry the responsibility. It's tough being a leader.

James: That's a good point. We should all be grateful for good leadership – grateful for those people behind the scenes who make things work, the administrators, statisticians, drivers, even hedge fund managers. I'm grateful for the people and systems who make sure that driving tests are fair to keep the roads safe. I'm grateful for the army of women who quietly run society. I'm grateful for those people who stand up to bad leadership and call power to account. I'm grateful for those people who strive to bring about continuous improvement and learning from the best around the world. I'm grateful for those who stand their ground and don't give in to the arbitrary whims of those who want change for change's sake or change to make their personal mark.

Dr Sugden appears at the door.

Sugden: Christine? Are you ready for the staff review meeting?

ENVIRONMENT, RESOURCES & SUSTAINABILITY

Friday, at last. I checked in on my inpatients before heading home for the weekend. Sitting in the nurse's station with Phil and Ayesha, I noticed something was different but couldn't put my finger on it.

'The Christmas decorations have come down,' he said.

'Yes, that's it. Why?'

Phil handed me the email. 'No displays of cultural allegiance are permitted on Trust property. Christmas decorations can be perceived as offensive by non-Christians. If you wish to offer seasonal greetings then use the term 'Happy Holidays!' Christine Pearson, Chief Executive Officer.'

'This has got to be a hoax,' I said. 'People have celebrated Christmas in England for over 1000 years.'

'No joke, she's serious,' said Ayesha. 'People scowl at me as if it's my fault.'

There was a card in my pigeon hole. I put it in my pocket.

'Aren't you going to open it?' teased Phil, eyebrows raised, half-smiling.

'West asked for weekend leave,' said Ayesha, 'he wants to do The Seven Sisters coastal walk.'

'Beachy Head?' I said, with worry in my voice. Everyone knew about Beachy Head — a notorious suicide spot. 'Should I be worried?'

'He's all right James,' said Phil. 'I've spent a lot of time with him and his suicidal impulses greatly reduced now.'

I wasn't happy, but I chose to trust their judgement. Nothing was going to be allowed to ruin my weekend. I tidied my desk and headed for the car park before anyone else could ask me to do anything. I relished the feeling of freedom from getting in my car, closing the door and driving out of the hospital car park.

I stopped off at the supermarket on the way home, and before getting out of the car I opened the card in my pocket. It had a picture of a Welsh Springer Spaniel long floppy ears and a shiny dome head. My heart skipped a beat.

'Dear James,' it read. 'I am so sorry that you got into trouble for seeing me. I am sorry I let you down at the Bombay Raj. I was all dressed up and ready to go but I got scared of getting in too deep, too quickly. Can we meet again but go slower? Please call, with love, Suki XXX.'

———◆———

Few people like getting up on a Monday morning. I was no exception. Seth ran me through the inpatients' list, filling me in on developments over the weekend. West hadn't jumped off Beachy Head. I could see him joking around with two other patients in the kitchen.

'I think he's ready for discharge, Dr Hill,' said Seth, tying his long black hair into a pony tail.

'I think you're right. I'll do the paperwork, you can put your feet up in the Mess.' Seth knew he was my favourite. Ayesha's eyes followed him out. West made his way over. Ayesha unlocked the meeting room.

James: How's things?

West: Fantastic, thank you. You've got a great team here. I'd stay for months if I could, subject to having a jacuzzi and private chef.

James: Did you walk all Seven Sisters?

West: I made it half way. The wind was freezing cold. I spent a while on the beach, watching the waves. I found a lovely old pub with a roaring fire.

James: Were you tempted to jump off Beachy Head?

West: I did go to the edge and look. I'd have to be very drunk.

James: Well, you were, on Waterloo Bridge.

West: I know. I'm sorry. I don't feel like that now. I've enjoyed being taken care of and socialising with the other patients.

West is glowing, but clearly not fully happy or confident.

James: Good. Was there anything on your trip that touched you?

West: I had a brief swim, first thing on Sunday morning.

James: It must have been freezing.

West: Invigorating! I did one of Ayesha's meditations. I connected with all the creatures in all the oceans of world. I got excited, feeling myself at one with the sea. It felt magical. I saw something out of the corner of my eye floating behind me. It was a beautiful grey seal, bobbing, watching me. I was stunned. I didn't know there were any seals in the English Channel. She looked straight into my eyes. She seemed curious and playful. I said, 'Hello.' She smiled playfully then disappeared.

James: Maybe she noticed the effects of your meditation.

West: I felt such a huge responsibility for the all the creatures in the sea. I felt ashamed of the rubbish, the pollution that I've dumped there. I normally never think about the ocean, but it came up to me and said hello.

James: Keep going.

West: I need to rethink the environment, sustainability, raw materials, food, oceans, atmosphere and climate change. The seal was giving me a message.

James: What was that?

West: That I need to look after the planet which is my home. That secure access to water, food, clean air and land is vital for life.

James: How do you want to respond?

West: Several voices keep arguing in my head. Some of them scare me with apocalyptic predictions. Others say everything is fine and we should carry on as normal. I'd like to find a common vision with all my parts on the same team. I need a practical strategy.

James: Would you like to do a Voice Dialogue?

West: I'm up for that.

James hands West the Spiral Dynamics Integral chart.

James: West, I want you to invite into the room all the different aspects of yourself. Greens, anti-environmentalists, corporates, ordinary people, scientists, anyone who needs to speak. We'll ask each part of you to take their turn, giving each the space to speak and be heard. Please don't censor yourself. When you're ready, step forward.

GREEN: I feel sick to the core. We've lived here for a million years. In the last 200, we've treated the planet like a rubbish tip. We're betraying future generations. People in developing countries deserve a fair share. When you're driving your four-wheel-drive to your comfortable suburban house, you don't think about the atmosphere, the disappearing forests, the melting Antarctic, the collapse of biodiversity, birds being covered in oil and whales eating plastic rubbish. All those beautiful forests full of beautiful majestic trees, huge biodiversity, vast ecosystems so complex and beautiful. It has taken millions of years for them to form. We're chopping them down like vandals. This isn't about sentimental attachment to fluffy animals, it's a matter of our survival. Our food is riddled with hormones and pollutants. The air we breathe causes asthma. We've nearly eliminated the remaining indigenous peoples. There are a few left in New Guinea and the Amazon, who still know how to live on the earth in harmony with nature. The world is massively overpopulated. We're running out of water. Greedy companies want us to be dependent on a handful of genetically modified crops. We'll will be vulnerable to disease and mutations. We've only got one planet. We're killing our life-support system. The developing world has been infected with Western Civilization.

West's chin quivers and his fists clench.

James: Who's next to speak?

West's stance changes. He appears to have shrunk in size.

PURPLE: I'm scared that there's an apocalypse coming. We're going to starve, we're going to have mass immigration of refugees due to climate change. If what she says is true, we need to dramatically change the way we live. I've got to pay the bills. I have to look after my children. It's no good ranting without telling me what I am meant to do about it. I'm not convinced that she knows what she's talking about. I need leadership from someone I trust.

West shakes himself and jumps to a new position. He looks self-confident, tall and assertive.

ORANGE: 200 years ago there was disease, endless war, high infant mortality, death in childbirth. People only had time for building shelter, searching for water, hunting and searching for food. They lived uncomfortable lives with no modern medicine, no lighting, no heat, no light, no security and disease. We're incredibly fortunate to live in such a clean, safe, free and prosperous land. The poor are wealthy by historic standards. We've plenty of time for learning, recreation and business. If you could go back to any period in time and tell them that you've free access to clean drinking water, easy access to cheap and nutritious food, physical security, strong and effective shelters, amazing health and education systems, they would swap places with you in an instant. Most of us live like Kings did in ancient times. This is all because of the Enlightenment, capitalism, the Industrial Revolution and science, the most amazing motors of human development. I love forests, I love seagulls, I want the oceans to be clean, I want the air to be fresh. Who wouldn't? You don't have any real solutions. You want to throw away 300 years of progress. If you unleash the creative power and potential of humanity with capitalism, science and democracy, all these problems are solvable. I want solutions, practical answers. These will be delivered by the market.

RED: I couldn't care less about the environment. I want sex, money and power. It's a dog eat dog world, a jungle.

James: Hang on. In nature, predators take the weakest members of the prey and have to nurture a healthy population of prey to eat. If they damage the population of the prey, then they perish themselves. In a human body, when cells refuse to collaborate with the rest of the system and use all the resources to grow, we call that cancer. Our bodies instinctively know that if one set of cells or organ is in trouble, the whole life is at risk. Help is sent to deal with it. It's essential to make sure the living system is healthy.

GREEN: We're connected to each other, to the earth and to the cosmos. We should love each other, we should love the planet.

West shifts position again, becomes less angry, more self-assured.

YELLOW: You know, there are people leading the way, coming up with solutions and innovations. For example, there's a man who watched on television the pictures of people lacking drinking water after hurricane Katrina. He invented a simple hand-held filter which enables you instantly to convert dirty water into pure clean drinking water. People like him change the world. We need to get the capitalist system behind these people.

ORANGE: I don't know if climate change is man-made. Emotional hysteria has corrupted the scientific research.

YELLOW: I don't trust either of you. I don't trust the corporate interests because they're thinly disguised RED, which couldn't care less about anyone else. Our wealth is languishing in the old systems, old transport networks, old energy sources, the old medical model, the industrial food system. You profit by creating scarcity. That's against national security, against the interests of our tribe.

PURPLE: Hear hear!

YELLOW: I don't trust you, GREEN. You've created an atmosphere of hysteria, aggression and fear around climate change. If anyone dares deviate from your groupthink, you vilify them. That's deeply unscientific and undemocratic. You've been caught tampering with the scientific evidence.

PURPLE: Stop idealising traditional indigenous cultures. If it's so good living in New Guinea with hunter gatherers, why don't you stay there?

RED: If they did, they'd get chopped up and cooked for dinner.

ORANGE: They couldn't endure the hardships and risks.

YELLOW: Scaremongering is counterproductive. Give up the zero-sum game. Western ingenuity has yielded vast wealth which did not exist before. We need environmentalists, scientists and business people to create opportunities and solutions together. We need active consumers.

BLUE: I have to watch these capitalists and scientists like a hawk because they've lost their moral compass. RED is polluting all over the place, tipping rubbish into rivers and putting horse meat in your food. I have to impose rules, regulations and laws.

James: There's another voice isn't there? Don't hold it back.

West smiles broadly.

James: Connect with your notion of God, ask him if he's willing to let you ask some questions.

ORANGE: Here we go! I don't believe in that old nonsense.

James: Just try. Think of God as the sum total of your intelligence – your consciousness, the unconscious, your body, your brain.

West falls silent, closes his eyes. He looks peaceful and serene.

West: How do we enjoy the growth of human potential in harmony with the planet we depend upon?

God: Listen to the feedback.

West: How do we live sustainably?

God: Treat earth like your home!

West: Can we make sustainable use of raw materials?

God: If you don't, nature will take care of it for you.

West: How can we eat more healthy, natural food, connected to its production while making it fun and practical?

God: Demand it, intend it.

West: How can we farm animals in a kind, healthy way.

God: Require it. Vote with your money.

James: Would you like to take this further in a meditation? Take it deeper?

West nods.

James: Make yourself comfortable.

West lays down on the sofa.

James: Breathe in to a count of three and out to a count of seven. Notice your breathing. Relax your tummy. Gentle breaths. Let your body guide you. Use your diaphragm.

Place your fingers over your sternum. Bring your attention to the sensations there, about an inch deep into your chest. Think of someone or something you love.
West looks more peaceful, letting go.

James: As that smile arises, smile back at your heart. It's like kindling fire. Can you feel that?

West nods.

James: Imagine that you can breathe in and out of your heart. Surrender to that heart feeling. Bring your attention to your heart and speak from there.

West speaks quietly, crying peacefully.

GREEN: Nature is crying out to us to reconnect.

RED: I protect myself, my family and my loyal allies.

GREEN: I can feel the beautiful, radiant love of the universe cascading through my crown, down my back into my heart. I can feel the hearts of the elephants. They're very wise.

West laughs.

GREEN: I can feel the hearts of the dogs! They're playful. They respect us. The seals want to know what's with all the noise, the pollution and the rubbish that we throw in the water. Why are we taking all their fish?

West pauses.

GREEN: I'm connecting with all the bacteria in the world. It feels like we're all one big blob connected. We're not any different to them. It feels tight. We're thriving. There's a background hum like a railway station when it's busy. It's full of life. We're a part of that.

West appears tearful, fearful.

ORANGE: I'm scared I'll have a heart attack and become a cripple. I've been working long hours, neglecting myself, putting myself under pressure. On my deathbed, it won't help me having money or success.

James: Allow your heart to open. See if it has a message.

ORANGE: 'Trust me. Let me guide you.' I'm used to using my gut reaction in business deals. It's instinctive to me. I've been disconnected from nature and from God. I was focused on numbers and objects. I lived in my mind. I need to get fit, to eat well.

James: What about the environment?

ORANGE: I don't have any answers right now. I'll work with GREEN if it can be less hostile.

James: Well done, West. Invite all the parts of yourself to return within yourself, one by one.

West looked serene. I let him rest for five minutes. There was a knock at the door. Phil needed the room. I suggested that West go back to his room to sleep and I said I'd collect him to take him to the Meadows in the afternoon to complete the session.

———◆———

At the end of my clinic, I returned to collect West. I told Seth he needed one more night in, that I'd drop him back when we'd finished at the meadows.

West was quiet in the car on the way. It was probably the aftermath of the last session. Or perhaps he had a sense that something important was about to happen. We wandered through the grounds down towards a field near the river. Four horses were eagerly grazing on the last of the year's grass.

'Which one are you most attracted to?' I asked.

West considered them for a moment. 'The mare in front, the white one with brown markings.'

The mare was busy eating, apparently unaware of us.

'Bring your presence fully into your body and spirit,' I said. 'Intend to make a heart connection with her.' A strange thing to say, but West was unphased.

For some time, the mare didn't visibly respond. West was patient. The horse inched towards him, a step at a time. She was slowly building trust. West raised a hand. She remained cautious. This continued for five minutes until she was a couple of metres away from him.

Startled by the sound of a passing police siren, she turned and left.

'What did you learn from that?' I said after a while.

'She connected with me a few minutes before she began moving towards me. She isn't used to people being that friendly or has good reason to be cautious. I felt love between us.'

'Anything else?'

'Her environment is controlled by people. She's not living according to her own instincts. All her power and instincts are still operational but not much used. She is used to being treated as an object. I wonder how much more of our environment is like that? The electric fences remind me of the hospital. Maybe the staff are like this horse, full of power and potential but controlled like objects.'

We walked through the field down towards the River Thames.

After a few minutes of silence I spoke again. 'When we hold strong attachments to ideas, structures and the past, we cheat ourselves of our future and present. An adaptive creature is alert and aware of the environment in which it finds itself, its needs, threats, opportunities and desires. It knows its strengths and weaknesses. When someone is depressed, they're often clinging to a loss in the past which they've not accepted. This could be a bereavement, a hope, a dream or the loss of their health, money, status or hoped for life. Part of the process of becoming well is to release what they've been clinging to. Then they can be free in the present.'

We sat on a bench and watched the river flow for a few minutes.

'If you could create the ideal environment,' I asked, 'what would it be like?'

West spoke at last.: 'All human beings would have clean air, clean water, plentiful, nutritious food, shelter, heat and light and fair access to all the raw materials they need. We'd live in harmony with nature, recycling or regenerating resources so that we can survive indefinitely and explore space.

'Consider whether you're prepared to make any commitments?'

A full ten minutes passed.

West: I'm going to champion success stories, role models, the creative visionary entrepreneurs who are inventing and implementing great solutions to environmental challenges.

I will bring together mature GREENs, mature ORANGE scientists and capitalists creative collaboration to invent, finance and implement solutions to my environmental challenges.

I commit to bringing clean water technology to all of humanity.

I commit to the exploration and colonisation of space to learn, seek new resources and become aware of other lifeforms in the universe.

I will to make it part of my defence strategy to ensure access to clean water, shelter, clean air and nutritious food.

I will innovate new ways of measuring value, risk and return on investment so that the force of capitalism can serve humanity's needs.

I commit to open minded scientific inquiry and challenging groupthink.

I commit to treating animals with proper respect, kindness and care with access to pleasant quality of the environment and nutritious food.

I commit to challenging pessimism and zero-sum game mentality and replacing it with a culture of confident, optimistic creation, empowerment and human potential.

I am part of nature.

I commit to relearning my ancestors' skills of intuition, sensing, wisdom, judgement, connecting and survival.

I commit to effective regulation, law and monitoring to detect acts of harm to our environment and to punish those severely, extracting compensation and restoration of the environment

I understand and respect that people in developing countries will inevitably have different values and priorities regarding the environment. I will try to work with them on that basis, neither forcing my own values upon them, unless it's a matter of survival or security, nor naïvely patronising them nor relating to them as a victim.

I commit to a massive effort to plant trees in our towns and cities for the benefit of our health and general well-being.

I commit to setting limits on waste and pollution.

James: Fantastic, West. That's amazing. You're fortunate to have seven billion people to help you with this massive task.

I drove him back to the hospital for one last night, to rest and to integrate the work he'd done.

———◆———

That evening I did my Christmas shopping online. Each year we had more and more presents. It could take the whole of Christmas Day to open them. I decided to get people experiences that they could share with me. Tickets to Warhorse for my parents. A dinner at the Jazz Cafe for my sister and brother in law. A trip to the coast for my grandparents. A day at the Royal Air Force Museum for my nephew. Those presents were easy to choose, especially my nephew – he likes the same kind of things I did as a child. The only person I couldn't think of a present for was my niece.

ENERGY

The next afternoon, I visited the Bernie Rosen Unit. The nurse in charge was Jenny. She was sincere but always flustered. I asked her about West.

'Mr West's for discharge today. Dr Seth needs to write up his drug chart.'

She had been in the morning handover meeting and doing the medication round. I'd always thought that 'handover' was an odd name for the meeting. It would have been more appropriately called 'Chinese Whispers.' I hadn't prescribed West any medication. It wasn't necessary. I checked the drug chart and to my horror he was written up for an antidepressant, a sleeping tablet and a low dose of an antipsychotic to be taken for distress. I tore up the chart and bleeped Seth.

I knocked on West's bedroom door. He invited me in. It smelled like a teenager's room on a Saturday morning. He was wearing a crumpled T-shirt and jeans.

'Morning Doctor. I feel great after that environment session. If I can do that for all the issues on my mind then I'll be right as rain.' West looked excited, as if we could do that within a week. 'I want to work on my energy supply next,' he said.

'Excellent. Tell me the story.'

'Can we go across to Bellini's for this? I'm desperate to get out of here. The man on the end was shouting all night and the staff were standing outside my room, talking loudly.'

'Before we go, have you been taking medications here?'

West broke eye contact. He opened the top drawer of his bedside cabinet. Inside were about 30 pills of different sizes. I laughed and nodded. I collected them up in a tissue and put them in my pocket. I let Jenny know where we were going.

We found a quiet table by the window in Bellini's and ordered.

'An Americano with milk and a cappuccino please, Miss,' said West.

'Thanks, that's thoughtful,' I said. 'Shall we start? What is it about energy that you want to discuss?'

West: I'm an addict doctor. I need energy for heating, cooking, refrigeration, transport, lighting, computers, health, education and water. Everything, in fact. I'm dependent on oil, coal and gas which are finite, dirty, becoming more expensive and not under my control. I'm driving faster and faster towards a cliff.

James: Energy is the foundation of every living system from bacteria to elephants, rain forests to civilizations.

West: Energy is a limiting factor on human development. If I do nothing new, I'll have economic collapse, famine and warfare. In 200 years I've burnt half of what took billions of years to form. Eventually, it will run out. I need to get the alternatives in place.

James nods, listening, sipping coffee.

West: I'm haemorrhaging money, my life energy, to gangsters, kleptocrats and religious imperialists. Their fingers are hovering over my carotid artery.

James: You're obviously feeling very insecure.

West: Russia provides 35% of Europe's energy. After six years of recession, they are in a weak position to oppose Russia's invasion of Ukraine. Eastern Europeans are nervous about their security again.

West drinks his coffee, looking out of the window at passers by.

West: The Middle East spends my oil money buying up my assets. I'm mortgaging our future. Some of the money finds its way into promoting conflict and fundamentalist religion. They bribe my universities to teach their propaganda.

West's posture is becoming more slumped.

West: I'm scraping the bottom of the barrel with tar sands, shale gas, fracking and deep sea oil drilling. They're buying some extra time, but they're not going to solve the problem.

James: What about nuclear energy?

West: Too dangerous. It creates radioactive waste for generations. Terrorists are looking to fill their suitcase bombs.

James: What about renewable energy?

West: Wind, wave and solar power is becoming more efficient and cheaper but it's still expensive and unreliable.

James: Let's run a Voice Dialogue.

West: What here?

James: Hang on.

They pick up their drinks and go to a quiet corner of the room for privacy.

GREEN: If we don't get clean, sustainable energy soon, we're going to have economic collapse, wars over resources, famine, and catastrophic climate change. ORANGE is destroying the planet for short-term gain.

James: What's the solution?

GREEN: We need to invest in solar, wind and wave power. Tax hydrocarbons and pollution. Close down the nuclear industry.

ORANGE: I'm already researching and investing in cheap, clean and sustainable energy for the long-term. I'm working on recycling, energy efficiency. We already have regulations against pollution. I'm using the best technology to exploit the remaining hydrocarbons. That should buy us time to find technological solutions for sustainable energy in the long term.

PURPLE: We're living on borrowed time. When oil and gas stop flowing, transport comes to a halt, the hospitals close, we run out of food. We're only ever a week away from anarchy. Every time you fill your car with petrol, you're giving money to enemies, criminals and terrorists. We're betraying future generations.

GREEN: Corporate cartels and financial interests delay the technological development of renewable energy because the transition to a new energy economy threatens their vested interests. The profit from scarcity. We must wrench control from these greedy corporate interests and do what's right for all of us.

BLUE: I'm doing my best with taxation, rules, regulations.

ORANGE: The last thing I need is more control freaks and red tape. Why don't you leave me to get on with the job?

RED: It's the survival of the fittest. We need to reduce the world's population. Let the nature take its course.

BLUE: That's evil.

GREEN: If ORANGE thinking was pure science and entrepreneurship, I could trust it more but it's riddled with RED's corruption, greed and abuse of power.

YELLOW: It's time to stop the blame game, complacency and selfishness. All life needs energy. Civilization needs energy. Let's be practical.

TURQUOISE: Abundant, free, clean and secure energy is a springboard to a new Age of Global Civilization.

ORANGE: In World War Two, technology leapt forward faster than ever. We can do that again. It requires urgency, leadership, science, entrepreneurship, finance, discipline and creativity.

BLUE: The Second World War was run by governments. It was run for the sake of the people in a life-and-death struggle. It wasn't run by companies for profit.

YELLOW: Let's be optimistic, have faith in human capability. We can generate wealth by mobilising to meet this challenge and through the massive benefits of having a new leap in civilization powered by abundant energy. Abundant cheap energy will allow us to build amazing homes, to garden the deserts and to empower the poor all over the world to improve the quality of their life. We can explore and colonise space.

> *The waitress appears, but a strange expression comes over her face as she takes in the scene at the table. Realising she is interrupting, she leaves.*

James: What are your practical commitments?

YELLOW: My governments will create the market, set the regulatory framework, invest heavily with their military and infrastructure budgets, offer prizes and set goals. We will stamp out cartel behaviour, rigging of markets, deliberate obstruction of research and development. I will put a World War Two level of effort into science, technology, commerce, creativity and capitalism to discover, develop and implement free, clean, sustainable, renewable, abundant and secure energy supplies.

James: Fantastic! Any dissenters?

West: None. That feels a bit too easy.

James: That's because it's a no brainer. Your challenge will be to overcome the vested interests and get the governments to invest the money. Easier said than done.

SEX, GENDER, FAMILY, CHILDHOOD

West arrived early for the next session. He was chatting to Jean in the waiting room, his hair combed and the tie knotted neatly.

James: Are you happy to be out of hospital?

West: It was a useful experience but I'd rather sleep in my own bed.

James: What do you want to talk about today?

West: I'm glad you asked, because I want to talk about sex. Sex, gender and feminism to be precise. And family, childhood, generations, old people. I'd like to use Voice Dialogue if you don't mind.

James: That's great. I'm impressed with your determination.

They clear a space and begin. West is straight into the first character.

BLUE (man): I don't know what the world is coming to.

RED (man): I do, it's all gays and feminists.

BLUE (man): Things used to be simple. You had men and women. Marriage was a sacred covenant before God and the community. Now they're corrupting it with gay marriage.

GREEN (man): Everyone has the right to make their own gender and sexuality choices without judgements.

RED (man): Yes! I ride anything that moves, any time I like.

PURPLE (woman): That's disgusting. Sex isn't to get a quick fix. You should honour one woman and nurture a family.

BLUE (woman): Sex is for married couples only. Marriage is the foundation of society.

ORANGE (woman): Society has progressed. We have contraception, abortion and the freedom to choose the life we want. I can try out as many sexual partners as I like and find the right match. Marriage is an agreement in which both parties commit to share property, duties, support. It's a framework to bring up children. It doesn't always work out so you need the freedom to divorce. Gay people have an equal right to pursue their chosen destiny.

GREEN (woman): Women are still oppressed. We get paid less than men for doing the same job. We are underrepresented in government, business, academia and the media. After 100 years of feminism we've still got a long way to go.

ORANGE (woman): Companies with female board directors perform better.

RED (man): Yeah, a few nice pairs of tits and arse to brighten up those boring meetings.

BLUE (woman): GREEN men are feminine, sensitive, unattractive.

RED (woman): They're sissies. A man should be a man and a woman should be a woman.

BLUE (woman): I want a monogamous man who will protect me and provide for the family.

PURPLE (woman): I like a man to honour me. I give myself to him.

GREEN (woman): Patriarchy has dominated women for 500 years.

RED (man): You could do with a shave, love. You might get more action if you wear lipstick, stockings and heels. Mind your wimpy GREEN man doesn't wear them while you're out with your lesbian friends.

ORANGE (man): Stop being offensive. There's nothing sacred about sex. It creates children and keeps relationships together. All organisms need to reproduce to survive, to pass on the genes. That's why there's so much competition to attract the best mate.

TURQUOISE: Sex is a sacred ritual, a rite of passage which unifies masculine and feminine energies, connecting with the earth, with the ancestors, creating new life.

RED (woman): I fancy powerful, sexy and wealthy men.

GREEN (woman): All human beings have masculine and feminine energies flowing through them. Men tend to be more masculine and women tend to be more feminine.

RED (man): You're more like a man than your girlie boyfriend.

GREEN (woman): I prefer him to a moronic thug like you. He is sensitive, kind, spiritual, in touch with his emotions.

RED (woman): My man could whip his arse any day of the week. Real men are independent, decisive and strong.

GREEN (woman): Is that why he beats you up? He isn't such a great role model for your son is he? He spends his time in his bedroom, looking at porn, afraid of his father.

RED (man): I'm ashamed of my son. He is weak.

BLUE (man): Sex is a sacred gift from God.

ORANGE (woman): I'm too busy working. I want more time with my children but can't afford it. I'm expected to perform as wife, mother, carer, fabric of the community and competitive career woman.

GREEN (man): Why don't you follow your heart, your intuition?

ORANGE (woman): I'd love to. The cost of living is too high.

BLUE (man): I told you so. If women go out to work, children are neglected, the old get left to rot in homes we can't afford and the streets are left to teenagers, delinquents and spongers.

GREEN (man): Feminism has liberated women to become slaves to capitalist masters rather than free to pursue their choices.

> *GREEN woman glares at him. He blushes, bowing his head.*

BLUE (woman): Sex is plastered across television, books, films, advertising. Even starter bras are padded. Excessive freedom has led to corruption.

GREEN (woman): Modern comedians think rape is material for jokes. Boys are addicted to porn which objectifies women. Young women feel pressured to dress like prostitutes.

RED (man): Better than your lot who all dress like men.

GREEN (woman): I want total equality and fairness. Equal representation in positions of power. No more porn. Equal pay. Severe punishment for sexist language and behaviour. Full gay, bi and transgender rights. Gay marriage the world over.

BLUE (woman): We should value motherhood. No sex before marriage. No abortions. No contraception. Castration for paedophiles and rapists. No teenage sex. No sex on TV. No promotion of homosexuality.

RED (man): You could do with 50 shades on those ample cheeks.

BLUE (man): Hold your tongue. Welfare and career women have reduced us to sperm donors. I have to work to pay the taxes to bring up the kids of the irresponsible RED ones. We need good male role models, fathers, male teachers, healthy male authority to get discipline and respect back into society.

PURPLE (woman): Childhood should be a magical, innocent time. We need to protect children from predators and bad influences. Children should respect their elders. They shouldn't be out with gangs indulging in sex, drink and drugs. They should be in the loving embrace of the family.

GREEN (woman): Back to the dark ages.

BLUE (man): Take their mobile phones from them. Turn off Facebook and texting. Back to proper education, boundaries, discipline and authority.

RED: You can only break up gangs if they're afraid of adults, if parents and the police are more powerful on the streets.

ORANGE: Children have more opportunities than ever to learn, develop, make connections and explore the world.

BEIGE: We've forgotten the purpose of sex and marriage; to have children, to reproduce and to survive.

ORANGE: We're not reproducing enough to maintain a stable population. PURPLE families used to have ten children. ORANGE and GREEN reduced to two children because they knew the children would probably survive. They both had to go out to work, got married later and had children later. Many don't even have children.

PURPLE: In Spain, Italy and Eastern Europe families only have one child. Children need siblings, an extended family.

BLUE: People are alienated and lack social skills.

PURPLE: Our tribe is collapsing. We're only holding up the numbers because of immigration. We're being replaced.

BLUE: We're killing millions of unborn souls every year. It's evil.

GREEN: A woman has the right to choose.

BLUE: People should keep their trousers on or take responsibility for their actions.

GREEN: The world is overpopulated. We take in people from poorer countries to share the wealth, create a global melting pot.

ORANGE: This isn't a Western phenomenon. Birth rates are collapsing globally. Russia's population will drop by 50% by 2050. China has 200 million elderly people to support but are giving up their PURPLE families which used to do it. India's middle classes are having fewer children. Iranians couples have only 1.4 children. Birth rates remain high where there's conflict, underdevelopment and lack of education for women.

PURPLE: Assertive minorities will take over Europe and America through immigration and high birth rates.

ORANGE: You're out of date. That seemed true in the 80s & 90s but ethnic minorities and non-Westerners are also having fewer children. After a couple of generations, immigrants have the same sized families as the general population.

TURQUOISE: At the moment we're overpopulated and are still drawing exponential graphs of booming population but they don't take account of the dramatic social and behavioural changes globally. Within 20 years it will flip to the opposite problem. Immigration slow down and may go into reverse as the rest of the world develops economically and they also suffer population decline. Economies will fail, social systems will break down and countries will compete hard for immigrants.

James: Are you worried about that?

TURQUOISE: Life is giving us warning signals. It's an opportunity and a warning. We've lived out of harmony with life. Either we adapt, realign with life, or we will suffer until we do. That's nature.

James: Tell me what constitutes a good man and woman?

PURPLE: A good man is strong, a hunter, protector, wise, kingly, a warrior, teacher, strong, brave, honouring tradition and tribe. A good woman is soft, loving, earthy, spiritual and carries the culture of the tribe, passing it on to the next generation. Relations between the two should be carefully socially regulated, with rules and intergenerational influence.

RED: Strong, capable men get the women. Weak men serve them. Women seek protection and reliability. A man penetrates a woman. Women dress to impress.

BLUE: I like those traditional roles. I enforce duty, shame and taboos. I like strict rules encoded into the law about marriage.

ORANGE: People live their life as they choose. People should be taken on their merits. Contraception gives people freedom and power over procreation, relationships and sex life.

GREEN: I've sought to break down the tradition of patriarchy. Men have abused their power as sexual predators, absent fathers and violent bullies. Women used to be pathetic, weak and oppressed. I've begun to liberate them. There's a rainbow of sexuality and potential gender roles and people should be free to choose their own path.

BLUE: Feminism is a destructive force, tearing apart family and society, castrating and abusing men. It has destroyed the family.

James: David Deida from the men's movement describes 1st, 2nd and 3rd man and 1st, 2nd and 3rd woman. The 1st position is the traditional roles of the masculine and feminine. Predominantly males are masculine and females are feminine although each contains both masculine and feminine energies. The balance varies. There are feminine men and masculine women.

YELLOW: I guess the 2nd position is the feminist woman and the New Age man?

James: Spot on. 1st man is confident, protective, capable, loving, penetrating, decisive, grounded, powerful, kind, wise and clear. He seeks freedom and independence. His action is spiritually guided. His shadow side of being abusive, bullying, controlling, dominating, isolated, predatory, egotistical, destructive and addicted to substances, money and power.

BLUE: Sounds like RED.

West: Yes, PURPLE, RED and BLUE. 1st woman is loving, compassionate, sacrificing, kind, yielding, interconnected, nurturing, interdependent, embodied, sensual and feeling. Her shadow is being weak, a victim, abused, overwhelmed with the needs of others, violated, codependent, anxious, needy and submissive.

GREEN: Exactly, hence the need for feminism.

James: 2nd woman, the feminist position arises through anger and rejection of both 1st positions. 2nd woman becomes independent, confident and free. She sometimes takes on those abusive masculine characteristics which she so hated in traditional man.

YELLOW: I guess New Age man is the son of the feminist, the son brought up to disown and repress his masculinity, taught to accentuate in his feminine aspects?

James: You've got it. The second man is sensitive, compassionate, spiritual, caring and cooperative but he's unable to defend himself, protect a woman, is fearful, wimpish and impractical.

RED: Highly unsexy!

James: Not necessarily. Opposite poles attract. 1st woman attracts 1st man and vice versa. 2nd woman, if she isn't too hostile, attracts 2nd man and vice versa. Where there's a feminine man and a masculine woman, the polarities are reversed and can work well. 2nd woman often craves 1st man, although she finds that desire unacceptable, so she experiences ambivalence and conflict. 2nd man often desires the first woman although he is unable to satisfy her and they find each other weak and unassertive.

YELLOW: This partly explains the collapsing birth rate! What's the best way forward?

James: Integrating the strengths of 1st and 2nd positions into a more conscious, mature 3rd.

YELLOW: Will gender distinctions fade away?

James: No. People are loosening their rigidities, allowing themselves to become who they really are but men and women are equal but different. There's a recognition that we've damaged the family, the community and there's a role for committed relationships and a strong family.

West: How can I integrate all that?

James: Winston Churchill said, 'There's something about the outside of a horse that's good for the inside of a man.' I'd like to take you back to the field with the horses so you can experience the masculine and feminine though interaction with horses.

West: Is that legal?

They laugh.

James: I'll introduce you to my friend Ellie. She will take you through it. Meet me at the Meadows at 10 o'clock on Saturday.

Saturday morning, we walked down from the Meadows' car park to the stables. It was a crisp sunny day with a blue sky. Ellie was the quintessential horsey woman, self-confident and physically fit – well-made for jodhpurs. She was brushing a mare and we talked casually to her about the horses while she finished the job. With that done, she called West over to stand next to her, near the horse, and she guided him through various Qigong exercises to raise his energy awareness. Half enjoying it, half uncomfortable, he was doing his best to embrace the experience with an open mind. He was confident in the horse's presence and soon acquired a feel for the safe way to approach it.

There were eight horses in total in the stable. Ellie took West through a body scan exercise with each of the eight. West was thrilled that he could instinctively detect where they had aches and pains, the character of the horse, their moods and their reaction to him.

Ellie asked him to choose one of the horses for the masculine and feminine leadership exercise. West chose Benson, a tall and muscular stallion with a beautiful grey dappled coat. Ellie led the house out and into the paddock in front of the stable block. I followed at a distance.

'Mares and stallions have different styles of leadership,' explained Ellie. She and West were together in the paddock. 'We'll start with feminine leadership. The Mare leads from in front with a feminine, Yin energy. Stand in front of Benson. Put your attention on your heart, in the centre of your chest, relax and make a heart-to-heart connection with Benson. Turn and face where you intend to go. Visualise where you want the horse to follow. Intend that he will to follow you. Maintain the heart connection with him.'

West looked sceptical, but within a few seconds, he was beaming with delight as Benson spontaneously followed him. West veered left and right. Benson faithfully followed. Then he stopped to eat grass.

'What did you do?' said Ellie.

'My mind wandered. It's amazing, Benson can read my mind!'

He tried again. After five minutes of trial and error, he got the hang of it. Benson was following as West intended.

'Well done,' Ellie congratulated him. 'Now, a stallion leads from behind with a pushing Yang energy.'

She demonstrated with her hands, the energy coming as a powerful penetrating force from the lower pelvis outwards. It was quite an attractive sight.

'Approach Benson from the front and get him to walk backwards,' she said.

Benson completely ignored West, who found himself pushing against Benson in an embarrassing gesture of impotence. We all laughed. Ellie approached Benson with sensitivity but she spoke loudly, clapping her hands to get his attention and pushed with great authority without touching him. He backed up five metres.

'Try to lead Benson from behind with your masculine Yang energy,' was Ellie's advice. 'Careful to keep out of the way of any possible kicks.'

I was impressed with Benson's patience as he happily played along. West got the hang of it quickly and was pushing Benson along like a stallion.

'Well done. How did that feel?' I said afterwards.

West thought for a moment. 'The masculine Yang leadership was more familiar. I'm used to that pushing energy. It felt like powerful thrust from my loins. The Yin leadership, the feminine energy felt softer, less familiar but, with practice I did know how to do it. It felt loving and deeply powerful. I need to use that much more.'

Ellie took us to her seminar room.

West: I recognised masculine and feminine leadership immediately. I use both in different people and different circumstances.

James: How does it relate to male or female?

Ellie: Males use the masculine Yang energy more and females use the feminine Yin energy more, but there's a huge crossover. How does that play out in sex? Well, Yin and Yang attract; a masculine man with a feminine woman or a masculine woman with a feminine man. The ancient Indian practice of Tantra has this refined to an art form.

West: Like Traditional Chinese Medicine?

Ellie: Yes, similar. There are seven chakras in the body, energy systems, several above the head and below the feet. They correspond to the parts of the body neurologically and hormonally – the brain, throat, heart, solar plexus, sacral plexus and perineum.

> *West raises his eyebrows in surprise.*

Ellie: Genitals. Your base. I won't go into too much detail as you need to experience it to believe it.

West: I'd like to experience it.

James: Let's do the inner union exercise.

> *Ellie puts on a soulful piece of music, a cross between an Argentinian tango and a modern jazz piece.*

Ellie: Stand up, West. Close your eyes and immerse yourself in your masculine energy, the powerful, penetrative energy, pushing out from the pelvis, drawing in from the heart, down the spine to the loins then out and back in a circular flow. Dance with the music. Imagining yourself as a young mediaeval knight, seeking to attract and impress your beautiful princess.

West was inhibited at first but kept his eyes closed and eventually just went for it.

Ellie: Now jump out of that state – just as if you could unzip it like a wet suit and leap into the feminine energy, the princess standing opposite the knight. Go deep inside to feel your heart, loving, intimately interconnected with the world.

A little more awkwardly, he dances. After a while, with more encouragement, he is in full feminine flow, hips wiggling, sensuous.

Ellie: See the male in front of you and use your feminine charms to connect with him. Receive the masculine energy in your base and allow it to rise up your spine to your heart. Let your love flow from your heart out and into the male.

At Ellie's request, West alternates between the masculine and feminine positions, each dancing with the other, embracing, then finally making love to one another. The male West is deeply penetrating the female West and she is opening her heart to him, allowing her love to flow out and into him as she receives him.

Ellie: Jump into the middle and feel them both simultaneously within you, merged as one.

She leaves him for five minutes to bathe in the ecstatic feeling.

West: That was mind blowing. I don't need to take drugs. It feels great, warm, blissful, peaceful. Aroused, excited.

Ellie: That's the union of the masculine and feminine energies, making love.

West: The masculine and feminine energies within me made love. I won't be able to tell anyone about this. They won't believe me.

James: Are you ready to answer some questions?

West nods.

James: What's healthy sex?

West: An open, learning and loving experience. The tender touch of a deeply loving couple. It might be the animal passions aroused and all the senses. It might be a quick, easy and generous gift to a busy, stressed lover. It might be a deeply spiritual connection, heart-to-heart, spirit to spirit. It can be conventional, playful or kinky.

James: What would sex be like in your ideal world?

West: It can be an amazing space of love, touch, connection, play, fun, safe place to bring out the deep and dark aspects of ourselves, a healing space, the place of blissful spiritual union, a way to relax, a way to get good exercise. Oh ... and a way to make children ... which is something that we've forgotten to do often enough.

James: How can we rejuvenate the family?

West: Do it or be replaced. The family and community will return as the cornerstone of society when the current system fails to provide food, security and care.

James: How can we revalue fatherhood and motherhood?

West: Honour it, experiment, share stories.

James: What are the differences between male and female?

West: Masculine psychology is more external, focussed, single-minded, action-orientated, objectifying, risk-taking, penetrating, aggressive, measuring, thinking and clear. Feminine psychology is more internal, broad, multitasking, being-orientated, integrating, feeling and complex. The feminine is more concerned with building and maintaining relationships, community, care, reciprocity, cultural-enforcement.

James: That's amazing progress, West.

West: Thank you.

SPIRIT, RELIGION, MEANING & PURPOSE

The last working day before Christmas, Jean was wearing a party hat left over from a Christmas lunch. A little tipsy, she held a piece of mistletoe over my head, stood on tiptoe and gave me a wet kiss on the lips. She had a small Christmas tree on her desk, a few left over chocolates and an inflatable Santa sitting in a waiting room chair.

'Don't tell the thought police,' she winked.

'Jean, why don't you finish early today? I'll lock up later.'

'Thanks James. Help yourself,' she said on her way out. We wished one another a Happy Christmas and in a flash, she was gone. As I was sifting through the bag of mini-chocolate bars, West arrived, wearing a Santa and Rudolph sweater.

West: Caught you!

James: Guilty as charged! Have a chocolate bar, West.

He shook his head, then changed his mind.

'You know, I'm really excited about the future. I feel a sense of urgency.' West didn't do small talk. 'A new world is emerging and I want to be in good shape. I can't afford to be divided or suicidal. I need to get my act together.'

We sat down, eating our chocolate bars.

West: I went to a graduate exhibition recently at St Matthew's College – that's one of the world's premier art colleges. I was looking forward to a diverse experience – cutting edge creativity, that sort of thing.

James: I've been meaning to go to that.

West: Don't waste your time. It was awful. Out of 200 pieces, only six could be called art. The rest were pretentious, narcissistic junk. I felt so sad for the students, deluded that they had created anything of value, having devoted three years and so much money.

James: Art reflects the mental state, the beliefs and culture of the time. What did the exhibition say to you?

West: The exhibits would have been bold and thought provoking 40 years ago. Eventually, maverick students will rebel against the prevailing orthodoxy and say, 'This is rubbish, pretentious, self-indulgent, self-hating, disrespectful, nihilistic rubbish, not art,' and some of them will create something new, genuinely inspiring and attractive.

James: West, it seems to me there's something important happening inside you. New seeds germinating. You know what your task is? To pay attention to those seeds and give them fertile soil.

West: Or like a chrysalis turning into a butterfly. The old structures are being gradually broken down, digested and the new life is emerging.

James: Very good.

West: My financial, welfare, health and education systems aren't well adapted for this emerging world though, and I can't shut them down until I can replace them with something better.

James: I noticed that same dynamic when I interviewed people about authority recently. People have lost confidence in their own authority and that of authority figures. There's no longer a consensus about right and wrong, truth and falsehood. Something is missing.

West: I've lost something in my spirit and my heart. People are wealthy by historic standards yet we're stressed. We've lost our roots. My public services have become heartless and soulless machines which don't care.

James shifts in his seat, looking at his watch.

James: You really choose your moments to get into this kind of heavy stuff.

West chuckled.

West: Just let me get this off my chest will you? It's been bothering me a lot – I feel so unprepared. Medicine has lost compassion and healing. Banking's moral compass disappeared in the 80s. Politicians lack passion, leadership and vision. We can't seem to sit still. We factory farm old people. I abort millions of human lives every year.

James: That's a big one isn't it. It's surprising how little reaction it gets.

West: For 2000 years, Christianity gave me a belief in the sanctity of life but at least half of me doesn't believe …

West pauses, unable to continue, overcome with emotion.

James: Yes? What's the matter West?

West: I have to tell you something. At the first sign of illness, I jump to the worst conclusion and I panic. When I get frightened, I pray. Everyday things seem trivial and I feel alone. I call out for my mum but she died 3000 years ago. That's when I wish I had a strong faith in God.

James: What's stopping you rejuvenating your faith?

West: There are so many different parts of me pulling in different directions. The world used to be simple. Children were taught about God, Jesus, the Bible, the Ten Commandments. They sang hymns, said prayers. They had a sense of togetherness and structure, a faith, even if it wasn't perfect.

West looked down and sighed.

West: Children get taught about the major religions. They celebrate the various festivals and rituals. They're left to work it all out for themselves and most of them end up believing in nothing much. We've lost the glue that held us together. We've cut the head off of the organism and it's slowly dying.

James: Bishop Nazir-Ali once told me that we're living on past spiritual capital, which we built up over 2000 years but is fading fast. Have you read 'American Grace' by Professor Putnam? Although there's a decline in Christianity in the West, there's a corresponding increase in the 'spiritual-but-not-religious' group.

West: Yes, especially among the young. It seems the spiritual-but-not-religious people have not yet found a popular way of replacing the community function of Christianity. The Churches are empty. The public space is for shopping, drinking and entertainment.

James: True. All true.

West: Look can we do a Voice Dialogue on this?

James looks at his watch.

James: Go for it.

West stands up and prepares himself.

PURPLE: Non-Christian religions are building places of worship at an exponential rate all across the West. They're always full, filling the vacuum left by Christianity but they only serve minority sections of the population. I think one of them will become the dominant religion of the West.

BLUE: That's happening already. In prisons, people are adopting fundamentalist BLUE religion in huge numbers. They're attracted by its self-confidence, clear assertions of right and wrong, the respect, protection and discipline.

James: Why did Christianity become less attractive?

ORANGE: It led us into two horrific World Wars. The old hierarchy of Monarchy, aristocracy, patriarchy, and Church told two generations of young men that it was their divine duty to fight for God, King and country. Millions died in a man-made Hell on Earth.

RED: Christianity was castrated on the battlefields of the Somme, in the gas chambers of the Third Reich, in the bombed out cities of Europe. Ever since, it's been a soft, feminine wimp, a pushover. Fundamentalist BLUE religion knows how to assert power. It doesn't tolerate disrespect. Christianity gets on its knees to pray for its enemies. Of course I don't respect it, Christianity is weak.

BLUE Christian: Jesus died for your sins on the cross, so that you may be forgiven and live a life in peace and joy. You've turned away from God. You'll be punished on the day of judgement.

ORANGE: Religion is superstitious wishful thinking. You can't measure it, you can't ever prove its existence. It's a comforting fantasy. There's no point in praying to an imaginary friend.

BLUE (Marxist): Religion is the opium of the people, superstitious stories peddled by the rich and powerful to keep the poor docile while they're being exploited.

GREEN: Science and spirit are coming together again. Our culture is stuck in the Newtonian world. Science long since moved on to quantum physics and beyond. The boundaries between matter and spirit, thought and cause, truth and complexity breakdown. We're all energy and consciousness. All spiritual paths are valid but none of them tell the complete story. There's no absolute truth. It's a mystery.

ORANGE: You can only know what your mind and brain are able to conceptualise. Trust only what you can directly experience.

GREEN: Open your heart, your wisdom and intuition. You will feel your spirit, your connection with all other beings.

ORANGE: How can you believe in thousands of Gods and fairy tales? There's no rational basis for it.

GREEN: I don't believe in all of that. Those are stories for uneducated people, like the stained-glass windows in Churches or Christmas Carols.

ORANGE: What do you believe then?

GREEN: God pervades the whole universe including each one of us. Through meditation you can reach higher states of consciousness, purify yourself and move towards a state of enlightenment. I respect everybody's truth. I follow my own path.

RED: Me too! The path of sex, power and pleasure.

BLUE: That's the problem. Anything goes. We've lost our sense of right and wrong. We've become spoiled and decadent. Human beings are divine, sacred beings. We must respect life. It's unacceptable to abort, to kill, millions of human souls a year because it's convenient. Greedy bankers need discipline and punishment. Have compassion for the weak, poor, lonely and sick. When people had faith in Jesus, we were free, righteous people with responsibility and authority who knew how to make judgements.

RED: Yeah, don't bend over to pick up the soap at the Church Summer Camp. Christianity is naive, weak and feminized.

GREEN: Christianity justified slavery, the oppression of women, horrendous poverty, colonisation and racism. It's an abusive power structure used by the powerful to dominate the weak.

BLUE (Marxist): Amen to that!

GREEN: Let's be grateful for what we have. Take a moment to feel in our hearts, to connect with the divine Goddess within.

BLUE (Fundamentalist Religion): No, that's forbidden. You're living in to the world of darkness wilful ignorance. You will face the day of judgement. There's only one right way. You must submit.

PURPLE (Indigenous): Why are all these foreigners sticking their oars in? West is Christian. They should keep their heads down like we have to in their countries. Christianity needs to get it's act together or they're going to take over.

BLUE (Fundamentalist Religion): God doesn't recognise borders. There's only one truth. Within a few generations, West will submit to the truth, God willing.

YELLOW: No one here has demonstrated the maturity required to provide an overarching truth. None of you have persuaded the majority to follow you. Younger Western generations don't believe rigid dogmas. Old religions are breaking down and slowly merging. Something new is emerging but it's not yet clear. In the meantime, we need to get along, so I'm going to set some rules.

RED: You can try!

YELLOW: Everyone is free to follow whatever spiritual path or religion they choose, free to believe in no religion and free to leave a religion. People have the right to preach, persuade and practice their beliefs but there must be an absolute ban on intimidation, violence or manipulation to make others follow your opinions. In a scientific, liberal democracy, all beliefs are open to scrutiny, debate and comedy. You must have the maturity and resilience for that.

BLUE (Fundamentalist Religion): Anyone who mocks me will be punished.

BLUE (Christianity): Why does he always get a free pass? I've been ridiculed mercilessly for hundreds of years by scientists, philosophers and comedians. That's not fair.

RED: Because you're a sissy wimp, of course!

YELLOW: As a matter of politeness and respect, we respect the right of others to hold their beliefs to be sacred. If you wish to have your sacred space treated with respect then you must respect others' right to reject your beliefs and to make their own choices and you must respect that which they consider to be sacred. No more bullying, no more victim games.

We're incredibly lucky to live within the West, to have the freedom of religions and beliefs. Anyone who disrespects this freedom does not belong in the West and should find somewhere else more suited to their beliefs.

PURPLE (Indigenous): About time!

YELLOW: You too must to respect the right of minorities and immigrants to choose their own beliefs.

PURPLE: OK, so long as there's strict prohibition of intimidation and violence and so long as people respect the indigenous culture. If everyone's doing their own thing, there's nothing to hold the community together, no shared rituals.

James: I'd like to know what you each hold sacred.

BLUE (Religion): God, the prophets, sacred stories and texts, places of worship, sacred sites, sacred rituals and prayer.

BLUE (Marxist): Workers' rights, justice, equality, secularism.

ORANGE: Democracy, freedom of thought, speech, assembly, and religion. Science, the right to pursue business, own property, secularism, separation of religion and state, individual liberty.

GREEN: Human beings, equality, freedom from oppression, nature, spirit, non-judgement, human potential, diversity.

RED: The freedom to do whatever I like, whenever I like.

PURPLE: Security, family, community, my land, my people, elders, ancestors, spirits.

BEIGE: Survival.

YELLOW: Survival, life, being, God, Spirit and love.

TURQUOISE: Life, consciousness.

James: I don't think that you will be able to agree on holding each other's sacred values to be sacred yourselves because that isn't honestly what you feel. You could all agree to show respect for what the others find sacred and to respect other's boundaries. That has to be fundamental.

BLUE: That will only work if the same rules apply to everyone.

YELLOW: The famous golden rule to do unto others as you would wish done unto you has a modern upgrade which is that you should do unto others as they would wish to be done to them.

James: Can you explain that?

YELLOW: If we only treat others according to what we hold sacred, then we're going to very quickly find that we're acting in a way which the other finds offensive. We have to show respect for what others find sacred.

PURPLE: This is my country, so what I hold sacred is sacred and if they don't like it, they can go somewhere else.

YELLOW: Societies are only going to get more diverse globally so you need to adapt to that reality, you can't go back to the past. However, you have the right to assert what you hold to be sacred and that should be respected by minorities and newcomers. If they won't respect that, then they've forfeited their right to live in the West. In return, you need to make space for that which they find sacred.

ORANGE: I won't compromise on Democracy. No religious group has the right to interfere with the rule of law, freedom of speech or democracy.

YELLOW: Fair enough, so long as you respect their religious rights and so long as BLUE strictly enforces the rules.

BLUE: I'd be delighted.

GREEN: Authenticity is a shared value.

RED: Hitler, Mao and Stalin were highly authentic.

GREEN: Fair point. Authenticity means simply being on the outside what you're inside. We have both good and bad in us. It's not realistic to be perfectly good, there's no such thing. We can do our best to heal and transform the dark side to integrate it healthily.

BLUE: We must make judgements about right and wrong, good and evil. We must have self-discipline, a moral compass to keep the dark side in check.

James: Compassion is surely a universal value?

BLUE: You haven't met RED have you?

YELLOW: It's your job to keep RED in line.

BLUE: That's impossible without a consensus on right and wrong. I won't have compassion towards evil. It must be destroyed.

YELLOW: Can God be a shared value?

ORANGE: God doesn't exist. It's a fantasy, wishful thinking. How can you ask me to respect other people's foolish beliefs?

James: Why did you say that freedom of belief is sacred to you?

ORANGE: I want to choose how I live my life with maximum freedom and opportunity. Because democracy works best.

James: Who said that?

ORANGE: I did, of course.

James: Who's that, who are you?

ORANGE: I'm a part of West, a way of thinking.

James: Yes and who is it that holds those beliefs?

ORANGE: I don't understand what you're saying.

James: You said 'I' and 'We.' Who is that? What is that? Place your attention on the 'I' and describe it to me.

ORANGE: I'm this body, this physical body and this mind.

James: How do you know that's true?

ORANGE: I can feel it, I can feel my body, look, I can touch it. I know my mind is there because I'm in it. I think therefore I am.

James: Who is it that's feeling the sensations, thinking those thoughts? Who's the observer?

ORANGE: My consciousness, my being.

James: Place your attention on it. Where does it begin and end?

ORANGE: It's a bubble. It includes my head and my chest, my heart. I seem to be able to vary it. I can imagine it to be like a small egg shape or I can make it big and be as large as the room.

James: You can directly experience it so it's empirical, scientific.

ORANGE: No, it's subjective. It's not testable or predictive. It's circular because I'm the thing which is experiencing it.

James: Isn't it self-evident that you're a being? Could you test a theory which assumed that you weren't a being?

West laughed, enjoying the exchange.

ORANGE: No, there would be nobody to do the experiment! So, I assume that I'm a being because I directly experience it.

ORANGE: I know that I'm a human being, but why should I accept this idea of God? It's just not necessary to explain the world.

BLUE: Because it says so in the scriptures. Because Jesus said so. Because God said so. Because religious authorities say so.

James: Hold on BLUE, that works for you but he won't see it that way. You have to talk to him in his own language. May I invite everyone who has faith in God to describe your experience?

PURPLE: I feel it in the top of my head, a hot pressure, especially when dancing, singing and praying. I sense God in everything.

BLUE: When I'm in the presence of God, I can feel my heart open, a heat in the chest. Sometimes it's a quiet voice inside me. Sometimes I feel God's presence when he is guiding me. Sometimes I feel God as a beam of light coming in from the heavens.

GREEN: That's fascinating! I get those sensations in meditation, connecting with nature and in tantric sex.

BLUE: Tantric sex? An orgy with the pretence of being spiritual.

YELLOW: Hey! Remember the rules? You must respect others right to express that which they hold sacred without ridicule.

BLUE: You keep shifting the goalposts. I thought you said that humour was OK.

YELLOW: That wasn't humour, that was a disrespectful put down.

BLUE: Sorry.

James: GREEN, describe your experience of spirit or God.

GREEN: My being is a warm presence, awareness around the core of my body. When I'm tired or fearful it can be small, the size of a football but when I'm joyful, it can expand as big as the cosmos and merge with everyone else.

James: How do you experience the others' beings?

GREEN: Sensations. I feel their pressure on my skin or a warmth in my heart. I feel life streaming through me when I'm in 'flow,' dancing, football, making love.

James: Do you experience God directly?

GREEN: I'm embarrassed to say. I normally disrespect BLUE's thinking but his description was accurate.

YELLOW: We put different labels on the same underlying truth.

James: ORANGE, do you ever get this experience?

ORANGE: I'm too busy to notice. I feel awe when I watch a beautiful sunset or a child laughing with joy. It was me praying earlier when I was afraid, but I put that down to feeling like a little boy and wishing my mum was there, a primitive defence mechanism.

James: Strip away the cultural baggage and experience the phenomena directly. Can you sense my presence?

ORANGE: Yes, like electricity in the air. I sense something alive.

James: That's reassuring! Turn on your attention inwards and see if there's anything there.

James: Is it possible that your assumption that the universe is non-living and purposeless is wrong?

ORANGE: Yes, of course that's possible.

James: Could you practice science with the assumption that the cosmos is alive, an interconnected conscious living system?

ORANGE: Yes, it's possible but science uses the simplest explanation possible. Why invent a more complicated theory?

James: Why did science leap from the simple assumptions of Newton to the complicated assumptions of quantum physics?

ORANGE: Newtonian physics couldn't explain or predict everything so people kept searching for more elegant theories.

James: Do your assumptions of a lifeless, materialistic, meaningless, purposeless universe explain consciousness, complexity, psychology, the economy, presence, life, love, placebos and fun?

ORANGE: No. Look, I'm willing to treat religious or spiritual ideas as hypotheses. But they only have value for me if they explain the world and make testable predictions.

James: I was taught at medical school that the heart is a muscle which pumps blood around the body and through the lungs. It has four chambers, four valves and an electrical system which controls its contractions and rhythm; it's controlled by the sympathetic and parasympathetic nervous systems; it has role in blood pressure; it secretes atrial naturietic peptide which has a role in fluid balance and blood pressure.

ORANGE: What's your point?

James: Research since then shows that the heart isn't just a pump with an accelerator and brake. It processes complex information, decisions, emotions and sends more nerves to the brain than it receives.

ORANGE: That all sounds very rational and reasonable.

James: People use phrases like 'winning hearts and minds', 'she was broken-hearted' and 'my heart isn't in it', but it never occurred to me that that might be true literally rather than metaphorically. I did some training in Tantra and energetics.

West winces.

James: That was my reaction too but, being a scientist, with an open mind, I was willing to give it a go.

ORANGE: Go on.

James: The Tantra students claimed to experience their hearts, as a sensation in the centre of the chest. That's where people feel angina or a heart attack so I tried the exercises. I was blown away by it. I could feel my own heart as a warm, tingling, heat in my chest. My eyes well up with tears.

PURPLE: I get that feeling at weddings and funerals.

BLUE: I get it with my family, with patriotism and prayer.

GREEN: I feel it when I connect with someone, heart-to-heart.

James: It's not always a pleasant feeling. People can feel pain in the heart from depression or a loss, like a bereavement or even the loss of homeland. The family and tribe, patriotism and religious feeling are felt in the heart. A wounded heart can unleash intense rage with extreme violence. Healing hearts is a big part of conflict resolution. If the heart isn't in a decision, it won't stick.

ORANGE: Where's the evidence for this?

James: It's a combination of empirical science, clinical experience and direct experience. Remember the heart mediation we did.

GREEN: We already know that brainwaves are very sensitive to our consciousness and influenced by what's going on around us. The HeartMath Institute in America have shown that the heart's magnetic field is 100 times more powerful than the electromagnetic field of the brain. Horses like Benson have huge hearts with an electromagnetic field which extends 20 metres. The heart is where we love, where we care. When someone speaks from the heart, it synchronises with others' hearts, being more persuasive.

YELLOW: Watch how flocks of birds, shoals of fish or herds of wildebeest synchronise with one another. Humans are similar.

TURQUOISE: I'm struck by the similarities between the apparently different positions. Everyone experiences themselves and others as beings. The heart is central to our love, judgements, decisions, relationships, our deepest wounds and pains. Mind body and spirit are all the same thing.

James: Does everyone experience joy, bliss, interconnectedness, oneness, transcendence and enlightenment?

RED: If you smoke the right substances!

James: TURQUOISE, what's the spiritual foundation of a global tribe?

TURQUOISE: We've separated mind, body and spirit. We've treated our bodies as machines which transport around our brains. The body is where we experience everything through sensations. We carry memory and perception, judgement and integration, sensing and intuition in our body. It's time to connect it all together, to be like the ancient hunter gatherer who lived as an animal and as a spirit being connected to his clan and natural environment. We're going to do that again but on a much more sophisticated level, incorporating the best of all the developments since.

ORANGE: I barely understand that.

TURQUOISE: You don't need to. Do what you're good at. Keep your mind open, keep challenging your assumptions and be creative.

James: What about God?

TURQUOISE: People experience God in a variety of ways – as a presence, voice, sensation, prayer, vision, ritual or a book.

James: I believe you've done research into fields and intention?

TURQUOISE: Everything has a field. The earth's magnetic field. The heart's electromagnetic field. The field of an idea, a company, or a social group. We are going to relearn how to perceive and influence these fields as did our ancestors. Hunter gatherers' awareness of the plants, animals, nature and humans involves capacities that the rest of us have long since forgotten. I think we're going to relearn them in a modern context.

James: Fantastic. Does anyone have anything else to say?

YELLOW: The Church of England is struggling to straddle all the different types of thinking from PURPLE through to TURQUOISE. It's weak in its traditional centre of BLUE which has moved to GREEN, being pluralistic, relativistic, open, sensitive and inclusive. It's lost its appeal to RED and BLUE. That's partly why fundamentalist BLUE religion is a strong competitor. Oddly, Britain, one of the most secular countries, is a theocracy and a monarchy, with PURPLE ways of thinking. The Queen is Head of State and the head of the Church of England, the official Church incorporated into the establishment including the House of Lords. It has done its best to reach out to other faiths, which have now become part of diverse Britain, trying to include them in various national and local celebrations and rites of passage.

James: Can you give an example?

YELLOW: The annual remembrance service at the Cenotaph. The Church of England leads and incorporates all the other faiths within the national structure. That's a fantastic example of YELLOW thinking with GREEN sensitivity and the BLUE state gathering to honour the fallen warriors of the PURPLE tribe.

West sits down.

West: That feels great but I'm tired. I'll sleep on that.

Thank goodness, I thought. I had planned to be away ages ago. I locked the windows and shut down the computer. To my dismay, there was a knock at the door.

'Suki,' I said, surprised.

She was standing in the doorway wearing a figure hugging Prussian blue dress.

'Hello James. Since you've been avoiding me, I decided to bring your Christmas present to you.'

She had a small hand bag, barely big enough for a purse.

'Close your eyes, James.'

I could feel her breath on my face, and slowly, tentatively, her lips touched mine. She smelled delicious. I put my arms around her and pulled her body into mine.

CHRISTMAS

Some clichés are there for a reason. The song 'Driving Home for Christmas', for me, was one of those. I was listening to it as I drove to my sister's house for Christmas. Faun settled down to married family life seven years ago with Brad, my brother-in-law. In fact, they were both in law, he a commercial lawyer and her a family lawyer. I was excited to see my niece, Mobu, aged five and nephew, Baz, aged seven.

I suddenly realised that I'd forgotten to get Mobu a present. I was on the motorway now. There'd be no shops till I arrived in Winchester where they live. I saw a tourist sign pointing to, *Alpaca World*. I veered off the motorway, causing righteous irritation to the driver behind me. After ten minutes driving down country lanes, I arrived at Alpaca World. It was a working farm which made clothes from Alpacas. It had a petting area for children. She'd love it. I bought an open family ticket with a stuffed toy baby Alpaca.

I arrived to a welcoming family atmosphere. We weren't religious. Nevertheless, Christmas wouldn't be complete without singing carols. At 23:15, we wrapped up warm to head to the Cathedral for the service. As usual, we were late and sat at the back with a poor view. We sang 'Once in Royal David's City', 'Hark the Herald Angels Sing' and 'Silent Night'. The service went on for much longer than we remembered, everyone getting rather restless during the long sermon. I listened much more carefully to the words than usual. West was right, we are disconnected from our roots, both Christian and ancient hunter-gatherer. Relief came with the final carol, 'Oh Come all Ye Faithful'. We filed through into the Church hall to consume mulled wine and mince pies. I felt guilty taking the church for granted without putting anything back. I wished Suki were with me.

As ever, I felt the excitement of a little boy on Christmas morning. It was a magical day which everyone did their best to enjoy. We loved giving and receiving presents. By the evening, we were all stuffed with turkey sandwiches, with room only for more alcohol and a few chocolates.

On Boxing Day, the drive to my grandparents took 15 minutes. Ever humorous, they were dressed up and ready to go out to their favourite pub for a hearty roast lunch.

The journey home seemed longer. A text buzzed in my pocket but I couldn't read it while I was driving.

FROM ECONOMIC DEPRESSION TO ABUNDANCE

The days between Christmas and New Year were quiet. Jean was on holiday, so I checked the appointments system myself. Only one patient, West. Right on cue, there he was, dressed in tweed jacket, green cords and a bright blue shirt. He looked physically well but unsettled.

James: Merry Christmas, West.

West: Merry Christmas, James.

James: How did you spend it?

West: I went to Bethlehem. Not much Christmas spirit there.

James: How come?

West: Christians are persecuted in most of that part of the world. It reminded me of the early years of Christianity under Roman persecution.

James: You look unsettled.

West: I feel frustrated – blocked. I can't pay the bills. While I'm in therapy, the others are working hard, getting richer.

James: Close your eyes. Observe the sensations in your body.

West: A lump in my throat. A headache. Buzzing in the chest – a tingling. Hot and cold flushes. I feel pregnant with something.

James: Allow those sensations to move up through you. Imagine you can allow whatever it is to come out in front of you.

West screws up his face and purses his lips.

West: It's a smooth parcel, rounded edges, grey paper cover.

He unwraps the parcel and holds something in his hand.

West: The paper fell away revealing an old stick that looks like the base of an old ceremonial mace. It's heavy. I could use it as a weapon.

James: Against whom or what?

West: Against the fear of financial and social collapse.

James: Tell me about that fear.

West: I feel sick. The gold price went gone up to a historic high because people were expecting the collapse of my financial system. It's gone down somewhat since the economy started to recover but the truth is that my financial system is still unsustainable. I've been running up enormous debts for years. It's caused by a combination of greed and deindustrialisation.

James: You might need to educate me.

West: Money doesn't exist. It's a confidence trick. People used to barter sheep, weapons, furs, whatever they needed. As society became more complex, we traded tokens of value such as gold and silver. My ancestors minted currencies on coins and we've been doing that ever since. In the 20s, when things really unravelled, I decoupled the currency from those precious metals, so, the value of my currencies is just a psychological contract. Money has value because everyone believes it does.

James: What's worrying you about financial collapse?

West: Democracy has enabled people to keep voting for short-term benefits and putting off long-term pain. I've lived on credit and now I can't pay it back.

James: A diet always starts tomorrow!

West: Democracy lets some people take the benefits while others feel the pain. Current generations can live well while deferring the payback to future generations. Those who receive benefits vote to increase those benefits. Few politicians have the courage to take responsibility for true budgetary discipline. In a democracy, the temptation is to be 'nice' which means expanding and cultivating a dependent victim class whilst others pay the bill.

James: Are you blaming the poor for the financial mess you're in?

West: No, everyone is responsible. We've all been living beyond our means. Much of my industry has moved to the developing world. They've sold me cheap products which

I've bought on credit. I've mortgaged myself to the hilt. Low interest rates and quantitative easing has created asset bubbles. Much of money I've spent on Chinese goods and Russian or Middle Eastern oil has been used to buy up my property, equities and infrastructure.

James: It's an exchange. What's the problem with that?

West: We've run up debts so high that it's not realistic that we're ever going to pay them back. Because I've de-industrialised, we don't have much to sell the rest of the world. Eventually, they'll realise this and then there'll be a panic, withdrawing funds. The dollar will lose its place as the global reserve currency and, like when the pound collapsed in the twenties, political power and stability will go with it.

James: I can see why you're feeling anxious.

West: Health, pensions, education and welfare are expensive. We're living longer and requiring ever more medical care. The population is top-heavy with dependent people. I've been plugging the hole with immigration. As the rest of the world gets richer, it'll be harder to attract skilled migrants. Energy costs are soaring through increasing competition for dwindling supplies.

James: So why not print more money to devalue your debt and make your exports more competitive?

West: I can get away with that occasionally but if I make a habit of it, people would lose confidence in my currencies. If you print more money, each note that you print is worth slightly less. You'd be eating away at people's savings. No, increasingly I'll have to compete on equal terms with developing countries. My living standards are already falling. Inequality is worsening. The rich are insulated but the middle class and poor are in for a rough ride. That's why I've been trying to put it off.

James: So, I guess we either prepare for the transition or it'll happen in a sudden and uncontrolled way, like in Greece, Ireland or Argentina.

West: France asked the Chinese to lend them money. They replied that Chinese workers worked in much harsher working conditions, harder, longer, for much less money. They suggested we live within our means.

James: You're speaking as if you were a powerless victim of the situation. You've got more well-educated and skilled people than ever. You've got by far the best communication systems. People can borrow money at low interest rates. The world outside the West is booming like never before. There's more knowledge and technology available than at any other time in history and it's unfolding at an unprecedented and increasing rate. What are you doing with the many millions of unemployed young people? What about their energy and creativity?

West: I feel sick. I feel guilty about it – such a waste of life.

James: You've overcome worse problems than this before. This is a problem of psychology. You said yourself that money is a psychological construct. Her Majesty the Queen asked her professors at the London School of Economics why none of them had predicted the economic crash. The answer is groupthink, mistaken assumptions, a world view which works for a while and then fails to adapt when the situation changes.

West: People want to believe that the good days will never end. They privately harbour doubts but assume that not everyone can be wrong. Then an event triggers the sudden change in sentiment so that it flips into a cycle of collapse, fear, loss of trust and so all the prices fall the other way.

James: Maybe it's nature's way of weeding out the weaker organisms, enforcing the discipline of hardship and reality so that the health of the overall system improves.

West is silent, chewing his finger nails and dwelling on something.

West: James, how do you treat depression and raise confidence?

James: Well, first of all you have to get all the facts on the table. Do you think you're depressed again?

West: I don't know, but I'm certainly lacking in confidence.

James: Let's give it a go then. Let's get it all out there – everything that's worrying you.

West: OK. I'm spending more money than I earn or create. I'm borrowing money to sustain a lifestyle I can't afford. I'm dependent upon global confidence in my economy and my currencies to retain stability and control. My assets are being bought up by those with whom we have a negative trade balance. We haemorrhage vast sums of money every year to pay for energy and raw materials. We're buying manufactured goods from the developing world where they have the temporary advantage of low exchange rates and cheap labour. Most of my economies have high rates of unemployment, have large, unproductive, inefficient state sectors. This is a massive historical aberration. I've held down interest rates in the core countries well below their historic average. When they return to normal level, it will throw many people out of their homes. I'm printing money to create the false feeling of confidence. We might look back on debt and mortgages in 200 years as a form of slavery. I want to find a better way. People keep voting for entitlements which we can't afford to sustain. There'll come a point when developing countries pull the plug on our economic position and we will have to compete from a position of weakness with an elderly population and little manufacturing base.

James: Now let's try and find your energetic, creative, optimistic parts. I have a question. What are the key challenges that have to be overcome if you want to get out of this bad situation you described?

West: How to innovate my way out of recession and into abundance? How to rebalance our economies to live within our means while remaining competitive and vibrant.

James: What are the limits to your abundance?

West: Energy prices. Land.... That's weird.

James: Go-ahead, don't censor.

West: Sunlight – the amount of sunlight is a limit to my abundance. All of my energy comes from the sun either directly or indirectly.

James: How much of the sun's energy are you using?

West: A tiny proportion. We could meet all the world's energy needs by capturing a tiny bit of the sun's energy. If we could do that cheaply and securely, it would unleash the most amazing boom ever.

James: What's stopping you? Why aren't you using the creativity of those millions of unemployed?

West: Investment costs money. I'm on a tight budget.

James: You told me money is imaginary, so why have you allowed it to get on top of you? What has happened to your confidence and imagination?

West: I don't know. Perhaps I just need to raise my sights a bit.

James: Maybe. What other limits to abundance are there?

West: My way of life is inefficient. The way we used to live is what people now call 'organic' as if it were something revolutionary and cutting-edge. All food used to be organic. Everyone used to live in a sustainable community. I could do it again.

James: Give an example.

West: Old people's homes. They are becoming unaffordable. It's an unproductive part of the economy. I feel awful describing old people as a burden. That's the way we treat them.

James: Could they be a resource?

West: They have lots of experience, knowledge and time. They're mature so less concerned about status or ego. I already have so many unemployed, it's not realistic to bring the elderly, even those who are fit and able, into the workplace.

James: Maybe the boundaries you draw between old and young, care homes and community are drawn too tightly. They're stopping you seeing something new.

West: Families used to care for their elderly. The elderly would look after the children, mind the home, do some jobs and be a source of wisdom.

James: When elderly people are stimulated, cared for, laughing and loved, they remain healthier, happier and active. Children who have a good relationship with their grandparents do better in life – are happier and more stable. Maybe you could achieve that again.

West: No chance.

James: But the simple fact is, there are more old people and fewer young people to support them. Either, you're going to have to find a cheaper, less labour-intensive way of caring for elderly people, or you're going to have to work longer. The poorest people in the world look after their elderly in their own homes at little financial cost. The cost is in effort and time, love and care.

West: I can't. Two adults have to work to gain an average standard of living.

James: You could experiment with different types of ownership. A community or groups of families could own particular homes. It could be expected as part of one's life-cycle that one would share the job of caring for the elderly and paying for the home.

West: It's worth thinking about.

James: There you go again. Pretending to agree with me but you're being depressive and resistant underneath, aren't you?

West: Not much gets past you. Care homes are a small issue compared to the massive economic mess that I'm in.

James: If you want a transformational solution, you've identified it already. Go for the World War Two level of effort and creativity to deliver cheap, sustainable, secure and clean energy.

West: I know.

James: Your current paradigms are reaching the limits of their effectiveness. The next boom will come from a new perception, new technology, something unexpected. Open up your creativity. Talking about care homes might seem mundane but what we're talking about is evolving from a top-down, machine-like, market capitalism model into a conscious living system, distributed, humane and wise. Aligned with life, affordable and sustainable. You will either do it by choice or by force. This is the message that your depression is trying to tell you.

West: What has that got to do with care homes?

James: The old model of care homes is that one group of people, the government or investors pay for a building and hire another group of people to organise and deliver the care for the elderly. So the financial incentives aren't aligned to motivate the best care or to make it affordable for all. Investors want a profit, the government wants to minimise costs and risks and the carers want an income. That system is like a machine with parts. Now perceive it as being alive, like a forest or a beehive. The care home is part of the ecosystem. Imagine if people trusted that in their old age, they would be cared for with love and kindness in a home run by their family and community.

West: That's a lovely fantasy, but it's not affordable.

James: You're adopting a victim mentality, being pessimistic, closing down options. You're the most amazing civilization ever to exist! You have billions of people, ever growing, ever broadening. What happened to your open mind, creativity, experimentation, scientific prowess? Why do you the same thing everywhere? Why do you use your creativity for mobile phones and software programs but not for hospitals, schools and welfare? You need to draw on your strengths. Get innovating. Experiment! True diversity is many different people in different places, trying out different ways of doing things. Eventually, something amazing, new and exciting will emerge. Snap out of your victim mindset.

West: Are you always so rude to your patients?

James: Usually ruder. But seriously, creativity is one of your greatest strengths. I want to help you experience that – but first we need to drive over to the Meadows. Take this notepad and pen and try to think of a question related to your problems – anything that seems particularly urgent. Don't tell me what it is. Just write it down while we're driving over there.

It was a drive of a few minutes over to the Meadows, and West had his pen poised over the pad all the way. Eventually I could see he was writing something. When we had parked, we didn't go into the unit, rather I led West round to the back of the building and walked off the path into the surrounding wooded parkland. The woods predate the hospital by centuries. Many of the trees are massive in girth and very tall. Some of them are said to be 1000 years old.

Our breath made clouds in the cold air as we walked. Overhead there was a beautiful blue sky, visible through the tree canopy, which was bare of leaves. After a minute or two of walking we stopped in a clearing. I told West to pick a tree and explained that he would be asking that tree his question. He gave me that eyebrow raise of his, but didn't complain. He chose a particularly broad-trunked oak with a knotted root system. The rough bark was covered in sparkling frost.

James: So, ask the tree your question.

West: Out loud?

James: Yes. Trust the process. No one else can hear.

West: OK, tree, how do I get my economy to thrive as an amazing motor to for human potential?

West waits for a response.

West: That's weird. It came as a quiet inner voice. Money is freedom, love and human potential, not a thing in itself.

James: Beautiful. Try another.

West: How do I balance my budgets and trade?

West waited for a response from the tree and spoke it out loud.

Tree: Be disciplined. Save. Stop buying junk you don't need.

137

James: Excellent! This tree doesn't take any prisoners. It has to live with strict discipline and the laws of nature.

West: How do I evolve capitalism to serve my culture and values making sure I value family, community, health, environment, education, security, freedom and human potential?

Tree: Value what's valuable. Measure what's important.

West: How do I clear my debts and live within my means?

Tree: Spend less. Truly live well.

West: This is amazing! Is it the tree talking or is it my intuition?

James: I don't know, it doesn't matter if it works.

> *They stand in silence for a few minutes.*

West: Money is a token representing human energy-human work, ingenuity, creativity, dynamism, time, ideas, solutions, enthusiasm, love and passion.

James: That makes sense.

West: Money flows between people, from investors to investments. An investment is human potential, a great business plan, a market opportunity with a brilliant leader or a good team. So capitalism is part of the architecture, the blood supply, the energy supply of human beings. Money is human energy flowing around the world.

James: How do you feel?

West: Excited. Shifting my perception made me feel optimistic.

James: Tell me more.

West: The next step is to think differently about how one values an asset or an investment. The traditional measure of an asset's value is a calculation of return on investment, risk, alternative investments, confidence in the leadership, supply and demand.

James: How could capitalism measure the other types of value?

West: BEIGE values survival. PURPLE values security, community, family, childhood, natural resources and spirit. RED values territory, power, excitement, status, sex, control, respect and reputation. BLUE values justice, righteousness, duty, sacrifice, discipline and order. ORANGE would continue to measure the financial returns and risks but would also factor in freedom, democracy, individualism, scientific knowledge and confidence. GREEN values fairness, equality, diversity, inclusion, the environment and human spirit. YELLOW values all of those priorities with the overall assessment of its value for the survival of the human race. TURQUOISE values all of those and the value to all life and consciousness.

James: Companies directors are legally duty-bound to maximise the shareholder value of their company. What could you do to take account of this new more holistic measure of value?

West: Include the stakeholders, community, customers and workforce as shareholders and non-executive directors.

James: Would measuring value holistically boost the economy?

West: I expect so because this way of measuring value closely aligns with motivation.

James: Give me ideas to stimulate the economy! Roll them off without any censoring.

West: I could go to war.

They both laugh.

James: What else?

West: Invention. Economic growth comes from innovation, productivity improvements and the creation of new markets. I need to measure the value of education and research holistically. I need to really get behind creativity, research and unleash the entrepreneurial spirit of the people.

James: How are you going to introduce business creativity into the academic system?

West: Business schools have entrepreneurial incubators. Silicon Valley, has it down to a fine art. Business television programmes are popular. I could have *Dragon's Den* or *The Apprentice* type processes running in every school, university and workplace. Make it fun. Make it cool. Make it pay.

James: What disruptive technologies are on the horizon?

West: Thousands. Too many to mention. It's incredibly exciting. Sorry, I was wallowing in self-pity and playing victim. I've got the most amazing opportunity, better now than at any other time in history. We need to recycle more, waste less, reduce costs, cut taxes, make sure people are incentivised to work productively.

James: Can holistic measures of value be used in the welfare?

West: Remember Deng Xiaoping. He allowed Chinese peasants to keep profits from excess production on their farms. It incentivised the people to work much harder. Productivity dramatically increased and the profits generated became the seed funding for entrepreneurial activity which has transformed China.

James: What's the application to welfare benefits?

West: A large part of society is incentivised to be unproductive and dependent. If welfare claimants make a profit, if they establish a business, work longer, harder or more effectively, they get to keep the profit and do not lose their benefits. That would boost the economy, free up labour and liberate human potential.

> *West looks up into the tree.*

West: My success has been based upon trust. BLUE thinking, righteousness, justice, regulation and punishment for wrongdoing is essential. That can seem boring or judgmental but a few more sheriffs in the banking wild west would have saved us from a lot of trouble. Places like the City of London thrived on that. Unfortunately the 'my word is my bond' culture degenerated into the 'I'm out for myself' culture. We need a moral renewal to guide our inner compass and the source of authority, structures and order.

James: What else?

West: Rather than see the competition from the developing world as an inevitable cause of decline, I should harness my strengths to rise with them, to serve those markets, thrive and help thrive.

James: What are your limiting beliefs?

West: I believe the future will be an extrapolation of the present. That causes pessimism and low expectations. I rarely foresaw previous booms, crises or innovations. Human creativity, communication and knowledge is greater than ever now.

James: The first five years of life is crucial for a child's health, character, future life chances. It makes sense to invest in making the very best of those years. If you measured every dollar, euro or pound spent on a preschool child, you would save lots later on health, police, justice and social services. It'd be better to invest in health promotion and fitness than on treating illnesses.

West: Very true. It's amazing how fast one's mood can shift when the perception changes.

James: A word of caution. When confidence in the economy returns, you should build in warning systems to limit the damage next time that greed and boom takes hold.

West scratches his head.

James: Is there anything else, which you've been avoiding, decisions you've been putting off, uncomfortable truths that you've not wanted to face? If so now is the time.

West: The most difficult one is going to be a different social contract between the government and the people. The industrialised model with the government acting as a parent is outdated. It's a limit to human progress and we're going to have to move towards a more holistic, bottom-up, community-oriented system. It will require political courage to step away from the parent-child model of government to a community-adult one.

James: Any other limiting beliefs?

West: That I'm limited to earth. If I colonise and mine space, the economy will boom, like when I settled the New World.

James: I noticed something you omitted.

West: What's that?

James: I'm surprised you didn't talk more about competition, positioning, strategy to outflank your opponents and competitors.

West: Competition is important at the level of the individual, a company, a product or service or even a city or country. It can bring out the best or the worst in people. It needs to be balanced with collaboration and used wisely.

West is beginning to shiver.

James: Look, we'd better get in out of this cold, you've done great work today.

James touches the tree and says a word of thanks. West does likewise.

I drove West back towards the hospital, but he asked me to let him out on the High Street. I wondered what he might be up to, but decided it would be best not to ask.

POWER, AUTHORITY, JUDGEMENT, RIGHT & WRONG

James: Morning West.

West: I've got a hangover. Too much German beer.

James: Are you fit enough for a session?

West: Yes, just about. I want to tell you about a brilliant example of healthy authority I saw yesterday.

James: Yes, go ahead.

West: I was sitting at a beautiful outdoor Tapas bar by the river. People were having drinks after work. A few families with children lingered there after a day by the river. There was only one table available right next to a couple kissing passionately. The woman had her legs around the man. They were virtually making love on the bench, making some of the other guests uncomfortable.

James: Right next to you in a family restaurant?

West: Yes, I assumed they would reign in their behaviour, out of politeness, when I sat next to them but they didn't.

James: Where's the healthy authority? So far it seems you behaved quite passively.

West: It didn't come from me, it came from the security guard. He was a large bald man. He made his presence felt around the bar in a very positive, friendly way, very respectful of the customers, doing his best to create a good atmosphere. He was a host, table clearer and security man all in one.

James: Not an easy job.

West: Quite. While the couple were eating each other's face, this man brought his considerable presence to bear in a very firm but sensitive way. He quietly whispered in the man's ear, pricking their bubble of romantic bliss and directed the man to take his feet off the bench.

James: This sounds like an everyday event. Why were you paying particular attention to it?

West: I was impressed by his sensitivity to not cause embarrassment to the couple during an intimate moment. He was firm but didn't humiliate or challenge the man in a way that might spark conflict or confrontation. He allowed his ego to remain intact but got them to adjust their behaviour.

James: Why did you notice that in particular?

West: My communities, schools and families are in dire need of more assertion of healthy, positive, natural authority.

James: Can you give an example?

West: The level of violence and disrespectful, disruptive behaviour in schools has increased dramatically since the 50s.

James: Older people say they used to be afraid of teachers, who used physical punishment. Would you like to go back to that?

West: No, but teachers are afraid of their pupils. Pupils are afraid of bullying, violence, knives, drug-taking and sexual assault at school. Some carry weapons and join gangs for protection.

James: Nature abhors a vacuum. The loss of adult authority created a security vacuum for the children. When the BLUE system of authority, truth, right and wrong, and discipline weakens, the RED system is liberated. Gangs are the natural form of organisation where the RED system dominates.

West: That's a cruel world. The law of the jungle. Might is right.

James: Teenage boys feel shame and anger when they haven't learned to project their own power and authority. Boys need positive role models to show them discipline and leadership to help them emerge into manhood.

West: Not just boys. Last week, on a bus, a group of teenage girls were shouting, swearing and intimidating the other passengers who were mostly women or elderly people. I was afraid of being attacked myself. The girls were aggressive like a pack of wild dogs looking for a victim. It was easier to look the other way.

James: I can feel your shame.

West: One girl, about 15, was swearing at the top of her voice. Part of me, probably the BLUE, authoritarian part was looking at her very angrily, wishing that I had the RED courage and the skills to take charge of the situation. I noticed that under her highly abusive behaviour there was a sad little girl. That doesn't excuse her behaviour but I could see that she lacked love and strict boundaries. She was desperate to be contained and loved which is the role of a parent, teacher or other authority figure.

James: I met a teacher from a tough inner-city school in Chicago. She said that many teachers struggle because the children don't respect them. Their words carry little authority and many suffer violence and disrespect from the pupils. She believed she had found a different way. She had actually chosen a role in that school. The children knew that she believed in them and cared about them, so she inspired trust and respect. She formed emotional connections with the roughest children in the school, engaging them in a way that the more authoritarian traditional teachers were unable to do. This gave her the trust and authority required to challenge the students when they crossed the boundaries she set. She got by far the best results in the school.

West: I'm thinking about the experience with the horse. It's like that. She combined masculine power, clarity and assertiveness with feminine connection, empathy and love.

James: Have you watched the TV show *The World's Strictest Parents*? They have a clear formula to transform disrespectful, disengaged and antisocial teenagers. They fly them to another part of the world to spend a few weeks living with some strict parents. Whether they're a liberal gay couple in Florida, religious Buddhists in Sri Lanka or traditional Ghanaian Christians, the parents combine strict parental authority with nurturing love. The out-of-control teenagers arrive, initially excited, curious. The strict parents meet them, welcome them very warmly and sit them down to tell them the rules. The children either laugh or are incredulous because no one has ever asserted a boundary. They sometimes run off saying that they won't accept it or, more usually, try to negotiate and then make an agreement which they fully intend to break.

West: That's the impulsive RED system?

James: Yes. Initially, the teenagers break the rules and have confrontations with the strict parents. Some of them respect the discipline and some play along for an easy life. Others resist. The teenagers are then invited to do some positive community activity such as working in a restaurant, volunteering in a home for the disabled or helping on a farm. Some love it and some hate it. At some point, something happens to crack open the heavily armoured, wounded heart of the teenager. This could be contact with someone who's very disabled, a feeling of self-respect gained through doing some work or it might be admiration for a role model they meet. The teenager usually breaks down, cries and all of those outward layers of aggression and defence come crashing down to reveal the loving child within. That's the turning point which leads to a whole series of realisations, changes of attitude and behaviour that can be profound or temporary.

West: That's what girl on the bus needs. There are many skills involved in that healthy adult authority.

James: Could you teach those skills to authority figures?

West: I asked the security guard that. He teaches in schools. He would inspire children's respect, especially the boys who would normally go off the rails.

James: Can you scale that up to a civilizational level?

West: Yes but it's the responsibility for each country, community, school and family.

James: If it were that simple, wouldn't they be doing it already?

West: Parts of me are antagonistic to authority and sabotage it.

James: Let's speak to them.

GREEN: Authority has been abused throughout history. Men have dominated women. White people have been slave masters, colonialists and racists. The rich exploit the poor. Parents have abused and neglected children. Doctors have exploited patients. Corrupt bankers have taken down the whole economy with them. I don't trust authority.

James: Don't you think crime, antisocial behaviour and disruption in schools are bad?

GREEN: Yes, but they're are the inevitable consequence of righting past wrongs, taking down the old abusive hierarchies. Authority must be heavily regulated, transparent with strict penalties for abuses to protect those who are under that authority. Everyone should be equal in authority with none having power over others.

BLUE: If you don't have positive authority figures exerting influence, enforcing rules and making decisions then the abusive impulses that you want to keep in check have completely free reign, the RED system takes over. The law of the jungle.

James: Can you give a practical example?

BLUE: We need a strong military with discipline and hierarchy to provide security.

GREEN: You're old-fashioned, living in the old, violent, hierarchical world. We would be better off if no one had any weapons.

BLUE: And what then would protect you from thugs, nationalists, criminals and religious fundamentalists at home and abroad?

GREEN: As Chomsky said, if you want to stop terrorism, stop participating in it. As Jesus said, love your enemies.

RED: Good luck with that, love.

James: BLUE, what's the current state of authority in the military?

BLUE: Officers increasingly walk on by when they notice a breach of rules. They let things go, letting standards slip.

James: Isn't that what older generations always say about younger generations?

BLUE: Officers used to inspire respect. The men were in awe of them, afraid. Now they let everything go

GREEN: That's my point. They used to operate on fear, domination and bullying. It's a good thing that that's less possible now.

James: Let's speak to RED in the military.

RED: I don't respect my Sergeant. He never listens. He treats me like dirt because he can. He hasn't praised me in three years. The old-timers say they thought of life in the Armed Forces as a vocation, but, to my generation, it's a job. Why should I work my guts out when they work the system to please themselves?

ORANGE: A marine can tell the Commanding Officer he's wrong, if he has a better idea. They operate in a complex, fast moving environment, doing whatever is necessary to get the job done. If that means challenging hierarchy, then that's their duty.

GREEN: Old style authority is finished. People nowadays expect to be treated with respect, like human beings.

RED: Warriors, young men full of testosterone, need discipline. They need to know who's boss and I need the power to enforce it. I can't do that with my hands tied behind my back.

James: What gives you the right to assert yourself?

BLUE: Military Law sets down our rules, the limits within which we operate. We have proper processes, procedures and justice.

James: True but that doesn't sound potent or awe-inspiring.

RED: Leaders have to earn respect through a track record – lead by example. People have to feel your presence and physical authority, to respect your character, believe in you. You have to know how to fight. They need to know you have the confidence and power to assert yourself. We train together in tough circumstances. You get to know who you can trust, who you'd want beside you in a battle.

BLUE: Justice, duty and sacrifice are the foundations of authority. You must put the group before yourself. You must put in the time, the hours and the sweat.

ORANGE: Authority derives from knowledge and skills. We're competing to be the most effective team. We're judged on our effectiveness, our ability to get results. We need an evidence base for what we're doing, to implement best practice.

GREEN: Authority is grounded in presence, connection, empathy, authenticity, being true to your values, especially under pressure.

PURPLE: Authority is tribal. A ship or regiment is a family. We respect the leader because he knows us, cares for us and listens to us. He treats us with respect and we respect him.

BEIGE: In an emergency, you need hierarchy and discipline. You can't have a debate. People must take orders. You need to do whatever is required to survive and defeat the enemy.

James: Together, all of your parts seem to have a good idea of what constitutes authority. What's the problem in making it happen?

BLUE: How can I enforce discipline when the officers have let theirs slip? There's so much paperwork, it's not worth the effort. My reports don't even mention leadership. It's all targets, process and risk assessments. Every time I discipline someone, they come back at me with human rights, health and safety, equal opportunities, bullying or another excuse.

PURPLE: We used to work on common sense and trust. Discipline was dealt with informally. Now its all legalised and bureaucratic. We're supposed to crack a nut with a sledgehammer. The pride has gone. The spirit is dead. It's a shell now. We used to learn leadership from our superiors by watching it done well or badly.

RED: I used to enforce discipline with my fists and a sharp tongue. If someone let the side down, I would give them a slap.

BLUE: That's exactly why we need the rules and regulations.

RED: It's never a problem on operations. People are pumped up and want to get the job done. It's only a problem with the misfits. They should kick them out.

BLUE: These days, soldiers, sailors and airmen have to look over their shoulder in battle, worrying what a GREEN lawyer, safe and comfortable back at home, might say.

RED: We should send GREEN to meet the enemy. That would give them a brown trouser experience.

ORANGE: The law and bureaucracy have got out of hand. There's not enough room for judgement. The compensation culture allows troublemakers and their lawyers to milk the system.

RED: English law used to say that you were free to do anything unless it was specifically prohibited. Now I'm tied up with rules and regulations. I used to be bold. I bought your freedom with my blood. ORANGE has sterilised us and GREEN has cut off our balls. Do think that Admiral Lord Nelson did a health and safety risk assessment before sending the French and Spanish fleets to the bottom of the sea? Do think the D-day invasion force did cultural awareness training before liberating a town?

James: If you want to project confidence in your authority then you need to know how to distinguish right from wrong. Tell me what's right and wrong from the perspective of each value system.

BEIGE: Whatever is required to survive is right.

PURPLE: What's good for the security of the tribe, family or group is right. It's a matter of tradition, ancestors, spirit. The chief is the decision maker. The shaman connects with the spirits and the ancestors. The elders share their wisdom and experience.

RED: Might is right.

BLUE (Religious): God, the scriptures and religious hierarchy are right.

BLUE Secular: Righteousness comes from philosophy, from rationality, reason and logic. It's codified in the law which is asserted by judges and police officers.

ORANGE: There's no absolute right or wrong. The best idea is the one that works best, delivers the objectives effectively.

GREEN: Value judgements are subjective choices, made by individuals perceiving through their own filters, with their own interests, based upon their own experience, in a particular context.

James: You never make any value judgements?

GREEN: I'm non-judgmental. I respect every person as an equal and do not impose my values upon others.

    The others laugh.

James: Why is it important to be non-judgemental?

GREEN: The powerful use their self-interested judgements to exploit the weak.

James: Is paedophilia OK?

GREEN: Don't be ridiculous, of course not.

James: You made a judgement, applied your values to others who have another perspective.

GREEN: Very funny.

James: It's not funny at all. You said we should have a world without judgement, without boundaries, without assertions of authority. That itself is a judgement. What makes you so sure that that is a good judgement? What about racism, persecution of minorities? Is that OK?

GREEN: You're playing games with me.

James: No, I'm showing you the inconsistency of your values. What do you consider wrong?

GREEN: You already mentioned paedophilia and racism. Discrimination. Murder. Abusing the environment. Intolerance. Inequality. Disrespecting others' culture and religion.

James: Some cultures and religions believe in discrimination based on sex, sexuality, age and nationality. Some cultures promote murder, accept paedophilia and institutionalise inequality based upon hierarchy, gender, religion, caste and power. Do you respect all of those cultures and religions?

GREEN: Don't be ridiculous.

James: Multiculturalism says you must respect all cultures equally, without judgement, giving no preference to any one culture and suppressing the native one.

GREEN: Yes that's right.

James: Do you think your GREEN values are superior within your own culture?

GREEN: Yes, of course. PURPLE is backward, hierarchical, irrational, male dominated, oppressive, discriminatory and exclusive. RED can be good or bad depending on the context. People who are abused or dominated have the right to strike back.

James: So crimes are excusable if they're committed by a victim against a perpetrator?

GREEN: Yes, it's like the distinction between a terrorist and a freedom fighter. Taxation is a form of theft. Property ownership is a form of theft. Racial inequality is a form of violence.

James: Do you judge your values to be superior to the BLUE and ORANGE systems?

GREEN: Certainly. BLUE is intolerant, rigid, authoritarian and judgmental. It excludes and does not honour diversity. It promotes hierarchy, judgement. ORANGE creates inequality between winners and losers. It voraciously destroys the environment and dehumanising heartless organisations

YELLOW: GREEN thinking is useful in breaking down the old hierarchies, challenging abuses of power, including all the perspectives, minorities and the marginalised voices. GREEN is useful in understanding complexity. It's spiritual, sensitive and caring.

James: I can feel a 'but' coming on.

YELLOW: The GREEN system finds it hard to accept power, hierarchy, judgements, assertions of truth, exclusions or boundaries. GREEN becomes highly intolerant, extremely judgmental if any of the other systems challenge its dearly held values. The GREEN system is excellent at facilitation, challenge and exploration but poor at responsibility, decision making and leadership.

James: YELLOW, what's right and wrong to you?

YELLOW: Right depends on whether something promotes the survival and wellbeing of the whole, including all the parts. We live in complexity and paradox. Different types of right and wrong have to exist alongside one another. We have to make the best of our life individually and collectively so we must make judgements moment to moment as to what's right and wrong. Individuals and groups will do that according to their value system and life conditions. This will inevitably be in conflict with others and we use judgement, dialogue, debate and mature leadership to make those decisions.

TURQUOISE: Whatever serves the highest potential of all life is what's right.

James: When is it right and fair for one individual or group to assert authority over another?

YELLOW: When it maximises everyone's chances of surviving and thriving. When it delivers results. It's a pragmatic judgement in every specific context. The most appropriate hierarchy and authority is determined by the particular task, context and value systems of the people involved. An entrepreneurial startup company composed of autonomous, freedom loving, self-motivated, highly educated staff can have a flat hierarchy with a charismatic leader who sets the vision, helps to inspire and engage, allowing individuals to self-organise. An Infantry Battalion needs to have a clear hierarchy so they can act cohesively as a group, with decisive leaders and obedient followers. A parent has higher authority than a child because they carry more experience, responsibility and knowledge and they are accountable for the upbringing of the child.

GREEN: Everything must be centred on the child, the child's needs and wishes must be paramount.

YELLOW: No, the adult must listen and take the child's wishes into account, but the adult must carry ultimate responsibility.

James: GREEN could you set out your principles on how to hold power and authority to account?

GREEN: Transparency. If parent-child, teacher-pupil, policeman-public, doctor-patient, officer-soldier relationships are open to public scrutiny then that acts as a force for... I can't believe I'm saying this... a force for good. When a person in authority knows that they're being watched by a powerful and independent body, they're more likely to behave well.

James: What else?

GREEN: Connection and relationship. Integrity. When power is exerted by treating people as objects, as numbers or faceless cogs in a machine then it's more likely that abuse will occur. With authentic human connection, we treat each other better.

James: That's true when people are ethical, but paedophiles, murderers and thieves, all exploit a connection to the victim.

GREEN: True. We need the BLUE system for regulation, watchdogs, audit, investigative journalists and public enquiries to catch out abusive behaviour when it happens.

James: RED, how do you deter abusive behaviour by others?

RED: Hit them where it hurts. Take away their power, money and property. Damage their status and reputation. Isolate them. Shame them. You have to fear that you will be punished and fear that you will be hurt if you break the rules.

GREEN: Most people operate from love and passion.

BLUE: Or duty and righteousness.

YELLOW: We must account for all of value systems.

RED: Use peer pressure to punish those who transgress and to reward those who behave as you wish.

PURPLE: Loyalty and togetherness inhibits bad behaviour.

BLUE: Initially, people do what's right because of the consequences and punishments enforced from the outside but, eventually, people internalise morality. They act morally because they want to live up to their own high standards, to be respected as an upstanding person by their peers, because they know that God is watching, or to have a clear conscience.

ORANGE: We should find examples of where regulatory systems, policing systems and scrutiny of power operates well, learn from that, identify the best practices. We need to experiment more.

James: Thanks. West, are you ready to reintegrate all parts?

West stood up, relaxed, closed his eyes and allowed all the different parts of himself to return inside. He took a deep breath and sat down, content.

West: You know, I think I get it now. Human beings and human society are complex beings and processes. There are many ways of perceiving the truth about a situation. Several people can take up apparently different and contradictory positions but they can be seeing different layers of the truth. Like a quantum particle, things can often go either way. Life isn't predetermined. Ultimately, someone needs to take on board all the information available to them, including their experience, logic, knowledge, intuition and wisdom and make a practical, pragmatic judgement and take responsibility for it. That's how we navigate complexity.

NEW YEAR

I normally prefer to spend New Year's Eve quietly at home with a few friends. It's a good time to review the past year and make a strategy for the next. This year, for the first time, I didn't feel the need to. I was on track, on mission, living by intuition.

I was in the bath on the morning of 31st December when I remembered I hadn't read the text message that arrived a few days previously, when I was busy. It was from Suki: 'Fancy spending New Year's Eve with me? Love Suki XXX.'

How could I have been so stupid? I tried ringing her straight away. It went to voicemail after a few rings. I left it a few minutes and tries again. Same thing. Was she busy or just punishing me?

Eventually I got through. I needn't have worried. She had been just as busy as me, and the delight in her voice told me that everything was OK. I arranged to meet her at a pub on Primrose Hill.

Walking up the hill from the station, I could hear the hubbub from the Duke of Wellington. I saw myself reflected in the window of the pub and wished myself good luck. The pub was packed with revellers. Suki waved from the balcony. I smiled, relieved and excited. I mimed, asking her if she wanted a drink. She held up a bottle of wine and waved me up. The staircase was a metal corkscrew. Emerging at the top, there she was. Utterly beautiful. Her long black hair was shiny and swept back over her shoulders. She stood to greet me in her stunning black dress. Suki pulled me in for a brief kiss on the lips. 'Hello James. Did you expect me to be here?' she smiled.

'I did wonder!'

We sat down. The room around us disappeared. For a moment, it was just the two of us, smiling, pleased, knowing but not speaking. Suki poured me a glass of her wine.

'Washington State, Pinot Noir. Where did you get that?' I asked.

'I fell in love with them in Vancouver at medical school.' The aroma was like plums and sweet blackberry pie. Suki was pleased with her choice. 'How was your Christmas, James?'

'A special family time, singing carols, exchanging presents. A feast and then board games, brandy and arguments.'

She laughed. 'That brings back distant memories. I was with my sister at her flat in Cheltenham.'

'Just the two of you?'

'Yes. My mum is dead and my dad is in Australia, Melbourne.'

'Oh, I'm sorry to hear that.'

Suki took a sip of wine and looked down onto the busy scene below. I stole a glance at her legs.

She continued, 'I grew up in Hong Kong. I was 20 when we were handed over to the Chinese.'

'37. The same age as my sister.'

'Good mental arithmetic, James. I didn't think psychiatrists did numbers!'

'How did it feel to become part of China?'

'We didn't trust them one bit but we knew they wouldn't kill the goose that laid the golden egg. They were thrilled to be handed the master blueprint for capitalism without democracy. They may have a chip on their shoulder about the Opium Wars but the British couldn't have given them a better present. Everyone was worried about the secret police. We were given British passports, though. I'm Australian anyway.'

'Is that where you're dad's from?'

'A banker. Yes, I know, boo hiss! In Hong Kong, they don't suffer from Christian guilt or socialist jealousy. Everyone works very hard, keeps their heads down and strives to be a success. It's more like America than Europe, without the open space and guns.'

'I went there when I was 25.'

'When was that?' she smiled.

'When it was still a British Colony. 1995.

'So I'm seven years younger than you, James. Are you going to exploit my naivety?'

'When I think of you, naive is not the first word to come to mind!'

She reached forward to hold my hand. 'What is the first word that comes to mind?'

'I don't get a word. I get a feeling.'

'And what is that?'

'I thought you wanted to take things very slowly!'

She smiled wryly. 'I seem to remember that was the plan, yes.'

'What about your mum?'

'She was Chinese. Born in Chengdu.'

'Where the pandas live?'

'Yes, but she only ever saw one in a zoo.'

'Why did she leave?'

'The Cultural Revolution. Her brothers were killed. Her dad was sent to a re-education camp and never returned. My grandmother was shunned by the community. She committed suicide. My mum escaped to Hong Kong.'

'How did she get there?'

'She never spoke about it. Too traumatic, I assume. They pretend it never happened. They prefer to remember the Long March, victory over the Kuomintang and Japanese war crimes. They're too busy having the world's biggest ever Industrial Revolution. One day those old wounds will rise to the surface and they'll need your services.'

'You say *they*. Do you feel British now?'

'Yes. Hong Kong was British. Australia was British. Canada was British. This country made the modern world.'

'It did but that's in the past. China is the future, isn't it?' I asked.

'Part of it, but there's massive social upheaval, exploitation of workers, corrupt officials and not much democracy. It's like the 18th and 19th Centuries here. And, of course, they're sitting on a militaristic time bomb. I don't want to be around when it goes bang.'

'You've obviously given this stuff a lot of thought.'

'Goes with my background really. Also, my dad taught me about history and politics. We used to talk philosophy and psychology when I was a teenager, before he left my mum.

'Oh?'

'Yeah, he had an affair with a woman back home in Australia. Mum knew but pretended not to. She carried on with the pretence of a marriage until she died of breast cancer when I was 28.'

'I'm sorry, Suki.'

'Don't be sorry. It's New Year's Eve. Enough of me. Tell me about you. What do you do for fun?'

'Fifteen minutes till 2014,' shouted the bartender.

I got us a bottle of Champagne. Everyone was streaming out onto the hill outside. We found ourselves a bench to sit down.

The crowd began to shout, 'Eight, seven, six,' I held Suki's hand and we stood up. 'Five, four, three, two, one, hooray!' I turned to hold her, kissing her. She had a tear on her cheek. I brushed it away, stroking her face and hair and then I kissed her again.

'Happy New Year, James!' she said, clinking my glass.

'Happy New Year Suki.'

We watched the fireworks all over London. The display from the river was spectacular.

'What are your New Year's resolutions?' she asked.

'To follow my intuition.'

'Mine is to pass my membership exam and to lose weight.'

'You are gorgeous as you are. Which membership?'

'Royal College of Surgeons. It's getting late. Will you walk me to the tube station, James?'

We walked slowly with our arms around one another, saying very little. I was thinking about the future – my future and Suki's future, and about the all those people who had shared New Year's Eve with us up on the hill. Feelings of confidence and contentment warmed me, expanding further and further out as we walked, encompassing wider and wider circles of humanity – people I had known and people I would never know. I was happy. But what about Suki – was her silence down to happiness or something else? I resisted the temptation to ask her what she was thinking and kissed her goodbye as we arrived at the escalator.

I awoke at 6 o'clock, alone. I waited a few moments to see if I had a hangover. I didn't, so I got up and made myself bacon and eggs for breakfast, turning on the television.

An American voice said, 'Hundreds of casualties have been taken to Jefferson County Hospital. Martin Schwartz, Madison Police Chief has asked people to stay at home until the situation at Roosevelt Mall has been brought under control. Eyewitnesses report seeing gunmen dressed in black, opening fire with submachine guns and grenades into the panic stricken crowds.'

I turned down the gas and rushed to see the pictures. It was still dark there, one hour into the new year. Twenty or so armed men, so far unidentified had executed a military style assault on the Roosevelt Mall in Madison. I felt sick. It was horrifying, seeing the carnage, the blood stained party goers running for their lives.

My phone rang. It was West, asking to come over. He was distraught. Under the circumstances, I agreed.

He arrived with red eyes, anxious, over breathing. He was wearing track suit bottoms, running shoes and a sweatshirt with food stains down the front. Like me, he hadn't yet shaven. I invited him up and shared my coffee with him. We watched the news.

A terrified woman, her hair matted with blood said, 'They herded people into the cinema. They've taken hostages.'

The reporter asked, 'who are the gunmen?'

'I'm not sure,' she said, 'some white, some black, most of them Middle Eastern looking. They're dressed like commandos. They were so cold, so calculating, asking who was a believer and who was not. They let the believers go. One man tried to save his family by kneeling down and praying. They shot him through the head in front of his children.'

Another clip showed a young man crying. 'My girlfriend is still in there. We got separated in the stampede. They were shooting and shouting religious slogans. I don't know where she is.'

'Mayor Jackson is due to make a statement.'

'I knew this was coming,' West said, his voice quivering.

'Knew what?'

'This type of attack. They did a practice run in Kenya last year. It'll be happening all over soon.' West was furious. I was scared. They had been enjoying the New Year just like Suki and me last night.

West pointed at the television. 'We go over to Mayor Jackson's statement.' The Mayor was dressed in casual clothes, having come out in a hurry. '2014 has begun with an evil act by evil men. The police and National Guard have regained control of the first three floors of Roosevelt Mall. They've isolated the gunmen in the Cinema on the fourth floor. They have taken several hundred hostages.'

'What are you going to do about it?' asked the ABC reporter, pushing a microphone close to his mouth.

'I can't give you operational details now. Our security forces will do everything they can to end this horrific scene with as few casualties as possible.'

'Mayor, Mayor Jackson, Larry White, CNN. Do you have any information on who these men are and what they want?'

'No, it's a kinetic situation. The People of Madison will never surrender to evil. No one will succeed in dividing the American people. These men do not represent religion. Religion is about peace. Thank you, that's all.'

The news cut to pictures of people celebrating in cities across the world. Crowds were jubilant, burning the Stars and Stripes, shouting 'Death to America.'

'I don't know what to do.' West grasped my forearm. 'This is happening all over the world. It's just the start, much worse is going to happen. Please help me.'

I felt sick inside. My heart was pounding. 'West, I am a psychiatrist. I'm out of my depth. You need to speak to the military, to intelligence, to community leaders, to experts.'

'James, I have advice coming out of my ears. I'm pulled in all directions. I'm overwhelmed. Please help me think clearly.'

'West, I'm sorry. I can't help you any more. A good doctor knows when he has reached the limits of his expertise.'

'James, I could have seen anyone, anywhere. I chose you.'

'I'm sorry West.'

'That's all right James. I understand.'

He left me his card with his telephone number.

I called Steve for some light relief.

'I did warn you, James. The guy is a fantasist, a bullshitter. If Sugden gets wind of this, you'll be out on your ear and struck off the register. You'll be a laughing stock for playing along with your patient's delusions. You'll never work again. Thank goodness you're rid of him. Forget it and move on.'

Monday morning, I headed for work. The traffic was light. The children were not yet back at school. I went about my usual rounds. Jean was upbeat as usual. I asked her to cancel West's next appointment and to free it up for a fresh case. 'Why's that James? Have you finished his therapy?' She looked doubtful.

'No, Jean. I decided I could go no further. I asked him to see someone else better qualified to help him.'

'That's unusual James.' She wanted to know much more but I closed down the discussion. 'Did you get the message?'

'Message? No, what's that?' I said.

'All non-emergency staff to attend a meeting with Christine Pearson at 17:30 in the main lecture theatre.'

'What's that about, Jean?'

'I don't know. There haven't been any leaks from the Meadows.'

The lecture theatre was two-thirds full. I sat at the back with Phil, Ayesha and Seth. Suki filed in with the ED team. She smiled at me discretely. Phil tapped my foot like a mischievous schoolboy.

The room fell quiet as the CEO, Christine Pearson, Medical Director Dr Sugden and Clinical Director Dr Prasad entered from the front. 'Good evening. I am sorry to detain you at the end of the day. I wish you all a very happy and productive New Year. I am moving on to pastures new.'

'Hallelujah,' whispered Phil.

Dr Sugden looked up at me and frowned.

'I am pleased to announce that I have been appointed as the Chief Executive of the National Council for Clinical Governance and Performance Management.' Some sycophants began to applaud. The rest of the audience joined in. I joined in for the last two claps.

'I have enjoyed my tenure very much and I'd like to thank you all for your support and hard work in achieving our corporate goals. I'll be leaving you in the very able hands of Dr Sugden, newly appointed Chief Executive.' The room let out a muffled gasp.

'That's you for the chop, then,' whispered Phil.

Dr Sugden, in his grey, shiny suit took the podium. The speech was a long list of planned changes and towards the end he announced Dr Prasad as his new Medical Director.

'Dr Prasad will be rolling out the Transformation Programme, starting in Psychiatry. The Bernie Rosen Unit will close and be replaced with the Worcester Community Treatment Protocols, a much more efficient and cost effective method of care delivery.'

Suki was watching my reaction from across the room.

'We will be ceasing all non-evidence based therapies immediately, and implementing the Worcester Community Treatment Protocols, which have manualised most clinical processes. Dr Hill ...'

I nearly fell off my seat. The audience turned to look at me.

'I want you to be a champion of the Worcester Community Treatment Protocols.'

The world seemed to contract and become a tiny space around me. I was no longer aware of the dozens of pairs of eyes staring at me expectantly, not even Suki's worried gaze. All I could see was Sugden standing smugly behind his lectern. Before I knew what was happening, I was on my feet.

'I'm surprised not to have been consulted about this. There's actually a very broad evidence base for our Personal Mastery and Inner Leadership Course.'

The atmosphere changed suddenly, as if dark clouds were brewing up for a storm.

'What's your scientific evidence base to justify these changes, Dr Sugden?' I asked calmly.

The audience muttered and stirred.

'I expect all staff to engage constructively with the Transformation Programme,' he said, looking straight into my eyes. 'Those who resist implementation will be transitioned out of the Trust. Thank you everyone for attending. If you have any questions don't hesitate to ask – my office door is always open …'

The moment was past. I sat down, suddenly alarmed at my own foolhardiness.

Phil whispered, 'You'll pay for that.'

———◆———

At the weekend, I fancied getting out of the city, but there was heavy snow. The Christmas Winter Wonderland was still operating in Hyde Park, so I invited Suki to join me there.

She arrived, wrapped up warm with a thick coat, scarf, gloves and bobble hat. I could just about get close enough to kiss her. She smelled gorgeous. The electricity pulsed through me. We wandered round, enjoying mulled wine, German sausages and fairground rides. Then we found a bench on a table next to a hog roasting and watched a folk band playing.

'I like her, she's great,' said Suki.

'Would you like to go to the front?' I asked.

'No, let's stay here, its warmer.' She shuffled closer to me and rubbed her cold nose against mine. 'James, are you going to resign or resist the changes to your ward?'

'I haven't decided. Maybe it's an opportunity to move on to something better. I can't imagine it being much fun to hang around.'

'People look to you to lead, James. You're one of the few they respect. If you leave, there'll be no one to protect them.'

'You can't swim against the tide for long, Suki. That's the way medicine is going. It's going to get much worse until the system finally fails. I'd prefer to go somewhere where they are creating the future that will come after that. I don't know where yet.'

We relaxed and enjoyed the foot-stomping sing-alongs. Suki knew the words better than me.

'Suki, can I ask you something? Ultra-confidentially?'

'Yes, of course, James, you can tell me anything.'

'You're going to find it very hard to believe.'

'You don't dress well enough to be gay. What is it?'

'Do you remember West?'

'Mr West, with the panic attacks and the suicide attempt?'

'Yes, him. Did he tell you about himself?'

'He's in his 40s, single I think. I don't remember.'

I told her the story. She looked at me as if I was teasing her.

'No, seriously, Suki. I mean it. He came to my house the other day in a panic when the terrorist attack happened in Madison.'

'You had a patient in your house?'

'He's not a normal patient Suki. I don't know how, but it seems true. I think he is the consciousness of Western Civilization.'

'Why haven't you told anyone about this? It's … it's … well, it's unbelievable.'

'That's exactly why. If I did, people would assume that he was psychotic and I was incompetent. If they believed him, he'd be all over the world's media or abducted by the CIA for scientific experiments.'

'James, I'm worried for you. You should get a second opinion.'

'No, I've discharged him. I don't have the skills to help him.'

'Oh! Good! I mean, not good really, but it's best to play it safe isn't it?'

Was she looking at me strangely? Trying to disguise the conviction that I had finally cracked under the recent professional strain? Maybe keeping me calm until she could make a break for it and call the authorities? I wouldn't have blamed her if she had thought that. But, strangely, I don't think she did.

———◆———

Wednesday evening, I drove home from work feeling low. I picked up a Lamb Biriani and some German weissbier. I was already in Dr Sugden's sights and now he was CEO and had wasted no time in humiliating me publicly by announcing the closure of my ward and termination of my Personal Mastery and Inner Leadership Course. I'd either have to lead the Worcester Community Treatment Protocols or find a new job during a recession.

I ate the Biriani on my lap, watching the television news with Nga. US special forces had stormed the cinema in Madison. All the terrorists were dead. The terrorists had held out till the last man and then detonated a series of bombs. Only a handful of the 350 hostages survived. The President spoke on the sidelines of a meeting with the Saudi Ambassador, ceremonially opening a new chain of Saudi-funded religious schools across America.

Washing up my plate, I wondered where West was, how he was coping, whether he had found someone else to help him. I switched on the kettle for a cup of tea. The lights went out. I used the torch application on my iPhone to navigate to the garage. The fuse box was dusty. I couldn't get the power back on. It was 19:15. I asked my neighbour to recommend an electrician.

An hour later, the doorbell rang. There was Alan Miller, an old patient of mine, dressed smartly in his electricians overalls, holding his toolbox.

'Alan, fancy seeing you!'

'Hello Doctor Hill, I thought I recognised your voice on the answering machine!'

'Call me James. Do come in.'

Within ten minutes, Alan had everything back up and running. I was embarrassed not to have been able to fix something so simple myself. I invited Alan to have a glass of beer with me before he went. 'No, thanks James, I'm driving. I'd love a cup of tea.'

I handed Alan his tea with a few chocolate biscuits.

'James, would you mind if I say something personal?'

'No, not at all, what is it?'

'You know, I'm not exaggerating when I say that you saved my life.'

I had no idea what he was talking about.

'When you treated my post-traumatic stress disorder, you asked me if I was suicidal. I didn't tell you the truth. I came very close twice. I didn't tell you in case you had me locked up.'

I smiled. 'It's common for patients to carefully manage what they say. It goes with the territory.' I listened, hoping he would feel comfortable enough to say more.

'One day I was planning to kill myself after seeing you but you asked me about my life's purpose, why I was here. You listened. You genuinely cared. I discovered my inner pilot light. I still felt suicidal but I knew I'd never act on it. That was my turning point. I took control from then on. Thank you for that.'

I was touched and embarrassed. I had had no idea what was going on inside this man, but I had made a difference all the same. I wondered how many more of my thousands of patients had stories like that? No one would ever know. Dr Sugden wouldn't have that data on his performance management dashboard.

'I'm getting married. Would you come to the wedding?'

———◆———

At the end of my clinic on Friday afternoon, I had an unexpected guest. Suki. Jean told her to come straight through to see me. It wasn't a social call, she looked very serious, like she had something to tell me. She closed the door behind her.

Speaking quietly, she said, 'James, I believe you.'

'Believe me about what Suki?'

'West. He presented to the ED last night. He wasn't suicidal but was in a terrible panic. He was fine physically. He asked to see me in the side room for privacy. He told me the whole story. I feel a bit mad saying this, but I believe he is telling the truth. He really is the consciousness of Western Civilization.'

There was a knock at the door and, before I could answer, Jean came in looking uncharacteristically flustered.

'I'm sorry James, I was listening at the door.'

I'd always suspected she did that.

'Dr Chen is right,' she continued. 'I think West is telling the truth. Why on earth did you stop seeing him? This is really important … for all of us.'

Jean and Suki were both looking at me, waiting for an answer.

'I'm a psychiatrist. What do I know about Western Civilization? How can I advise him on the economy, counterterrorism and immigration? That's nothing to do with medicine. It's too much responsibility. Besides, if it went public, that'd be the end of my career. The media reaction would make Sugden look as soft as a bunny rabbit by comparison.'

'James, I have known you since your first year in psychiatry, 20 years ago,' said Jean. 'Frankly, I don't know anyone better qualified.'

Suki said, 'He doesn't need an expert in geopolitics or economics. He's already an expert himself. He just needs your help to think clearly, to overcome his anxiety, to integrate his conflicting parts and find his voice.'

Jane picked up: 'He needs your help to reach his highest potential, James. You are the best person for the job. If you don't help him who's going to?'

'He has seven billion people to choose from,' said Suki, 'and he chose you. Don't you think that means something?'

I looked them both. They were waiting for a decision. I went over to the window, looking out at the trees, watching people walk past. 'OK, OK, I'll do it. But this has to remain secret. No one outside this room must ever know about this.'

They agreed.

'He gave me his business card. I'll bring it in tomorrow,' I said.

'No need, I've booked him in tomorrow at four,' said Jean.

RELIGIOUS EXTREMISM

My morning clinic had been light, so I went for a walk and had a late lunch at La Rochelle. West was waiting for me when I returned. Jean was looking pleased with herself.

James: Thanks for coming, West, please come through.

West was wearing his navy blue suit with chalk pinstripes again. He had polished his black brogues this time. His collar was undone, too small for his neck, his multicoloured silk tie, attempting to cover that up. He sat down, scratching his nose, then his head.

James: I am sorry that…

West: No apology necessary. I'd do the same in your situation.

James: You look unsettled West. What's up?

West: I am really worried about religious extremism getting out of hand. I've suffered many terrorist attacks here at home and many more all round the world. Religious extremists are asserting their beliefs and way of life all over the world. Some try to take over my schools, prisons and communities. Others have subverted democracy with election fraud and voter intimidation. Some use the legal system insincerely to advance their power under the guise of human rights and anti-discrimination legislation. Religious extremists routinely make appearances on university campuses and their followers use all means available to shut down free speech.

James: You have laws against violence, intimidation, election fraud, discrimination and terrorism. Why don't you just apply those?

West: I do but it's more mixed up that that. I believe in religious freedom and protection of minorities' rights to choose their way of life. I don't want to be seen to be singling out any particular religious or ethic groups for criticism. I want to be seen to be fair. Besides, I am afraid of provoking a violent reaction and economic sanctions from foreign powers.

James: Surely, there is nothing wrong with asserting your values of freedom, democracy, pluralism and diversity in your own countries?

West: My desire to be fair and culturally sensitive is being exploited. It's hard for me to distinguish who is a sincerely religious person and who is a religious extremist. It's a supersensitive subject because people get very angry very quickly. Religious extremists are very well organised and adept at hiding behind the language of anti-racism, multiculturalism, religious freedom and human rights. If I don't get a handle on this soon, then there will be an ugly backlash from the mainstream population.

James: You must be feeling awful, so soon after the attack in Madison. Let's run a voice dialogue.

We cleared a space for West to Voice Dialogue.

PURPLE: Don't say I didn't warn you about this. I saw this coming in the 60s and 70s but GREEN changed the law to silence me. These religious fundamentalists will rule us within 30 years if we don't act now to protect our way of life.

GREEN: I brought in political correctness and multiculturalism to overcome past abuses and inequalities and to ensure that discrimination, imperialism and racism were consigned to history. The whole point of political correctness was to enforce rules to make sure that people will no longer permitted to speak in tribal, ethnocentric, nationalistic, racist ways.

BLUE: You don't apply those rules fairly and equally. You turn a blind eye to the activities of some types of totalitarian fascist.

James: GREEN's values are very well-meaning yet have created unforeseen problems. Can you see a better way forward?

YELLOW: I can see many potential futures, some wonderful, others catastrophic. The future is not predetermined. We have the opportunity to influence the outcome. It depends on my mood how I see it. One day I have apocalyptic nightmares about civil war, terrorism and religious fanatics taking over. The next day I travel around my great cities and see people from different backgrounds, races and religions getting on well together and I sense a general confidence that things will work out for the best.

GREEN: We're creating a new global, multicultural civilization. PURPLE is just an old fashioned, reactionary and wants to take us back to an imagined past. We have to embrace globalisation. I'm scared that PURPLE will take us back to racist, ethnocentric mentality, persecuting religious minorities. I won't allow that.

ORANGE: We're at an amazing stage of global development. These are natural teething troubles while people adapt to the modern world. All over the developing world I see dynamic, thriving people, embracing education, science and capitalism. There are conservative and traditional religious forces, but they're finding their way in the world. All the religious countries I've visited are very friendly. They make you feel very welcome, much more so than Europeans who look down on foreigners. This phase will pass. Focus on trade and education and everything will be fine.

James: That rational, optimistic, scientific and business mentality is one of your strengths. The rest of the world is embracing that.

YELLOW: When traditional societies take on the beliefs and practices of the modern world, it's very challenging to their BLUE and PURPLE systems of thinking. We had the luxury of doing this over 500 years and yet we stall had wars, revolutions and all kinds of upheaval. The non-Western countries have had to do it much faster, with us in the driving seat, in some cases forced upon them by imperialism and globalisation. It's no wonder their PURPLE and BLUE systems push back with fear and anger. Anti-Westernisation or anti-Americanism is a misnomer. It's a conservative, traditional backlash against this social, spiritual and structural breakup of the old way of life. We need to be much more compassionate about that, yet, we must not accept the role of being their scapegoat. We're just further ahead on the developmental path. We must be more mature and magnanimous.

PURPLE: I can understand that. ORANGE and GREEN have undermined my security here at home, so I understand the way these religious fundamentalists feel. It's just that I don't want them in my country. They should go to live in countries where people share their beliefs and not try to colonise me.

BLUE: We're strong in apparent financial and military power but, on the inside, we are weak spiritually. That makes us vulnerable to the imposition of religious fundamentalism by determined, committed, well funded, well organised groups.

James: Step into that way of thinking and speak from there.

BLUE-RED Religious Fundamentalist: Westerners are materially wealthy but when you look into their eyes, there's no sparkle. I can feel it in their hearts. They're dead. Working, commuting, going to the supermarket, watching TV, going to the movies, paying taxes, doing DIY, going to football games, filling their bodies with burgers and chips. They thought that they'd abolished slavery but they've chosen it as a way of life. They ignore the word of God. They've chosen eternal damnation. They spend billions on medicine to avoid dying but they don't spend ten minutes in prayer to submit to God. They don't use their freedom to look after their family, to discipline their children. To anaesthetise the pain, they ply themselves with alcohol and drugs. They lecture others about human rights but send their elderly to die in soulless homes. They send young men to prison but they don't teach them God's power, they don't teach them how to submit to the truth. They're weak to the core, a paper tiger. They must submit to God or perish.

James: Do you have a strategy to bring that about?

BLUE-RED Religious Fundamentalist: It's God's will. We will keep offering the non-believers the truth, the opportunity to make the right choice. If they refuse, they condemn themselves to never-ending war. We will harass them wherever they are. We will strike fear into their hearts. Their high tech weapons are useless in asymmetrical warfare. They cannot bomb an idea. Believers are thriving in the West, showing them the way by living among them. While they neglect their families, we will look after ours, we will have children and look after our elderly. While they watch television we will pray. Our way of life is superior so it will naturally become dominant in the world.

James: Why don't you bring about your ideal in a country where your believers are the majority?

BLUE-RED Religious Fundamentalist: We're blocked at every point by dictators, spies and commercial interests. With a couple of exceptions, we've been unable to take control from the Western-backed thugs. As soon as there's any sign of a religious government, the West strangles it at birth. Therefore, we must fight the devil at its source.

James: What's your strategy?

BLUE-RED Religious Fundamentalist: We will provoke you into endless wars until we drain your energy and money. Your material power is no match for our spiritual power. We believe in God, you believe in nothing other than your freedom and wealth. We will use your lawyers to tie you up in knots. Your high tech weapons cannot protect you from God. Your military cannot fight beliefs. We will show you the right way to live. Your people will follow us because they see the truth.

James: What gives you this self confidence?

BLUE-RED Religious Fundamentalist: Westerners are either converting to the truth or accommodating us and retreating. Your universities are teaching our syllabus and giving platforms to great preachers. Your media is spreading our message and silencing non-believers. Your prisoners are our recruiting grounds. We are punishing the forces of evil and darkness all over the world. Your leaders are desperate to be sensitive, tolerant and accommodating. Your banks and companies will do anything for money, so we use the wealth God has given us to mould them to his wishes. In their hearts, Westerners know that their materialism is evil and that they must eventually return to God. They will do so very fast now and the world will finally be free to live under God's law.

James: How effective is your strategy?

BLUE-RED Religious Fundamentalist: Excellent. Your governments have passed laws to make it illegal to criticise religious beliefs. As our numbers increase, your politicians are desperate for all the votes they can get. You Westerners think as far ahead as the next election or the next news bulletin. We think over hundreds of years and on into the next world. Time is on our side. God is on our side, eventually you will come to follow the right path. We will bring God's law to your empty hearts. Your only choice is when to submit. I pray that you do so quickly.

BLUE Convert: I've converted to religion because religious people know right from wrong, protect their women, don't allow teenage sex, are religious, ban drinking and gambling. They respect their elders and the family. They support each other and live in a community. West used to do that but we gave up believing.

PURPLE Religion: You don't speak for me. This is not the traditional religion. You have got mixed up with the desire for worldly power. You have become intolerant and extreme. You must return to your family and community to seek guidance from the elders.

BLUE-RED Religious Fundamentalist: You are mistaken and naive. You have let ORANGE exploit and pollute you. I will not stand for that. It's time for revenge, righteousness and justice.

GREEN Religion: Religion is about peace, love and harmony. There are many different paths up the spiritual mountain. Each should choose their own path. We must include all faiths and spirituality in our diverse and complex world. This BLUE fundamentalist expression of religion is not authentic. It has no right to force it's narrow, intolerant views on everyone else.

BLUE-RED Religious Fundamentalist: You are an unbeliever, corrupted with Western thinking.

ORANGE: Let's be practical. We can agree to disagree about the facts and focus on the results. People should be free to choose the brand of religion which best satisfies their needs. It's up to each version of religion to compete to get the most followers. Let's get wealthy and then we can debate about religion in comfort.

James: Why don't we hear much more from GREEN, ORANGE and PURPLE Religion?

All three broke eye contact, looking down, scared of the RED-BLUE fundamentalist.

James: What can West do to enable you to have a more productive dialogue about how to sincerely live according to your religious beliefs in the modern world?

PURPLE Religion: You need to make it safe for us to talk and express our views.

ORANGE Religion: You need to make sure democracy and freedom of speech are protected so that we are safe to choose our own destiny.

GREEN Religion: West, you see that religion is a vibrant, dynamic way of life, diverse and complex. Your prejudices about religion are stuck in the past. Religions have many voices, many perspectives from different people in different countries, places and circumstances. You must listen to all the voices and not treat us as if we're all the same. You need to make it safe for us to live without intimidation and discrimination from either the RED-BLUE Fundamentalist Religion or your PURPLE and BLUE world views that want to exclude us all.

James: West, how does that make you feel?

YELLOW: The RED-BLUE Fundamentalist version of religion is a conservative, reactionary, absolutistic world view powered by warrior fighting spirit. It feels that it has been wounded, violated and it is determined to take power to assert itself. It's angry that it has lost control of its spiritual, religious and social foundations. It's very genuinely pious but has mixed it up with the desire for power, domination and revenge. It doesn't like other people interfering in its business. It sees the West as the cause of its problems. It's coming from a victim position, feeling violated and blaming others for its shortcomings.

GREEN: All religions have fundamentalists. You must treat all religions equally. Christian fundamentalists are dangerous in America too. Their apocalyptic beliefs encouraged George Bush and Tony Blair to invade Iraq. They promote extremism, terrorism and intolerance. They want to take away women's rights and the right to choose an abortion. Jewish fundamentalists have caused all kinds of harm to the Palestinians.

ORANGE: Creationists are trying to stop me teaching evolution.

BLUE Fundamentalist: Abortion is murder. Murderers will go to hell. Evolution is a lie, a conspiracy to deny God.

James: A BBC programme on religious fundamentalism read out a bloodcurdling speech by President Ahmadinejad of Iran about the will of God, the evil enemies out to get them, the day of judgement, and an apocalyptic war to destroy the unbelievers. The presenter revealed he'd played a trick on the listeners. The speech was actually made four centuries ago by Oliver Cromwell!

West took on a new persona, looking lively and chirpy, pointing his finger at me.

PURPLE: I don't want Oliver Cromwell and all his mates back here again, kitted out with AK-47s, thank you very much.

RED: I can't believe we're so weak as to let these religious fanatics take over.

ORANGE: We used to have free speech. Now if you criticise religion, GREEN calls you a racist and sends the thought police round. Religion is a set of beliefs, a faith, not a race. In a democracy, everyone has the right to assert their own beliefs and challenge others in the marketplace of ideas.

PURPLE: We'll be living under foreign religious rule in a few years. I worry for my children. Any time anyone criticises these fundamentalist beliefs, they become angry and violent and our politicians, pathetic weaselly little worms that they are, get on their hands and knees and appease fundamentalist religion. It took us 500 years to get rid of fundamentalist religion and now our elite is opening the door to it again under cover of the Trojan horse of multiculturalism.

BLUE: Give 'em an inch, and they'll take a mile.

GREEN: You went over there to colonise them so you can't complain when they come back to colonise you.

RED: At least they had the self-respect to fight back. We're lying down and taking it. I don't know what our government is up to. They appease and surrender at every opportunity.

GREEN: Most religious people are ordinary people getting on with their lives, being your doctor, your nurse, a taxi driver like you, running businesses, obeying the law, paying taxes, suffering prejudice and intolerance from people like you.

James: Is there any way to make a success of it, to make it work?

PURPLE: No mate, this country has gone to the dogs. All we can do is to keep out of their way and let them get on with it. I'd go to Australia if I could but they won't have me.

PURPLE (Australian): No point, mate, it's the same here.

James: What are you going to do?

PURPLE: Once my old mother's dead, I'm off to the Costa del Sol, Spain.

James: So you'll be an immigrant? Do plan to learn Spanish and become a Catholic?

He smiled and winked.

BLUE: These religious extremists are right-wing, fascist, fundamentalists who use terrorism, intimidation and manipulation to force their way of life on everybody else. Why can't GREEN see fascists every bit as evil as Hitler when they're ethnic minorities?

GREEN: You want to take us back to the dark days of racism, slavery and colonialism. Your elitist and supremacist views led to the Holocaust. I reject racism. Terrorism is a reaction against 300 years of Western domination. You can't hit them and then complain when they hit you back.

YELLOW: We get so wrapped up in the strong emotions of the moment that we fail to see the big picture. It's no surprise they're angry. It's got little to do with religion. It's the trauma of emerging into the modern world. We've come from hunter gatherers 10,000 years ago through to an amazing global Civilization. It has got nothing to do with race or nationality. It's our shared human story. It's about consciousness, beliefs and ideas. We've had a turbulent 500 years on this journey. In the West, we've experienced modernisation and globalisation in the driving seat.

PURPLE: My grandparents were born into a world with radically different values, family life, sexual behaviour, social standards, religion and economy. The West has changed beyond recognition in a lifetime.

YELLOW: Take the Germans. They gave us Beethoven, Bosch and BMW. They're an intelligent, sophisticated, civilised people. Yet, only 70 years ago, they got whipped up into a fanatical frenzy of PURPLE tribal, racial pride, RED lust for power and BLUE Fundamentalist Nazi Ideology. They started a war that killed 55 million people. It's a massive trauma for human beings to undergo these radical changes to our way of life and sometimes, in fear, we take a step back, we try to reclaim the past, we hunker down in our families and tribes, cling to our traditions and structures more tightly and sometimes we become rigid and intolerant. Many others followed this path; the Imperial Japanese, the communists, the juntas in South America and the Chinese Cultural Revolution. If you blame religion for the terrorism and conflict, then you're picking a fight with God and you will never win that, you will drive that hugely diverse religious population into one corner and you will help the fascists among them to bring about the apocalypse which they desire.

GREEN: When people are under pressure, they scapegoat others. The Germans blamed the Jews. Communists blamed the bourgeois. Religious extremists blame West. I don't want West to respond by scapegoating religious people.

ORANGE: Religions have always caused conflict and war. They have always persecuted people who don't believe in their version of religion.

GREEN: There you go again, prejudiced, judging all religious people by the action of a few.

RED: How do you think religions spread around the world? It wasn't only trade and pilgrims. It was warriors, intimidation, migration and conquest like they're doing now all over the world.

YELLOW: Just because GREEN has become sensitive and inclusive doesn't mean the rest of the world has followed suit. Authentic diversity means acknowledging the full range of value systems in all people, including those we disagree with.

BLUE: Most people are resigned to it, depressed and angry about it or they're too busy to notice. GREEN perceives resistance to its multicultural ideology as evil. The religious extremists will support human rights and political correctness long enough for them to take over. Naive middle class and rural people are insulated from it. They don't want to see.

GREEN: Most religious people don't support the use of force to spread their religion.

BLUE: How do I distinguish a religious person who genuinely believes in democracy, science, freedom, the rule of law from a fundamentalist?

PURPLE: Most Germans weren't Nazis. Most Russians weren't communists. The extremists were initially just every small, determined, committed groups. People said they didn't matter. But they still took over. The current religious extremists are well on their way to reaching their objectives.

> *West moved across the room to the window, expanding vastly. He paused. There was a profound silence.*

YELLOW: The cities of the West now contain a huge diversity of people including followers of all the world's religions. They represent many different strands of thought among whom there's debate, discussion and creativity. The freedom of the West, the democracy, the safety, the rule of law is incubating both religious enlightenment and renaissance. This goes unnoticed because the aggressive fundamentalist RED-BLUE voices are loud and alarming. Hosting all these newcomers does constitute a risk but it also represents an amazing opportunity. The West allows religious people the freedom of speech and association which will help us to evolve and adapt new ideas quickly.

ORANGE: It provides a free space in which terrorists and fundamentalists can optimise their skills, knowledge and become more effective.

YELLOW: It provides a quieter space for religious people to work out how to live their beliefs in a modern, democratic, pluralistic context. There's no guarantee of a positive outcome. It may be a Trojan horse that takes over. It may be a springboard to a renaissance, reformation, enlightenment and positive flowering of religion in a modern, constructive, adaptive form.

ORANGE Religion: We need the freedom to think, debate, experiment and to adapt our faith to the modern world. We can't do that if there's a climate of fear generated by the conservatives and zealots who hold us in the past.

YELLOW: Relativism served a useful function in opening up diverse perspectives, being willing to see complexity from different points of view, deconstructing the old abusive hierarchies. It has gone too far. There's still right and wrong, true and false. Human beings have the capacity to make judgements based on their reason, intellect, intuition, experience and wisdom. This is what creates a free, independent human being able to stand in their own authority, to be a free being, aligned with life. West needs to become comfortable with having boundaries again. We need a clear moral compass so that freedom can be used responsibly.

TURQUOISE: There's only one God. The arrival and assertion of the world's other religions on our shores is a gift, a challenge and an opportunity. We need to separate out the different layers because not all of what we see is pure religion. Some of what we see, is nationalistic behaviour, tribal thinking, anger, woundedness, revenge, frustration and difficulty adapting to a fast changing world. Show compassion for those parts because they struggle as we struggle and have struggled in the past.

James: What's the gift, the challenge and the opportunity?

TURQUOISE: We have lost our spiritual centre, separated from God, separated from life itself. Nature abhors a vacuum and God has come knocking at our door. We don't have to accept the specific cultural manifestations of religion but we do need to wake up to God and to life. Continuing with materialism is futile. We've no choice but to re-enchant our universe, to live as the spirit beings which we are. Our only choice is about how we're going to do it.

BLUE: How do we do that without being forced to submit to other's assertions of religious belief?

TURQUOISE: Distinguish between the underlying deep truth, the spiritual message, from rules, laws, traditions and ethnic culture. I'm not pretending that it's easy but if you fight God, you will lose.

James: If you created Heaven on Earth, how would religion be?

TURQUOISE: We would live fully at one with God, the divine, the life within, the spirit within and between us!

YELLOW: The world is globalising and we have to live with each other in a way that we didn't have to in the past. It's a basic rule of global civilization that minorities, wherever they are, must be protected and have the same rights as the majority in whichever country they are. Minorities also must respect and protect the culture, values and rules of the country which gives them those freedoms and rights in which they live or choose an alternative home.

James: What do you need to do to get along together?

YELLOW: Strong, healthy boundaries. We must protect democracy and freedom of speech for all. Respect each other's space and territory. When you're a minority in one another's country, you must defer to the laws, culture and customs of the locals while the majority must respect your equal rights and you must be free from harm or persecution. People everywhere have the right to practice their religion and have freedom of thought. The West must make it clear that it respects all religions, distinguishes between terrorists and ordinary religious people.

PURPLE West: We can only do that if they do the same for us, stop trying to impose their beliefs us.

YELLOW: Very true. West must stop using military force inappropriately such as in Iraq and Afghanistan. Non-Western states must step back from their own imperialism by ceasing to fund fundamentalist religious schools and extremist groups in other countries. If you wish to live by your own rules in your own country, you must respect others right to choose how they live in their country.

BLUE Religion: You need to treat us like we're part of your country, so we can be full Americans, Australians and Germans. Stop treating us as foreigners, a fifth column.

YELLOW: In the West, religious people who have become part of the country have full citizenship and full status and equality. They have the right to practice their religion and to be treated as an equal member of society. Vilification of religious people is totally unacceptable and will be punished. Equally, within Western countries, religious people have the duty to accept Western culture and values, democracy, liberalism, diversity and pluralism. They must accept that they have no right to force their beliefs or behaviours upon anyone else. They must give their loyalty to their nation of choice not to act as agent for other countries or transnational groups.

BLUE: How can I enforce that?

YELLOW: The pure faith of religions is a good thing. However, it's not acceptable for anyone to force their opinions on others. It's not acceptable for anyone to use violence in a democracy to get their way. People are entitled to believe that they're right and say so. People are entitled to try to persuade others of their opinions. People are entitled to criticise and challenge others' positions and opinions. These are the rules of democracy and freedom.

BLUE: How are you going to stop GREEN from appeasing religious fundamentalists?

YELLOW: GREEN means well but has fallen short of its ideals. GREEN should treat all forms of totalitarianism and fascism equally. GREEN should treat all races equally. GREEN should stand for authentic diversity and recognise that others really do think differently. GREEN must be honest that it does make value judgements and assertions of truth. GREEN must sincerely engage in dialogue with those with whom it disagrees and not close down debate by vilifying others and imposing groupthink. People with fundamentalist beliefs need strict boundaries to prevent them from harming others or using force to impose their beliefs on others. It's totally unacceptable to indulge any forms of violence, imperialism, racism and fascism.

GREEN: That's OK so long as there's no racism, no persecution of minorities, full religious freedom.

James: Thank you all very much. Would anyone like to say anything further before we finish?

> There was silence. West looked tired. One by one, he invited each of the different voices, the different value systems back within himself and integrated them all. He sat quietly.

James: Brilliant, West. I'm proud of you. I reckon you could do with a walk and a good sleep.

West: Thanks for taking me on again, James. I won't let you down.

SECURITY, DEFENCE AND PEACE

It was good to have West back in the consulting room, enthusiastic and raring to go.

West: Good Morning, Doctor.

James: Welcome back. How are you?

West: Knowing that I was coming in today I slept wonderfully deeply last night. I feel relaxed and I want to get to the root of my security fears.

James: Excellent. When you're ready we can start. What's the background to your recent crisis?

West: I have the most powerful military force in history. I spend much more on defence than all the others. Democracy and capitalism are accepted by more people around the world than ever. Part of me feels confident that it's a matter of time before we're one global Civilization.

James: I'm waiting for the *but*.

West: In 1919, Britain invaded Iraq through Basra up to Baghdad, imposed a puppet ruler and subdued the tribes under British influence. They did that at the same time as having a military which straddled a global Empire, having exhausted their economy in the First World War. It took only 30,000 men. Most of the 5000 casualties were due to disease. 90 years later, a force ten times the size with vastly more powerful weapons, communication and trillions of dollars of investment was incapable of having the same effect. Military power isn't enough to be secure any more. My military might is great for bombing installations, sinking ships, eavesdropping on communications and destroying weaker forces, but even the mighty United States and its allies have been unable to bring security to Afghanistan, one of the weakest, poorest, most underdeveloped countries in the world. What happens if we ever had to fight stronger, more technologically advanced countries like China, Pakistan, Iran, North Korea or Russia?

James: Keep going.

West: To fight a war, you need an industrial base and control over energy and resources.

Much of my industry has moved to the East. My energy supply is in the hands of countries which don't share my values. My whole system would come to a standstill within days if the energy supplies were cut. I'm vulnerable.

James: And finance?

West: It's a house of cards waiting to blow down. If my competitors withdraw funds from the Dollar or Euro or equity and bond markets, they could have me on my knees within days. America did it to Britain in 1956 during the Suez crisis. That was the final castration of the British and they have been America's poodle ever since. America is at risk of suffering the same fate but, if America falters, there's no powerful liberal democracy to become the new bigger brother. If the Alpha chimpanzee loses control, the rest fight until a new hierarchy is established.

James: What about India? It's an English-speaking democracy, with the rule of law, vibrant capitalism, education and science.

West: I see India as an emerging pillar of Western Civilization. That sounds counterintuitive because nowhere on earth is more exotic to a Westerner than India. Yet, it is the world's largest democracy, which is amazing given its immense diversity and internal challenges. India upholds the rule of law, an independent judiciary. India is a leader in science and medicine, increasingly in technology and engineering. India has a vibrant, pluralistic media. India has a booming middle class and growing domestic market. India is diversity in action.

James: There are many places like that. Eastern Europe, South and Central America, Malaysia, Singapore, Hong Kong, Turkey, Indonesia, Japan, South Korea, sub-Saharan Africa, Thailand, the Philippines, Taiwan. You've been so successful in spreading your ideas that you've forgotten where your boundaries are.

West: Good point. Together we may protect our shared values.

James: Is the world moving towards a future of peace, consensus and cooperation?

> *Without it even being suggested, West stands and closes his eyes, preparing himself for Voice Dialogue.*

RED: There will always be competition for resources and status between different power bases.

ORANGE: The First and Second World Wars were between countries with Western values. They had modern ORANGE-BLUE Western values superficially but regressed to a more primitive PURPLE-RED form. The Germans were highly sophisticated and yet the Nazis descended into deep barbarism. It's important to uphold democracy and freedom.

GREEN: Democracy and freedom are your fig-leaf to cover the real motivations, the desire for power control, domination and exploitation. It's time for us to move on beyond tribes and wars. That's why we must pursue peace, international harmony, international law, the United Nations. We must demilitarise, stop threatening other countries and promote peace and consensus for a fair world.

BLUE: We need strong boundaries or others will take what we've got. Just because you've become an accommodating pacifist, don't assume everyone else has.

RED: Power brings freedom. The fittest, most dominant, best organised warriors with the best fighting spirit, the most powerful alliance call the shots. The only thing that stands between the weaklings and foreign domination is armed force, the military.

GREEN: Why do you think Iran wants nuclear weapons? Why are the Russians always posturing for power and position? Why do you think religious fundamentalists keep attacking you? It's because they're tired of you dominating them, interfering, and disrespecting them. Learn from history. Be peaceful. Be the first to lay down our arms and promote international peace through dialogue, mutual understanding, respect and a fair distribution of wealth and resources.

James: There's an inconsistency in your beliefs and values – in the way that you apply them to the West but not to others.

GREEN: I don't follow.

James: You're highly critical of PURPLE, RED, BLUE and ORANGE thinking in the West, yet you don't perceive those in others, or for some reason, you treat them differently. Of course, the RED system operates in the West. There's a long history of the projection of power, control, adventure and assertion along with its dark side of abuse, exploitation, shame, domination and selfishness. No doubt about that. Why are you naive when you look at non-Western people? Why do you treat them differently?

GREEN: The West has been so powerful for so long, all the others have been on the receiving end of our RED values, and they feel the need to defend themselves. I want us to stop threatening them, to show them love, acceptance and willingness to share power equally and fairly. If we do, they will behave differently.

James: That's well motivated but you're not living up to your own expressed values. If you genuinely believe in diversity then you must acknowledge that there different types of people with different positions, beliefs, motivations and characteristics in different places with different circumstances behave in different ways. Have you ever met members of the Iranian Revolutionary Guard? Have you spent time with young officers in the People's Liberation Army? Have you invited any KGB agents to dinner?

GREEN: I don't like your tone. It's patronising and disrespectful.

James: I'm challenging you to live up to your own values. You've allowed your own guilt, shame and self-hatred, to distort your judgement. You apply different standards and values to different races, cultures and religions.

GREEN: How dare you? Take that back!

YELLOW: You treat people from non-Western countries differently to those from Western countries. You assume that everyone thinks and acts like you. When you see a RED-BLUE nationalist chauvinistic thug who happens to be a South American president, you hail them as an inspiration. When someone with exactly the same values is within the West, you call them bigots, racists, fascists or rednecks. You treat racist, imperialistic, violent fascist religious zealots who comes from outside the West, as freedom fighters, misunderstood victims of Western hegemony. When you see exactly the same values from a Western person, you vilify them. It's time for you to heal your emotional wounds and be more mature, to walk your talk.

> *GREEN looks uncomfortable, red-faced, brooding, angry but unable to muster a defence.*

YELLOW: You know, BLUE values peace as highly as you do, maybe more so because it has suffered the pain of war. You don't seem to value security, you take it for granted because you've always had it even though you never built it yourself. It's about time that you, GREEN, showed some respect and understanding, did some listening, engaged in dialogue like you keep talking about.

James: West, what's worth defending? What's worth fighting for?

BEIGE: A fight for survival, to stay alive.

PURPLE: My family, territory, people, resources. Security.

RED: Control, power, status, revenge, freedom, my property, my allies, fun.

BLUE: My nations, truth, righteousness, the rule of law, the Constitution, order and stability and justice.

ORANGE: Democracy, individual liberty, freedom, the right to pursue your own destiny, business and science.

GREEN: Equality, fairness, human rights, anti-racism, women's rights, gay rights, social justice, environment, diversity and pluralism.

YELLOW: All of those, and we must fight for all to survive and thrive as we're all in the same boat now.

TURQUOISE: All of those, and we must defend life, all life, all humanity.

James: What threatens you? Let's hear your worst fears.

BEIGE: Famine and disease, pandemics. Nuclear weapons, especially in the hands of terrorists and psychopathic dictators.

PURPLE: Colonisation through immigration and foreign imperialism. Religious extremism.

RED: Loss of US hegemony leading to conflict. China is building a blue water Navy with the capacity to project power. They're colonising Africa and South America by buying up assets, buying land, bribing governments and sending settlers. There are more Chinese in Nigeria now than there were British when it was a British colony. They've got their eyes on Australia and Canada.

ORANGE: Our financial system is unstable and insecure, very vulnerable to shocks. We're hostages to our creditors. Most of them don't have Western values.

PURPLE: The Arab Spring is unleashing nationalists and religious zealots. We'd be stupid to think that Europe is insulated from that. Do you remember the Algerian war? That's what Europe will look like in 20 years but the Europeans won't have anywhere to run to. North America has its own problems and will close its doors.

RED: The Russians are chauvinistic nationalists looking to expand the Russian Empire.

BLUE: Religious fundamentalists. Those who control our energy supply control us. That's dangerous.

RED: What's happening in Syria will come to Europe soon. We invest money on high-tech weapons but they are no defence against religious extremism, guns, knives, fists, intimidation, hate speech and the Internet. Colonel Gaddafi saw immigration and high birth rates as a strategy for colonisation of Europe.

BLUE: We've lost confidence, our fighting spirit. People are spoilt and complacent. They take everything for granted. They're not willing to defend what they have.

GREEN: The huge inequality in wealth, resources and power make us a target.

BLUE: What's happening in Syria is terrible but that's nothing to what could happen if Israel fights Iran, or if the Sunnis and the Shia start fighting each other. If Pakistan collapses, who will get their hands on the nuclear weapons?

RED: When North Korea implodes, it will be dangerous. Their paranoid leaders have got their finger on the button. They would think nothing of nuking Seoul or Tokyo.

GREEN: America is a rogue regime, bullies who make up the rules to suit themselves. We need international law.

PURPLE: Settlers with PURPLE and BLUE thinking are pouring in. In the United States there's a risk from Hispanic nationalism and fragmentation. In Europe, there's a risk of submission to religious extremism. GREEN is racist so it refuses to admit it.

West sits down, sighs and takes a deep breath.

James: Thanks. That's a lot of fear to carry around with you. Tell me your strengths.

West: I have an open, diverse, vibrant society which engages enthusiastically in business, science and democracy. Even if they don't like my countries' foreign policy, people all over the world are attracted to my values. My interconnection, ability to self-criticise and learn quickly gives me power. My strength is in the incredible knowledge I've amassed.

James: And your weaknesses?

West: Loss of confidence and morale. Spiritual weakness. Emptiness, alienation and meaninglessness. Self-hatred, self-loathing and excessive self-criticism. Disconnection from the land, dissociation of the community and breakup of families. Disunity. Inability to make judgements, to distinguish good from bad or right from wrong. Inability to lay down a boundary, to exclude, to say no.

James: What about external, systemic weaknesses?

West: My complexity makes me vulnerable to attacks, emergencies and shocks. Food, transport, energy, health, finance are all incredibly interdependent with a huge support system. Individuals and communities, even countries are no longer resilient and independent. People don't know how to grow their own food.

West sits forward in his chair, suddenly looking pale and weary.

West: That's enough for today. I need to get some fresh air.

———◆———

Two days later, the telephone was ringing when I opened the office door at 8AM. It was West of course.

'I'm sorry to bother you,' he said. 'I'm in a real panic. I can't sit still. I have a dry mouth and pins and needles in my hands and around my lips. My bowels are really unsettled. My pulse is bounding at 120 beats per minute.'

'Do you have any chest pain? Breathlessness?'

'No, nothing like that, I can walk up and down stairs, no pain, no cough. I want to come and see you, can I come before the next appointment?'

'Yes, certainly,' I said, sounding less than convincing. 'Come straight away.'

I slumped in my chair. Weary – although the day had barely begun – and full of doubts. What was I expecting? That everything would be plain sailing now that I had a couple of cheerleaders in Jean and Suki? Of course not. *Believe in yourself James* I said internally. What was the alternative, anyway? The Worcester Community Treatment Protocols?

I busied myself clearing some necessary admin. West arrived 15 minutes later. To my surprise he looked fine, pink, alert, speaking normally, fully mobile, but anxious. He was certainly much better.

'I'm so sorry Doc. I suddenly noticed my heartbeat was very fast which made me panic, thinking the worst. I still have this horrible anxiety feeling in my chest.'

'Let me examine you.'

He sat down and took off his shirt. His pulse was 90, regular, sinus rhythm. Blood pressure 130/85. The heart sounded normal. The chest was clear, normal breathing sounds, no other signs.

James: Did anything bring this on? Any worries?

West: I was relaxing after the last session when I started to get intrusive images of all those fears we discussed.

James: OK. I want to introduce you to a powerful technique called Eye Movement Desensitisation and Reprocessing, EMDR. It helps to clear the emotional charges from past traumas. You identify traumatic events in the past which carry a heavy emotional charge and then use bilateral stimulation, moving your eyes from one side to another or being tapped alternately on the left and right knees. Your mind then naturally reprocesses the information and releases the emotional charge.

West: Sounds weird. Does it work?

James: Often. When it works, it's amazingly effective. It promotes a natural healing process. It's different during each bilateral stimulation. Sometimes, there's a release of tension, an emotional shift, a new awareness, new idea. Sometimes you run through 20 different images in a flash. Sometimes nothing happens. Sometimes you get strong sensations in your body. Sometimes your mind jumps back to past events. Sometimes you get a new perception or a new way of looking at things. Your mind does it's own thing but the general direction is towards healing of emotional wounds, releasing of emotional blockages.

West: Are there side effects?

James: You're mature and robust and have good coping skills so I'm not too worried about that. EMDR can unlock things which have been long repressed. Emotions can be very painful.

West: Is it like brainwashing or hypnosis? Would it erase memories or insert thoughts?

James: No. You will remain in charge always and my role will be as a facilitator. We will probably need to do several sessions. We need to clarify the target. We'll be trying to narrow it down to a clear image, memory, negative beliefs about yourself, positive thoughts you'd like to have, emotions and sensations. Then we can get into the therapy.

West: I'd like to try it.

James: I'll direct me to a particular image, thought, emotion or sensation. You give me a nod when I'm ready. I'll move my fingers back and forth and you follow them with your eyes while letting your mind go free

West: Got it. Sounds weird but I'll have a go.

James: First, I will read out the whole of the target to you and invite you to take yourself deep into that state. Then when you're ready, give me a nod and we will start the eye movements. Then, it's like rolling the ball to the top of a hill, I want you to let go of it and watch wherever it happens to go.

West: How long do we do that for?

James: I'll guide you for about a minute or so. I'll be watching your reaction closely. The aim is that you do as much processing naturally, without interference from me, as possible. My aim will be to facilitate that and stay out of the way as much as I can. First, we need to establish a safe place that you can take yourself to if you become distressed. You'll go there at the end of the session. Think of a time or place when you felt safe.

West: Sunbathing on a beach.

James: Take yourself there and describe it in detail.

West: Lying on a sun bed, eyes closed, the sun beating down on my skin, listening to the waves of the sea. There's a gentle breeze over my skin. I can smell suncream and sweat. I can taste salt on my lips. I take a sip of a cold drink.

James: How do you feel?

West: Safe. Peaceful.

James: Excellent. Choose a word to use as a trigger to take yourself there if you need to.

West: Beach

James: Good. Now, what's the worst image that comes with these feelings of anxiety and panic?

West: An apocalyptic civil war. My countries overrun with terrorists, men with guns, breakdown of civil order, riots, bombs, kidnappings, complete collapse of society. Brutal gangs. Religious fanatics. Foreign powers providing weapons and money.

James: Float back in your memory to the first time you felt this way.

West: It's something way back, the mediaeval period, maybe prehistory, I'm not sure.

James: What's the worst image?

West: Women and children cowering in a bombed out house with gangs roaming outside, seeking revenge, looking for people to rape and decapitate. Seeing the terror in the face of the mothers unable to protect their children as the men burst in.

James: What beliefs do you have about yourself in that context?

West: I am powerless. I am weak. I am defenceless. I can't protect them. I am alone.

James: What would you like to believe about yourself?

West: I am safe. I am strong. I can defend myself. I can protect my people.

James: What emotions come with that?

West: Terror. Fear. Hopelessness. Rage. Hatred.

James: What sensations do you get in your body?

West: That horrible, tight feeling in my chest, a buzzing.

James: Rate how true, out of 7, is it to say, 'I'm safe?' 7 out of 7 means you believe it 100%. 0 out of 7 means you don't believe it at all.

West: 3 out of 7

James: How true is 'I can defend myself?'

West: Again, 3 out of 7.

James: How intense is the fear out of 10?

West: 5.

James: Focus directly on the sensation in your chest. Follow my fingers with your eyes from side to side and allow your mind to go free, like letting a ball go and watch it roll down the hill.

> *James moves his fingers from side to side across West's field of vision. West follows with his eyes.*
>
> *Bilateral stimulation.*
>
> *His face twitches. He lets out an odd squeak, like a baby's whimper. He looks distressed.*

James: What did you get?

West: I felt like a baby, afraid, vulnerable.

James: Put your attention on the sensation. What thoughts about yourself come to mind?

West: I'm not safe. Fear, anxiety, tearfulness.

James: Go with that.

Bilateral stimulation.

West is clearly distressed, tearful and anxious. His left upper lip twitches and his face screws up.

James: What did you get?

West: I keep hearing a nostalgic song.

James: Go with that.

Bilateral stimulation.

Tears roll down West's cheeks.

James: What did you get?

West: I'm afraid to let go of my past. Everything is so scary, changing so quickly. Things that used to make me feel safe are slipping away. I can tell that I've let go of the attachments that make me feel safe. I'm having to open up to all of these foreigners, these other cultures. We've been separate in the past, mixing at the edges, mostly trading or fighting. Where we've come together for the last few hundred years, I've dominated them because I've been in a position of power so I felt safe. They're asserting themselves, they're coming here, they're coming to live among me and I'm having to move aside to accommodate them.

James: Go with that.

Bilateral stimulation.

West looks happy, joyful, smiling.

James: What did you get?

West: I was thinking of happy songs, my grandparents, dancing, playing when I was a child, it was joyful. That was a very long time ago. I feel lonely. I miss my family. I miss my ancestors.

James: Go with that.

Bilateral stimulation.

West looks initially very happy, even joyful, but then it turns to tears, sadness and distress.

West: I was getting happy memories of my family, of my childhood. I was remembering when we used to sing hymns in church, when we used to believe in Christianity. Everyone was the same, we have a real sense of togetherness, of safety. I miss the certainty and safety. Everything is chaotic and complex now.

James: That's what each of the value systems have felt when the next one has arisen. When RED values broke free from PURPLE tribe, that provoked fear and uncertainty. When the BLUE system arose to control the RED, the RED felt the loss of its freedom. When the ORANGE system emerged, BLUE felt a loss of certainty, right and wrong, truth and order. As the GREEN system emerges from the ORANGE, the ORANGE system finds itself frustrated that the rules keep changing, it keeps being judged and interfered with, its meritocracy and its wealth regulated and redistributed against its will. Now, as the YELLOW system of thinking begins to emerge from the GREEN, all the old systems are re-emerging and asserting themselves everywhere globally, GREEN loves the diversity and complexity but hates to have the values of all those other systems imposed upon it. GREEN does not like rules, tribe, success or boundaries.

Notice also that that's how everyone else in the world feels. You've heard the voices of religion from PURPLE to RED to BLUE to ORANGE and GREEN who are feeling dislocated and insecure. This is the challenge of your time, when you must turn fear into the courage to rise to the YELLOW system and TURQUOISE leadership that the world needs.

West: I'm feeling calm. I feel like having a drink to relax.

James: Go with that calm feeling and tell yourself, 'I'm safe, I'm safe and secure.'

Bilateral stimulation.

West looks distressed again.

James: What did you get?

West: I was remembering the First World War and the Second World War, not the horror of it but there's a feeling of safety, knowing that we had overwhelming military superiority in the end, it was like daddy had come to save the day. The masculine, the powerful military. I wondered for a moment if that was like having God as Father.

James: Go with that.

Bilateral stimulation.

West: I could feel tears welling up and a warm feeling in my heart like it wanted to open. I realised that I had put up walls to keep me safe. Now those walls are breaking down, it's very intense. I want to open my heart but it feels dangerous.

James: Go with that.

Bilateral stimulation.

James: What did you get?

West: People in other countries and new migrants who have come to join me must be feeling these fears, insecurity and pain. I must be compassionate to them, even when I feel fearful. I should be kind, because I've led the way, they will hold me responsible partly for pulling them into the discomfort, the anxiety which I myself am feeling. Someone has to show leadership.

James: Go with that.

Bilateral stimulation.

West: I felt a huge surge of pride, of self-respect. I thought back to my successes in the past, the times when I rose to the challenge of the time and I felt proud of myself for getting this far. I said to myself 'I'm good enough.'

James: Go with that.

Bilateral stimulation.

West: I thought back to times in the past. I felt nostalgic, but, at the time, from the perspective of people living back then it was anything but nice. All generations have had to be brave, courageous and rise to challenges. I felt so proud, I felt my solar plexus activate, heat in my belly, the courage which I've had often and I must have again now. The only difference is that the pace of change has accelerated hugely in every way imaginable. I need more courage than ever now, but I must be humble because so many past generations have suffered intense hardship way beyond anything we experience today.

James: Go with that.

Bilateral stimulation.

West: I need all the friends I can get. I thought of the people around the world. If we're all fearful, defensive and prickly, we're not prepared to help each other through what's a very challenging time. I wish we could all be friends.

James: Go with that.

Bilateral stimulation.

West looks bittersweet. Tears, joy and sadness altogether.

James: What did you get?

West: Sadness, a heart feeling and tears.

James: Go with that.

Bilateral stimulation.

Some tears, but looking expansive, warm, smiling, proud.

West: I'm ready now. I've got no choice but to lead, to go forward and face into the fear with courage. I have a strong impulse to go out and meet all the other countries, talk to them, listen and open like never before. Confident in myself, strong in my values, confidence in my patriotism, my science, my technology, my economy, my strong family, my ancestors behind me, God above me guiding, my heart warm and open, friendly, loving and compassionate, open to the mystery and courageous enough to leap into the cauldron of the future with the rest.

James: Well done! You look glowing. I think that's enough for today. Come back next week and we will do exactly what you say – we will meet the other countries in a new way.

I couldn't help hearing through the consulting room door that West chatted to Jean for a few minutes before leaving. They were laughing about something.

———— ◆ ————

The Bernie Rosen Unit as a whole had become depressed. Ever since Dr Sugden announced the Transformation Programme, the staff and patients alike had developed a strong sense of foreboding.

'Twelve patients have discharged themselves prematurely,' said Phil. 'They've sought help elsewhere. Kylie Morrison is in ITU. She took another overdose.'

'Sorry to hear that. Is she OK?'

'Yes, fine. Ayesha's down about it, but it wasn't her fault.'

'How are the staff?' I asked.

'The Personal Mastery and Inner Leadership Course team have all gone. Penny, Judy, Salim, Alison and Sujata. Ayesha has applied to train in the Worcester Protocols. Dancing with the devil.'

'Going with the flow. Very wise. How about you Phil?'

He paused, with a lump in his throat. 'Early retirement. I'll get a golden handshake. Well, a plastic one!'

'I feel ashamed.'

'Oh James. Come on ...'

'No really. I should have been able to protect the Unit, or at least the course. I nurtured it like a child, and now the best I can do is try to protect the patients and staff from the worst effects of this bureaucratic change.'

'What about you James? What does the future hold?'

'I haven't decided yet. If I stay I'd be redeployed to lead the implementation of the Worcester Community Treatment Protocols, which I don't believe in. I don't have much time to look for a new job because the clinic is so busy. The patients are so unsettled about the changes that they're decompensating. I'll take a holiday once the place is closed.'

RUSSIA

Suki was on holiday in Melbourne. She had decided to visit her father for the first time in years. It just occurred to me that it was slightly odd, her surname being Chen, when it was her mother who was Chinese, not her father – obvious really, I couldn't think why I'd missed it. She sent me a few emails and pictures, and seemed to be having a lovely time, although she didn't mention her family at all. She had been offered a job on the surgical rotation in New South Wales. Maybe I could join her, I suggested. Her messages dried up.

———◆———

West arrived for his appointment looking better than I'd ever seen him before. He was a little smarter, slimmer and he stood taller. His posture was more confident. His tie still didn't fit, so he had an open collar.

James: Good Morning West, how have things been?

West: You promised last time that we would do something to improve my international relationships. I've been thinking a lot about that, to be honest.

James: Excellent. Where would you like to start?

West: Russia.

James: OK. Give me an overview of the relationship.

West: We've had centuries of competition with Russia. The French fought them several times in Europe. The British Empire competed with Russia for control of Asia, the Middle East and the Eastern Mediterranean. Germany fought them twice. I pitted my whole self against them in the Cold War. Since the defeat of Communism, they haven't joined the West as I had hoped. Hey kept me out to some extent, and they've slipped back to being authoritarian, nationalistic, suspicious and prickly. They snipe at me from the sidelines rather than being my friend. President Putin has become increasingly like a Czar. Russia is reasserting its influence in the former Soviet republics. They invaded Georgia and now they've annexed Crimea and massed forces on the border with eastern Ukraine. My presence in Eastern Europe and the Baltic is under threat. I am worried that I'll be dragged into a new Cold War with them. In my nightmares, they invade the countries of Eastern Europe again, leading to Armageddon.

James: Right, let's run a process similar to voice dialogue where you imagine leaving your own Western consciousness and step into the consciousness of Russia.

West: Like having empathy for Russia?

James: More than that. Actually trying to step into Russia's consciousness and perceive the world from there.

West: How is that possible?

James: Don't think too hard about it or your intellect will block the process. It's an intuitive thing. It's like imagining you are your father or like a salesman getting into the mind of a customer. In fact, Gandhi did it to you.

West: How?

James: He practiced the skill of entering the perspective of the British Empire, the various players in the game. It gave him a huge advantage over his adversary. He realised that the British valued fair play and wanted to be seen as just, enlightened rulers. He exploited that to the maximum. He knew they had lost their belief in their right to rule and the Indian elite had learned enough to become conscious of their equality and demanded self-determination and personal opportunity.

West: I remember it well.

James: Exactly. His intelligent approach help facilitate transition to independence with the minimum of suffering. Britain and India remain good friends to this day.

West: All right, you've sold it. Let's do it.

We cleared a space on the carpet for West to move about.

James: Let's take a journey with your imagination into the consciousness of Russia. I'm going to lead you into the shoes of Russia. Imagine you could step out of Western Consciousness. Unzip it like a wet suit and let it drop. Leap forwards into the Russian wet suit. Put it on. Zip it up. Close your eyes and experience what it is like to be Russian consciousness.

You're Russia, the largest country on earth. Feel the soil from the deserts of the South to the tundra of the North, from the European plains to the wild east. Sense the vast resources in the land: the oil, the gas, mineral wealth and agriculture, the forests, lakes, rivers. Immerse in the spirit of the 200 million Russians. Look into their eyes, see who they are, become part of them. See them at home, notice the habits, join them for weddings and funerals with their families. March with them on May Day. Celebrate Orthodox Christmas. Feel the power of their industry, many cities, the vast infrastructural network, the large navy, the proud air force, the mighty Red Army. Listen to Shostakovich, folk dances and Pussy Riot. Connect with the ancestors of the Russians, taking yourself through their layers of history. The rise and fall of the Soviet Union, the chaos and corruption, the thugs and the oligarchs and the powerful President Putin. Bask in the pride of the Soviet era, the global superpower, its nuclear arsenal. Mourn the defeat in Afghanistan, the loss of pride, the shame of losing an Empire. Recall the mutual paranoia with the West, the Cold War, Mutually Assured Destruction. Submarines colliding in the deep oceans. Mourn the 20 million dead of the Second World War. Feel the brutality of the Nazi invasion, Barbarossa, the hell that was Stalingrad. Think of the delicious victory, arriving in Berlin, the capital of the Nazis as the new master. Think of the oppression, the Gulags, the KGB, knocks on the door in the middle of the night, privileges for the party members. Recall the turmoil of the revolution, the overturning of the old imperial, agricultural Czars, the hope followed by the terror and the pride. Float back deep into the folk memory beyond, close to land, the survival, the harsh winters, the hot summers. Remember the terror of the Mongol hordes. Remember the Vikings. Imagine the surge of pride as you see Russian troops retake Crimea, feel your chest swell with pride as you sing the national anthem along with the choir of the Black Sea Fleet, the white, red and blue flag hoisted once more over the sacred motherland.

Russia: I'm there. There's a bittersweet mix of sadness, melancholy, loss with pride, power and tragedy, deep wounds from past traumas. There's a struggle to thrive, a desire to break free and to live one's life without the heavy burden of history and the dark forces of human nature to hold one back.

James: Look to the west to Europe. Look north and east to Canada and America.

Russia: These people are privileged. They have a higher standard of living, more wealth. Things work better. They're better organised. I feel jealous and ashamed. I feel proud because I'm tougher than them. I've had much bigger challenges and I'm strong and resilient. I'm afraid of being left behind by globalisation. I'm not going to let them cut me out. I make myself as powerful as I can be, so that am treated with respect. I have fantastic natural resources, land and military power. I notice that West is filling his cities with foreigners. Why would he do that? That looks dangerous. I remember my own insecurity. Chechnya, Dagestan, sitting on top of the world's most unstable region. To the East, the Chinese, vastly numerous, incredibly industrious. They covet my land, if they get the chance, they'll take it. I must be very strong. My people drink too much and have too many abortions. My population is collapsing. Vladivostok is like a foreign city to me now. I must have more children.

James: Can I ask you something that puzzles me?

Russia: Be my guest.

James: I don't understand why you, Russia, perceive West to be your greatest threat. Your diplomatic and military behaviour suggests that you still have a Cold War mentality. Surely you know that West isn't planning to invade you. He couldn't, he's not powerful enough. The Chinese could. They're walking over your border as we speak. What you did in Crimea, they will do to Siberia. A third of your army is non-Russian. You have fundamentalist insurrections in the south, not far from Syria and Iraq. Like the guns in British Singapore, aren't you facing the wrong way?

Russia: I'm an orphan. I'm European but they treat me as if I'm a barbarian from the East. I'm ashamed that I've found it hard to compete with Europe and America. If it wasn't for my natural resources, they would have rolled over me by now. Look at what they tried to do to Ukraine. They filled it with spies, liberals and moneymen to tempt them to betray their Russian brothers. Now I have the resources and the money, the boot is on the other foot. I have to sort out my own psychology and demography, get on top of corruption and cronyism for sure. I'm alone. America is protected by two oceans. I have to be incredibly strong to deter all of those who would like to dominate me.

James: What do you want from West?

Russia: To be treated as an equal. Respect for my sovereignty. I've had enough of them ruling the world in their own interests. That's why I ally with others to counterbalance West. I want him to stop interfering, invading other countries.

James: What do you have to offer West?

Russia: All my heart, all my power. They missed a trick at the end of the Cold War. I was magnanimous, I was willing to give up, listen, admit that Communism had been a mistake. That was very shameful. I was willing to do it because I had no choice. They could have embraced me as a brother, showed respect to me and treated me as an equal, inviting me into NATO and the European Union. I trusted them and they treated me like a colony to be exploited. Never again.

James: You seem angry.

Russia: I won't forget it. I'm like the poor relation, the dysfunctional family. They don't invite us to weddings or Christmas because they're ashamed of us. Why should I give them anything?

James: Are there any opportunities or challenges which motivate you to work with the West for mutual interest and benefit?

Russia: Defusing North Korea. Stability in the Middle East. The whole area could go up in flames. Neither of us will benefit. I would like to work with the West to keep a lid on it, to stop it blowing up in our faces.

James: Anything else?

Russia: I would like them to balance China's power in the Pacific and in Asia. If the Chinese have a free hand, they will start picking off the Spratly and Paracel islands, the Scarborough shoal and their oil reserves, Taiwan, Mongolia, Philippines, Australia, New Zealand and Indonesia. Their people are hungry for land. They've aborted so many female foetuses that they have 40 million surplus single men who are looking for women, unless they're all going to be gay like you Westerners. I don't want to make the Chinese paranoid. I couldn't win a war with them without going nuclear. I want them contained.

James: Global warming?

Russia: I don't believe in that. Besides, I can move north.

James: So will the whole of Asia. What can you do to improve your relationship with the West?

Russia: We could talk more. We might be able to find room for manoeuvre but trust is an issue. The main thing I can do is to be strong, to revive my culture, the sort out the corruption and renew the spirit of the people so that they choose to start breeding again. It doesn't matter how strong my military is or how abundant resources are if I don't have the young men to defend it.

James: Is there anything else you would like to say to West?

Russia: No.

> West stands up, moves around and resumes his persona as the West. He straightaway becomes more relaxed, allowing his body to soften.

James: West, how do you respond to what Russia had to say?

West: Well, she gave an accurate description. It's weird because I'm not Russia. How can I know so much about them?

James: You've lived and interacted with Russia for centuries so you know each other well. When we allow our own ego to drop, we can more easily empathise with others. TURQUOISE can access all consciousness if we activate that capability.

West: Is it for real? Did I actually access Russian consciousness?

James: I'm not sure. It seemed authentic to me. What can you do to improve your relationship with Russia?

West: Treat Russia with respect. Have strong boundaries with them. They're prickly, easily slighted and always on guard, so I have to be sensitive. I certainly am not going to yield any power to them. Not until they eventually become genuinely democratic.

James: What about their suggestions for things you can work on? The Middle East, China?

West flips back to Russia.

Russia: It's very hard to cooperate on the Middle East. On the one hand the West is all about power and manipulation to maintain their oil supply. On the other, they have this ridiculously naive idea that they can transplant democracy everywhere even when people aren't ready for it. How many times do they have to fail with that before they realise that countries have to develop at their own pace, in their own way?

West: Yes, I need to be more mature in future.

James: And China?

West: When the Chinese economy falters or when the people demand more political power, the government will stoke up nationalism, international disputes and a classic distraction by war. We could never win that. We mustn't box them into a corner because it would be like Japan in the thirties, they would feel the need to break out, so we need to be strong and cooperative and friendly at the same time. I don't think directly working with Russia would be clever as it'd make the Chinese fearful.

James: Is there anything else either of you would like to say?

Russia: I'd like to see an end to the double standards. West speaks about me as if I'm a power hungry thug and they talk about themselves as if they're the enlightened beacon of democracy and freedom, acting in the best interests of humanity. It's nonsense. I'm interested in power, security, respect and influence, who isn't? I would appreciate it if they would admit that they do the same and not dress it up in fake liberal clothes.

West: I half agree with that. You were talking about RED thinking. Yes, we both do that and we both must do that in a healthy way. But we do sincerely want to promote freedom, democracy, human rights and security.

Russia: Then act sincerely and with integrity. Then I might trust you better. Improve your own democracy. You point fingers at others but you're far from perfect. You've clamped down on the freedom of speech of your people, you use the police and the security services to suppress protest in your countries. You spy on your own people on a scale which the Stasi would be proud of. Those in glass houses shouldn't throw stones.

West looks irritated, blushing, somewhat shamed. After a pause, he nods.

West: You're right. I accept that. Thank you. I will try to do my bit.

James: Brilliant, well done. Let's take a break.

THE PSYCHOLOGY OF INTERNATIONAL RELATIONS

West: It's odd. I've used the term 'International Relations' for years but I'd not been aware of the relationships between my own consciousness and others. I'd focused more on the relations between leaders and institutions. Now I see that international relations is about relationships between people, groups of people each of which has its own psychology and consciousness. Traditionally, diplomacy and foreign policy was all about geopolitics, economics, sociology, law and the military. I used to send gun boats to China. Now I have to relate to them as people, not objects at a distance. It's more like genuinely being in a global village now, genuinely having relationships in real life rather than some distant, intellectual, rarefied high politics. Increasingly, we're interdependent and interconnected.

James: What does this mean for your foreign policy?

West: Nowadays we interact continuously on so many levels – individual, group meetings, inter-organisational, mass consciousness through the media. My diplomats have had excellent skills as regards intellectual intelligence, analysis of interests, positions, geopolitics. But my institutions have had blind spots, Achilles heels in emotional & social intelligence.

James: All relationships, whether between husband and wife or between China and Japan have three dimensions. First, physical power, aggression, violence, force. Militaries will remain vital for the foreseeable future. Second, rational cooperation. The very familiar world of trade, law, negotiation and treaties. That too will remain very important. Third, emotional connection. Empathy, trust, affiliation, loyalty, respect, compassion, love, commitment, inspiration. Hate, contempt, mistrust, paranoia and suspicion. This is the area that previously was dealt with in an implicit way but now is needed as a third pillar of diplomacy. You could call it Psyplomacy.

West: I'm already well versed in public diplomacy.

James: What's that?

West: Take my relationship with China. I survey what the Chinese think of me, decide what I'd like them to think about me, subtract one from the other which gives me my 'key messages.' Then I identify 'target audiences' to whom I wish to project these 'key messages' and then do that through the media and PR.

James: Do you know anything about the Chinese?

West: Yes, we've been dealing with them for centuries, we meet them all the time, trade with them, visit them, exchange students, monitor their media, read their newspapers. We've been increasingly connected them over the last couple of hundred years. I don't pretend that we know them back to front but we've got a very good idea about them.

James: Do you think that the Chinese know anything about you?

West blushes, but can't bring himself to speak.

James: Yes, I suppose they know exactly who Westerners are, what they're like, how they think, how they act, what they've done in history, how they do business. They've been watching carefully. I'm not saying that they're without prejudice or that communication couldn't be improved. Of course it could. It's completely unrealistic to imagine that you can sell your country like soap powder. In the modern world, you can forget political spin and manipulation. People see straight through it. They're not stupid and don't appreciate being treated as such.

West: What do you know about diplomacy, you're a doctor? Besides, propaganda is an ancient art which is alive and well. Take Ukraine. Both sides are masters at it.

James: I'm not talking about negotiating treaties, spying or influencing governments. That's an area of special expertise. I'm talking about relating as one group to another as human beings. If you want to have good relationships with other countries, you must have a very clear sense of yourself, who you are, your values, your beliefs. What's true and false, what's right and wrong, what you care about, your strengths and weaknesses? From that position of self-confidence and self-awareness, you can be strong but open simultaneously, and sincerely connect with the other, genuinely listen. People are used to being talked at and manipulated. How do you feel when you get a cold call from a company trying to sell you something you don't want? Do you believe the gloss in a corporate brochure?

West: No, I get the point. I do this stuff implicitly, through experience. Take the French and British. They're very different and very similar at the same time. The British are pragmatic empiricists; the French are rationalist idealists. The French like to sit down and discuss the big picture, philosophy and grand schemes while the British like to focus upon specific practical issues and get things done briskly. The British want to get to the point, say what they think and get a result. The French are always left feeling that they've not been listened to, not taken seriously, are unloved and that the British are not committed to them or the EU.

James: How do British diplomats learn to handle that difference?

West: They let the French talk, give them space, join the discussion, acknowledge what they say, genuinely and the French, if it's sincere, open their hearts and the relationship goes to a deeper level. That's on a one-to-one level with diplomats, that's always been part of their skill set. How can it work with whole nations or civilizations?

James: That reminds me of the inner union tantric exercise! When you lecture people in other countries about human rights and democracy, what's the most common come-back?

West: Some welcome the support but often we do get an angry response, complaining of double standards. It's very difficult to influence others if you don't walk the walk yourself.

James: Exactly. In the modern world, interconnected by travel, the Internet and the media, you've no choice but to be sincere. Everyone, everywhere can see what you're up to and you will have no credibility unless you live your values and if your values are sincere. You're no longer manipulating small groups of people at a long distance, you're effectively living in the same home, the same village and they know you, they see you, you have a track record and reputation.

West: I should lead by example and focus on making my own countries the best they can be. Because of mass immigration, international students and the internet, people from countries all over the world have directly experienced the West, learned what we're like and taken on our values and then they take them home with them. Leading by attraction is more powerful than manipulation. It's like the feminine leadership with the horse.

CHINA

After a break, West chose to repeat the exercise with China.

James: Stand up. Move around. Loosen up. Imagine now that you can separate your awareness from the substance of Western consciousness. Imagine, playfully that West is a wetsuit you can unzip and step out of, leaving it on the chair.

West is already ahead of the instructions, with his eyes closed and head bowed.

James: You are standing at the centre of the world, the vast land mass of China in East Asia. Take a moment to connect with the collective consciousness of 1.5 billion people. From the Han majority to the Uighur, Mongol and Tibetan minorities. Feel the unrelenting dry heat of the Gobi desert sun on your back. Shiver in the deep winter of the north. Wipe the drips of sweat off yourself in the misty jungles of Yunnan. Wash down a fine Chinese feast, with a sweet, delicate Jasmine tea. Pinch yourself as you walk through the streets of Shanghai, reminding yourself that you are not in New York. Meditate with a Buddhist monk on a Tibetan mountain. Listen carefully for the police at the door in the middle of the night. Listen to someone secretly whisper to you about the slave labour camps and the torture. Feel enraged as your property is demolished to make way for a new development, courtesy of a bribe paid to local officials. Feel your heart burst with pride as you celebrate the Beijing Olympics as the world once again pays homage to its greatest civilization. Send a short message on Weibo to mock the communist officials, spouting propaganda while lining their pockets. Bow your head with respect as you say thank you to the traditional Chinese doctor who keeps you well with acupuncture and herbs.

To your north is the vast, empty cold expanse of Siberia and Mongolia. To your west are the Central Asians, the Turks, the Indians and Pakistanis. To your south-east are the humid jungles of Thailand, Vietnam and Burma. To your north east is paranoid, awkward North Korea and to their south, the hugely dynamic South Korea. Across the sea is your once prodigy, then colonial abuser, now competitor-collaborator, Japan. Spit with incandescence as they manoeuvre their navy around your islands out at sea. Know that you will punish them one day. As you look out East into the Pacific you see huge tracts of water sprinkled with many islands. You feel sore, knowing that foreigners have long dominated these seas and hemmed you in. Across a short channel is part of the motherland, recalcitrant Taiwan. It breaks your heart, hurts your pride and angers you to be separated from your brothers and sisters.

While West was living in mud, poverty and superstition, you were a vastly powerful, technologically advanced economic and cultural powerhouse. The rest of the known world kowtowed to your Emperors. You had no need to travel overseas or colonise anyone because you were the centre of the world. Your cities, rivers, canal systems, civil service, science and manufactures were the envy of the world. You set out to explore India, Africa and the Middle East but changed your mind and closed yourself to the outside.

You were rudely awoken from stagnation by the Portuguese, Dutch and British boats impertinently arriving in your docks. You dismissed them arrogantly at first little more than gnats on a giant dragon but before long they used their superior firepower to force open your markets. They exposed your weakness.

You smile, pleased at least to have reclaimed Hong Kong from the British who bullied and exploited you in the 19th Century with their overwhelming firepower, money and industrial power. They took Hong Kong and ran Shanghai until the Japanese decided it was their turn in the 30s. Your once proud Emperors were shown to be a sham as the Japanese Imperial Army raped and dominated your once proud land. No Great Wall could protect you from their aeroplanes and tanks. Feel the gut wrenching trauma of the violation of World War Two followed by the immediate leap into civil war. Sense the exhaustion and exhilaration of the people as peace finally came at the end of Chairman Mao's Long March. Feel the overwhelming dislocation of an ancient 5000 year old civilization being meticulously and ruthlessly reconstructed as a Marxist, Maoist experiment. A dream for some, a desperate nightmare for others.

Let your chest swell with pride as you recall forcing arrogant West to a ceasefire in Korea and Vietnam. Imagine the surge in self-confidence knowing that never again would you submit to foreign occupation. Armed with your nuclear might and your People's Liberation Army, backed by the solidarity of the Chinese people, in their uniforms, committees and the Communist Party. Let the tears roll down your cheeks and feel the lump in your throat as you see Deng Xiaoping watch the parades in Tiannenmen Square.

Travel to the dark side, the deep fear of revolution, famine, the fanatical intolerance and violence of the Cultural Revolution. Feel the sickness in your gut, knowing that the party members ate well while the peasants starved.

Others know that when the Chinese Dragon awakens from its deep sleep, the whole world trembles. What the British Industrial Revolution did 200 years ago, you have done on a scale 30 times larger in as many years to become the world's centre of manufacturing. You have brought more people out of poverty than any Marxist of the old days. Countless millions of workers travel to work in tens of thousands of factories. The West is a hollowed out shell. Your banks are full of their gold. You reach across the world from Asia to South America to Africa as the emerging superpower. Your time has come.

China: I'm very powerful, very dense, very exciting and potentially explosive. I'm hot, crowded and hemmed in. It feels like a black hole with so much gravitational pull that I can barely see out to the outside world.

James: What's on your mind?

China: I'm tired. I've been working so hard, everything is changing so quickly but I can't rest for one moment for fear of what would happen. If the people stop raising their living standards, the whole thing could unravel. I have so many wounds in my history, with the most catastrophic experiences that I cannot face the possibility, I will do anything to avoid it.

James: How do you feel about West?

China: Japan is a necessary evil. They've done us great harm but we need them, we will need them for another 30 years to get to full strength. I've never forgiven them for what they did to me.

James: And the West in general?

China: As in Aesop's Fable *The Tortoise and the Hare* I was the Tortoise leading civilization for thousands of years. I sent ships and traders all over Asia, the Middle East and East Africa before the Europeans ever ventured to the Americas. I turned inward, closed myself off and went to sleep, complacent and old-fashioned. The Europeans overtook me in the 18th Century. I got a very rude awakening when the Portuguese, the Dutch and the British started knocking on my doors, demanding to sell me things I didn't want. They forced my door open and I lost my self-confidence. They didn't manage to rule me but they did humiliate me and I had to dance to their tune until Chairman Mao united and modernised us. I feel shame for those centuries of weakness.

James: Quite a lot of resentment too?

China: No one likes to lose, do they? Especially when they've been a winner before. West is going to feel that too, within 30 years. I will be the centre of the earth again and West will dance to my tune. I will keep your doors open and dictate to you the terms of trade.

James: You publicly talk of harmonious rise and equality, a multipolar world.

 He smiles.

China: The Western elite are very naive. I'm hardly going to give you the ammunition to keep me down any longer, am I? The future won't be like the past. Your ridiculous adventures in Iraq and Afghanistan have demonstrated beyond doubt that the age of imperial rule by military force is over. My people are the most industrious, disciplined and sacrificing. You used to call it the Protestant Work Ethic but now you laze about, borrow money and live off the achievements of your ancestors while your rotten structure creaks beneath you.

James: The consciousness of your young people is changing and will change very rapidly in parallel with the economic development, media and travel. Maybe there's a new China emerging?

China: There will be a new China but the young Chinese are not like Westerners. They will not become selfish and decadent. They know that we need to stick together to survive.

James: Do think that that could apply to the whole of humanity?

China: Yes, but you can forget trying to dictate to us with your patronising NGOs, human rights activists, interfering busybodies. Sort out your own troubles, your economy. Discipline yourself.

James: What would like to ask West to do to improve your relationship?

China: Keep your nose out of my business, stop imposing your values on me and the rest of the world. Work hard and treat others as equals with respect. You will be in deep trouble in a few years. I've already learned most of your knowledge and expertise. There are more Chinese than British graduate students in Britain! Within 30 years, you will be the periphery and I will be the centre. Accept it with grace. It's the natural order resuming after your brief, albeit spectacular, firework display.

James: Is there anything that China could do to improve the relationship?

China: It's already improving. We're becoming more powerful economically, technologically, militarily and politically. We've already spread all over the world, buying up parts of Africa and South America, getting influence in every country in the world. We play the long game. We're not a bunch of impulsive pirates like you. We're focused on stability and building ourselves up.

James: Thank you.

West physically leaps out of China and back into his own skin.

West: That's scary. I thought they would be much more conciliatory. I'm not sure we got the whole picture there. It's a big place and changing quickly. I think you were speaking to an old nationalist voice, with a chip on the shoulder. The emerging generations will determine our future relationship.

James: What would you like to say to the younger Chinese, and the future Chinese?

West: I'm going to have to share the world with them in a way that I haven't had to for the last few hundred years. I'd like to do that as equals. I hope that they will choose the path of democracy, pluralism and an open, friendly society. I'm scared because I can feel that resentment and aggression and I don't want to provoke it.

China: Make sure that we have free access to oil and natural resources and don't do anything to interfere with our economic development. It's in your interest to have a healthy, happy China. If things go off the rails here, you will know about it.

West: Point taken. We need full access to your markets. It's not sustainable to have such a massive trade imbalance. We need you to become consumers as well as producers. We need the exchange rate to be fair to give our exporters a chance. We want you to re-spect intellectual property, to stop cyber attacks and spying.

China: You don't like losing control, do you? We will balance things out when we've reached your level. You've no right to tell us about what's fair after the way you treated me historically.

West: We're concerned that you're building a blue water navy with the capacity for power projection and bases around the Indian Ocean. We notice your very active space program.

China: Get used to it. We're only interested in protecting ourselves and ensuring the free flow of trade and access to raw materials. We've no history of imperialism. We live and let live. Don't expect us to be weak or to submit to you any more. We intend to be as powerful as you and to have our fair say about how the world runs.

James: West, there must be some overarching goals, some shared interests which can foster cooperation and bring out the best in you both.

China: We want continued economic development, access to raw materials, peace and stability, honouring of your loans and we would like you to avoid interfering in our pri-vate business.

West: It's in our interests that you continue to develop economically although it needs to be in a sustainable way. It can't all be one way anymore. Unless we balance our trade, we aren't going to be able to pay back your loans. We cannot stand by if you seriously violate human rights.

China: When we've achieved equality, we will consider your requests. In the mean-time, we need to do what's right for us. When you talk about human rights, you've forgotten the ladder that you've had to climb. Remember the turbulence, strife and sacrifice required to bring about your current prosperity and freedom. We're squeezing 300 years into 50.

West: Will you help me stop the spread of religious extremism?

China: I don't want to get involved. You stirred up the hornet's nest. I don't intend to get stung. We have problems in Xinjiang but I aim to keep a lid on that.

West came out of role and sat down, tired. We agreed to finish there for the day and resume the following week. If had been a thought-provoking session. After he left I sat for quite some time with the light fading around me. The days were beginning to lengthen at last and the end of winter was in sight, bit it was still dark 6PM.

Suki was back from holiday. We planned to meet at the National Portrait Gallery the next weekend. She seemed cool, more distant. I wondered what had happened in Australia.

The ward was feeling empty now. We had just four inpatients left, awaiting transfer to specialist private units. That didn't make financial sense, but we had to put their safety before the budget. My clinic was correspondingly much busier with many of our old patients turning up as emergencies.

Dr Prasad was leading a Significant Event inquiry into West's near-suicide on Westminster Bridge. He wasn't qualified to do that as a non-psychiatrist but I wasn't worried. West was alive and well and would happily vouch for my good care. Perhaps that was why Prasad cast his interview net much wider than would have been standard practice.

NORTH KOREA

Jean had taken to blocking out the final hour and a half of my clinic for West's appointment so I didn't need to watch the clock. West arrived looking worse for wear, dressed in a red jumper, collared grey shirt and blue jeans.

West: Afternoon Doctor. Before you ask, I've had a dreadful week. I woke up several times with nightmares.

James: What were they about?

West: It started with me fighting off two dragons. They were attacking from both sides. Then lots of small people, like in *Gulliver's Travels*, overwhelmed me and tied me down. The two dragons merged into a double headed monster and laid a giant egg beside me. The monster flew up into outer space and watched as the egg hatched to reveal a ticking time bomb, a massive nuclear bomb strapped to my chest. I woke up screaming.

James: What do you make of that?

West: I'm not sure who the dragons are.

James: Close your eyes, immerse into the scene.

West: North Korea and Iran.

James: Tell me about North Korea.

West: It's half of Korea, the Northern part left over from the Korean War. It's frozen in time. There's nothing wrong with the Korean people, as a trip to South Korea will demonstrate. Unfortunately, it's a brutal Communist dictatorship with a fanatical personality cult. They live in a fearful state of mass hypnosis, choreographed by the demagogue.

James: Very sinister. I've heard the testimonies of escapees on TV.

West: They have an enormous military. I'm worried that in some impulsive moment they will use nuclear weapons. There's nothing to gain from war with them and everything to lose.

James: Can you help them adapt to the modern world?

West: I don't know. There is little official contact with the outside world. It's one of the most tightly controlled states ever. The Chinese are the only ones they'll listen to and even they don't carry much weight.

James: OK, let's do the exercise.

West stands, makes sure he is relaxed and allows his attention to focus.

James: Stand beside the river that marks the border with China. Notice the border guards, the security checks. Be aware of the change of atmosphere as darkness comes. Join a smuggler bringing in thousands of USB sticks full of Western films, showing the isolated people a very distorted view of the outside. Feel the unbearable hunger in your belly as you discreetly scavenge for food, prepared to trade your last possessions for something to eat. Whip yourself up into a patriotic frenzy, proudly recounting the victory over West who tried to defeat you and colonise you from the treacherous south. Watch the news with pride as you see the leaders of the world get together to try to negotiate with your small but proud and powerful nation, the true inheritors of the medieval warrior spirit. Put yourself in the shoes of the President and the Generals. Not so long ago the President was at a Swiss boarding school and university, enjoying the best that the West has to offer. Now he is playing with nuclear missiles as if they are a toy. He can execute anyone on a whim. Those who raise the slightest doubt risk instant death or decades in the barbaric slave labour camps. It's a billion miles to the other side of the border in the South where the people of the same race, language, culture and history live in freedom and prosperity thanks to their embrace of industrialisation, education, science, Christianity, democracy and very hard work. Your old uncle China has long since given up Communism but you haven't moved with the times. You know that the brutal slave system is a charade but you daren't admit it. China, Japan and the West talk tough in public but give you suitcases stuffed with money under the table in the desperate hope that you'll find a way out of your self-induced nightmare. You are immensely proud of your vast military forces. Admire the immense discipline of the thousands of dancers and marching soldiers. You're not ready to give up the dream or end the nightmare.

West nods slowly as he stands with his eyes closed.

James: What do you feel?

North Korea: Highly paranoid. It's volatile and dangerous, frozen with fear. If you put a foot wrong here, you're in trouble.

James: What do you need?

North Korea: I need to feel safe and strong. I need to be respected to maintain my status and power, otherwise I'm in danger.

James: How are your people?

North Korea: Mind your own business. If you threaten me I will destroy you.

James: What do you need from West?

North Korea: Money. I can't back down. I'd be humiliated. South Korea would dance on my grave. I'd lash out. I need money to get out of this mess while keeping control, saving face.

James: West, is there anything you would like from North Korea to improve the relationship?

West: I'd like a private channel of communication with the leadership so that we can keep each other safe, so that I can tell the difference between bravado and genuine threat.

North Korea: That's not realistic. The President and the Generals don't trust each other. No one can afford to show weakness or be accused of treachery or disloyalty.

James: Thank you both. I wonder if there would be a way to engage the North Koreans in a visioning exercise, envisioning a future Korea, united, strong and successful together? Or maybe, if that's too threatening, may be simply offering them whatever assistance they ask for. Somehow, you need to be magnanimous enough, as well as strong, to allow them to back down from this position and they can only do that if they feel safe.

IRAN

West released himself from North Korea and stretched. We took a break for coffee, but while I was away at the vending machine he carried on pacing around the office, impatient to continue.

James: Immerse in Iran, the ancient civilization of Persia, stretching back thousands of years. Feel its magnificence and pride. Take yourself from the lush valleys of the Caucuses through to the wild expansive plains and deserts down to the bottleneck at the Straits of Hormuz, sitting opposite the US 5th Fleet in Bahrain. Hear the cacophony of sounds in Tehran, bustling with traffic, an ancient capital with a potent mix of intellectuals, deep cultural sophistication enmeshed with a deep religious conservatism. Imagine the polarisation in the West between liberals and conservatives and multiply by ten. Vast oil and gas installations once owned by the British and Americans, nationalised after the decadent Shah was deposed by the religious revolution. Take yourself back to that heady time, when the people rose up to remove the corrupt regime with great dreams of democracy and justice followed by fundamentalist terror and religious dictatorship. Enjoy the self-respect which came with this independence, throwing off centuries of foreign domination, the once mighty Persian Empire humbled by the British and Russians, no longer a sphere of influence but an independent and patriotic state under the law of God. Feel the sweet, sensual, openhearted culture combined with the harsh rule of the puritans. Suffer the wounds of the Iran-Iraq war, every bit as horrific and futile as the First World War. Imagine being hemmed in on every side, by the Saudis bristling with weapons, by Iraq under Saddam, by America then by the chaos of war on every frontier. Afghanistan ruled by the Communists, the Russians, invaded again by the Western imperialists then left to chaos again. Pakistan, once British India, the Mogul Empire before that, now a land of extreme paradoxes, nuclear armed, infinitely complex. Take yourself back to the time of your ancestors, the Greeks and the Romans who knew the Persians as a grand and proud civilization. Remember Alexander who rolled back your once mighty empire and humbled you. Immerse yourself in the youth culture, the modern Iranians, educated, entrepreneurial and very well aware of democracy, very well aware of Iraq, Egypt and Syria, not wanting that hell for themselves.

Iran: I'm there – hemmed in, boiling. Conflicted. I'm very proud of my heritage. I feel the loss, a disconnection but along in for the regal, imperial spirit of Persia, a desire to fully embrace science and the entrepreneurial world, to resume our place as one of the great countries of the world, unique and proud but deeply torn between conservative and liberal, religious and secular. Surrounded by chaos and enemies.

James: How do you feel about the West?

Iran: I respect the West for its success, wealth and power. I resent it for pushing me around, exploiting me in the past, for not treating me as an equal with due respect. I want prosperity, military power, respect and honour but part of me is deeply religious and conservative and will never allow the likes of the Shah or his parasitic cronies to use this proud land as their playground. I admire democracy, human rights and capitalism but I utterly reject the double standards, the two-faced manipulation from the West which I've dealt with for 200 years. I intend to be powerful and independent, never pushed around. They implanted their Zionist colony to divide us.

James: Do you want to erase Israel from the map?

Iran: No, of course not. Some of my nationalist hotheads would do but zealots in every country would love to destroy the their enemies. Jews used to live here happy and free. They were successful. I had to be hard line to get you out of my country, to take charge and be secure.

James: What could West do to improve his relationship with you?

Iran: Treat me with respect, as an equal. Respect my sovereignty and territory. Stop trying to undermine me. Stop interfering in my neighbourhood. I want safety, security and respect, how complicated can that be? Isn't that what you want? Lift the sanctions, trade with me fairly. Stop lecturing me about democracy. Do you think I want to go down the path of Libya, Egypt and Syria? Sort yourself out. You're not that democratic.

James: What can you do to improve the relationship?

Iran: We can be strong, proud and united. We need to grow our economy beyond gas and oil. You respect my boundaries and I will respect yours. Help me to thrive. Pakistan and Saudi Arabia are your enemies, constantly plotting against you. I can be your friend. My people are educated and sophisticated.

James: West, what can Iran do to improve the relationship?

West: Stop exporting terrorism to Syria, Lebanon, Israel and to the West. Stop your nuclear weapons program. Stop plotting with China and Russia to undermine me.

James: They do those things because they feel threatened. Can you help them feel secure?

West: I would like to guarantee their borders and make the regime feel secure but I dislike the regime. They're fundamentalists and nationalists. I don't think they serve the

Iranian people, the Iranians people are proud, pluralistic, sophisticated and cultured people who are being ruled by hardline religious conservatives. It's hard to show respect for that.

Iran: That's why we will never show weakness, never stop defending ourselves until you back off, and back off you will, because you're getting poorer, weaker and we're getting stronger and more confident.

James: Thank you. Is there anything else to say before we finish?

There is no response. West looks tranquil.

James: West, well done again for some good work. You've opened up new ways of looking at things – areas for exploration.

West: I'm not sure I'm going to sleep tonight. This is exciting. Can't we just carry on?

James: Well I …

West: Only joking. I'll see you next week. Thanks again James.

———◆———

Something wasn't right with Suki. That Saturday, she met me at Charing Cross Station and we walked through Trafalgar Square up to the National Portrait Gallery. She was quieter than usual. There were uncomfortable silences. I sensed her distress. I suggested a detour. We went into St Martin in the Fields Church, a very grand neoclassical building with a huge spire and massive Corinthian columns at the top of a flight of grand steps. Inside, it felt more modest, like the 18th Century Protestant churches in America. We slipped in during a service and sat discretely at the back. Bizarrely, the service was in Cantonese. The church had a special service for Chinatown on the other side of Leicester Square. Suki's eyes welled up with tears. I held her hand, albeit though her woollen glove. Suki shook her head when the usher indicated it was our turn to walk forward for the Eucharist. She closed her eyes and sobbed quietly. I guided her to light a candle. She lit three.

'Let's skip the gallery and go for lunch,' I suggested.

'My trip to Australia was awful. I've been distant from my father since he cheated on my mum. I had been forced to grown up fast when I had to care for my dying mum and my younger sister. My father left for Melbourne to be with his new woman by then. He hadn't attended her funeral. That's why I took her surname. I didn't speak to my father for five years.'

I just listened, holding her had as we walked.

'In Melbourne, I stayed with my father and his new wife and my half-sister. I'd intended to stay for two weeks but felt uncomfortable so I left after five days and went to the Hunter Valley vineyards and the beach at Foster. I swam with a dolphin in the surf!'

I told her about West's experience with the seal. We held hands as we walked around Leicester Square with an ice cream. She licked the chocolate off my top lip before she kissed me. She wasn't in the mood to talk much so we went to the cinema. Afterwards, at her bus stop, she clung to me tightly. I would have loved to invite her home with me but she was still tearful. I could taste the salt in her tears when we kissed goodbye.

INDIA

While Suki was away in Australia I wondered when was the right time to invite her to meet my sister Faun, brother-in-law Brad, nephew Baz and niece Mobu. After the gallery date, I felt confident that an invitation wouldn't scare Suki off. As it turned out, she was delighted when I asked her to join us for Sunday lunch. In fact she was so excited, she immediately asked if we could make it the whole weekend.

Introducing Suki and the family was an exciting prospect. A natural motherliness came out in her, which I hadn't seen before. Within half an hour, she was covered in paint and sparkly glitter, laughing heartily with Mobu. Baz had already developed a crush on her, unable to look at her directly without blushing.

—◆—

West was on a roll now. I knew there was much more to do but he seemed to be on a more even keel. He arrived early and I could hear him laughing with Jean. I opened the door to find them both smiling. Jean was showing him her Christmas family photos. West was holding himself with confidence.

'Greetings West,' I said jovially, wondering what they had been talking about together.

'Afternoon James, how are you?'

'Good, thank you.'

'And how is Doctor Chen?' he asked, exchanging a look with Jean.

So that was it.

'Fine,' I said with a frown. 'Fine as far as I know. Shall we get started? I think it was India today. That's what we agreed I think.'

James: OK, unzip your Western consciousness and jump into the consciousness of India. Close your eyes. Listen to the cacophony of sounds. The car horns honking, the bicycle bells ringing, chatter in dozens of languages, tropical birds. Take in a deep breath of hot, midday air. The smell of the tuk-tuk exhausts, the spices from the stall beside you and the Masala Dosa of the man eating in the window of a restaurant. Sit and drink a hot glass of sweet chai as you watch the cows wander down the street, oblivious to the cars and mopeds streaming around them. Sit on the banks of the Ganges and take in the spectacle of thousands of people going about their timeless rituals, some washing and praying, others seeing off their relatives with a cremation besides the sacred river. Notice the vultures overhead, ever present, reminding us of our earthly fate. Walk around the grand imperial buildings in Delhi still hot in the evening sun. Visit the statues of the old Raj, their heads and noses knocked off, covered with dust and bird excrement. Look out of a luxurious five star apartment complex onto the people far below in the shanty town, making their way out to the fly ridden swamp edge for their morning ablutions. Take a tour of the shiny skyscrapers of Mumbai, old Bombay and then turn into the ancient back streets leading to a fishing village, the children barefoot and the old women 500 years from the street you just left. Sit for nine hours in Varanasi railway station, waiting for the train from Patna. Try to catch some sleep as the Bollywood film screeches in your ears on the night bus to Calcutta. Be pulled along with the flow of humanity at the giant Mela. Enjoy a concert of music with different rules and tones to your own. Join in the celebration of the most colourful and long wedding you can imagine. Feel the intense frustration of the entrepreneur, bound in red tape, his hands cuffed by the local police while scores of hands grope around is his pockets for baksheesh. Celebrate with your friends when you graduate from the Institute of Technology in Hyderabad, just before you take up your new job as a software engineer in Bangalore.

Immerse yourself deep into the hot red earth. Feel the hooves of the Mughals' horses riding down from the distant mountains to the north. Run for your life as the mob turns on your community during partition, desperate to get to safety. Enjoy the splendour and sophistication of the ancient courts. Pray to a thousand Gods as the life of the living universe flows throughout you. Hear the call to prayer from the early morning to dusk. Immerse yourself in the tales of the Mahabharata. Remember the insignificance of the tiny European enclaves. Awaken to find that little England has conquered all Bengal and is poised to take the rest. Experience the growing pains of 300 years of modernity alongside the deepest and most spiritual life you can barely imagine. Breath the fresh mountain air over the waterfall in the Himalayas, your boundary with the wild north beyond. March with pride with the Punjab Regiment, your heart full of love and your belly full of courage. Feel the timeless connection to the warriors of old. Cry with despair as you mourn the dead from the famines. Roar with exultation as the midnight sounds, 15 August 1947, tears streaming down your face. Close down your computer after a day's management consulting and head off to Chowpatty beach with your family.

West looks serene and peaceful.

James: How are you?

India: Vast in all dimensions. Time, space, people, classes, history, culture, spiritual and scientific. Vast potential.

James: How do you feel about your relationship with the West?

India: Mixed. Oddly, I feel part of the West in some ways. Having lived with the British for 300 years, I have absorbed most Western ideas, technology, science, law, democracy, media, education, the English language, bureaucracy, a global perspective and a global diaspora. Yet I am so much more. I have taken much of what was worth taking and integrated it with everything I am. I have a vast population, a huge educated middle class and resilient political infrastructure. China has raced ahead but I will thrive long after it has past its peak. I will take longer to get there because of my complexity but it is that very complexity which positions me perfectly to thrive in this globalised world. I am at home in London, New York, Toronto, Sydney, Hong Kong and Singapore. The British Empire didn't finish, it transformed into the global community in which I am one of the main pillars.

James: So you see yourself as part of the West?

India: You need to clarify what you mean. If you mean the global, democratic, capitalist, scientific, entrepreneurial, geopolitical, pluralistic, aspirational, free, just and fast evolving consciousness of the world, then yes, most certainly. I will naturally, organically become its central hub whilst China will remain detached, arrogant and controlling.

James: Do any historical wounds need to be healed?

India: Not really. There is the legacy of Westerners treating us as their exotic inferiors and of the rich exploiting the poor. However, I am not the sort to hold grudges. I am extremely magnanimous and ...

James: And what?

India: I was about to say 'and wise' but that sounds arrogant. I don't mean it that way. I mean that I do not behave like a little child. Well, OK, I do sometimes, especially with Pakistan, but generally I am mature and deep. I am spiritually wise, so I don't waste my energy on resentments from the past. I am too busy with survival, modernisation, education, building infrastructure, personal and global competition. Besides, I forgive those who have harmed me in the past. The list is too long to mention. What human has never done any harm? I am focused on striving to be the best I can.

James: West, would you like to ask anything of India?

India: Actually I want to ask something of West. How can you help me to thrive and to support the development of all my people?

> *West shifts back into Western consciousness, moving to a different position on the carpet.*

West: That's a very good question. I'm not sure. I could reel off the usual things like security, education, intellectual property and support for your institutions, but that's the old me that thinks I know what's best for others and treats them like children. You're doing an amazing job yourself. I'd rather ask you what are your challenges, then we can work together on them. Actually, I expect that you're going to be leading innovation in science and medicine, not to mention your cultural and spiritual strengths.

India: Careful not to patronise me in the other direction, treating me as an exotic, wise sage. Just relate to me as equal but different and we won't go far wrong.

West: Can you help or advise us how to deal with religious fundamentalism?

India: Keep out of its way if you can. Fundamentalism is a maladaptive reaction to the modern world and is based in anger and fear. The problem is an emotional one. You should ask Dr Hill. Each person is responsible for himself. Those who are angry, fearful and wounded must find peace in their own hearts. You cannot do it for them. So my advice is to not react, to show as much equanimity as you can and allow them to find their own way. If you do your Western thing of attacking it head on, you will give it energy and force and you will make things much worse. Be compassionate.

West: That sounds very good but what do we do about terrorist attacks, kidnappings and attempts to impose an alien way of life of me in the West.

India: It is a competition of ideas, of ways of living. You must make your democracies as good a crucible for experimentation and debate as possible and together you will find the best outcomes. More democracy, more talking, more science, more debate. Believe in yourself.

James: That requires security, rules and boundaries.

India: Sure. I said a strong crucible.

James: Is there anything else either of you would like to say?

India: Yes, West. You are going to need to nurture you communities, families and culture, your PURPLE because it is not strong enough to hold you together through the turbulent times ahead.

West: Any idea how?

India: No, I fear the same is happening to me. You're much further along the curve. It's up to you to experiment. You can ask me for help any time.

West: Thank you.

'That was fantastic,' said West after I had guided him through the reintegration process. 'I am just amazed at what comes up. I would never get to those answers through the usual rational, analytical approach.'

'You're not wrong. So, what's next?'

ARAB WORLD

West: The Arab world.

James: You'd better define that first.

West: The Middle East and North Africa, excluding Israel and Iran. There's some overlap with Central Asia and parts of Africa.

James: OK, I want you to stand under the high sun, under a clear blue sky and scoop up a handful of dry dusty earth. Allow it to run through your fingers, blowing in the gentle breeze. You are a caravan trader far from home – spend the night by a fire under the billions of stars. Beware of the scorpions and insects. Hear the deck of your ship creak and the canvas flap in the wind as you sail from ancient Alexandria to Tangiers. Wander through the narrow white streets bustling with traders and travellers, following the smell of spices to the market. Arrive at the Sultan's Palace, rich and opulent – beyond your wildest dreams. Listen to the birds sing in the immaculate peaceful gardens of Cordoba. Take pride in the invention of algebra, the magnificence of religious architecture and the intricacy of religious art. Visit the ancient past, going back to the time of polytheism, superstition and even further to the first migrants from our common African home. Marvel at the knowledge held in the great library of Alexandria, lost and forgotten by your Greek ancestors – admire the ancient scrolls on their shelves. Enjoy the status of being the most sophisticated culture in the Middle Ages while looking across the Mediterranean at the barbarian Europeans, endlessly fighting one another. Ride a Barbary pirate flotilla as it raids the European coast, your heart beating faster and your blood rising as you strike terror into the hearts of the natives, collecting the next shipment of slaves and hostages for ransom. Feel the pride of being the cradle of civilization from the very first human cities in Mesopotamia 10,000 years ago. Feel the weight of the stone blocks, levered laboriously into position as you help to build the great Pyramid of Giza. Pray in a hundred different ways, before the advent of monotheism. Shout in a crowd that is celebrating the expulsion of the ancient Jews. Feel the ambivalence of watching them return and thrive in your lands. Hear whispers about the birth of the Son of God under the rule of the Roman Empire – about the spread of his Church as it takes shape. Tell the good news to everyone you meet – rich man and servant. Stand at the very top of a towering minaret, looking out over a city and call the faithful to prayer. Show respect to the Prophet who told us the final word of God. Ride with him to the Holy Places and follow the one righteous path. Spread God's truth wider and faster than ever before, to the far ends of the known world.

Cower in fear from the despot who rules you. Change your allegiances to survive the shifts of power. Trade with all the known civilizations. Feel the shame of losing your leading position to the Europeans, now advanced in technology, finance and organisation. Cling to your dignity as your lands are colonised and dominated. Get accustomed to the experience of having others meddle in your affairs. Ignite with the spark of nationalist consciousness, fight for your freedom and independence. Applaud the great Nasser and sigh with resignation as great hope turns to despotism and despair. Relish the opportunity to take control of the West's oil supply, once more a player in the game. Expel the Jews once more – another crowd shouting in the street. Try and fail to take back Palestine then mourn your sons as you bury them. Enjoy the fragrant subtle flavours of a lamb tagine with your friends on the banks of the Mediterranean. See yourself in a framed photo, graduating from university as an engineer – so young and so middle class. Shake your fist at a rank of armed police – representatives of the corrupt authorities. Watch in despair the news reports as you see your people killed in one bloody war after another. Dance with joy in the streets when the American bully is given a bloody nose. Wipe away your tears as you try to protect your family in Syria, as civilization descends to barbarism before your very eyes. Post a Facebook message to your university friends. Listen to the rumours in the souk. Watch carefully the actions of the other sect. Never let your guard down.

West is deeply immersed.

Arab World: Get out of my land, leave my people alone and respect my religion.

West shifts back to Western Consciousness.

West: How can I do that when I keep getting attacked and when I need your oil and money?

Arab World: I am determined to restore my self-respect. You've had me on the run for centuries but you will never defeat me. I will keep going until I'm successful, united and proud once more. Look at the mess you've made of Iraq, Israel and Libya. I have millions of young people who want jobs, food and dignity. How do you expect me to sort out all these problems?

West: It's not my responsibility. I colonised you briefly but that's not why you're in trouble.

Arab World: No? It's not just a few years of colonisation, it's two centuries of meddling, manipulating and exploiting. I don't forget all that. You are going to pay. I see you are weakening now. The others are rising and we will punish you.

West: In that case, I can't just get out and leave you alone, can I? I have to stop you taking revenge, trying to dominate and colonise me. Is there a way that we can be friends?

Arab World: Friends? You want to be friends now that I have you on the back foot? I don't trust you. Why should I? Get out of my countries and keep your nose out of my business.

West: I'd like to stay away from you too but we have to live together. We have to share the same neighbourhood and resources. We need to trade to thrive. You often ask me for help.

Arab World: You mean you exploit my divisions. Stop it, keep out and show due respect. Maybe in 100 years we can be friends but for now I am angry. I will trade with you but won't be your friend.

James: Is there anything that West can do to support you?

Arab World: I need to sort out my own problems. I need security, order and jobs. Many of my people are in your lands. They can learn from your technology and democracy but do not dare corrupt them with your atheist materialism. Why have you strayed so far from God? You are so sophisticated in your science and organisation but your spirit is weak.

James: I understand that you are experimenting with religious science and religious finance.

Arab World: Yes, in my richer parts I have plenty of money to finance science with, and I'm going to use it to resume my scientific and entrepreneurial leadership – without bankrupting myself on the inside like West. West will perish if he doesn't submit to God.

James: Is there anything that you can do to help the West?

Arab World: What more does he want from me? He took my ancient inventions. I provide much of his energy supply and invest in his economy. I provide him with young people who work in his cities while his young people indulge in drink, drugs and sex and don't even bother to marry and have children. My people are showing him the right way to live, the truth of God. What more can he want?

West: I'd like you to respect my boundaries too.

Arab World: The hypocrite speaks! That's like the serial burglar complaining about security. You must be joking.

West: I know I've violated your boundaries in the past.

Arab World: And in the present. Still you try to influence my people and my governments. Still you have military bases in my land. Still you send spies to manipulate me.

West: I can't let down my guard if I feel threatened by you. I fear that you are trying to spread your people, power and religion in my lands. I feel your hatred, shame and desire for revenge. How can I show you weakness and compassion when all you respect is power and force?

Arab World: You don't like the taste of your own medicine, do you?

West: Maybe so but if we are going to get along, we've got to find forgiveness for the past and respect and security in the present.

Arab World: Hollow talk. I will not trust you until I see that your actions match your words. Come back to see me when that is true. For now, that is enough. I am busy.

West unclenches his body and sits in the chair, clearly exhausted.

James: That was fascinating. What conclusions did you draw?

West: He's very angry with me. He feels intense shame because I overtook him and exploited my position. He feels violated and part of him wants to get powerful and take revenge.

James: That explains your fear. So, given that you acknowledge that you have harmed him in the past, and given that you want to be friends now, how can you move forward?

West: He told me what he needs. He said he wants me to show him respect, to keep out of his business, withdraw militarily from his land and ensure that my behaviour matches my words.

James: Later, I'm going to teach you about the victim triangle and the empowerment dynamic, a very simple but brilliant model. For now, suffice to say that I think you are both caught in the victim triangle. You each feel that you are a victim of the abusive behaviour of the other. You both consider the other to be the perpetrator. You both have been and are perpetrators. You both want the other to change before you are willing to do so yourself.

West: Forgiveness is the answer.

James: You saw that in abundance of forgiveness from India and your relationship with them is excellent as a result, but the Arab World generally is not in such a forgiving frame of mind. You acknowledge that you have been a perpetrator and would like to step out of that role. You are going to have to be the magnanimous one, to eat humble pie and try not to rise to the bait when the Arab World gets angry with you. If you flash every time you have an argument then you'll remain trapped. Take charge of your own emotions.

West: What do I do about terrorism, about manipulation of my energy supply and attempts to colonise me?

James: Those are all real threats, so you can't pretend they're not there. However you need to be strong yet magnanimous. Enforce effective boundaries, especially around religion and democracy. Respect his boundaries. You already committed to a World War II level of global effort to discover and implement clean, sustainable, abundant and secure energy supplies. That's vital. Rather than attack with criticism and manipulation, be a respectful challenger. You can ask inspiring, empowering questions rather than get into name calling and interference.

West: He's so sensitive. The slightest criticism makes him go ballistic.

James: You'll have to live with that until your relationship improves and until he feels happier in himself. Be supersensitive and do what you can to show respect and maintain his dignity.

West: OK, I get that but part of him wants revenge on me.

James: You have to live with that for now. Break the cycle of conflict. Maintain a strong defence and control your borders. You do have to be powerful and compassionate at the same time. This is going to take a long time. Try to listen, allow him to tell you how he feels. Really, truly listen until he feels heard, acknowledged and respected. Eventually his heart will open and he will forgive you. It may take a generation or two. Before you know, he will be your warmest, deepest friend. He has a warm heart. It is a wounded heart. A wounded heart closes off, becomes cold, angry, violent and desires the destruction of those who it perceives violated it. Be patient. Open your heart as much as you feel safe to do and show him love and kindness without letting your guard down or showing weakness. You can show emotional vulnerability at the same time as being physically strong. Eventually, you will embrace and put the past behind you. You are much more alike than you think, like two competitive brothers.

West: Thanks James, I appreciate that. I had no idea I could end up feeling so hopeful about this.

AFRICA

James: Who's next?

West: Africa. Sub-Saharan Africa.

Somewhat recovered, West resumes his position standing in the middle of the room. He closes his eyes, preparing himself to jump into another culture.

James: Take yourself to Africa, that enormous landmass, brimming with people and wildlife. The vast plains and endless blue skies. From the lush tropical rain forest to the Sahara Desert. From oil-rich Equatorial Guinea to pirate and terrorist infested Somalia. From teeming, money-making Nigeria right down to the home of Nelson Mandela, the rainbow nation. From the San Bushmen in the Kalahari to the Indian entrepreneurs of Nairobi. Feel the heat baking the rich red soil. Hear the call to prayer in Mali at dusk. Watch the wise, ponderous elephants play in cool river mud of a Botswana flood plain. You heard that, once, Europeans called it 'the dark continent' because it felt mysterious, impenetrable, exotic and full of disease and bandits. Is it mysterious or dark to you? Certainly not – its colours and light and song are your definition of home. Look back to the very origins of humanity. Here in Africa the slow, inevitable forces of evolution have shaped humanity – more so than anywhere else on earth. Now you are the earliest man standing upright on the plains, watching for predators and carcasses to scavenge. Feel the influence of evolutionary forces on your body and mind, shaping you like a potter shaping a clay jar. Your cultural history is littered with fundamental inventions and discoveries: cooking, fire, fishing, currency, tribes and thousands more. Advance through time to the many kingdoms of Ashanti, the Zulus and the great Empire of Mali. Feel the whip of a slave master on your back: African, Arab or European slavers, you're just a commodity to them. The wise rule of the chief gives you a feeling of security, and the witch doctor's powers help you feel less afraid of the world. The elders sitting under the baobab tree are also very good. In your imagination, soar above the African continent with an eagle's eye. Now you can see one of the world's most amazing fractal patterns – the African Village laid out in a form that is tens of thousands of years old. Enjoy a rich delicious lamb stew in Alexandra township, watching a fleet of BMW's drive past. Feel the dramatic shock of the arrival of the Europeans, the excitement, turmoil and disruption caused to the ancient rhythms and customs. You are angry – angry at the exploitation by Europeans, Arabs, Chinese and, not least, by your own corrupt elites. Can you feel hope? Maybe. Africa is beginning its renaissance.

Africa: My young people, tentatively optimistic, forward-looking and very excited are looking to West for opportunities, ideas, education, as a market, as somewhere to migrate. They appreciate China with its settlers, infrastructure, investment and products. They respect the Japanese for their technology and vehicles that plough up and down this great continent. The older generation have seen it all before, hopes and dreams quashed by coups and criminals. They're tired of the do-gooder aid worker come to pat us on the head like children and use us to feel good about themselves. I want good governance, discipline and order, like the British and the French brought here.

James: How do you feel about West?

Africa: Mixed feelings. I admire West for his wealth, technology and culture, order and security. I remember the colonisation in the 19th Century. I resent the exploitation of the multinational companies who would buy up our mining interests. Because our governments are weak, the strong external forces can easily exploited us. We can't say no because we need to trade and cooperate to develop ourselves.

James: What would you like from the West to improve the relationship?

Africa: Open their markets to my agriculture. I have this massive garden of organic food, a vast population which could feed you ten times over but instead you pay your farmers huge subsidies to give you expensive artificial food. Open your mouth and your hearts, let us feed you and build our economy. We need your technology, education and ideas to help us thrive. Give us access to your universities via the Internet on cheap tablet computers. Bring Oxford and Harvard to each village and bustling city. Share your pharmaceuticals. We don't need you to come as a parent but we do need your experience to help us develop strong governments, justice, taxation, regulation and security.

James: Can you forgive Europeans for slavery and imperialism?

Africa: Life moves on and we're focused on opportunities ahead. This continent is young in humanity and ancient in civilization. We're taking off in some places like the Chinese did 50 years ago.

James: Thank you. West, is there anything you would like to ask?

West: Don't be colonised by stealth by China, Brazil or the Gulf states. Keep ownership of your land and your resources. Imperialism isn't a European thing of the past, it's a human thing in the present.

Africa: It's up to me to protect my people from predators of all varieties.

James: West, what can you do to improve the relationship?

West: Treat them with respect, like adults. I've spent far too long treating Africa like a child to be patronised, a victim to be rescued, a hopeless case to be pitied that I may, if I'm not careful, miss out on the boom – the new opportunities. I could open my markets to their food but I need to consider my food security.

James: Thank you very much.

West: James, I've done enough for now. But, you know, this technique is powerful stuff – really incredible. Now you've shown me how to step in and out of other viewpoints, I'm definitely going to do it a lot more.

James: I can tell it's having a profound effect. But I'm not sure we're quite done yet. What about South and Central America and the Caribbean? Are they part of you or could you step into them as well?

West: The Caribbean is definitely part of me – an integral part. South and Central America is mostly part of me but with one foot in, one foot out. It's a hybrid, like India or Russia. I spread there through Spain and Portugal and a lot of immigration since then. They have followed their own path, diverging from the English-speaking and European West. Because of economic, religious and political differences they've grown up semi-detached. But we're all part of the same family. America and Europe have exploited them for sure, but now they're exerting a big influence on America through migration.

I noticed, when West had gone, that the session had overrun quite seriously. It had been compelling stuff and I just hadn't been aware of time passing. Consequently I had to drive home, shower and dress for going out all within 45 minutes.

———◆———

Suki had invited me out to meet her best friend Elizabeth and her husband Ajit. We met for a drink at the Cumberland Arms on the river at Chiswick, not far from the Meadows. I'd had many an evening there as a younger man with my university friends. Suki was early again, this time chatting to a man at the bar when I arrived. I was jealous but faked being unconcerned. She introduced him as Jake, an old friend. He was annoyingly cool and self-assured. It took five minutes to walk up the suburban roads to Elizabeth's house. They had an Edwardian Villa, three stories high. Elizabeth was a dermatologist in training. Ajit worked in the City. They worked well together. Suki seemed very proud to show me off to her friend. I sensed her measuring me up for size. I tested out West's financial ideas on Ajit. He said they hadn't learned much from the financial crash, other than to be more cautious, and, most worryingly, he said that optimism and thus greed were returning again. Finance might be a tough culture to crack. Maybe that's just the way of the world, like the inevitable rhythm of the tides and the waves. Elizabeth kept looking at the red patch on my nose. I wanted to ask her what she thought of it, but was embarrassed to bring my health anxiety out into the open on a social occasion.

Suki and I shared a taxi home. The driver was from Karachi. He was proud that his son was at medical school. Suki told him to drop me off first. When we pulled up outside my house, she got straight out of the car and stepped through my front gate.

'Can I come in?' she said.

'You are very welcome.'

Nga dashed in with us, introducing herself to Suki. As I was pouring us some brandy in the kitchen, Suki put on some music. She had found my dance practice CD. 'Cha cha cha! I didn't know you were a dancer, James!' She clicked through the tracks until she found *Sway* by Michael Bublé. 'My parents used to dance to this when I was a girl.' I placed my hands on her hips and kissed her, then took her hands and guided her in a cha cha cha.

'Copy me,' I said. 'Mirror what I do.' She looked down at my feet and tried to pick up the thread of the steps. She was a fast learner.

'My dad taught me in Hong Kong.'

We danced around the room until the tracks got too fast for us.

———◆———

I woke the next morning to the sound of Nga purring. She was standing on my pillow over me, sniffing my forehead. I must have forgotten to let her out. I remembered that I hadn't let Suki out either. I turned to see her wrapped up in the duvet, just her head above the surface. I crept out of bed, trying not to wake her and went downstairs to let Nga out. She looked out of the door, looked up at my face, turned and went back upstairs.

'Mmmmmmm coffee,' said Suki's voice as she walked into the kitchen, wearing just my blue T-shirts and her blue silk knickers. She came straight over for a kiss. She had that just-got-out-of-bed smell. I kissed her neck and caressed her thighs. 'Milk, no sugar, please.' She wandered off, exploring my house. She was in no hurry to leave.

POLITICS & DEMOCRACY

In the end, Suki stayed till Monday. I dropped her home on my way to work. The romantic spell was broken when I arrived at the Bernie Rosen Unit. Phil and Ayesha were dressed in casual clothes, sorting through files to archive. The last patient had been transferred out on Friday. We had been booked on a course at the Worcester Institute, to learn the protocols.

Jean was busy, trying to find outpatient slots for people. She kept sniffing as though she might be crying.

West arrived five minutes late, dressed smartly in a blue blazer, grey trousers and his black brogues. Seeing him raised Jean's spirits, but he seemed utterly oblivious to the upset and disruption going on around him. He seemed excited about something to judge by the jaunty way he entered the room.

James: Good Morning, West. How are you?

West: Splendid thank you very much. I had a very unpleasant dream.

James: Go on.

West: I was trapped in an ugly 60s university building with many corridors. I was there with a group to secretly meet someone about something. It wasn't clear what but it was some positive social advance. We were under constant attack by a small group of violent protesters. It was taken for granted that they would always be there throwing eggs, hurling abuse and threatening violence. It was very intimidating.

James: How did you feel, being trapped like that?

West: Scared. Courageous. But it felt futile. Very frustrating. The violent protesters were convinced that they were righteous and progressive. In fact they were prejudiced, bigoted people, full of hate and judgement. Most of them were young. Some well-to-do and others unkempt. What they had in common was intolerance, hatred and abusive behaviour.

James: Why were they angry? What were you meeting about?

West: That wasn't clear, but it's a pattern that I recognise. I've seen it in most eras. There's always some kind of groupthink – a set of beliefs that are accepted unquestioningly by the elite, and there's a strong taboo against challenging those ideas. Any dissent leads to brutal attacks. In every age, of course you also get mavericks – who go ahead and challenge the groupthink anyway, with the inevitable results. When that kind conflict gets emotionally charged, the for and against positions become extreme and polarised. Both poles are self-righteous and hate the other, convinced that the annihilation of the enemy is the route to salvation. The particular content of the arguments varies, but the pattern remains the same. Debate gets shut down. The conflict is so intense that it blocks any reasonable outcome.

James: Was there any guidance in the dream?

West: I felt that my energy is wasted on these polarised conflicts.

James: Where is this polarisation process going on now?

West: Racism and anti-racism. Authority and anti-authority. Egalitarians and meritocrats. Climate change believers and deniers. Welfare claimants and welfare haters. Religious fundamentalists, democrats and naive appeasers. Capitalism and anti-capitalism, peace campaigners and the security establishment, liberals and conservatives, abortion and pro-lifers, pro and anti-gay marriage and pro and anti-immigration.

James shows West into the office and shuts the door behind them. The walls are bare and the books from the shelves have been placed in boxes. Luckily there are still chairs.

James: Does your oppositional political system encourage polarisation?

West: Not necessarily. These polarities exist in countries with proportional representation and a tradition of coalition government. It encourages disagreement for the sake of it rather than collaborative, constructive leadership.

James: I thought you prided yourself on democracy?

West: Just because people vote doesn't mean that there's a democracy. Who chooses the candidates? Who in the media decides to whom to give air time and who to exclude? Who are the vested interests who pull the strings behind the scenes?

James: Can you imagine improvements to democracy?

West: I'd like to see a deep democracy, a culture of mature inquiry, exploring issues deeply, integrating the best of all perspectives, including those who have been marginalised and silenced.

James: Are some views and behaviours beyond the pale?

West: Do you know where that phrase comes from?

James: No, tell me.

West: British-ruled Ireland. The Pale was the area around Dublin where their rule was strong and 'beyond the Pale' meant beyond control, dangerous, bandit country; to be excluded.

James: Given the subsequent history of separation polarisation, violence and hatred, that's not such a good model to choose then

West: The peace process had to engage and include the extremes, those who most hated one another.

James: Often consensus seekers shut down the extremes and confine the debate to the moderates in the hope of finding a reasonable outcome. In my experience, the challenge is to incorporate all the elements, to listen carefully to the extremes while detoxifying the hatred, making it safe.

West: America is super-polarised too. The bipartisan system encourages debate, challenge and accountability of the government but it also enables destructive partisanship as a tactic and habit. The electorate are cynical because they believe politicians will say anything to get elected or play games to attack each other.

James: Similar to the disrespect people have for the law where the adversarial system incentivises lawyers to use dirty tricks and technicalities to win a case as opposed to genuinely seeking justice.

West: In some of my countries, they have proportional representation which theoretically better represents the diversity of opinion within the population and breaks the monopoly of the party machines. Political parties have to negotiate, make deals and alliances to form a majority to take power. That's a very democratic process but, around the edges, it means that relatively small parties and narrow interests exploit the opportunity to exert disproportionate influence by holding the majority to ransom.

James: Is there a more intelligent way to draw together different shades of opinion?

West: What do you have in mind?

James: I was brought up to believe that democracy was something that we'd already achieved. Now, I see it as a process in constant evolution, like a garden that needs to be tended to bear fruit and bloom.

West: Politicians do make bipartisan agreements. In foreign policy and security, it's very common.

James: But are there any peacetime examples of mature bipartisanship?

West: In Britain right now there's a coalition between the Conservatives and the Liberal Democrats which came about because no party won an overall majority in the first-past-the-post electoral system. For the first time in generations, the highly adversarial politicians who, only days before, had been rubbishing one another as mistaken and incompetent had to form a government.

James: That takes mature leadership.

West: Political parties themselves are coalitions of a broad range of people with different priorities and desired policies. Some try to capture the middle ground by combining the views of their more partisan members with those of the moderate wing of the other parties. Tony Blair and Bill Clinton tried to take ownership of certain Conservative and Republican values like the free market, private enterprise and consumerism, combining them with their more left-wing values of equality, social justice and state provision of services.

James: Who was left out of that arrangement?

West: The Labour Party and the Democrats abandoned their traditional working class supporters. Traditional values of patriotism, family values, strong borders and worker protection were neglected, leaving those people disenfranchised because their parties were more interested in constituencies among minority groups, identity groups and public sector professionals.

James: What makes you think democracy could be improved?

West: For example, the majority of the population of the West since the 60s has been in favour of a stricter immigration policy. During that period, there has been immigration into the West on a massive and increasing scale. There has never been any proper democratic accountability for that.

James: Every political party has an immigration policy and the voters can choose.

West: The voters don't get a true choice of policies and candidates.

James: Anyone can stand for election.

West: Anyone can stand for election but unless they're part of one of the major political parties, the media ignore them and in the countries with the first-past-the-post system like the US and Britain, they have little chance of breaking through.

James: If the people had genuinely been strongly against immigration then, that would've been reported in the media. Voters would have complained to politicians on their doorsteps. Politicians would have adjusted their policies to win. Surely you have the freedom to make those choices?

West: On a subject like the economy, the debate is open and raucous and people have the opportunity to choose between distinct positions. On controversial subjects like immigration, the cultural elite who dominate politics, the media and education use their power to restrict the boundaries of debate. They tend to be strongly in favour of open borders, multiculturalism and pluralism while the less powerful, less well-educated part of the population tend to value strong borders, patriotism and security.

James: Any other challenges to democracy?

West: Money buys power and influence. In some countries, corporate and vested interests control the debate by buying advertising or sponsoring pressure groups.

James nods sadly.

West: Back in 1984, everyone was reading about Big Brother and feeling very smug that we in the West have a fantastic democracy while those poor people in the Soviet Union and Eastern Europe had the totalitarianism of Communism. Shockingly, many of the things in the book have since become true in the West.

James: You mean Big Brother is spying on the Internet and bugging your telephone calls?

West: Yes. It used to be commonplace to say, 'We live in a free country.' That feels ever less true. Now the police are routinely policing people's thoughts, arresting people for making ordinary comments on Twitter or Facebook. The state is using increasingly sinister techniques to disenfranchise people from their right to protest, assemble and organise. The security state is routinely monitoring law-abiding people, criminalising them for dissent, controlling what they can and can't say. It feels sinister to me.

James: Democracy has never been perfect. There's always a tussle for power between the elite and challengers. Protest has been one of the prime drivers of your evolution from the rights of nobles and clergy in the Magna Carta, the rights of peasants after the Black Death, the American Declaration of Independence, emancipation of slaves, workers rights, decolonisation, gay rights and women's rights. If people care about these things, they can protest. If they don't then their complacency is their vote to give away their freedom.

West: Freedom is precious. Most Westerners were lucky enough to be born into democracy so it's easy to take democracy for granted, as the natural order. Witnessing the Arab Spring reminds me of the generations who have fought, sacrificed and protested to earn our freedom and democracy.

James: You're speaking for part of the West there. What do the other parts think?

West: Part of me thinks you can trust the people. Part thinks people don't know what's best for them and they need a wise elite to lead them. If we had pure democracy, most of my countries would have capital punishment, public floggings, no gay marriage and no immigrants. Most of great advances like civil rights, the emancipation of women and the welfare state have been driven by a minority of passionate activists.

James: Any other parts?

West: Part of me is preoccupied with money, power and status.

James: What do you consider to be the purpose of politics?

West: Decision-making, alignment of effort, accountability, representation, conflict resolution, collaboration and leadership.

James: The human being is a social animal as well as a conscious being – in other words, we're part of you, West – part of the group consciousness. If you look at a shoal of fish, migrating herds of wildebeest or a beehive, you see the amazing way in which they coordinate as a cohesive group, a collective intelligence.

West: True. But aren't human beings mostly only aware of being conscious individuals?

James: Although we're individuals, each of us has an inner compass, similar to the birds navigation system. We carry a map of the world, our model of how the world works and we have an inner compass which gives us continuous feedback on our place in the world. We use our inner compass to make choices, decisions, judgements and to align with others. Politics aims to define the map and calibrate the compass for the best result.

West: So, I guess its during that compass-calibrating process that the fights kick off – battles over which metaphors best describe how our social relationships should work.

James: I think you're right. In politics, people have to do their best to condense the complexity down to some straightforward visions, policies and actions. We do that's by simplifying things with generalisations, ideologies, slogans, metaphors and political parties.

West: The metaphors are often simplified down to left and right wing. Is there any real difference between left and right-wing people or is it just about metaphors?

James: Authoritarian people tend towards the view that you need central, top-down control and that that's necessary for safety and effectiveness. Libertarians believe that human beings should be as free as possible. Some people prefer to think of us as individuals and others tend to look for the group explanations. Human behaviour and motivation can be driven by internal factors such as our character, values, free will and intentions and can be driven by external factors such as community ethos, culture, institutions.

West: Where are left-wing people on that graph?

James: The left tend to see external factors as most important and the right tend to see internal factors is most important. Both left and right can be at different positions on the authoritarian-libertarian spectrum. You can have socially liberal conservatives and authoritarian socialists.

West: Let's take crime as an example.

James: That's actually a very good example. A conservative believes that a criminal has chosen to break the law of their own free will, manifesting their character, values and morality. Socialists tend to assume that criminal behaviour is caused by external factors like unemployment, racism, inequality and poverty. A liberal religious world view sees the criminal as one of God's beautiful children who has exhibited their natural sin but who must be forgiven and shown love and compassion. The state as nurturing mother, to coin a metaphor. The modern liberal has secularised this view. A conservative religious person instinctively likes the strict father idea of the state and believes strongly in punishment, boundaries and discipline.

West: There are so many dimensions to this. It's a lot to juggle.

James: That's why it gets oversimplified into left and right. But individuals are different and unique. Why shouldn't politics reflect that? There are many dimensions on which we all have our own position. Masculine-Feminine. Individual-Group. Authoritarian-Libertarian. National-Local-Global. Separate-Interconnected. People have different preferences for stability or change, evolution or evolution, consensus or confrontation, responsibility or paternalism, being rational or emotional, seeing the big picture or a narrow focus, being intuitive or empirical, theoretical or practical, religious or secular, open or closed, fundamentalist or pragmatic.

West: I couldn't put up with 5000 political parties.

James: You don't need to. Everyone has a unique place on multiple dimensions. We just have to be honest about the complexity of our beliefs.

West: For most of my history, politics has been top-down — power-based. People were more free in the past because the state took no interest in their private lives so long as they paid their taxes and didn't threaten the established order. Why can't we just go back to that?

James: You're not wrong. There are so many unhelpful entrenched political conflicts, and it's important that you understand why.

West: Shoot.

James: Well, let's look at the historical context. Over the centuries, protest movements have liberated huge numbers of people. That's great, but as a result, the dominant way of thinking in the anti-authority part of you, West, is the victim-perpetrator-rescuer consciousness. Traditionally that made sense because there was plenty to feel sore about: women were dominated by men, slaves were owned, workers were exploited by capitalists and so on. Well-meaning people saw this sought the role of rescuer for those victims.

West: That's a good thing, surely?

James: Sure, the victim-perpetrator-rescuer consciousness is good for attacking and breaking down the current order but not for envisioning something better. Such people know what they're against but they don't know what they're for. A leader needs a positive vision.

West: There must be something more powerful driving this than a simple desire to act like a knight in shining armour, surely.

James: There are some deeper psychological orientations, yes. People can make decisions with their head, heart, guts or spirit. Some like stories, others prefer statistics.

Some want equality, others diversity. Some lead, some follow, some criticise. Some like to be told what to do, others prefer autonomy. Some prefer action, some prefer thinking. Others like intuition and relationships.

West: What determines those different values?

James: Different experiences of life, parents, family, school, culture, different bodies, character and emotions. Some of the most intense feelings come from past emotional wounds. Abuse, ridicule or judgement can have a powerful impact. If someone has been dominated and controlled, they may well go on to become a dominating controller, an authoritarian control freak. Alternatively, they may rebel and go to the opposite extreme and become a human rights lawyer, a freedom fighter, an anarchist.

West: When someone posts a political picture on Facebook, it elicits a huge outpouring of negativity, hatred, jealousy, judgement, racism, jealousy, resentment, envy and greed. How come?

James: It's a political version of the Rorsach ink blot test.

West: It's funny sometimes, because the people who write aggressive posts are very often exactly the same ones who would pride themselves on saying, 'I'm non-judgmental.'

James: That's the shadow, the repressed, unconscious side of their politics coming out with all guns blazing.

West: Should we exclude people who are angry or extreme?

James: You can't safely have dialogue with someone who's violent or threatening. However, people can become angry because they feel disrespected, not heard, disempowered or violated. If you exclude them then that's adding fuel to the fire.

West: Like in the 90s when the religious fundamentalists won the election in Algeria. I worried that they were going to install an Iranian-style theocratic dictatorship so I overturned the election result. The consequence of excluding those people from the political process was an extremely violent and brutal civil war.

James: Can you think of an everyday example from your direct experience?

West: Welfare. Virtually everyone agrees that there should be a safety net for the elderly, sick and unemployed. As soon as you get into the detail of deciding who's eligible and who's gaming the system, rationality goes out of the window. Part of me assumes welfare claimants are scroungers, lacking awareness or compassion for suffering. Another part is so wracked with guilt and victim-rescuer thinking that it responds to any criticism of welfare like a hippopotamus protecting its baby. The polarisation makes it hard to have a sensible discussion and get beyond the stereotypes into some practical solutions. So many subjects are controversial like that like immigration, abortion, racism, crime and taxation.

James: Take a look at the Assimilation-Contrast Effect. This is a brilliant model proposed by Sherif and Hovland in 1961.

> *He digs down into a box and eventually finds the book he is after. Using the contents page he locates a specific diagram and passes it to West.*

James: You see, for any particular issue, there is a spectrum of views. In the middle are conciliators, pragmatists and moderates and either side are the polarised ideologues, zealots and flamethrowers. Conciliators hold their views lightly. They can see things from all perspectives, very GREEN. They search for consensus, common ground and seek to include everyone. Pragmatists are practical. They do what works.

West: So that's the ORANGE value system?

James: Yes, ORANGE and GREEN. Moderates hold their beliefs more strongly but can still see the other positions. They have ORANGE and BLUE values. Ideologues are true BLUE believers, absolutists, with firm convictions and rigid boundaries. Zealots are highly partisan, fiercely evangelical. They think in black and white, all or nothing RED-BLUE. Flame-throwers are aggressive, violent, and predatory, with RED thinking and intent on destruction, attacks, and eliminating the enemy.

West: How do they interact?

James: For an issue which is uncontroversial or quiescent, the majority are in the middle. The few people at the edge have little influence because even though they're heard, they are easily dismissed as extreme, unreasonable or mistaken. Either way, people don't feel strongly about it. When a subject is highly charged and strong emotional wounds are involved, large numbers of people gravitate to the extreme positions and energy is spent fight. Zealots and flamethrowers perceive moderate people on their own side of the argument as being traitors. A communist will see a socialist as being right-wing. A religious zealot will see a religious moderate as being an enemy non-believer.

West: It seems to me that the extremes can be dangerous, so I understand why they get shutdown by political correctness. That's why we have anti-hate speech laws, to outlaw prejudice and inciting violence.

James: The anti-racism laws and policies have made racism taboo in public life, but we know that at least 30% of people are still privately racist. Do you see any problems that have arisen as a result of limiting free speech?

West: Absolutely. It's impossible for conciliators, pragmatists and moderates to have a balanced conversation about race and religion, immigration, crime and terrorism because they immediately get shut down by zealots and flamethrowers who call them 'racists.' It's the ideologues and zealots on one side of the argument who have taken control of the debate. They've established a groupthink, to use your phrase, and they do it through peer pressure, threats of violence, removing people's livelihood and establishing laws that control people's thoughts and speech. So, even pragmatists and moderates on their own side who want to discuss the inflammatory issues have to treat the subject very carefully. Even the slightest deviation from the ideologues' position can unleash a torrent of violence and abuse.

James: This suppression of democracy – is it working for you?

West: In a word, no. I can't have constructive discussions about immigration, religious extremism, social justice, social problems in particular ethnic groups. It means that perfectly ordinary decent people are denied the right to be patriotic and to have an identity. We are storing up very dangerous problems.

James: So why do you keep a lid on all this?

West: What else can I do? It's highly explosive stuff.

James: Let me tell you a story. I went to a conference on the subject of immigration once. There were Members of Parliament, representatives of minority groups, academics and journalists. I expected they would all follow the standard groupthink favouring mass immigration, anti-patriotism and multiculturalism. Privately 80% were extremely worried about immigration, integration of newcomers, regretted the denigration of national identity and alarmed by religious extremists. They knew that the public were becoming increasingly uneasy about these subjects and they wouldn't be able to keep a lid on it much longer.

West: That's exactly what I mean. Sit on the lid, do whatever you have to, just don't let the contents see the light of day.

James: But the thing is, what those people said in public was not the same as their private utterances.

West: I'm sure. Only a tiny handful of ideologues and zealots are honestly in favour of mass immigration. They're the ones who want to erase domestic national identity.

James: At the same conference, one left-wing Member of Parliament told me that he felt physically scared of his constituents as he canvassed before the election, especially the working class people who have to live with the consequences of mass immigration directly. They were intensely angry with him, asking why he had flooded the country with immigrants, complaining about security, housing, crime, religious extremism and suppression of their identity. He was afraid. He couldn't see a way out of it. He knew that the status quo, the establishment groupthink ideology, was wrong but he couldn't see how to move beyond it into something that wouldn't appear racist. Look at the diagram in the book. He was a moderate on the side of pro-immigration and multiculturalism. He could understand that the moderates on the other side of the argument had some good points and he wanted to be able to engage with them but dare not for fear that the zealots and flamethrowers on his side would attack him as a racist and identify him as an enemy on the other side of the argument.

West: Yep, this suppression of democracy thing is a serious problem.

James: Basically, freedom of speech inhibits creative solutions, positive vision, healing and cultural evolution. I once asked a very senior TV executive why, given their duty of impartiality, did the media unquestioningly promote the ideologues' and zealots' positions on multiculturalism and immigration, aggressively attacking dissenters? To my surprise, they said that it was impossible within the TV company to allow any anti-immigration, patriotic voices to speak because within minutes there would be a torrent of abuse from the flamethrowers and zealots both within the TV company and beyond. The career of the journalist in question would be threatened. They might suffer physical violence.

West: This makes me so angry and frustrated. How can my democracy function better to sort this out?

James: Vigorous debate, freedom of speech, determined enforcement of the law to prevent crime, violence and intimidation. Deep dialogue, healing emotional wounds, challenging taboos and a powerful commitment to creating an exciting positive vision of who we are, we're going, our supra-ordinate goals.

West: Oh, come on, those things can work in a safe, professionally facilitated consulting room but out on the streets, with rough and tough people who are not necessarily very eloquent and who are highly fearful or angry, that stuff isn't going to work.

James: Sorry. Democracy requires order and security. That's a must.

West: Could we use professional facilitators for to make democracy work better?

James: Yes, certainly they could help. It's actually one role of journalists to facilitate democracy. They ought to be trained in the skills required to get beyond superficial positions and to get underneath into the complexity. All too often they take up an antagonistic position, seeking to make a fool of the person interviewing, find the point of weakness or, they give the politically correct position an easy ride. I'd like to see more authenticity and appreciation, giving people the chance to speak beyond the soundbite, giving them space to speak sincerely.

West: Politicians are slick operators. They need aggressive interviewers to catch them out otherwise they spout propaganda.

James: A good interviewer needs to be able to do both simultaneously, giving an appreciative space in which they genuinely listen to the other person, allow them to speak from the heart, express their passions and offer their highest vision, making them feel safe enough to express their fears, their worries and to open up their vulnerabilities. Equally they need the forensic logic, scepticism and analytical skills of a rigorous barrister or scientist.

West: I'd like to see donations to political parties seriously capped to the amounts ordinary people could afford to prevent companies, rich individuals, pressure groups and unions for exerting disproportionate influence.

James: Would you pay for political parties from the tax?

West: Certainly not! Politics should raise money and volunteers by inspiring the population. Big money corrupts the democratic process by favouring the positions of the powerful.

James: What else?

West: Erm, give me a clue.

James: Comedy. It's meant to challenge taboos, get under the skin of establishment groupthink and laugh at ridiculous ideas and policies, fearing to tread where politicians are too timid. Comedy has become tame. Comedians stick within the boundaries of political correctness which is precisely what they're not meant to do.

West: You're right. It's fear of those zealots and flamethrowers – enforcing thought control with emotional violence, or physical violence.

James: Comedians are censored whenever their material stands a chance of offending anyone, particularly advertisers or vested interests. It's time for comedy to offend people. Often.

West: Do you really think comedians are being gagged? It doesn't seem like it to me when I watch TV. They can be quite offensive.

James: OK, well, it could also be that comedians are largely drawn from the GREEN world view and therefore fail to do full-spectrum comedy! So, let's move to sum up. What would your ideal democracy be like?

West: It would engage the global brain. It would harness collective intelligence. Transpartisan politics would integrate the best of all the different positions to design intelligent strategy and generate vision that reflects the diversity and complexity of our world.

James: Go on.

West: I'd have safe spaces for dialogue on the hot topics to be professionally facilitated in order to achieve the best outcome. All levels of society would engage in dialogue, healing, conflict resolution, visioning, strategy and leadership.

James: Brilliant, West. Let's leave it there for today. Next time we're going to get practical.

When West had gone, I started reading the notes of my next patient. Jean appeared in the doorway. 'James, Dr Prasad asked you to pop over to the Meadows to see him when you have time.'

I hadn't talked to Dr Prasad since he became Medical Director. He had taken over Dr Sugden's office, overlooking the gardens.

'James, old chap, please do come in, welcome.' His friendliness made me suspicious.

'Hello Vinay, you seem to have settled in nicely here. Are you still doing any clinical work?'

'No, James, I'm fully focused on the Transformation Programme. I'm relying on you to champion the Worcester Community Treatment Protocols.'

I nodded noncommittally.

'However, I haven't called you here to discuss that.' His tone was more serious. 'I have completed my Significant Event Analysis for the near-suicide of your patient Mr West.'

'Oh, really. You didn't speak to me about it. Wouldn't that have made sense?'

'Under normal circumstances, yes, James.' He paused, taking a deep breath, shuffling his notes. 'I'm going to have to pass on the report to Dr Sugden. Mr West nearly committed suicide and has been under your care since the autumn. He has been an in-patient, outpatient and a frequent attender in the Emergency Department. Yet, you haven't kept back all records of your clinical sessions and assessments.'

I felt sick, knowing what was coming.

'I am told that you have allowed this patient to visit your home twice, that you have conducted a session in a café and that you have received a gift from him without registering it.'

'Vinay, West is a unique patient. He asked me to keep him off the record because he is very concerned about confidentiality.'

'James, I trust you,' he said not very convincingly, 'but I have to consider how this would look if it became public. You have broken basic rules of medicine and disregarded the hospital regulations. We're not in the old days of doctor-knows-best. You are accountable and so am I. This will be on Dr Sugden's desk shortly and you need to have some very good answers.'

I thanked him for the warning and made my way to the door.

'James,' he said to my back. I turned. 'I think you'd better cool it off with Dr Chen.'

I nodded and left. I wandered out and down to the river to visit Ellie and her horses.

———◆———

That evening in the pub, Steve was unsympathetic. 'I warned you. Don't mess with those hyenas. They'll relish the opportunity to hang you out to dry. If you want to keep your job, you have to eat humble pie, champion the Transformation Programme and make them look like a success.'

'They're sending me on the training course next week. I can't pretend to support something I know to be harmful. Are there any jobs going at the private hospital?'

'Dr Prasad and Dr Sugden are on the board there. You may have to move to a different area.' We took a sip of our beers. 'I hope this Suki is worth it, James. Watch your step.'

———◆———

The following Monday, I got up very early to pick up Phil, Seth and Ayesha on the way to Worcester. It felt great to get out of London. The trees were coming to life. There were daffodils on the grass verges. We arrived two hours before the course was due to start so we took a walk around the town. Just 150 miles away from London, it felt more friendly, slower and more gentle. The magnificent Cathedral overlooked the River Severn, the longest in the country. Young people were playing on the grass outside and couples were embracing beside the river. I sent a text to Suki, wishing she was with me.

I could hear the organ playing inside. There was a service going on. The stained glass window was awesome. I walked as quietly as I could along the edge to take a seat near the altar, next to a large tomb. On top was a wooden effigy of a King, lying in state. It was King John, the King against whom the nobles and clergy rose up to demand the safeguarding of their rights, privileges and liberties, leading to the signing of the Magna Carta in 1215. The 800th anniversary was next year, I noticed.

It was Ash Wednesday, a feast whose meaning I only dimly understood. A service was unfolding around me in the light and space of the cathedral: some colourfully dressed priests, organ music, singing of a half-remembered hymn and then an echoing sermon, which explained that today was the start of the Christian penitential season of Lent. When the sermon had finished – in fact it lasted barely five minutes – cathedral ushers appeared and invited the congregation, row by row, to come up to the front. On impulse I rose and followed, kneeling in front of the altar with a dozen other – mostly accidental – worshippers. The Bishop worked his way along the row, marking a cross on each forehead with ash. As his thumb made two short strokes on my forehead, I heard him say the words 'Remember that you are dust and unto dust you shall return.' It made me feel tearful, although I didn't quite know why.

———◆———

The course was a cult induction and a high pressure sales talk combined. As a small act of subversion I kept the ash cross on my forehead throughout.

The Worcester Community Treatment Protocols made sense logically. They present-ed all the latest data. The business case made sense. The only fly in the ointment was that human nature doesn't work the way the model assumes. I kept my mouth shut. My colleagues, like me, had to adapt to the changes so there was no point in being a cynic. This had been mandated at government level, driven by academics and politicians. It was easier to go with the flow than to resist the tide. No doubt, some ivory tower would rediscover the value of common sense at some point and we'd be sent on a new course to learn that.

ENDING THE CULTURE WAR

West appeared for his regular appointment and seemed quite unaware of my post-Worcester malaise. In fact he was on something of a mission.

West: Hi James. I've realised something. I've been wasting too much energy fighting culture wars between conservatives and liberals. Can you please help me resolve this once and for all?

James: That's a tall order but we can experiment. We can try to take the charge out of the conflict with EMDR. Let's access the consciousness of the zealots and flamethrowers on both left and right.

They clear a space on the carpet for West to move.

James: Stand there. Get yourself into a conservative state of mind. Immerse yourself in the BLUE values of tradition, order, duty, sacrifice, the Church, righteousness, patriotism, the military, the police, justice and truth.

West closes his eyes, breathing deeply.

James: Dive deeper into the PURPLE values of security, togetherness, protection, family, community, tribe, territory, spirits, mysticism and safety.

West looks peaceful and powerful.

James: Add in the values of ORANGE. Entrepreneurship, business, meritocracy, democracy, science, hard work, skills, pragmatism and success.

Now unzip that part of yourself and jump forwards into the Liberal-Left part. Turn around and close your eyes. Really immerse yourself into those GREEN values of fairness, equality, compassion, diversity, sustainability, spirituality, inclusion, human rights and peace.

West is glowing.

James: And now unleash the RED system, free from the constraints of BLUE and PURPLE. Feel the freedom, the lust for sex, power, money, status, immediate pleasure, domination, courage, risk-taking and warrior spirit.

West chuckles and smiles broadly.

James: Open your eyes and look at the Conservative self. Notice your emotions, thoughts and sensations as you look. What do you get?

Liberal-Left: I see a racist. A bigot. A control freak. A nasty, intolerant person who judges others. I see an inflexible fundamentalist. A nationalist. I see a selfish corporate parasite. I see a homophobe, a backward zealot who wants to undo all the progress of the last 60 years. I see an abuser.

James: How do you see your Liberal-Left self?

Liberal-Left: I'm a protector of victims. I protect minorities, women, gays, minority religions, workers, the poor, the developing world and the environment. I'm authentic, compassionate, holistic, fair, non-judgemental, spiritual and inclusive.

James: Thanks. Unzip that part and jump into the Conservative. Look back at the Liberal-Left. Tell me what you see and feel.

Conservative: I see a naive idiot. A privileged freeloader who hasn't done a day's work in their life. A wuss. A tyrant. A childish bully. They think they're so moral but they want to tear the world apart, unleashing all the criminals, spongers, parasites and colonisers. If they get their way, I will be insecure, the world with be unjust and our enemies will take advantage.

James: And how do you see your Conservative self?

Conservative: I'm the defender of the nation, the faith, democracy. I stand for making the world fair for the strivers.

James: What about the Liberal-Left most infuriates you?

Conservative: They want to take away the wealth I've earned. They make excuses for criminals. They want to overwhelm me with foreigners and religious fundamentalists.

James: What are the worst images which come with that target?

Conservative: Being mugged and burgled. The streets full of aggressive foreigners. Losing my home and job. Being sent to prison for resisting the religious fundamentalists trying to take over my country. Tearing down my flag. Riots.

James: What thoughts about yourself cross your mind when you have those images in your mind?

Conservative: I am not safe. I am violated. I can't protect myself.

James: How do you feel?

Conservative: Scared. Angry.

James: Rate those out of ten.

Conservative: Scared 8 out of 10. Angry 9 out of 10.

James: What sensations do you have in your body?

Conservative: Gritted teeth. Clenched fists. Tearfulness. Stomach churning. A lump in my throat.

James: What beliefs about yourself would you like, reasonably, to hold when those images are in your mind? Rate how strongly you believe them out of 7.

Conservative: I am strong 3 out of 7. I am powerful 2 out of 7. I can defend myself 2 out of 7. I am free 3 out of 7.

James: Excellent. Remember your safe place?

Conservative: The beach.

James: Good. Now make the image as strong as you can. Bring up the emotions and sensations. Nod when you're ready.

West nods.

James: Now let your mind go free, let it go wherever it wants.

James the bilateral eye movements. West screws up his lips. His eyes fill with tears.

James: What did you get?

Conservative: I felt vulnerable and very sad to have lost so much and scared to be violated. Then I thought that the world is changing and I need to adapt.

James: Go with that.

Bilateral stimulation.

Conservative: I saw myself trying to fight off muggers and thugs. I lunged at the religious fundamentalists with a sword but GREEN tied my feet together so I fell over. They overwhelmed me.

James: How does that feel?

Conservative: I'm overrun. I've surrendered. It feels shameful and frightening. There is a certain peace to surrender but I'm now at the whim of criminals and enemies who want to dominate me.

James: Go with that.

Bilateral stimulation.

Conservative: I see myself as a small child sitting on the floor with bad adults walking around me. There is no father to protect me. No police officer, no good authority.

James: Go with that.

Bilateral stimulation.

Conservative: I'm a child on the floor, crying. The Liberal-Left is looking at me. Now I am a victim, they feel sorry for me, guilty for having been naive to have allowed this to happen. But they are weak so they can't fight off the attackers. We're defenceless.

James: Go with that.

Bilateral stimulation.

West weeps and contorts his face.

James: What did you get?

Conservative: I felt sad. The Liberal-Left's naivety caused us all terrible harm. They regretted it too late.

James: Go with that.

Bilateral stimulation.

West looks sad still, but calmer.

James: What did you get?

Conservative: I saw the Liberal-Left as an adolescent or young student. Very sincere, idealistic and well motivated but very naive. It's not safe to let them run things. They are immature. Liberal-Left individuals can make their own mistakes but it's not acceptable to let them take us all down with them.

James: Is there anything you can do to support the Liberal-Left?

Bilateral stimulation.

Conservative: I notice that their main motivation is to protect people they see as victims but their beliefs create new victims. So there is potential common ground if only they would be open to find more effective ways of achieving their objectives.

James: Imagine yourself doing that.

Bilateral stimulation – slower

West looks sad and angry again.

James: What did you get?

Conservative: They won't listen. They are arrogant.

James reviews West's beliefs again. I am strong. 6/7. I am powerful 5/7. I can defend myself 5/7. I am free 5/7. Scared 3/10. Angry: 3/10.

West: That's interesting. When we reviewed the target, I still saw the bad things happening but I felt less afraid, stronger and less angry about the Liberal-Left. I was more able to accept what was going on and could stand my ground confidently, letting the wave roll over me and I was still standing.

James: Fantastic! That's fast progress. I think we need to turn the tables now. Take yourself to your safe place, the beach and rest for a few moments.

West relaxes.

James: Now take yourself into the Liberal-Left part of yourself. What about the Conservative most infuriates you?

Liberal-Left: I see all the victims they create. Victims of racism, sexism, homophobia, capitalism, police brutality, indigenous peoples, minorities. I hate them for the suffering they cause.

James: What are the worst images which come with that target?

Liberal-Left: I see slaves. I see boats of immigrants sinking. I see bigots with guns shooting at Mexicans crossing the border. I see child labourers in Bangladeshi factories working 14 hour days. I see the horror of Iraq and Afghanistan. I see the coming climate change catastrophe. The Conservative is complacent, mean, selfish, nasty, brutal and an abusive thug.

James: What thoughts about yourself cross your mind when you have those images in your mind?

Liberal-Left: It's my duty to protect the victims 7 out of 7. I am the only one who can save them 5 out of 7. I am ashamed to be associated with the Conservative 7 out of 7.

James: How do you feel?

Liberal-Left: Angry 9 out of 10. Indignant 9 out of 10.

James: What sensations do you have in your body?

Liberal-Left: Gritted teeth. Blood rushing in my chest. Heart pain.

James: What beliefs about yourself would you like, reasonably, to hold when those images are in your mind? Rate them out of 7.

Liberal-Left: I'm already happy with my beliefs.

James: OK. Now make the image as strong as you can. Bring up the emotions and sensations. Give me a nod when you're ready.

West nods.

James: Let your mind go free, let it go wherever it wants.

James begins bilateral eye movements. West frowns.

James: What did you get?

Liberal-Left: I hate the Conservative. They are evil and must be stopped for there to be a better world.

James: Go with that.

> *Bilateral stimulation.*

> *West looks tearful.*

James: What did you get?

Liberal-Left: My father bullied me. I hate the abuse of power.

James: Go with that.

> *Bilateral stimulation.*

> *West looks more tearful. His lip is quivering.*

James: What did you get?

Liberal-Left: I feel vulnerable to my abusive father. I'm scared. I want to get away from him. Power is wrong. Authority is bad.

James: Go with that.

> *Bilateral stimulation.*

> *Still sad, West lightens slightly.*

James: What did you get?

Liberal-Left: That's surprising. I realised that I'm being hypocritical. By stepping in to protect victims, I'm asserting authority myself. By hating the Conservative so much, I am being judgmental and intolerant, fundamentalist just like them.

James: Go with that.

Bilateral stimulation.

Liberal-Left: So I do believe in power, right and wrong and authority. I believe that I am right and the Conservatives are wrong.

James: Go with that.

Bilateral stimulation.

Liberal-Left: I felt my heart. I felt compassion for the Conservative. They're trying to protect what they hold dear. I should be kinder.

James: Go with that.

Bilateral stimulation.

West looks cross again.

James: What did you get?

Liberal-Left: I can be compassionate but I will never tolerate their abuses against others, so I won't compromise.

James: Look at the Conservative again.

Bilateral stimulation.

Liberal-Left: I see that they want safety and fairness. But they can't have that at the expense of others.

James: How can you cooperate with them?

Bilateral stimulation.

Liberal-Left: I should be using empathy, listening and engage in dialogue. But I won't compromise on fairness.

James: So, you're BLUE yourself! Fundamentalist, certain that you're right. Casting the enemy as evil, worthy of destruction.

West blushes and laughs.

Liberal-Left: You're right. I need to walk the walk, don't I?

James: Let's revisit the target and score the emotions and beliefs. 'It's my duty to protect the victims. I am the only one who can save them ...'

Liberal-Left: Oh my God, I hadn't seen it before. How arrogant of me. I am speaking for the victims – the perceived victims – but I haven't even consulted them. I have taken it upon myself to be their rescuer. I should empower them.

James: Go with that.

Bilateral stimulation.

James: What did you get?

Liberal-Left: I saw the ethnic minorities, the women, the poor. I should empower them, not treat them like victims.

James: Go with that.

Bilateral stimulation.

West looks pale and stunned.

Liberal-Left: I saw those I've treated as victims. Many of them have very unpleasant habits. Some were criminals. Many had traditional tribal, patriarchal, religious and Conservative beliefs. Many had problems which weren't fault anyone else's. I should make wiser judgements.

James: Go with that.

Bilateral stimulation.

Liberal-Left: I see why the Conservative is so angry with me now. They could see what I couldn't. I feel like an idiot now.

West points his finger at James.

Liberal-Left: But I won't let the racists, sexists, abusers or exploiters off the hook.

James: What will you do?

Bilateral stimulation — slowing

West looks powerful and serene.

James: What did you get?

Liberal-Left: I didn't expect that outcome. I will develop my own healthy BLUE! I will develop my own positive authority, enlightened leadership. I'll learn how to empower those who need it. I will discipline myself to use my skills to the full with the Conservatives, treating them with respect. I don't think I'm going to let them take back power but I am going to try to provide justice, right & wrong, security, leadership and authority. I will endeavour to overcome my naivety. I will treat people equally and not naively or arrogantly classify people as victims in need of my rescue. I will cultivate good judgement and wise action. Thanks James.

James: That's my pleasure. Can you step out of the Liberal-Left and back into the Conservative now?

West jumps to the opposite position.

James: Did you see that? Take a look at the Liberal-Left now.

Conservative: I feel like they have incorporated me. I feel strong and safe. I will watch them like a hawk but I trust them now. I can see that they have got skills that I haven't got which can be useful. I am willing to be led by them if they truly carry BLUE and PURPLE for me.

West jumps into the Liberal-Left position.

Liberal-Left: I didn't say anything about PURPLE! We're not going back to tribal patriotism and ethnocentrism!

They laugh.

James: I'd like to you reintegrate both those parts. Similar to the inner union exercise with the masculine and the feminine.

At James's suggestion, West alternately stands in the Conservative and the Liberal-Left positions, immersing himself in each by turns, looking at the other, then finally merging as one.

James: How was that?

254

West: Powerful. I can feel the strong essence of both of them inside me. Each bring such strengths and together could be a constructive force for good.

James: Well done West!

EQUALITY, JUSTICE & FAIRNESS

The Bernie Rosen Unit had been renamed the Pearson Centre. The finance department had moved into the middle two floors. The Audit and Performance Management teams were on the ground floor. Pride of place went to the Transformation Programme on the top floor, with the best view. The new furnishings reminded me of a smart hotel.

Back at my clinic, it was refreshing to see West again. He had become a familiar fixture in a fast-changing environment.

James: Welcome back, how are you?

West: Very good thanks.

James: Right, I said we were going to get practical, so let's practise your transpartisan skills.

West: Remind me what transpartisan means.

James: Integrating the best of all dimensions. Left and right. Liberal and conservative. Traditional and modern. Masculine and feminine etcetera.

West: While we're doing that. I'd like to explore how people can become truly equal.

James: OK. Off you go.

West: All human life is equally valuable. Every child should have an equal opportunity to thrive, make its own choices and reach its full potential. There won't be any discrimination according to race, gender or sexuality. Everyone will have a fair chance in life.

James: What steps can you take now in that direction?

West: Remove the barriers that get in the way of equality and fairness. Fully empower those who are at a disadvantage.

James: Why do you care about this?

West: Everyone deserves a fair opportunity to thrive. I hate injustice, discrimination, unfairness, corruption and exploitation.

James: Why does it matter?

West: A child doesn't choose where it's born and that fundamentally isn't fair. Some children are born into a prosperous country with freedom, security, education, health and employment opportunities. Some are born into war-torn, poor, crime ridden places full of inequality and injustice. Some children are born into loving families who are supportive, kind, caring and do everything they can to stimulate and empower their child. Others are born into broken families or suffer neglect, abuse, mistreatment.

James: A child's first five years heavily influence its life course. Does *equality* mean equality of outcome, equality of value or equality of opportunity?

West: I value both equality and diversity but, by definition, diversity means difference whereas equality means things are the same. Human beings all have equal value both legally and morally but differ in many ways. Everyone should have an equal opportunity to thrive and lives as they choose and we have to accept that there will be a huge diversity of outcomes. I could insist that outcomes must all be the same; same housing, money, health, services, clothes, same life. They're all different types of equality.

James: What makes people different?

West: Male and female, old and young, rich and poor, black and white, religious and secular, happy and unhappy, successful and unsuccessful, good-looking and not, healthy and unhealthy, lean and overweight, independent and dependent.

James: Keep going, don't censor.

West: Thriving and stuck, passionate and bored, optimistic and pessimistic, popular and unpopular, connected and disconnected, sociable and unsociable, liked and disliked, free and controlled, loved and unloved, abused and protected, disciplined and lazy, home owner and tenant, homed and homeless, vegetarians and meat eating, imprisoned and free, oppressed and privileged.

James: Keep going until you run out.

West: Sexual and asexual, sexually attractive and unattractive, fertile and infertile, shy and confident, gregarious and solitary, city and countryside, indigenous and immigrant, private and public sector, employee and employer, employed and unemployed, employee and entrepreneur, saver and spender, impulsive and cautious, courageous and cowardly, intelligent and stupid, modest and extravagant, powerful and weak, insider and outsider, professional and worker, gay and straight, masculine and feminine, heterosexual, homosexual and bisexual. Male, female and transgender, single and married, cohabiting and married. Parent and child. Parent and childless. Creative and not. Efficient and inefficient. Cruel and kind.

James: Keep going.

West: Western and non-Western, religious fundamentalist and democrat, couch potato and athlete, animal lover and not, aggressive and peaceful, assertive and passive, dominant and submissive, responsible and irresponsible, caring and callous, forgiving and resentful, magnanimous and arrogant. Envious and grateful. Reactive and passive. Harsh and compassionate. Left brain and right brain. Scientist and artist. Rational and emotional. Logical and intuitive. Socially skilled and inept. Disabled and able. Do you want me to carry on?

James: Do you notice different types of difference?

West: You don't choose your race or gender but you do choose whether to commit a crime or work hard. You don't choose whether you're born into a loving family or not but you can choose whether to be cruel or kind.

James: I'm not sure the distinction is as clear as you think.

West: What do you mean?

James: In any moment, an individual can choose to commit a crime or not. When you dig down deeper, there's not such a clear distinction between free will and determinism. Ask each world view what makes someone commit a crime?

West stands up, entering his well-rehearsed routine for Voice Dialogue..

BEIGE: Someone commits a crime because they need to survive, eat, get shelter or in self-defence.

PURPLE: Someone commits a crime because they disrespect the community, elders and the chief, because they're selfish, their family is bad or because they're possessed by evil spirits.

RED: People follow their impulses, do what they want. It's a game. Everyone would be a criminal if they could get away with it.

BLUE: Criminals are bad. They lack guilt, shame and integrity. They have bad character, values and upbringing. People commit crime when there isn't proper discipline, punishments or when monitoring, regulation and policing fail.

ORANGE: People commit crime because they see an opportunity to improve their lives or achieve their goals. People commit crime because they lack the skills to succeed another way. Crime is a rational strategy, calculating risks and rewards.

GREEN: Criminals are victims of poverty, racism, unemployment, exploitation and inequality. People's behaviour is determined by the situation, environment and culture much more than character or free will. We have a culture of greed, entitlement and materialism. There are winners and losers in that heartless game. People who have been dominated and exploited eventually fight back.

YELLOW: I agree with all said so far. People commit crimes because the GREEN system has undermined the BLUE morality with its non-judgement and relativism, anything goes. People commit crimes because the ORANGE system has undermined the truth and encouraged selfishness, not duty or community. The BLUE system has lost its clarity, self-confidence in asserting what's right and wrong. The PURPLE system, community and family, the bonds are weaker so the connections, the transparency, the feedback, the trust is much less than it used to be. We need all the value-systems to operate effectively.

TURQUOISE: The RED system is a necessary part of every life. Without RED, life would not exist, there would be no courage, risk-taking or sex. Without RED there will be no warrior to protect the vulnerable from predators. Without RED there would be no boldness to harness the environment. The shadow side of RED is cruelty, sadism, selfishness, greed, resentment, shame, jealousy, and entitlement. Two sides of the same coin. We need a healthy system at all levels within individuals, families, communities, processes, institutions, laws and actions to minimise the dark side and to maximise the positive. If you have total freedom, the dark side is free to abuse and exploit. If you have an authoritarian system then life itself is stifled and corruption finds another way. The devil is creative.

James: Excellent, West. Let's drill down to a more specific aspect of equality. Pick one.

West: Welfare and poverty. I support the welfare system in helping the sick, disabled, elderly and disadvantaged to survive and thrive. There's a huge disparity between rich and poor, workers and capitalists, developed and developing countries.

James: Why does that matter to you?

West: Inequality is unfair. Some people cheat, some exploit others, some work the system and that's not fair on those who lose out. Some inequality and wealth is due to inherited privilege and that's not fair on those not born to privilege. Societies with large disparities in wealth have more crime, unhappiness, insecurity and lack a feeling of togetherness.

259

James: Imagine you're someone who works hard, long hours, sacrificing your freedom, delaying gratification, saving, playing by the rules and paying taxes. You own your own house. Your neighbour lives on welfare. They have the same home, school, health service, police, roads and justice. They smoke, drink and go on holiday. When you go out to work, they're still in bed and when you go to bed, they're up late, playing music loudly. You were mugged by members of their children's gang. Your neighbour burgled you, while you were at work, to steal money to fund their drug habit. How do you feel?

BLUE: I'm angry. The people next door have everything but give nothing back in return. They commit crimes, create climate of fear, throw rubbish in the streets and bully my children.

James: What should be done about it?

BLUE: They should be punished for their crimes and made to live by the rules. They should have their benefits taken away, forced to work, or do voluntary work to contribute to the community.

James: Let's speak to the RED system in that family.

RED: I'm entitled to my benefits. I can't get a job. I'm depressed. My doctor signs me off sick.

ORANGE: You could learn some skills to improve yourself.

RED: I've got emotional problems. Education is expensive and boring. I don't want a menial job like sweeping the streets. Mind your own business.

GREEN: This man grew up in a poor family, in a poor environment. He was beaten as a child. His alcoholic mother neglected him. His abusive father undermined his self-confidence. He went to a rough school where he had to join a gang to protect himself. He got into drug taking which was a sign of bravado in the gang. The crime pays for his drugs. His school didn't pick up on his special needs or neglect. He was allowed to play truant and ended up with no qualifications. Whenever he did try to get a job, he was turned away because people prejudiced about his accent, looks and manners. You can't blame him for being a bad parent, he had very poor role models.

ORANGE: Why should I pay taxes to support him? There are opportunities available which he doesn't take. He should get some training and be entrepreneurial.

PURPLE: This family is a parasite on the community and is a source of crime and violence. Where are the elders to guide him, to provide role models? Where's the chief to provide leadership and discipline? Where's the shaman to heal this man's spirit? Where are his peers to support him and hold him to account?

GREEN: He gets a visit from the community psychiatric team which tries to help with his drug addiction and depression but it's not easy. Those things are deep-seated and hard to treat when the system is stacked against someone.

BLUE: I come from a poor background, I had poor parenting, I came as a refugee to this country but I've knuckled down and worked hard. You have no God, no justice, no right and wrong. It's all about money to ORANGE and all about self-righteous political correctness to the GREEN system. This man needs discipline, boundaries and morals. You're not helping him. There is inequality here. I have to work hard for my lifestyle. He gets his for free and harms everyone else. That is deeply unfair.

James: You have elements of the solution in each of the value systems. The challenge is to integrate those and make it practical. You have to identify the overarching, supra-ordinate goals which are going to unite these people and the wider community.

West: All the value-systems are self-righteous but none of them has all the answers alone.

James: What's your highest vision for this situation?

West: I would like to see these two neighbours respecting one another without crime, fear of violence and ideally being friends, good neighbours and part of a thriving community. I'd like to see the man who's working feel content with his situation and to feel that society is fair. I'd like to see the unemployed man become empowered, self-confident, happy and thriving, finding a role in the world in service of the wider community, being responsible, earning his way and feeling self-respect. I'd like to see all of their children thrive and meet their potential.

James: Now identify the incisive, empowering questions which generate new possibilities and give rise to the actions and strategies which will achieve your vision.

West: What does the unemployed man want? What are his motivations, desires and needs? What can those around him, his neighbour, the welfare system, community psychiatric team, the police officer and wider society do to give him responsibility for his actions? What support, resources and structure are necessary to help him achieve his goals? What can I do to make the welfare system fair to taxpayers, workers and recipients? What can the school and the community do to support and engage his children, make sure that they're thriving and to make sure that they don't lose out in their own life chances as result of this poor parenting? If this man isn't capable of working because of his character and habits, what is it reasonable and desirable to expect of him as a minimum contribution to society in return for his benefits? Is there anything which he or his psychiatric team can do to help him break his addictions and improve his mood and motivation?

James: These are excellent questions but mostly from the rescuer-victim perspective. He doesn't respond well to criticism or judgement. What could you ask to inspire him to raise his game?

West: What kind of father and man would he like to be?

James: Great. I'd like to get to know him, his story, listen to who he is and what he wants from life, how he sees himself and then we could elicit his frustrated dreams, his shame, how he would have liked things to have turned out. With careful listening, you could find out what he cared about, engage his heart intelligence. He has thick armour to protect his wounds so you have to be sensitive. That can easily trigger violence but if you tread carefully, he will melt, cry, open up to his inner guidance system.

West: You forget that you're highly trained to do that. Anyway, he'd probably tell you where to go.

James: True. Even when people are motivated to change it can be very hard work. I'd ask him what makes him proud of himself, what his strengths are, what he cares about, what he values, how he envisaged his future unfolding? I'd like to ask him if he saw any opportunities for himself. What does he do for fun? I'd try every angle to tap into his motivations, get under his skin to stir things up. What would you ask the neighbour, the psychiatry team, the school, the police, the local services, the local businesses and, maybe, carefully and his wife?

West: I'd ask the neighbour if they have any common interest that could be used to improve the relationship. Are there any men who could provide support, friendship, security, discipline, encouragement and accountability.

James: What questions would you have for the welfare system?

West: How do they assess his fitness for work and capabilities? What support do they offer to help someone into the discipline of work? Is there was a way to provide mentoring, training and support for the man? Are there role models to inspire him? Maybe people who have been in his situation and improved themselves, someone that he might respect and wish to emulate. What does the welfare system do to incentivise people to work? How do they detect people gaming the system?

James: What about the criminal justice system?

West: How do they support local people to self-police, to assert authority on the streets? What has the Council done to deal with the nuisance of music being played late at night?

James: I would like to know about this man's spiritual beliefs. With sensitivity, you can find the soul in everyone. They might talk about relatives that they've lost, their experience of illness, their beliefs about fate and what happens after death. Often it opens up someone spirits and gives you and them a clear way forward. People fall in between the cracks of our industrialised, dehumanised systems.

West: My organisations need to evolve to be a living, human, conscious, interconnected system which more accurately maps onto the complexity of the situation, based on relationships. You can't run the world from a spreadsheet in an office. I haven't put the world to rights in one day but I can see a better approach, thank you.

James: My pleasure. See you again soon.

West: I won't be here next week. I'm going to spend a week in Greece. All this therapy has whet my appetite to explore my roots.

James: Fantastic. Kos is where Hippocrates set up the very first medical school at Asklepion. You could go on a tour.

West: I was planning a few days on the beach, but I'm sure I could drag myself away for a few hours.

James: See you soon. Book before you leave — the clinic slots are getting heavily booked now.

———◆———

Jean wished me good luck, knowing that I was on my way to Dr Sugden for a dressing down over my record keeping and probably about Suki too. 'Be careful what you say James, you know he's just itching to get rid of you.'

Dr Sugden kept me waiting for half an hour. He had moved into Christine Pearson's old suite in the grandest rooms at the back of the Meadows. 'Come,' he shouted through the door. As soon as I entered, I knew something was wrong. Sitting beside Dr Sugden was Bill Taylor, the Trust Legal Officer and Penny Jameson, Head of Human Resources. They didn't stand up. There was one chair set back a metre from the large table which separated me from them. I could see over their shoulders to the beautiful trees in the grounds beyond. West's oak tree was swaying in the breeze.

'Doctor Hill, please sit down.' Dr Sugden was wearing a brand new suit. Still grey, still shiny, still smelling of cigars. There was an ash tray on the window sill outside with a half smoked cigar, freshly trailing a grey-blue ribbon of smoke. 'I think you know Mr Taylor and Ms Jameson?' I nodded. 'I have to suspend you today without pay pending referral to the General Medical Council.'

The blood drained from my face, my heart was in my mouth.

'You're joking?' I said, knowing that he wasn't.

'No. Dr Prasad has already explained the reasons. You have seen Mr West, without keeping any records, without keeping any personal details or writing to his GP. You have deliberately concealed him from your colleagues. I have been told that the patient is clearly psychotic with delusions of grandeur yet rather than treating them, you have colluded with the patient, indulging and elaborating these fantasies. Whilst under your care, Mr West almost committed suicide as a result of your inaccurate diagnosis and lack of adequate treatment. I have been informed that you have entertained the patient twice in your home and once in a coffee shop. You have been using non-evidence based treatments. He consulted his notes. Spiral Dynamics Integral. Voice Dialogue. Meditations. Talking to trees. Tantric mumbo jumbo. Doing something with horses in the fields out there. Talking about politics. Getting the patient to carry out bizarre rituals like having sex with the woman inside himself. Dr Hill, I knew you were unorthodox but I did not know you were an unprofessional charlatan. You leave me no choice but to refer you for a Fitness to Practise Panel of the General Medical Council with the recommendation that you be struck off the Medical Register and banned from practice.'

My heart was pounding. I felt tearful but wasn't going to give him the pleasure of seeing that.

Ms Jameson cleared her throat. 'Dr Hill, you have abused your power and position in the Trust, initiating a sexual relationship with Dr Chen who is junior to you. This is an unacceptable violation of Trust regulations.'

Mr Taylor, a usually affable chap put on his stern face to say, 'Dr Hill, I have reported this matter to the police. Sexual harassment in the workplace will not be tolerated in the Trust. I must ask that you cease your relationship with her pending the police inquiry.'

'How ridiculous! She's 37. She's an intelligent, assertive woman.'

They stared at me in silence.

'West is a highly unorthodox patient. A unique case. He begged me from the start to keep his case off the record. He is very famous. If this his treatment became public it could be a disaster for him. Please respect his confidentiality.'

Dr Sugden replied, 'You are not to see him again. Dr Trenton will be taking over his care. Do not communicate with him. Clear your desk and go home, Dr Hill. Do not return to Trust property until the GMC and the police have investigated this fully.'

'That could take months. How am I going to survive on no pay?'

'You should have considered the consequences of your actions before transgressing.' He pressed his intercom. 'Julie, can you call security to escort Dr Hill to clear his office?'

———◆———

Jean was in tears. I hugged her, saying that it would be all right. She wanted to talk more, but the security guard was breathing down our necks, so I cleared my desk and we said our goodbyes. Leaving with a cardboard box of possessions, I was escorted to my car by Derek, the security guard. As I drove out, the car park attendant avoided eye contact.

———◆———

Suki called me soon after I arrived home. 'I'm being transferred to the Bateman Hospital.'

'That's miles away. North London, isn't it?'

'Too far to commute. I'll have to get a room in the hospital.'

I apologised for the trouble I'd caused her. She wouldn't accept the apology. 'James, I went into this with my eyes fully open. You have done nothing wrong at all with me or with West. Trust the investigations. It will all come out in the wash.'

I didn't share her confidence in the system.

———◆———

Steve called to say he was right behind me, that he would lend me money if I needed it. Phil called to offer his good wishes. He said the staff were behind me but that they'd been told not to visit me. I called my brother-in-law, who suggested I rent my house out and go live with them until it had all blown over.

———◆———

The following week passed slowly. I went to North Wales to do some walking. On top of Mount Snowdon, I could just about make out the hills of Ireland. It was an exceptionally clear day. Maybe I should go across there one day, I thought. Some of my ancestors came from there. I knew little of my family's past. Phone reception was poor but I got emails from Suki. She had moved out of her flat and into a room at the Bateman.

The drive home always seemed longer. It was raining The North Circular Road was busy even in the early hours. Arriving home, there was a car in my driveway. Nga wasn't there to meet me. Suki's shoes were in the hall way. Her coat was on the bannister. Her bag in the kitchen. I put my bags down in the lounge and poured myself a glass of water. I made my way to the bedroom quietly, hoping not to disturb Suki. The spare bedroom was full of cases and boxes.

'James, is that you?' she called out from the bedroom.

I couldn't have been more overjoyed. At the lowest point of my professional life, I had come home to find the smartest and most beautiful of women in my bed. Apparently she had also moved herself in, a development that had not been communicated to me in advance, although that fact did not seem important right now.

'I hope you don't mind James. I found the key in the flower pot. I can't face living in a single room in a hospital again.'

I slipped into bed. 'Suki,' I whispered, 'you are welcome to stay for as long as you like.'

IDENTITY, RACISM, DIVERSITY AND PATRIOTISM

It was a Saturday. Suki and I lay in bed long after waking up. We were beginning to get restless but neither of us had made the effort to be the first to get out to make the coffee. The doorbell rang.

'Who's that?' I said.

Suki rolled over to cuddle me. 'Leave it, James.'

The bell rang again. I could hear voices. I put on my dressing gown and went down to find out.

Phil and Joyce were at the door. Something was wrong. They looked like they were in a hurry. 'James, can we come in? There's something we need to tell you,' said Joyce.

They followed me upstairs to the lounge. I put the coffee on. Suki came down the stairs in a T-shirt and tracksuit bottoms. 'This doesn't look like a social call,' she said.

Between them, Joyce and Phil told us the story. West had run into trouble in Greece. After a few days in Kos, he visited Athens. He'd been wandering around the red light district and got mugged and badly beaten up by an Albanian gang. He narrowly avoided being stabbed, saved only by a Greek gang who came to his rescue. The police put them all in the back of a van. Upon noticing West's injuries, they took him to hospital. He was concussed and told them more than he should have so they diagnosed him as psychotic, pumping him full of drugs.

'Five days ago, he was transferred back here with two police officers. They said he'd been aggressive whilst trying to resist the injections,' said Joyce. 'He's been under Dr Trenton on the Intensive Care Unit. He's on a Section 2 with a diagnosis of schizophrenia.'

'This is awful,' I said, 'but why are you telling me? I'm suspended. I've been told not to see him.' Suki brought in the coffee.

'Look, we know he's not psychotic, James. We believe him when he says who he is. We smuggled him out. We reported him absent without leave. The police are searching for him as we speak,' said Joyce.

'You're joking,' said Suki, laughing.

I walked over to the window, pulled back the curtain. Jean's car was parked outside with West in the back. Jean waved from the front seat. West kept facing forward, wearing a blanket and hat.

'You're nuts. What are you playing at?' said Suki.

'We want you to look after him here. Get him well and keep him out of the limelight. He wants to continue therapy with you James,' said Phil.

'I appreciate the risk you've taken but I'm responsible to the GMC and the Royal College of Psychiatrists, not to mention the law. If I take him in while he's AWOL from a Section 2, diagnosed with schizophrenia, I'll be struck off for good and with a police record, I'll never get a job. I'm not going to drag Suki into this either.'

'James, we're not talking about a psychotic patient who needs medical treatment. West is the consciousness of Western Civilization who is in distress and needs your help to sort himself out. What happens if we don't take him in? Consider that,' said Joyce.

'I could go to prison for this. So could you.' I said.

Everyone looked at me, waiting for my response. I drank some coffee.

'I'm not promising anything. Let me see him. Bring him inside.'

Jean followed West inside and up the stairs to the lounge. His eyes were glazed, his arms stiff. His face was bruised. His top lip swollen. 'I'm sorry James, I couldn't bare to see him in this state. You know what will happen if he stays under Dr Trenton.'

I sat back in my chair and looked at West, sat down on the sofa next to Suki. He was wearing his blue sweatshirt and grey tracksuit bottoms. His shoes didn't match. He was staring into space.

'West, how are you?' I asked.

He grunted, pointing to his cuts and swellings.

'How are they treating you in hospital?'

He shook his head, moaning.

'Can you wait a few months till I'm cleared by the GMC?'

His face dropped. He mumbled, 'If I go.' We tried to make out what he was saying. 'If I go under.' He took a breath. 'If I go under, you will all go down with me.' He started to cry. 'The economy will slide. The dollar will fall. All the frozen conflicts will burst open. Dark forces will be unleashed. A global unravelling.'

My gut tensed. We each looked at one another.

'Food will run short. It will be a choice between foreign domination, anarchy and totalitarianism. The GMC won't matter. Your hospital will cease to function. Your pensions will disappear.'

He sobbed again. Jean looked worried.

'Help me get back on my feet. I have a few days before my enemies notice.' He gritted his teeth and hit his fist against his leg.

I said, 'Does anyone else know he's here?'

They each said no.

'No one can know about this. If they do, none of us will ever work again. We might go to prison and West will be captured as a madman on the run and sent to a secure hospital, probably never to escape. I need everyone here to swear to absolute secrecy.'

In turn, each of them promised.

'West, that goes for you too. You have to stay inside and keep away from the windows. You mustn't make any calls or log in to anything personal on the internet,' I said.

'Yes, I promise,' he said in slightly slurred speech.

'Where's your phone?'

'It's in his locker in the hospital,' said Phil.

'If you come here, you must leave your phone in the hospital or at home and you must check you're not followed. The police will be looking for West.'

West started to cry. He reached out to hold Suki's hand. She stroked his fingers kindly.

———◆———

Over the following days, West gradually returned to normal. I weened him off his anti-psychotic medication and sleeping pills. His body became flexible. He slept for hours. He dutifully kept away from the windows. Suki and I took turns to get him the food and clothes he needed. I saw Suki's maternal side again. I also saw West's strength. He turned himself around quickly.

After five days, West was feeling more himself. Suki started her new job at the Bateman.

On day six of West's stay, he was ready to resume his therapy. When I came down in the morning he had made bacon butties.

'Good Morning James,' He said cheerily, thrusting a coffee into my hand. He was bright eyed and energetic, and I could tell what was coming next.

'I was wondering if it would be OK to start therapy again.'

'I don't see why not,' I said through a greasy mouthful.

'I want to deal with the most delicate and explosive subject on my mind. Racism, immigration, patriotism and identity.'

'Excellent. Let's run a voice dialogue … as soon as I've finished this and had a shower.

———◆———

Standing in the middle of the room, West is red in the face, his fists clenched.

PURPLE (White): I feel like a foreigner in my own country. I used to feel safe. I felt like I belonged. Everyone was poor, but we looked after each other. We had a sense of who we were, what we stood for. In those days people had a feeling of confidence. We used to sing songs to which everyone knew the words.

West looked reluctant to go on. He looked torn, conflicted, unsettled. I wondered if he might suddenly get up and go.

James: What's it?

West: I'm blocking it. GREEN won't let me speak.

James: Let me speak to GREEN directly. Tell me what's going on.

GREEN: He's about to go into a racist rant. It's a tired old stuck record. It's not acceptable. I will not tolerate racism.

PURPLE (White): We know how the Native Americans, aborigines and Maoris must've felt when the Europeans arrived.

James: Who's *we*?

PURPLE (White): White people.

GREEN: You see, he's a racist, I told you. Shut him up.

James: GREEN, you say you believe in diversity, empathy, compassion, respect, hearing all voices and healing. Isn't that true?

GREEN: Yes but I'm not going to let racism go unchallenged.

James: What's racism?

GREEN: Racism is when someone with power and privilege treats someone else differently because of their race.

James: Why do you feel so strongly about this?

GREEN: White people have dominated and abused all the other people of this planet for the last few hundred years. White people shipped millions of Africans across to the Americas as slaves. The Germans exterminated six million Jews. Europeans colonised the other people of the world with their so-called civilising mission which was thuggish racial supremacism.

James: Those things are in the past, aren't they?

GREEN: White people still dominate the world. They're still racist. They exclude others. They think they're superior. White people have an unfair share of the worlds' resources. Workers in sweatshops round the world might as well be slaves. White people interfere in other people's business, invading their countries.

James: This is touching a raw nerve, an emotional wound.

GREEN: That sounds like racist psychiatry to me.

James: I'm observing that on this subject, you have lost your balance, your reason and emotional sensitivity. You've activated your threat system, your amygdala and sympathetic nervous system. It's overriding everything else in you. When we have an intense emotional trigger like that, it often acts as a block to our well-being and human potential. When we carry wounds around, they distort our perceptions and stop us moving forward.

GREEN: Why don't you do some psychotherapy with PURPLE (White) to cure their racism?

James: Can you think of an example where you hold the space for someone, seeing the very best in them, giving them unconditional positive regard and listening, deeply listening?

GREEN: Yes. I volunteer in a prison, befriending a woman who killed her children. I can see past the crime to the wounded soul, the broken person in need of love.

James: Excellent. Imagine yourself in that role. Run it like a video through your mind seeing, hearing and feeling yourself operate with the highest level of love, compassion and non-judgement. Notice your attitude, sensations and intention.

GREEN: OK, James. I get the point. I'll listen. I want to hear from the full diversity of perspectives.

PURPLE (White): In the 60s I felt safe as a young woman. I used to think nothing of walking back from a night out at two in the morning. It never crossed my mind that I might come to any harm. Suddenly, immigrants moved in. There was only one or two at first. Soon, thousands came. They started mugging people, breaking into houses. It was scary. My parents asked, 'Why did we bother to fight in the war against Hitler? What was the point of all that if they can come in and take over?' The police were meant to protect us but they didn't. Now they arrest you for daring to complain about being a second class citizen in your own country. It's getting worse and worse.

GREEN: Don't you realise that we're all human beings? Distinctions of race and nationality are only superficial.

PURPLE (White): The GREEN world view thrives in pleasant places, in people who are insulated from the crime and threat. They don't have to queue up in the doctor's surgery or down at the benefits office, feeling like a foreigner in their own country. Immigration to them means cheap labour, ethnic food, interesting people at their dinner parties. They don't see the dark side of it.

James: Tell me about the dark side.

PURPLE (White): My mother used to work at the Race Relations Board in the 60s. While GREEN was going to its meetings about racism and discrimination by white people, my mother was an ethnic minority in the kitchens there. She said, 'They dislike each other more than they dislike us. The West Africans disrespect the West Indians, the Indians look down on the Africans, the different religions don't get on and the Chinese won't even work there.'

James: What was her point?

PURPLE (White): Human beings are tribal. We stick together with our own. They didn't like us going over there colonising them and we don't like them coming over here colonising us. They're not stupid, they know the game. It's only naive GREEN that lives in a fantasy land where we're all the same. When they are the majority, we'll be persecuted like in other countries and there'll be no human rights protesters or anti-racism campaigners to protect us. We'll be like the Aborigines.

James: Have you never met a non-white person you could be friends with, treat as an equal?

PURPLE (White): Of course. They're human beings like you and me. The point is that underneath all the niceties, humans are tribal and, when the chips are down that means trouble. Look at Rwanda, Yugoslavia and Syria. I don't want that to happen here.

James: It's a democracy with laws. Racism like that isn't allowed.

PURPLE (White): That will last while white people are the majority, because white people believe in that stuff, but within 30 years we're going to be an ethnic minority in our own country and it'll be like a patchwork of colonies manipulated by countries overseas. When the civil war kicks off, wealthy GREEN and ORANGE will get on a plane to safety and leave us to suffer our fate.

James: West, you said it yourself, it's not about black, brown or white, it's about BEIGE, PURPLE, RED, BLUE, ORANGE and GREEN! Surely, it doesn't matter if white people become an ethnic minority? What matters is the values of the people and the institutions.

PURPLE (White): Many minorities have a chip on their shoulder, full of rage and resentment. It's dangerous when they get the upper hand. Look at the crime and gangs in the inner cities.

James: West, we need to do some work on victim thinking, West. You're riddled with it and it's getting in the way of a solution.

West gritted his teeth and pointed his finger at me.

PURPLE (White): Look, Mr Posh doctor, don't patronise me. Ethnic minorities have got more rights than me. They can do anything they like to us, and we have to keep our mouths shut otherwise GREEN comes down on you like the Gestapo.

James: Do you have any evidence for that?

PURPLE (White): Come and live with me. It's been getting worse for 50 years. In the 90s, GREEN opened up the floodgates to all the asylum seekers. The first-generation kept their heads down. They've seen the real world. They know which side their bread is buttered. Their children grew up being taught by all these GREEN teachers to hate us and celebrate the places they come from. They teach them that we enslaved them, destroyed their cultures, took all their resources and pushed them around. So they want to get their own back. If you complain about it, you're called a racist. If we're so bad, why do they all want to come over here? Who's queuing up to get into their countries?

GREEN: You can't complain. You went over there and colonised them. Now the boot's on the other foot.

PURPLE (White): I've been silenced by GREEN for 40 years. All over England, there have been gangs of mainly Pakistani men, paedophiles, grooming, abusing and raping white children.

GREEN: You get paedophiles in all racial groups and backgrounds.

PURPLE (White): Yes you do, but the point is that the perpetrators were virtually all Pakistani. The children were virtually all white. The men said that they saw white people as inferior to them. Can you imagine what would happen if white men were selectively grooming and preying on Pakistani girls. The whole world go up in flames, the whole of the state apparatus would go into action... and so it should, but for those white girls, it didn't. For years, the authorities allegedly colluded with the paedophiles because they were scared of being called racist. The 'you're a racist' weapon is so strong that it can allegedly deter a police officer or social worker from protecting a young girl from a racist, rapist paedophile. How sick is that?

BLUE: It's only since 9/11 that anyone has dared to criticise the totalitarian ideology of multiculturalism. If you dissent, they arrest you or you lose your job. All cultures are equal and to be celebrated apart from our own in our own country. GREEN vilifies us.

James: Are you sure that's not a touch exaggerated?

PURPLE (White): GREEN keeps talking about fairness and equality. I don't see that. Wherever you look, housing, welfare, quotas for jobs, immigrants are getting priority. GREEN keeps inviting in more an more foreigners and then we get treated as second class citizens in our own country.

James: Are the rules not fair?

PURPLE (White): No, love, the multiculturalism rules only apply to the natives. They don't apply them to the others. I'm not allowed to be patriotic, to celebrate my culture. I'm told its exclusive and racist. If I put my flag up, GREEN screams I'm a fascist.

James: Some people find flags offensive, even threatening.

PURPLE (White): I find it offensive that my country is being taken over by foreigners. I find it offensive that I have to suffer crime from PURPLE-RED minorities but GREEN won't let the police do their job. I have to suppress my identity and celebrate theirs, treating them as sacred, beyond criticism.

James: GREEN is seeking to protect people from racism.

PURPLE (White): GREEN itself *is* racist. The ruling class is repeating what they did when they ruled the Empire. From the position of a minority they manage to rule the majority. This time, we're the natives and they're bringing in colonists to divide and rule us. The GREEN wants that so it can impose its equality fantasy on us and assuage its guilt. OR-ANGE is happy because it pulls down wages and workers' rights so it can better exploit us.

James: I'd like to hear more evidence for these assertions.

PURPLE (White): Take that Salman Rushdie business. If you had a load of white right-wing Conservatives burning a book, the full force of the law and media would come down on top of them. When the right-wing conservatives happen to be from ethnic minorities, they protect and appease them.

> *GREEN looks uncomfortable.*

PURPLE (White): What about when a GREEN (Sikh) playwright put on a GREEN play in Birmingham? A mob of PURPLE-RED (Sikhs) went to the theatre and used intimidation to close it down. GREEN gave in to them. They let a violent, PURPLE-RED minority impose their will by force. The police got down on their knees to talk to these self-appointed community leaders instead of enforcing the law and upholding freedom of speech. They surrendered democracy and freedom for the sake of a quiet night and to avoid the risk of being called racist.

James: Shouldn't the police talk to community leaders?

PURPLE (White): What's a community leader? Isn't it meant to be your MP? These old-fashioned men, whose minds are still living in the past in the country that they came from, want to act like tribal leaders, extracting concessions and making threats against their weak GREEN overlords. GREEN acts like it's the magnanimous Viceroy of India, handing over power to Gandhi. It isn't. This is England, our home. We're not de-colonising the Empire any more, we *are* the natives.

BLUE: We need a Mrs Thatcher from a minority group to sort things out.

James: GREEN, thank you for your patience.

PURPLE (Indian): I'm a financier for Bollywood films visiting London. Every time I come over here, I see ever more foreigners. Your television is full of programmes cele-brating other cultures. This is one of the best countries in the world. Don't you realise that it only took 2000 British civil servants and 100,000 British, soldiers to rule 350 million Indians for a 200 years? What makes you so arrogant to think that that only works in one direction? India is going to become very powerful and you're getting weaker.

ORANGE: Let's be objective. We live in a global marketplace. Business needs to have the best people with the best skills to compete. I don't care what nationality, colour or religion they are. I care about their skills, the character and attitude. Why do you think immigrants make better workers? They're disciplined. They're willing to work hard. They've got what we used to call the Protestant Work Ethic. Many people thought they've got some divine right to be at the top of the hierarchy. Wake up, smell the cof-fee. It's time for them to get off their lazy backsides and get themselves educated, be disciplined, be creative, focus on solutions not problems, take risks and take charge of their destiny. Everyone is equal now and if you rest on your laurels, you will be left behind in the dust. The future doesn't have any tribe, nations or races.

ORANGE-PURPLE (Canadian-Indian): I came to Toronto to do a Ph.D. in elec-tronic engineering. I did well in Hyderabad but I knew that over here there were more opportunities, better pay and I wanted to see the world, I wanted to get away from my family for a while, make some money and get on in life. I took up a job in IT.

James: Are you Indian or Canadian?

ORANGE-PURPLE (Canadian-Indian): My passports are Indian and Canadian but, in my heart, I'm Indian, a Hindu. I'm close to my family and feel kinship with other Indians. I'm feeling more Canadian. I love the culture here. It's so friendly, open-minded.

James: What did you think of what PURPLE (White) said?

ORANGE-PURPLE (Canadian-Indian): I understand it. I'd feel the same. People are moving all over the world. We may as well get used to it. It won't be long before we're global citizens. I'm not interested in taking over Canada, but I can understand why they might worry that others might be.

ORANGE-BLUE (Nigerian-British): I grew up in Lagos, went to a British school and an Anglican church. We speak English. My father was a judge trained in English law. My mother is a nurse, educated in the British system. I grew up watching British TV programmes. It was only natural that I would want to come to England.

James: Has your British dream come true?

ORANGE-BLUE (Nigerian-British): Yes. I found a lovely British wife and have two children now. We live in Peckham – little Nigeria. It's very lively. I love my local church. I am British.

James: What do you like about your new home?

ORANGE-BLUE (Nigerian-British): The honesty, the rules. The people back home are more alive. This British can be reserved but Britain is safe and you know that you can trust the authorities, they're not corrupt. That makes a big difference. You are free to pursue your own destiny.

James: Thank you. Is there a voice from the BLUE system?

BLUE (British-Arab): Hello.

James: What brought you to London?

BLUE (British-Arab): I come from a large wealthy family. I could have stayed at home and never worked, but I couldn't bear the oppressive atmosphere in my family or society. I love England because the law protects your human rights and you can trust it. It doesn't get twisted by the government, by bribery or who your uncle knows. The whole atmosphere is secure. I can think whatever I like, say whatever I like. That's not true at home. I can see a great future in London. You can be yourself, you can feel comfortable in your own skin without constantly justifying who you are. Women have got rights. The schools educate my children rather than teaching them about religion.

James: Are you still connected with your family?

BLUE (British-Arab): Yes, I visit them and they visit me. My husband went home. He was used to throwing his weight around back home because he was wealthy and connected to the right families. He hated being boxed in by all the rules.

RED-PURPLE (African-American): At least the PURPLE (White) is honest, she says what she thinks. ORANGE is colour-blind but doesn't realise how much privilege they have, how they're already established with all the skills, knowledge, networks, family money and schools. How can I compete with that? This isn't a level playing field. GREEN loves to have me as a pet victim. That suits them fine until I want to go out with their daughter or move next door to them, then they show their true colours, deep PURPLE.

James: You feel excluded. The cards are stacked against you?

RED-PURPLE (African-American): You bet. If ORANGE spoke to me the way it spoke to PURPLE (White), I'd tell him a thing or two.

James: Like what?

RED-PURPLE (African-American): They tell us to shape up, pull our bootstraps up, play the game, but how would they like to play the game with one hand tied behind your back and the other players starting half way to the finish line – and if you dare challenge them, they get the rulebook out and stitch you up?

James: I wouldn't.

RED-PURPLE (African-American): If you're born black in America, you're a second-class citizen. You grow up with poor housing, crime, poor schools, violence and drugs all around. The police hassle you, but don't protect you from the street gangs. If you go for a job, people see your address, your name or your face and tell you that the position is filled already. Then they complain when they get mugged.

James: Do you think that white people deserve to be mugged?

RED-PURPLE (African-American): They've mugged us for hundreds of years, every day of the week. It's payback time. Time for them to give up their privilege. Latinos too. The border is like a sieve. There are more Hispanics now than African-Americans. They're pushing us out, taking our jobs. They're carrying on as if they're still in Latin America, speaking Spanish, all sticking together. At least many of the whites feel guilty for the way they treated us.

James: What about the other minorities?

RED-PURPLE (African-American): Everyone is out for themselves. The Jews, the Japanese, the Koreans, even the Indians are like honorary white people, getting on and leaving us behind. We need reparations for slavery. We need that historical crime put right. White people must pay for the crimes of their ancestors.

PURPLE (British): Every culture has been involved in slavery and colonialism at some time. The difference between us and the rest is that we stopped it and then went about stopping others doing it. GREEN can take credit for that.

James: Don't you think it's reasonable to pay African-Americans and the Caribbean countries reparations for slavery?

PURPLE (British): Why? I didn't do it. My family didn't do it. How is it that all white people now have to bear the responsibility for what a few white people did 200 years ago? No one wants to take responsibility for all the crimes that are going on right now in our city. That's racist. It's like saying that because someone who knew your great-great-grandfather committed arson, you deserve to have your house burnt down.

James: That's true, it's victim mentality, but it's not that simple. Modern-day Westerners benefit from the institutions, the advantages and the wealth of the country which was partly contributed to by the profits made from slavery and colonisation.

PURPLE (British): If we're playing this game, the Romans, Dutch and Normans owe us for the death, destruction and exploitation during their occupations of Britain. The Danes and Norwegians owe us for Viking plunder and pillage. The Spanish owe us for coastal raids and unfair trade barriers. The Germans owe us for two devastating World Wars. The Japanese owe us for killing, torture and occupation in the Far East. The Moroccans, Algerians and Tunisians owe us for taking European slaves for centuries. The Russians owe us for the immense cost of the Cold War. The Americans owe us for their profiteering during World Wars I & II and commercial exploitation since.

How much should we pay the Arabs for mathematics? How are the Syrians going to put a price on written language? I have half Irish blood so do I have to compensate myself for the actions of my ancestors against my ancestors? You see, this approach is never ending. It turns everyone into a deserving victim who demands compensation from imagined perpetrator. It encourages people to be victims and to be racist. It's a recipe for resentment, violence and conflict.

James: You mentioned the positives. What are they?

PURPLE (British): Americans, Australians, Canadians, New Zealanders, South Africans, Singaporeans, Hong Kongers and the rest of the world owe us about 100 trillion by now for providing their ideas, culture, technology, language, people, security, economy, law, institutions, education, liberal enlightenment, science, railways, Civil Service, military and democracy.

James: Slavery isn't just a historical phenomenon. It's going on today in many forms? All over Africa and the Middle East. Even here at home in the shadows.

RED-PURPLE (African-American): You mean like Boko Haram in Nigeria abducting those 200 schoolgirls for marriage?

James: Yes, but that's the tip of the iceberg. There are millions of slaves across Africa. Chattel slaves. Sex slaves. Owned servants. Here in the West there are women trafficked and held in slavery for prostitution. The Middle East and Asia have many slaves today, out of sight, out of mind.

RED-PURPLE (African-American): I didn't know. That's awful.

James: Now you do, what are you going to do about it?

RED-PURPLE (African-American): I'm just one poor person. I have no money, influence or power. I'm busy with my own life. It's up to governments and the police to deal with slavery.

James: Do you think that all of your descendants should be held responsible for your inaction on current day slavery? Do you think that all future Africans in Africa should be eternally shamed for the inaction of current day Africans to end the current day slavery?

RED-PURPLE (African-American): Of course not.

James: You are wealthier, better informed, more free, better educated and more powerful than the vast majority of people who lived at the time of the Atlantic Slave trade? You are free to demonstrate in the streets. You can organise and protest if you really care.

GREEN (German): No one has mentioned the 'F' word. Forgiveness. The Nazis killed 6 million Jews in a calculated, planned act of genocide. They killed 50% of the world's population of Jews within living memory. Yet, the large majority of the living people who suffered and lost relatives have forgiven the German people in their own lifetimes. It has been a painful process but they have got on with their lives and quickly got back on their feet to be one of the most successful, dynamics, tolerant and creative people on earth. Germans and Jews are friends once more. It's astonishing. The Jews both in Israel and in the West have got on with their lives and become a successful and integral part of society.

PURPLE (Native American): My grandfather told me the white man had brought the seeds of his own destruction with him. He saw that the way that they lived wasn't right.

James: What did he mean?

PURPLE (Native American): Before they came, we used to live in harmony with nature, in small groups. The immigrants were well organised and had money and weapons. They defeated us and broke our spirit. We turned to drink and gambling.

James: What did your grandfather mean the white man had brought the seeds of his destruction with him?

PURPLE (Native American): You can see it in their eyes. They've lost their spirits, like we did. All the science, technology, possessions and activity. They're desperate to find themselves but they won't sit still and listen. It's what happens if you detach from the spirits to live in the material world like a machine. We used to be majestic beings, like a soaring eagle or magnificent bear.

James: Can we recover in time?

PURPLE (Native American): Yes but not while ORANGE has its hands on the controls. Get back to nature, connect with the divine.

James: What are the steps in the right direction?

West shifts in his seat.

ORANGE: James, from your medical training, are there any biological differences between racial groups?

James: The quick answer is *no*. There are a few differences for medical purposes. We should treat race as unimportant, a confounding variable.

PURPLE (White): What's a confounding variable?

James: It means that race can appear to be a cause but it isn't, there's some deeper cause. If you look at the statistics for crime, poverty and employment, you will see variations between racial groups. These differences have little to do with the colour of someone's skin and are caused by other variables. Focusing on race gets in the way of solving underlying issues and creates hostility and division unnecessarily.

RED-PURPLE (African-American): That's easy for you to say. They *do* treat me differently according to the colour of my skin. That affects my health, wealth, freedom and opportunity. We have got to stamp out racism.

PURPLE (White): Let's start with yours.

James: Stop right there. BLUE, we haven't heard from you.

BLUE: Everyone wants to live in the nicest places with the best jobs and highest quality of life, that's natural. Anyone can get on a plane and be anywhere within 24 hours. If I opened the borders, we would be overwhelmed with millions overnight. How do I keep order amidst the chaos? How could I run the housing, health, welfare, education and taxation? We need strict boundaries.

GREEN: It's time you embraced the rich diversity of life.

BLUE: We need cohesion too. We can't all live separate lives, loads of different people coming and going as if we were travellers in Heathrow airport.

James: 50 million people pass through there every year, Heathrow airport is well run. It has one of the most diverse bunches of people ever and they all get along very well.

BLUE: Yes, but Heathrow is neither an anarchy nor a democracy. It's a highly organised, top-down hierarchy with rules, structures and strict security. No one is allowed to be there unless they have a clear role or unless they've paid for the privilege.

James: Can I speak to British PURPLE?

West nods and goes straight there

PURPLE (British): We're a tribe. We love football, sport, Shakespeare. We have the oldest universities in the world. We have a long tradition of freedom of thought, being a safe haven. That's why our financial sector is so strong. People trust us. The Queen is our Chief, a magical mummy, our fairy Godmother. She embodies the tribe. Bizarrely, it's more democratic to have a Queen because she is there for all of us equally and the politicians, those RED parasites, have to kneel down before her and be reminded that they're just passing through. Our Parliament and democracy run deep. The British have asserted their freedom ever since Magna Carta in 1215, the will of the people has been towards ever greater freedom and democracy. That spirit to challenge authority while respecting authority has helped us to evolve and mature democracy.

James: There was nothing democratic about the British Empire.

PURPLE (British): That's very true, and in a very typically British way, it's also not true.

James: Explain.

PURPLE (British): By definition, an Empire isn't democratic. It has an Emperor or Empress at the top and a pyramid of warriors underneath, enforcing their will. In those days, most people in the world were still in the PURPLE tribal stage of development. That's why the British were so successful. We were aggressive, well-organised RED warriors, harnessed by BLUE organisation empowered by ORANGE finance and technology. So, it was relatively easy to dominate the world by kicking the local chiefs off their perch and replacing them with one of our own. PURPLE thinking people accepted that. That was the way the world was.

James: It still isn't sounding very democratic to me.

PURPLE (British): It was asymmetrical. The amazing developments of the Industrial Revolution, the Enlightenment, science and medicine freed people up to go into the ORANGE system themselves and make the best of their life. The British settlers in America, Canada, Australia, New Zealand and South Africa advanced faster than the British back home because they didn't have so much heavy BLUE and PURPLE to hold them back. In the end, the colonised peoples emerged from PURPLE to RED. This ignited their drive to fight for their freedom and satisfy their impulses. They were no longer willing to be told what to do, particularly by foreigners. They acquired their knowledge and the economic ability to push for independence. We had put in place all the systems such as law, justice, transport and education which enabled them to climb the ladder. GREEN thinking had already begun to take root in the upper classes who lost the belief in their right to rule. They became embarrassed about imperialism and tribal superiority and they lost the RED fire in the belly.

James: You're saying that, by accident, the British Empire pushed the world towards higher levels of development and, indirectly, democracy?

PURPLE (British): Yes. I'm very proud of that. It wasn't just indirectly either. Britain established representative assemblies and local democracy in its colonies. The assumption was always that the locals would get educated and rule themselves. The only debate was over the time scale.

ORANGE: If you want to be patriotic, if you want to emulate the values of all of those inventors, scientists, explorers and adventurous warriors, then wake up to the world as it's now, stop living in the past. If any of them were alive now, they wouldn't be wasting their time wallowing in the faded glories of history. They'd be out, competing, innovating and trying to get ahead now.

James: Thank you very much. Any other voices?

BLUE(British-Ugandan-Indian): I came here 40 years ago when Idi Amin kicked us out of Uganda. I had to leave behind my businesses and possessions. We were very lucky, because we knew the British system and respected it. I learnt a lot from the Jews. They had arrived 40 years before me and they had made a real success of themselves. I saw that they valued hard work, education and, above all, integration.

James: What's integration?

BLUE(British-Ugandan-Indian): We respect the British way of life, laws and customs and mix the best with our own.

GREEN: I've held my tongue for long enough.

James: Please go ahead.

GREEN: White people have caused so much harm to others. I've spent years deconstructing whiteness, Western hegemony, patriarchy, racism and the imperialist mindset. We need multiculturalism. It's the best way to hold down all those old primitive racists and nationalists, so we can give the others a fair chance – allow others in without forcing them to assimilate into a racist culture.

James: You speak as if you're not white or Western – as if you're somehow separate from it all.

GREEN: I hate being associated with those past abuses. I want to have nothing to do with it. I want to permanently destroy that evil culture so that it can never take hold again.

James: Do you hold yourself personally responsible for the sins of the past?

GREEN: Of course not. Most of me wasn't around then. It was GREEN values that helped to undermine all of those old structures from the inside.

James: It sounds like you're still carrying guilt and shame – maybe still some repressed racism?

GREEN: How dare you say that? I've spent my life vigorously opposing racism.

James: Did you hear RED (African-American)? He doesn't trust you. He thinks that you're still racist underneath the pious surface. Maybe that's why you're so aggressive when challenged?

GREEN: Who could be more devoted than me to eradicating racism, imperialism and injustice? I've done the best I can to redress inequalities. There's much more to do. Every time a fascist or racist voice is raised, I aggressively slap it down.

James: Your sincerity is obvious. I sense that in your desperate rush to distance yourself from the past, you've not fully processed it or completely let it go.

GREEN: That's ridiculous. I suspect that you're a racist.

West gives a shudder as GREEN storms out. He looks much more calm now.

James: The GREEN value system is fantastic but it's not mature yet. We've got to help the GREEN world view release its shadow racism, shame and guilt which it has repressed and projected onto others. That's the key to enabling GREEN to make healthy judgements, assert healthy boundaries and distinguish adaptive and maladaptive behaviour.

West: And what does the PURPLE world view need to do?

James: The old ethnicities like German, Italian, Canadian, Australian have to let go of a lost past, a real past and a nostalgic, romanticised past. They must make room for new people, and invite ethnic minorities to join them in a new emerging tribe.

West: What would you do if a patient came to you and said that they hated themselves and wanted to kill themselves because they weren't perfect and they done some bad things in the past?

James: I'd want to know exactly what they did, in what context with what intent. I'd want to know what has happened since then. Have they apologised? Have they sought and received forgiveness? Have they let go of their guilt and shame? Have they changed their ways and lived in a better way since? I'd want to appreciate all the strengths and virtues of the person.

West: That's exactly what we need here.

James: We can't rewrite history, heal every wound or to right every wrong. Forgiveness is required so that all of your parts are free to reach their fullest potential and most adaptive expression.

ESCAPING THE VICTIM-PERPETRATOR-RESCUER TRIANGLE

Suki had begun to settle into her new job well. She was able to spend three nights per week at my house. She was comfortable around West. Nga was more wary. She would sit at the other side of the room and observe him with interest.

West had settled into my home surprisingly easily. I thought he might be too intense but he was happy to watch TV and surf the internet. He slept like a teenager. He was helpful with household chores and respected my privacy.

As the second week passed, West started to become more irritable. He would stay up late into the night and was erratic in his eating habits. He polished off my brandy one night and the following day I took an opportunity to corner him in the kitchen.

James: How are you, West?

West: I'm going round in circles, feeling angry and hopeless. There are three loud voices that are bothering me. The anti-immigration, fearful one, the anti-racist, multi-culturalism voice and the angry minority voice. They know every argument, every counter-argument and seem to enjoy the fight.

James: Imagine those three voices. What do they look like?

West: All three are puffed up like giant dragons, breathing fire at each other, with hate in their eyes.

James: Now imagine yourself asking them, 'I know what you're against, what you don't want, but I'd like to know what you DO want? If you could fast-forward to a world in which all your beliefs, dreams and values come true, what would that be like?'

West closes his eyes. He stands silent for several minutes. Eventually he begins to laugh.

James: What's funny?

West: I asked the anti-racist one. He visibly softened, relaxed and appeared to shrink in size. I don't think he had ever considered that question before. He answered 'a world without racism.' Then I asked what else. He said, 'a world without sexism.' He went on to say, one by one, a world without all the -isms. I then said, 'I agree with you on those but those the absence of something bad. What positively would that world be like?' He completely deflated like a windsock with no wind. The giant dragon had become a little man, with no idea what he wanted.

James: What about the others, how did they respond?

West: At first they were incredibly smug, especially the anti-immigration one. But he then said to the anti-racist one, 'I've spent my life hating you for what you've done and feeling powerless to stop you. If only I'd realised that that little question could make you lose all your power and fall silent. The only problem is that I can't answer that question myself either!' The wronged ethnic minority voice laughed and said, 'Me neither.'

West is looking peaceful, like a burden has been taken off his shoulders.

James: Have you heard of the book 'Games People Play?'

West: Yes, by Eric Berne. We all have scripts about how the world works. We get stuck in those patterns, playing games.

James: That's it. For example, the victim script. Dr Karpman described the Drama Triangle where the victim, the perpetrator and the rescuer get stuck in an ongoing cycle of fighting each other.

West: You're saying the three voices are in the victim triangle?

James: Yes.

West: Isn't that patronising? Victims exist. Bad things do happen.

James: Of course they do. If you're a victim of a fire you certainly want the fire brigade to come to your rescue. Bad things do happen to people and they need help. Sometimes we all, me included, get into victim mentality where we get stuck in the psychology of the wound and it blocks us from healing or from getting a resolution, stops us with getting on with our lives.

West: Can you give an example?

James: I had a patient with depression. When I visited his house, the lounge was like an office, crammed full of files on shelves all over the walls. He was furious that he'd been wrongly dismissed from his job 30 years earlier. He was determined to tell me every detail as if it had happened yesterday. He pulled down many files to show me the evidence of the wrongful dismissal. He kept saying how he would never let it go until he had got justice.

West: I can understand that.

James: He had already pursued all the legal avenues open to him and had been told that there was no case for compensation. He wouldn't accept that.

West: No wonder he was depressed.

James: I asked him what he'd been doing with his life otherwise over the 30 years. He had never found a new job, never made a relationship stick and had little pleasure. He couldn't get over his loss and so he relived the wound every day. Life passed him by.

West: Could you help him?

James: I tried to persuade him to let it go and focus on what he did have and on his future but I could tell that he still wasn't ready. You can't make someone change. They have to discover it for themselves. My colleagues had tried antidepressants and cognitive therapy but to no avail.

West: How does this relate to racism and immigration?

James: Each of the players have got their own emotional wound..

West: Is it possible for me to do a voice dialogue on this? I'm not sure what characters to summon up for this one. It's not a simple case of GREEN or PURPLE or whatever is it? I mean, people's emotional wounds are very personal.'

James: I don't see why we shouldn't use voice dialogue all the same. Don't worry about the characters, just let them come. There are hundreds of millions of voices inside you just waiting to express themselves..'

West finds some space in the middle of the kitchen prepares himself.

James: Ready? OK. Ask each voice to choose a particular character and come forward.

Agatha: I'm Agatha from Africa, a PhD student at the London School of Economics.

Peter: I'm Peter an anti-racist, pro-diversity campaigner.

Patricia: I'm Patricia, a housewife and mother from Essex.

James: Excellent. Agatha, tell me about yourself.

Agatha: I'm 28, I'm doing a PhD on International Development. I love London because it's so diverse, such a global hub of activity. I love the freedom and opportunities. There's a great cultural life.

James: How do you view the other characters?

Agatha: I don't like Patricia. She doesn't like me. She's a racist. She is careful not to say it out loud but I know that I'm not welcome, that she would send me back home if she could.

James: And Peter?

Agatha: Peter is a nice guy. It's because of people like Peter that I can come here and be treated fairly well. Nice as he is, these British will never let us join them. I'm happy being African. There are so many foreigners here that it's more of a global city. Only 45% are white British now. They're a minority already and among the young, even fewer.

James: Thanks Agatha. Can I talk to Peter?

Peter: Hi. I'm Peter. I'm a liberal, more towards the left. I love the diversity we've created in London. It's exciting to be in a place buzzing with so many languages and cultures. It's so much better than the old white Britain of the past. There's still racism in our institutions and among the white people. Some pockets of the country are still horribly white but we're getting there.

James: Thanks Peter. What do you think about the other two?

Peter: I warm to Agatha. I celebrate her courage to move to another country and to overcome the barriers of racism to study at a top university. I welcome the enrichment she brings to London with her different perspectives. Patricia, I don't like. She is stuck in the past. She's the bad old Britain we're trying to get away from. Racist, prejudiced, parochial, fearful, wanting to take us back to the past. I'm determined to stop her.

James: Thanks Peter. And Patricia?

Patricia: The feeling is mutual. I don't wish Agatha any harm. She's probably a pleasant lady but I'd rather she went home. There are too many foreigners over here.

James: What about Peter?

Patricia: He is a nasty piece of work. I don't understand him. Why is he so determined to fill our country with foreigners and make us British second class citizens? I feel powerless because people like him run the media, education system and government. They pump out propaganda and vilify anyone who disagrees with them.

James: Does it bother you that they both dislike you so intensely?

Patricia: They've been ganging up on me for 50 years so I'm used to it. I can't lay down and let them walk all over me. This country will be like Bosnia or Syria in 30 years. I'm afraid for my children.

Agatha: West came to Africa, as adventurers, missionaries and traders. He took our land, resources and imposed his rule by force. He exploited us and denigrated our culture. We had a proud and rich culture but West treated us as second-class citizens. West taught us that his ideas were superior. He advanced Christianity though we had our own spiritual traditions.

James: Were there any benefits of West coming to Africa?

Agatha: No.

Patricia: What about science, technology, the rule of law, democracy, connection to the rest of the world, trains, hospitals, modern medicine, education, modern agriculture, a global language, mining, a police force, the suppression of slavery, Christianity and investment?

She laughs.

Agatha: Is this a Monty Python sketch? West brought those things for their own benefit so they could exploit us more. It would be better if West had never come to Africa. We would have developed without them in our own way.

James: How does it affect you, 50 years after independence?

Agatha: I suffer racism every day. I feel it under the surface. Westerners will never let me become one of them, even if I wanted to. There's always a barrier. They still think that we're inferior.

James: What about Peter and people like him?

Agatha: They're trying to offload their guilt. They like to have black friends so that they can say they're not racist.

James: Why did you come to London?

Agatha: LSE is one of the top universities in the world.

James: What is your Ph.D. about?

Agatha: Governance in Africa as a foundation for democracy and economic development.

James: Tell me about your family.

Agatha: My father owns a copper mine. My mother teaches in Singapore. One brother's in Sydney learning law. My sister's an accountant in Cape Town. Another brother's in Silicon Valley.

James: How did your family come to do so well?

Agatha: Under Western rule, my grandfather received an education and became a judge. My other grandfather owned some tribal lands where a Western company found huge copper deposits.

James: Where did you go to school?

Agatha: A boarding school in England.

James: I've heard the Chinese have taken an interest in Africa.

Agatha: They're building things and doing business. There are main customer for my father's copper. They keep to themselves.

James: What happened to the indigenous people back home?

Agatha: We are the indigenous people.

James: I mean the hunter-gatherers who were driven off the land, like the North American Indians.

Agatha: That wasn't taught at school.

James: Were you aware that Africa was dominated by Arab and African Empires before West arrived?

Agatha: Three wrongs don't make a right.

James: West, I'd like to lay out my hypothesis as to whats going on and then suggest a way forward.

West: Go ahead.

James: In Agatha's world, she is a victim of racism, exclusion, imperialism. Patricia is representative one of the racist perpetrators and Peter is an anti-racist rescuer, though she suspects he is a closet perpetrator using her for his own purposes. In Peter's world, Agatha is a victim of racism, imperialism, patriarchy and class oppression. He sees himself as a rescuer, her protector against the likes of Patricia who's the perpetrator, the racist dominating majority. In Patricia's world, she is the victim. She sees herself as someone whose country has been invaded, taken over by Agatha with the collusion of co-perpetrator Peter. She wishes she had a rescuer-probably an anti-immigration, nationalist politician.

West: Which one is right?

James: All of them and none of them. They each are right from within their own perspective but none of them genuinely understands the others and none of them are able to find their way out of the deadlock. All three add fuel to the fire. People move between positions on the drama triangle between victim, perpetrator and rescuer. It's unusual for anyone to think of themselves as a perpetrator. When they attack someone, they believe that they're getting in there first to avoid being made a victim or they're getting revenge or retribution for a perceived injustice.

West: Nice.

James: Victims often become perpetrators. People who have suffered abuse often go on to be abusers. It's a self-perpetuating cycle.

West: With a high level of immigration plus low birth rates in the majority population, Patricia will soon be an ethnic minority so will have less power.

James: That's true, but won't solve the problem. If you do nothing, the tensions will become greater as Patricia feels ever more frightened. Besides, the same dynamic is likely to be operating between all the different ethnic minority subgroups, so you do need to get a grip on this.

West: It has been very hard to do because the GREEN system has vigorously suppressed any discussion. Peter has made it taboo if not illegal for Patricia to speak and has used the state apparatus to enforce his value system.

James: Sure. That's why you're here. If I'm right, I think that Patricia, Peter and Agatha all have got some emotional wounds.

West: How can you say? They're imaginary characters.

James: I know. They represent the wound in your group consciousness. Patricia feels that her security and identity have been violated and she has lost her past, partly real, partly imagined, in which she felt safety and togetherness. She blames the others for this and is acting out of this wound which causes her both anger and sadness. The fear is linking to some primitive circuits in her limbic system, including the amygdala and this triggers her sympathetic nervous system.

West: What's that go to do with it?

James: When she is thinking about race and immigration, she loses her objectivity, feels intensely threatened and relives her wound in the present. In that fear state, she can't hear the others, can't think rationally and blocks the loving human connection which is necessary for people to operate at their highest potential.

West: It's not pleasant to be with someone who's angry or fearful.

James: Exactly. Her anger triggers rejection and hostility in the others so she never feels heard or acknowledged, which in turn makes her more angry.

West: That's a recipe for violence.

James: Yes. As a junior doctor I was called to many violent incidents. In most cases, a simple formula worked. Security must come first. Everyone has to feel safe. The nurses are very well trained so they can bring down a huge, aggressive man in a safe and humane way. Usually that wasn't necessary. The number one priority was to get the aggressive person to feel acknowledged, respected, heard and understood. Nine times out of ten, the person would relax, settle and become available for a reasonable conversation. Often the problem was something simple like an argument over their feeling of being slighted.

West: This is why Peter uses political correctness to shut down Patricia. He's afraid that if she unleashes her fear, anger and prejudices, then violence will ensue.

James: He's right to be very cautious because this subject is inflammatory. Dismissing people disrespectfully and ignoring their legitimate concerns stores up trouble. I'd like to take each voice in turn, release the emotions, try to heal the wounds.

That evening, Suki went out to collect a Thai takeaway for the three of us. West and I watched the news. The doorbell rang. West got up to let Suki in. I stopped him. I opened the door. My heart leapt. Two police officers were standing there.

'Hello Officers,' I said as loudly as I could. 'How can I help?'

One was a man in his 20s, PC Strode, thin and naive looking. man The other, Sergeant Bingham, a woman about 35, more savvy. 'May we come in?'

I've never seriously broken the law before. A few speeding and parking fines. I led the way up the stairs. The game was up, I thought. As I opened the lounge door, West had gone. The police officers sat down. I offered to make them a drink. They said no. I made an excuse to go to the toilet. Upstairs, West was hiding under his bed. I mimed to him to stay put. I flushed the toilet and returned downstairs.

Sergeant Bingham said, 'I expect you know why we're here?'

I nodded. 'Have you found West yet?'

'No, do you have any idea where he might be? Does he have any family or friends for example?' said Sergeant Bingham.

I said, 'I don't know. I believe his parents are dead and he has no partner or children. We never spoke about friends.'

'Do you know his address, Doctor Hill?' said PC Strode.

'I'm sorry, I never asked and it wasn't recorded,' I replied.

'Isn't that very unusual, Dr Hill?'

'Yes, very, but West is an unusual patient. He wanted very strict assurances about his confidentiality and I respected that.'

Suki arrived back from the takeaway. I met her on the stairs, putting my finger to my lips silently. I introduced her to the police officers.

'That's a lot of takeaway for two!' said the Sergeant.

'I love to have the left overs cold the next day,' replied Suki.

'If you hear anything about him or if he makes contact with you, please let us know.'

'We certainly shall,' I said. 'Let me show you out.'

'Actually doctor, there is one other matter. We have come to take a statement from you both regarding the allegation of sexual harassment made by the Meadows Trust against you.' She asked to speak to us separately and took a statement from each of us. 'Thank you doctors. I'll have to report this to my seniors but it all sounds reasonable to me. Probably a misunderstanding.'

'It's not a misunderstanding Sergeant,' said Suki. 'It's a deliberate misrepresentation by Dr Sugden who has been looking for an opportunity to drive James out of the Trust. He is completely innocent. It's me who pursued him, me who telephoned him, me who initiated the relationship and me who chose to move in.'

'I should watch out, Dr Hill, if I were you,' joked PC Strode, winking at me. His senior frowned at him. They thanked us both and left.

When they had driven away, Suki waited five minutes then called West down. We ate together in silence. The Thai green curry was amazing.

PATRICIA: FROM FEAR & ANGER TO LOVE

After three weeks, my savings were already running low. Suki offered to pay the bills. I took her out to the cinema to try and restore my self-respect. When we returned, West was nowhere to be seen. We drove around searching for him.

An hour later, he slipped in the back door. 'Only me!'

'Where the hell have you been? You'll get us into terrible trouble.'

'I was desperate for some fresh air. Sorry.'

'If you want to go out, it must be at night, to a discrete location.'

'It's all right. I made a few phone calls while I was out. The section has been lifted and the police won't trouble you again.'

'Who did you speak to?'

'It's best if I keep some things to myself, James. I'm going to go home now. Would you mind coming to a hotel near me to complete the therapy? I'd cover your costs. What do you think?'

'All right. It should only be a few more sessions. Where do you live exactly?'

'Windsor. I'll book a suite tomorrow afternoon at the Magna Carta Hotel on the river.'

———————————◆———————————

The following morning Suki arrived home from a night shift to find me snoozing on the sofa. She looked tired. She didn't say hello to me but walked straight into the kitchen. I heard her open the fridge. I jumped out of my skin as she bellowed, 'James, there is nothing to eat. You have eaten everything.'

'Sorry love, I've been busy.'

'Busy? Busy with what? I've been working my arse off in the Emergency Department for three days and I come home to you sleeping on the sofa and an empty fridge.' She walked quickly out of the kitchen and stomped down the stairs. 'Maybe you should get a non-medical job while you're waiting for the GMC,' she shouted. The front door slammed. Her car door slammed. She drove off.

While she was out, two letters arrived in the post. I opened the official looking one first. 'Please attend the Fitness to Practise Panel at 9am on Monday 14th April. Be aware that the proceedings are open to the public and the media.' I felt deeply sick. I didn't trust them one bit. How could they even begin to believe West's story? I wouldn't if I hadn't met him.

The other letter was in a fancy envelope. It was a last-minute invitation to the wedding of my old patient Alan Miller and his fiancée, Janet. They must have had drop-outs, but I didn't mind being an afterthought. I just really fancied getting out of the house to have some fun, and hoped Suki would feel the same. I wondered whether my suit still fitted. The wedding was on the coming Saturday and there might not be time to look for another. I'd put on quite a bit of weight around the middle since its last outing – I'm a terror for comfort eating.

A text arrived while I was rereading the invitation. 'Sorry darling, x. Run me a bath and put the oven on.'

Suki returned home with several shopping bags. She put them down in front of me in the lounge. 'James, pack that away and make me some dinner. I am going to take a bath.' As she left, I gave her the invitation card to read. She took it without comment.

She came down after her bath in my dressing gown and showing signs of a much more relaxed mood. 'Mmmmmmm what's cooking?' she said.

'The roast chicken,' I said. I handed her a glass of white wine and some pistachio nuts.

'That's very exciting about the wedding,' she said, stretching out her foot for me to massage. 'To be invited as a couple I mean. Will you come shopping with me on Thursday night?' she asked and pointed to my expanding midriff. 'You're going to need a bigger suit.'

<hr>

We drove over to the Magna Carta Hotel in the afternoon. It had a magnificent position on the banks of the River Thames at Runnymede. I went out the back to the veranda from where there was an excellent view of the river. There were trees on both sides. It gave a hint of what the scene may have looked like in the days before the human population exploded. Something caught my attention. I couldn't believe my eyes. West was rowing himself across the river.

'James, welcome to Windsor!'

I caught the rope and gave him a hand out of his boat.

'I live over there.' He pointed to a red houseboat moored on the other side of the river on a small island.

'So, the Magna Carta was signed somewhere round here was it?' I asked.

'Yes, there on the river bank of the Thames at the base of Runnymede hill. I remember it well.'

'You were there?'

'Of course. I can take many forms James, like a chameleon.'

'You could have saved me a lot of worry if you had changed form when the police were looking for you.'

'Sorry James. I wasn't myself. That medication and head injury knocked me off balance.'

We were shown to our suite by a porter. He gave us an odd look – two men and a rather attractive young woman occupying a suite during the day – but the room was fine for our purposes. Suki sat on the bed while West and I occupied the desk chair and an armchair.

James: This session, we'll work on Patricia's fears. Take a few moments to immerse into her perspective.

West closes his eyes and prepares himself.

James: Patricia, we need to choose a very clear target for the EMDR. Can you describe your very worst fear?

Patricia: My identity has been vilified and disrespected. We are being systematically replaced by foreigners. I don't feel at home in my own country. I used to feel a strong sense of belonging and security and that has been taken away from me. Teachers and the media tell my children to hate their culture and history. They teach the new population to feel superior to us natives. Ethnic minorities commit a much higher proportion of violent crime, but the police and media censor the figures. GREEN gives them excuses rather than holding them to account. The police forces won't actually police the minorities' for fear of being called racist. They police our thoughts instead. If we don't celebrate our own colonisation and replacement then we're called racist. They force what they call diversity on us which is actually conformity, everyone must think the same. My area is full of crime and foreigners while the nice liberal people live in safety among nice people, protected from the consequences of their ideology. They discriminate against me. They give preferential treatment to the immigrants. They're the new privileged class. The minorities are racist and they look after their own. So-called antiracism actually racism against white people. The so-called anti-fascists are the closest thing we have to fascists after the religious extremists. Multiculturalism treats all other cultures with reverence but ours is marked for suppression and elimination. They tell us that our culture is inferior. If that's true, why are the rest queuing up to come here?

James: What's the worst case scenario?

Patricia: We become an ethnic minority in our own country, oppressed, suffering crime and discrimination. Our civilization falls and anarchy ensues. Foreign countries get involved and we end up in a civil war like Syria or Bosnia.

James: What are your beliefs about yourself in this situation?

Patricia: I'm not safe. I've lost my home. I can't protect myself. My identity has been violated. I have no future. I'm alone.

James: Now find a positive belief which you would like to hold about yourself in the current situation.

Patricia: That I'm safer and respected in my own country. I'm confident in the knowledge that my country still leads the pack. I'm free to express myself.

> *At James's request, Patricia rates the degree to which she actually subscribes to the positive beliefs:*
>
> *I am safe 2/7. I am free 2/7. I can protect myself 2/7. I have a greater global family 1/7. We are leading the world still, in different ways 2/7. I can create a community anytime 3/7. My home is where I make it 3/7. I have a beautiful future ahead of me 1/7. I'm grateful for the opportunity to live in this exciting time 3/7. I live my own life in the present 3/7.*
>
> *Patricia then rates her emotions about her situation.:*
>
> *Anger 10/10, Sadness 10/10, Loss 10/10, Rage 9/10, Fear 8/10, Violated 10/10, Resentment 8/10, Resignation 8/10.*

James: What sensations do you feel in your body?

Patricia: Tension in my shoulders, clenched fists, a sick feeling in my stomach, pain in my heart, tears in my eyes.

James: Patricia, thank you for sharing all that. I can see why you feel so bad. It's a heavy burden to carry around. Remember your safe place?

West: The beach. Am I doing this as Patricia or West?

James: West. When we get into the EMDR, the moment you start processing, the whole of you will be integrating.

West: Let's do it.

James: OK. I want you to immerse himself deep into that state; target, the negative beliefs, the emotions and sensations.

> *West nods and James begins the bilateral eye movements.*
>
> *West's eyes fill with tears. His chin rises up like a little baby and quivers. He is breathing more deeply.*

James: What did you get?

West: I felt incredibly sad, a deep sense of loss. I went right back to the beautiful memories of safety and togetherness, but with an overwhelming sense of loss, like a bereavement.

James: Go with the feeling of loss.

Bilateral stimulation.

West starts crying much more. Tears are rolling down his cheeks.

James: What did you get?

West: Deep sadness that I've lost my past. Like losing a loved one. Very painful. I felt all the new people, young people coming up around me which at first was threatening because they couldn't see my past and didn't care about me. I started to be curious who they were. I felt I was missing out and wanted to find out what was going on.

James: Go with that.

Bilateral stimulation.

West appears to be quickly shifting between different states. His face is changing expression rapidly.

West: That was fascinating. Weird. I was desperately clinging onto a big heavy stone which represented my past. I had this image of a black person trying to take it from me. At first, I assumed they were threatening but then I could see in their eyes that they were very loving, smiling at me. I relaxed and they changed form into a midwife, a plump middle-aged black lady with gold-rimmed glasses and a very old-fashioned uniform. It felt like she was helping me give birth. I cried like a newborn baby.

James: Take yourself deeply to that place again, as the newborn baby, looking at the midwife. Go with that.

Bilateral stimulation.

West closes his eyes and takes himself there. He nods.

James: What did you get?

West: I can't tell you that. It sounds strange.

James: You can say anything, don't make any judgements.

West: I was a new born baby, asking myself how I could be safe. I felt small and vulnerable. The midwife took me and held me to her chest. I had a strong sensation of love in my heart connected to her heart. It felt nice, like a cuddle. Then, I started suckling on her breast. It felt soothing.

James: Beautiful stuff. You're going deep. Don't block it. This is about security and that takes you back to this very young age. It's natural and healthy. Are you ready go again?

West: Yes, OK.

James: Go with the love feeling.

> *Bilateral stimulation.*

> *West looks very calm and peaceful, but then his expression becomes distressed. His chin and lips screw up. He frowns. His breathing becomes fast and shallow.*

James: What did you get?

West: It was lovely with the midwife, feeling safe and peaceful. I remembered my family that I had left behind. I saw them and we were holding hands but they were being pulled away from me. We were trying to hold on, I was trying to grip their hands to stop them being taken away from me. It was horrible, like a horror film. They turned into corpses. I could see their skulls.

James: How do you feel?

West: Sick. I felt repulsed and let them go.

James: Go with that.

> *Bilateral stimulation.*

West: That was very upsetting. I felt sick. I saw the faces of loved ones, distraught that I would never see again. I felt I might see them after I die but that passed off quickly and went back to the intense feeling of loss.

James: Go with that.

Bilateral stimulation.

West: I got this image of myself as a dog whose owner had died, pacing up and down, knowing that they had gone but not understanding it. Then I had the image again with the lovely black midwife and myself as a baby. That was comforting for a few moments but I then got a lot of resistance. I wanted to find my family, to go back to the past. It wasn't there.

James: It looks like you're feeling something now?

West: The sick feeling, sadness and a lump in my throat.

James: Put your attention on that.

Bilateral stimulation.

He moans in a constant high pitch whine like a baby. It is distressing to listen to. He doesn't cry but his face is contorted. The left side of his lips is raised up while the right side is relaxed. He is holding his body tense.

James: Where did you go?

West: I didn't get any images that time. I had an intense feeling of sadness, of loss, of distress. It felt unbearable. Horrible.

James: Go with that.

Bilateral stimulation.

West continues to contort his face and whine intermittently. After a minute or two he changes state. He looks afraid.

West: At first I was in the same state of distress, feeling alone. I felt like a baby desperate for its mother but she wasn't there. The midwife tried to comfort me. Then, I found myself at night time in the inner city, surrounded by a gang of immigrant boys. I felt vulnerable, alone. Scared.

James: Go with that.

Bilateral stimulation.

West continues to look very fearful. After 20 seconds or so, he looks physically uncomfortable and wriggles in the chair.

West: That's weird. This gang of boys came close to me. One of them put their hand in my pocket and took my phone and another took my wallet. Then one of them sat down and started writing something I was inquisitive to know what it was. I didn't feel threatened anymore. I've got this sudden intense discomfort in my left heel.

They take a break for West to walk around. He does some stretches to get himself comfortable again.

West: As I was doing my stretches, I realised that people like Patricia are insecure, afraid and fearful, like that little baby and people like Peter are being very abusive and not compassionate. That isn't the right way to treat someone is it?

James: You said it! Let's leave that until we deal with Peter. For now, let's stick with this target.

West: I'm inquisitive about what the boy wrote.

James: Go with that.

Bilateral stimulation.

West looks peaceful, even joyful at first. But his expression changes after a few moments. He looks sad and surprised.

James: What did you get?

West: That was disappointing. I expected the boy to be writing something beautiful, like those love feelings that I had with the midwife. As I was moving my eyes from side to side, I saw him erasing my history, rubbing it out. He was taking my history away from me. He wrote, *SLAVERY* in capital letters. He wrote a long list. He showed it to me. I couldn't see the words. He was like a police officer, writing up a charge sheet. He was telling me why I had been mugged, why I have no rights. The others crowded round me angrily, each one shouting bad things that they felt that I had done to them. They had a lust for revenge.

James: Go with that.

Bilateral stimulation.

West looks tense, his eyes bulging, obviously fearful.

James: What did you get?

West: I felt afraid. The boys were shouting at me crimes they say I've committed and must pay for. It was like being in a court room with false accusations being thrown at me and the judge was shouting 'guilty, guilty, guilty!' That made me angry and frightened. I was trying to explain that I wasn't guilty but no one would hear it. I saw Peter encouraging them to attack me, telling me that I must be ashamed and punished. Why? I'm that innocent little baby. I didn't do anything wrong.

James: Of course, individuals who have been born after the past abuses of slavery, the Holocaust and colonialism are not personally in any way responsible, they're as innocent as the newborn baby, as you say. We're talking about you, West, the consciousness of West. You live in people and across time. You *were* responsible for those actions as well as being responsible for all the good things too. Will you take responsibility? Sit with that thought for a moment and when you're ready, give me a nod.

West nods.

Bilateral stimulation.

West: I'm sorry. I see it now. Patricia isn't responsible at all. She was born after those things and cannot be held accountable for them. I, the consciousness of Western Civilization, I'm responsible. I did do those things. I saw images of slaves being taken across the Atlantic. Evil brutality. I saw the Europeans who did that. It's strange but they didn't know that they were doing wrong. Life was cheap back then. Most people lived in awful conditions. I'm responsible and I'm sorry. It was evil. I was immature, that's the way I used to think.

James: Immerse in the sorrow.

Bilateral stimulation.

West: I've got loads of images of concentration camps and of slavery. There's no getting away from it. I did do it. It's in my past. No wonder many people don't want anything to do with me, want to pretend that they're not part of me. What can I do to help them? I don't want people to have the feel the guilt and shame for ever. How can I forgive myself? How can others forgive me for what I did so that no more newborn babies have the guilt put on them by Peter or Agatha?

James: Go with that.

Bilateral stimulation.

West: I've always tried to defend myself by saying that when I did those things, it was bad but everyone else was bad too. Africans and Arabs did slavery. Many people have had wars and conquered others. That's true but that isn't going to get me out of this. The shift needs to happen in my heart.

James: Pay attention to your heart, the centre of your chest. Relax, pay attention to the sensations there, open and allow whatever needs to happen.

Bilateral stimulation.

West: That religious stuff is right. I have to love myself and love others and be strong enough, compassionate enough to absorb the aggression from Peter and Agatha. I did do wrong and they're still very angry about it. I would like them to heal but Patricia can't do that for them. That's their own journey and I have to respect that. As West – that is, the West as a whole – I have to take responsibility for what I did. I need to purify my heart.

James reviews West's positive beliefs, taking his scores:

I am safe 5/7. I am free 6/7. I can protect myself 5/7. I have a global family 5/7. My country is leading the way 7/7. We are leading the world still, in different ways 6/7. I can create a community anytime I choose 6/7. My home is where I make it 6/7. I have a beautiful future ahead of me. 5/7. I'm grateful for the opportunity to live in this exciting time 7/7. I live my own life now 5/7.

West's emotions:

Anger 0/10, Sadness 3/10, Loss 1/10, Rage 0/10, Fear 3/10, Violated 2/10, Resentment 0/10, Resignation 0/10.

James: What's stopping you from scoring security 7 out of 7?

West: There'll always be some risk.

James: You've rated 'I have a beautiful future ahead of me 5 out of 7.' What needs to happen to get that the 7 out of 7?

West: I experienced forgiveness and heart opening with the very loving midwife. It's not complete because Peter, Agatha and those boys who mugged me haven't let go of their anger and resentment, so I'm still on my guard.

James: I'm so impressed. I think you've done amazing work here. Let's leave it there for now.

From the car park outside, I called the GMC. 'May I speak to Dr Foster, Chair of the Fitness to Practise Panel?'

'Yes, who is it speaking please?'

'Dr James Hill.'

'I'll put you through.'

'Dr Hill, hello, what can I do for you?' said Dr Foster.

'I need to speak to you confidentially about West.'

'That has to wait for the hearing.'

'My patient is a public figure with huge responsibility. It's essential that the hearing be held in private. His story is unique and if it becomes public, the GMC will be responsible for the consequences.'

'Very well Dr Hill. I will let the committee clerk know that. We have been unable to contact Mr West so far.'

'Thank you Doctor Foster. See you on the 14th.'

'Ready?' Suki descended the stairs, like a princess. She was wearing a striking red cocktail dress with shoes and hat to match.

'How do I look?'

'Stunning, darling. Gorgeous.' She walked over to me, reaching forward to adjust my tie.

'Perfect,' she said, kissing me on the lips. I let my hands wander down to her hips but she intercepted them before they could go any further. 'There's no time, we're going to be late for the wedding.' She rubbed the lipstick off my lips.

We arrived just in time to hear the vows. Alan and Janet were very much in love. Suki looked at me with excitement and a beaming smile. After dinner, when the new couple finished their first dance, Suki pulled me by the hand to the dance floor. The cha cha cha practice paid off as we enjoyed the jealous glances of other couples.

We both had rather more to drink than we ought to have done. Jeremy, a builder in his 40s asked Suki to dance. His wife, Karen, an attractive blonde woman in her late 30s said, 'I guess we'd better join them.' At that very moment the music changed to a slow dance. Jeremy went outside for a cigarette and Suki sat down, but Karen put her arms around my neck and pulled me close. I could feel Suki's eyes burning a hole in the back of my head. I made my excuses and led Karen back to the table. Before we sat down, Suki got up and walked out.

'It's nice to have an adult evening out without the kids,' said Karen. 'Do you have any?'

'No, Suki and I have only been together six months,' I replied.

'James, she's stunning,' Jeremy said, winking at me. Karen kicked his leg playfully, faking a frown.

'Where is she?' asked Karen. 'That's a long trip to the toilet.'

Suki was outside in the garden, barefoot, drinking some whisky. Her makeup was smeared down her face. I sat down beside her, putting my arm around her. She pulled it straight off. 'I saw the way you held Karen.'

'Darling, it's just a dance at a wedding.'

'If you want to flirt with other women then you'd better tell me now and I'll pack my bags and you can find some other mug to pay your bills while you mess about with West.'

Nothing I could say could turn around her mood. The taxi ride home was in silence.

AGATHA: FROM SHAME TO GLOBAL FAMILY

The next morning I woke with a steaming hangover and a recollection of last night's argument. It might have been the slamming of the front door that had woken me, but I couldn't be sure. Suki was nowhere to be seen. That didn't necessarily mean anything – she was working today.

There were no notes from her in the kitchen or elsewhere, so I sent her a text message: 'Going shopping later. Any preferences for dinner tonight? Jx'

It took fifteen minutes for the reply to come. 'Can't possibly think of food right now.' That was encouraging. She was talking at least.

My mind at rest, I showered and dosed myself with pain killers. It was 8 o'clock by the time I was dressed and ready to start the day. Time to go over to Windsor again for another session with West.

It was a sunny day, the warmest of the year so far. I arrived at the hotel to find West sunbathing in a deck chair on the lawn.

'Good morning,' I said, mustering as much cheerfulness as possible.'How are you?

'Morning James. Raring to go. You look dreadful though. Are you all right? We can reschedule.'

'No no. Bit of a cold that's all. Did you book the suite again?'

'Something slightly different this time.'

He led me inside and down corridors to a bright seminar room facing the river. It was perfect. There were comfortable chairs and plenty of space for voice dialogue. I wished I'd always had access to a consulting room like this.

West: I've been thinking about justice – who owes what to whom. I can't help feeling that we've been giving too little weight to crimes that occurred in the past. I mean, if someone were the victim of a serious crime, you would want them to see a police officer and maybe a lawyer to get justice wouldn't you? You wouldn't insult them by sending them to see a psychiatrist.

James: Sometimes people need both. Where justice can be done, it should be done. Where a perpetrator can be punished, they should be. Where something can be put right, it ought to be. People can be harmed by their psychological reaction to traumas. Patricia was stuck, endlessly reliving her wound of insecurity and loss of togetherness for very understandable reasons but, having released the charge, she feels much better and is ready to create a more positive future.

West: Shouldn't we first focus on putting right the wrongs and punishing perpetrators?

James: How is that working out for you so far?

West: We've had partially effective anti-racism campaigns, the civil rights movement which brought about desegregation and equality. I dismantled the European Empires, I helped the Jews to get their own homeland. I encouraged mass immigration to create diversity. I've imposed multiculturalism.

James: Have you finished? Is the job done?

West: No. Racism and inequality still exist. Many resist diversity and multiculturalism. Anti-semitism is returning in a new form.

James: There are psychological barriers to overcome.

West: So can we do the EMDR for Agatha?

James: Sure.

> *They carry out the usual preparations, standing, clearing the space and beginning to focus..*

James: Focus upon that part of yourself which Agatha represents.

> *After a few moments, West smiles.*

James: Agatha, were you watching Patricia's EMDR therapy?

Agatha: Yes, I was amazed. It looked very weird but I was very impressed how much she shifted from racism to love.

James: You know the form then. We need a target for the exercise. So, tell me about your negative feelings. The things you really fear.

Agatha: I don't want to be treated as if I'm inferior one moment longer. My identity and culture have been violated and disrespected. West is more advanced, successful and powerful than me and all I can think of is those white colonialists telling Africans what to do, treating them with disrespect, taking their land. White people's privilege and power eats at me day and night and I'm glad to see them coming down in the world – getting a taste of their own medicine. I feel unwelcome in the West, I can see them looking at me with suspicion, but I don't belong at home either – I've lost my roots. I wouldn't say I'm happy to accept West's money, knowledge & infrastructure, but it's a necessity given the slow pace of change at home – there's also vested interests & corruption that hold back development. I'm part of that, I know — I feel ashamed of my own wealth & privilege.

James asks Agatha to score her negative feelings:

I'm inferior 3/7. I'm a second-class citizen 7/7. I cannot succeed because the world is against me 5/7. I'm a victim of white people 7/7. I have lost my home and culture 5/7. I have lost my roots 6/7

James: And what are the positives? The things you wish characterised your life.

Agatha: In a word, opportunity. Each generation becoming freer and freer with more and more options to interact with the world. I want to be proud and respected like anyone else, of course. That would help me feel at home both in Africa and the West.

Her marks for the positive images are as follows:

Positive cognitions: I have more freedom & opportunity than any previous generation 2/7. The world is open to me 1/7. I can choose to do whatever I want 2/7. I am proud of myself 3/7. I am at home in the West and in Africa 2/7. I am equal to anyone 3/7.

She rates her negative emotions as follows:

Shame 8/10, Humiliation 10/10, Embarrassment 7/10, Revenge 9/10, Anger 9/10, Sadness 4/10

Agatha is very tense, sitting hunched up, with gritted teeth, clenched fists and legs twisted around one another.

James: Thank you very much Agatha. Now I'm talking to West again. West, I hope you were listening. I want you to bring all that to mind — the feelings and images I just discussed with Agatha — and make it intense. OK? Now follow my fingers and let your mind go wherever it wants.

Bilateral stimulation.

West: I was in a traditional African village with dancing and a feeling of togetherness and belonging. I felt sad to have lost that. I resent West for that.

James: Go with that.

Bilateral stimulation.

West: I resent the fact that Westerners lord it over Africans. The have an easy lifestyle which they haven't earned. Africans are struggling to deal with the dramatic transition to modernity on West's terms. They tell us what to do, what's best, what to think. They're so patronising. I wish they could the feel pain.

James: Go with that.

Bilateral stimulation.

West looks angry at first but then his lip begins to quiver, his face screws up and he looks tearful.

West: I'm stuck in a game where West controls the rules and the pace. I'm running to keep up. I wish they'd respect us. I felt bad when I realised that I don't respect myself.

James: Go with that. (Bilateral Stimulation)

Bilateral stimulation.

West: I want to feel as if I'm part of the story of the modern world, but their stories exclude us. We're the primitive ones, the losers who are trying to catch up. That doesn't feel very nice. I wish we could tell the story as our human story, our human progress so that I could feel a part of it.

James: Go with that.

Bilateral stimulation.

West: I want to belong. I want to feel a part of something, this journey that we're on together. I hate those politically correct ones like Peter. They pretend that they're helping me but they're making me feel like a victim, telling me stories to keep me separate. They're not my true friend.

James: Go with that.

Bilateral stimulation.

West: Peter and his sort are using me to get rid of their guilt. They pretend they're helping me but they're really helping themselves. How can I join a team that hates itself?

James: Go with that.

Bilateral stimulation.

West: I was a shy person in school longing to be accepted. I couldn't join the group because half of them were arrogant, looking down on me. The other half were negative, self-loathing, always bitching and saying how much they hated everything. I crave belonging to a happy group, with a sense of togetherness.

James reads out Agatha's original statement – her fears and negative emotions. West thinks about it for a few moments in silence and then nods.

West: I'm upset about losing my roots. I realised that everyone is losing their roots in the modern world, including West, including Patricia, and it's unsettling for everyone. I had a sensation in my pelvis. A fullness, a heat. I felt my roots going down into the earth like a plant. I wondered how collectively we would be able to re-imagine or rediscover our roots.

James: Go with that.

Bilateral stimulation.

West: That felt a lot nicer. I felt a connection to the millions of years in which most of humanity was African so we're all one family. I saw the ancient emergence of people from Africa into Asia and Europe. I saw West arriving back in Africa. It felt like a homecoming, like this giant organism had spread out all over the world but its parts had lost awareness of one another but that came back when West arrived. It was like the family coming home, the long lost relatives returning. I felt grateful to them for being the ones who spread all over the world to reconnect our human family. We're emerging as a conscious species. I felt proud of West, like my children who had done well and return to their parents to show them their achievements. I felt ashamed for having been angry and jealous that they were the first to globalise the world. They are my children returned home.

James: Go with that.

Bilateral stimulation.

West: I had a feeling of joy of connection and welcome home when West came to Africa. It turned to sadness when I saw they hadn't recognised us as their family. They were treating the people as an inferior species. The Africans also didn't recognise the Europeans as their family. They were weaker militarily and economically so they came off

311

worst. Then I had the feeling of awakening which we've been experiencing for several generations as we realise that we're one family. That's a nice feeling.

James: Go with that.

  Bilateral stimulation.

West: I was enjoying a warm feeling of being part of one big global tribe. The African and European tribes are part of that greater tribe. Living together requires us to put the greater human tribe first while still fully respecting our local tribes. I felt proud that Africans had been responsible for all the first stages of development; the discovery of fire, axes, language and so on. Then I found myself feeling competitive with West, disappointed that my tribe hadn't been the most successful. If I think of myself as global then the European tribes are part of my tribe, and I don't need to be resentful or feel inferior. No living being was responsible for discovering how to make a well or the first writing or algebra. We're all beneficiaries now and it doesn't matter which particular tribe found at first. Future generations won't care about that. It's the present and the future that matters.

James: Fantastic stuff, West, that's a huge shift. You look tired.

West: You're right, that's plenty for one day. I'd like to take a rest there.

'Will you stay for dinner?' said West as I put my dictaphone in my pocket and rose to go.

  It was tempting, but I wanted to be at home when Suki came back. 'I'd love to,' I said, 'but I need to spend some time with Suki. Another time.'

  'You must bring her here to stay here one weekend,' he said with a wink.

———◆———

The traffic home was awful. The M25 was more like a car park than a motorway. I bought ready meals at the supermarket and pulled into the driveway not long after 7PM, looking forward to a TV dinner curled up on the sofa.

  Suki was just leaving as I came through the door. She looked very sexy indeed.

  'Hi Darling, where are you off to?

  'Out with the girls. See you later.'

  I shared my dinner with Nga. Channel hopping, I found myself watching the financial news. There had been a 5% drop in the stock markets during the time West had been in hospital.

  Suki didn't come home that night. No reply to my messages.

312

I was restless without work to do and without the money to go on holiday. I prepared myself for the GMC hearing as best I could. Dr Prasad had couriered over a copy of West's records from the Emergency Department and a copy of my colleagues' statements. None were critical.

One thing kept nagging at me. I couldn't understand how Dr Sugden knew details of what had gone on in my sessions with West.

PETER: FROM GUILT TO NEW WARRIOR

'**G**ood Morning!' I said, turning to greet West as he entered the hotel meeting room. I had been gazing out at the view from the large picture window, and the River Thames had worked its magic on me. I had no special reason to be happy given that I hadn't heard from Suki since yesterday evening, and given that a GMC hearing was rushing up at me. But the sparkling water and the parade of pleasure boats had a particularly English sweetness that was irresistible.

West looked like he could do with some of the same treatment. Unshaven, tieless and slightly green-looking, he placed a cup of coffee carefully on the table and dropped into an armchair, then weakly raised a hand.

'Morning,' he said.

'Are you hung over?'

'I'm afraid so. Stayed out late last night with friends.'

'That's OK, you're allowed to let your hair down. What was the occasion?'

'Oh nothing in particular, I was just excited the EMDR stuff we did yesterday.'

'That's great. And today we're focusing on Peter, yes?'

'I suppose so.'

'If you're not feeling up to it …'

'Oh no, no. I've been looking forward to this session. I wouldn't miss this one for anything.'

'What's special about this session in particular?'

He coughed and took a sip of his coffee. 'It's my guilt about the past that's holding me back, isn't it? I need to overcome that before I can move on.'

'And you think Peter might hold the key.'

'Let's see shall we?'

James: Immerse yourself in the consciousness of Peter.

On this occasion West does his preparation sitting down.

James: Did you watch Agatha and Patricia's EMDR sessions?

Peter: Yes. I was sceptical, so I was astonished to see both of them expressing such beautiful sentiments. It gave me hope.

James: You'll know then that we need to select a target – the very worst images, thoughts, feelings and sensations that you experience regarding this issue.

Peter: Where to start?

James: Just let the images flow. Don't censor.

Peter: You asked for it.

He buries his head in his hands for several minutes. When he speaks he is almost whispering. Seemingly he can't bear to take his hands from his face.

Peter: African slaves tied up in the hold of a ship crossing the Atlantic. There's sweltering heat, the stench of diarrhoea, people groaning with sea sickness and fever. Those who aren't sick are listless with hunger and dehydration. I can see white men on plantations, standing over the Africans with whips, cursing and lashing out – brutalising, sexually abusing and humiliating.

I see a terrified family of Jews in Nazi Germany – spat at, made to wear yellow stars and moved out of their comfortable apartment into a ghetto. Travelling on cramped, hot, waterless trains day after day. Naked and afraid they stand in a shower room, The gas starts to flow – and people start screaming. Others are gunned down – bullets tearing up women and children. Bodies dumped in mass graves. Still others are kept alive for forced labour or sadistic medical experiments.

Indigenous peoples witnessing the arrival of Europeans. Their bodies riddled with new diseases. Powerful weapons cut them down mercilessly. India now – I can see famine dead and flies are everywhere, but on the quayside there's food bound for Britain. Hong Kong – a young Chinese man screams for opium. Australian Aborigines, Maoris, people of the Americas all crowding round me, dull eyed – they've been deprived of their land and broken in spirit. Whole tribes lie dead around me in heaps – Tasmanians, the Bushmen, the first people of Newfoundland.

A black South African, staggering under the weight of a great racial hierarchy that sits on his shoulders – a white man is sitting on top of the pile.

Subtle, self-justifying words explain why democracy and freedom are for white people only. Words shamefully taken from the Bible. Pseudoscientific theories of racial hierarchy, eugenics and the racial cleansing.

Poverty, unemployment, crime, poor health, an early grave- the lot of many non-white people today. Terrifying neighbourhoods, awash with drugs and blood. A cold, embarrassed look in the eyes of a potential employer.

As in previous sessions, James asks Peter to score the intensity of his beliefs: I am ashamed of being white 7/7. My privileges are unjust 7/7. I do not deserve what I have 6/7. I am unfairly advantaged 7/7. My comfort is based on the suffering of others 6/7. I deserved to be punished 4/7. I deserved to experience revenge 5/7. I have contempt for white people 5/7.

315

James: And what's the opposite of all that Peter? The dream. The ways you would like things to go.

Peter: I'm forgiven. The weight of history is off my shoulders. I'm free to relate normally to the rest of the world and the world can see me for who I am — a lover of justice and peace and opportunity.

> *Marks given by Peter that show his level of confidence in this positive of the future:*
>
> *I forgive myself 2/7. I am forgiven 1/7. I am safe 4/7. I am good 3/7. I am an agent for justice 5/7. I am one of the good ones 6/7. I am putting bad history right 7/7.*
>
> *Peter's emotional state:*
>
> *Emotions: Shame 10/10. Guilt 9/10. Fear of retribution and revenge 6/10. Fear of loss of privilege 5/10. Anger 7/10.*
>
> *Like Agatha before him, Peter seems knotted and twisted with tension. He has the same gritted teeth, tense arm and constricted breathing.*

James: So, now come out of Peter and speak as West again.

> *West is still slumped over.*

James: West, are you OK? That was truly amazing stuff. Very well done indeed. Best yet.

West: I'm suffering with this hangover.

James: We should stop.

West: No. Do the EMDR, I want to get this over with. I want to move on.

James: Well, OK. But say if it gets too much for you.

> *James begins the bilateral stimulation.*
>
> *West sits up in his chair with some effort. His eyes are closed, face pale and unshaven, brows knotted.*

West: I got an overwhelming feeling of sadness — a massive burden of guilt and the desire to get rid of it.

James: Go with that.

Bilateral stimulation.

West: I'm finding it difficult to keep my eyes open. My eyelids are very heavy, I want to sleep. It feels like I want to block it out.

James: Scan your body sensations now, what do you notice?

West: A lump in the throat and a desire to cry.

James: Go with that.

Bilateral stimulation.

West: I want to share my wealth around so that I can be forgiven and reduce the burden of guilt.

James: Go with that.

Bilateral stimulation.

West: I'm scared they will take revenge, be violent and take what I've got, that history will repeat itself with the boot on the other foot. I'm scared they won't be magnanimous so I can't let go.

James: Go with that.

Bilateral stimulation.

West: I'm sorry that I've created new white working class victims, to make myself feel better, to blame others and avoid responsibility. I have to do something to deliver fairness and the way I've done it might be a continuation of racism in a different form. I'm ready for something new.

James: Go with that.

Bilateral stimulation.

West: There's a paradox. To put right the inequalities resulting from past racism, we've been applying racist solutions, dividing people according to their races and treating them differently. I'm desperate to unload this overwhelming shame and guilt.

James: Go with that.

Bilateral stimulation.

West: It's overwhelming, confusing, so many bad feelings that I want to get rid of. I want to get on with life but I don't know how to let go of the past.

James: Scan your body again for any particular sensations

West: Tension in my jaws.

James: Go with that.

Bilateral stimulation.

West: It's not as simple as redistributing wealth and power to non-white people. Two wrongs don't make a right. The success of the West is and was down to many things, not only imperialism. I can't put history right. How much do Japan and Germany owe for the Second World War? How much does Turkey owe to the Armenians for the genocide? How much does the Chinese Communist Party owe the Chinese people for the Cultural Revolution? Who kept records of what the North American Indians did to each other before I turned up? Where is the guilt and shame in the Arab world for its many centuries of colonisation, persecution, racism and slavery?

James: Go with that.

Bilateral stimulation.

West: What about poor white people? If you follow their history back, they could easily construct their own victim story. The game of blame, shame and guilt leads nowhere. I need to release this burden so I can be free to thrive. It's no good me lying on the ground, asking to be kicked. Those who would benefit not my superiors, I would be surrendering the field to people operating at the same moral level as the racists and imperialists of the past.

James: What's most live in you now?

West: I've gone into my head, being intellectual, I've lost it a bit.

James flips through his notes andI reads back the account of Peter's fears.

West: I've been hating whiteness, deconstructing it, vilifying it because of my shame and guilt. I meant well but that's turning previous racism on it's head, it's not moving

318

beyond racism, it's a new vengeful, self-harming form of it. The world won't advance by making white people hate themselves or by encouraging others to resent them. I feel so stuck. I can't bury my head in the sand. I did do all those bad things, that's true. I did good too. I can point to the misdemeanours of everyone else, but that still wouldn't release me from my guilt and responsibility. It's not right for future generations to be burdened with this. That won't serve humanity. It's not as if I could destroy myself and give way to something better. The others are no better. Hating myself is self-destructive. Treating others as victims isn't showing them due respect or recognising their responsibility.

James: I wonder if this is linking to something earlier? Take yourself deep into this wound, into that feeling of being stuck, the heady, oppressive guilt, shame and the feeling of being wrong. Float back in your memory. When was the first time you felt it?

West closes his eyes for several minutes.

West: I went back through different eras in my history. First was the puritanical Christian guilt in the late Victorian period and in the time of the Puritans in the 1500s. I spent years being very afraid of the Moors and Turks who took Spain, Byzantium and the Balkans from me. In a flash I went back to prehistoric times. I've been fighting for survival throughout my history. I saw images of sadistic and brutal things that I did in prehistory. To have slaves was normal in Greek times. It was normal to have a hierarchy dominating the masses in the mediaeval period. The Arabs, Africans, Chinese, Aztecs, Egyptians, Japanese, all my peers fought each other, for resources, land, prestige and power. Until modern times, it was normal to treat the outsider as an alien, suspect, sometimes an enemy and it was normal to capture women and take slaves. That's how people thought at the time.

James: Maybe you can give yourself some credit for the advancements that have taken place.

Bilateral stimulation.

West: I'm worried that this is another psychological trick to avoid guilt and responsibility. In the same way that I polarised between good guilty white liberals and bad nationalist white racists to offload my bad feelings. I'm worried that taking credit for the advances is another quick way of pushing it down, leaving the wound unhealed.

James: What do you feel right now?

West: Tension in my chest.

James: Go with that.

Bilateral stimulation.

West: I feel bad for judging the people in history. They lived in different contexts. My present world sits on their shoulders. It's my duty to do my best now, not to judge past generations by present-day values. My job is to do what's right now. I started to feel guilty, as if I was letting them off the hook for their crimes.

James: We know that the Aztecs and ancient Egyptians practiced slavery, domination and exploitation and some extreme rituals including human sacrifice. How do you judge those people?

West: I can't judge them. It would obviously be wrong in the present world but I can't judge people so far back in history whose world I don't understand or know.

James: Imagine that you took an Aztec, an ancient Greek and a hunter gatherer from New Guinea in a time machine to 1750 on a Jamaican sugar plantation where slaves are forced to work for the profits of their owners. Let them see, walk around and notice how they see you, the West.

Bilateral stimulation.

James: What did you get?

West: That was interesting. The Aztec felt very much at home. He recognised the slave system and agriculture. He didn't judge it. The Greek was familiar with slavery. They were impressed by the scale of it and wanted to learn about the technology, organisation and finance. They also didn't judge it morally. The New Guinea hunter-gatherer was overwhelmed by the scale of it. He wasn't used to so many people. He found it frightening and wanted to go home. I felt nervous in the time machine with all three of them. I wouldn't turn my back on them. They were no angels.

At James's request, West rates his belief in Peter's positive cognitions: I forgive myself 4/7. I am forgiven N/A. I am safe 2/7. I am good 4/7. I am an agent for justice 6/7. I am one of the good ones N/A. I am putting bad history right N/A.

He rates his emotional state: Shame 10/10. Guilt 9/10. Fear of retribution and revenge 6/10. Fear of loss of privilege 5/10. Anger 7/10.

James: Can you explain those figures?

West: I can partially forgive myself, but I don't think I've fully released it. I can't say that I'm forgiven because I'm not in control of that. That's a matter for others, their choice, their responsibility. I don't feel safe because others feel resentful towards me, some of them have a strong victim mentality. I encouraged that. Everyone is good and bad, we're a mixture. It's more appropriate to say, *I accept myself.* That way I can accept myself as I'm without needing to be perfect. I'm an agent for justice. It no longer feels right to say that Peter is one of the good ones. That was based on me creating a group of scapegoats, like Patricia, upon whom I could heap all my guilt and shame. History is way too complicated with so many layers and dimensions. You can focus on particular things through particular lenses but then you lose the whole picture. What's done is done and is responsibility of those people who lived at the time. What I can do is to do my very best now.

James: How do you rate yourself now then on those questions?

West: I accept myself 5 out of 7. I think that's the best that can be expected.

James: Why? What's stopping you getting to 7 out of 7 for that?

West: I'm not doing everything I can to liberate the potential of humanity. I could do a lot more, especially if we stop wasting energy arguing between Peter, Patricia and Agatha.

James once again reads over Peter's negative vision..

West's chin quivers. He nods.

Bilateral stimulation.

James: What did you get?

West: I'm shocked. Something I didn't expect. I'm afraid that the ethnic minorities are going to come for revenge and attack me. I'm scared.

James: Go with that.

Bilateral stimulation.

James: What did you get?

West: Again. Weird. I felt overwhelmed by attackers and felt like a vulnerable child. I saw a big powerful warrior with a sword, defending me. I was horrified. I reject their bad old ways. I realised that I haven't been relating to the minorities. Like before, I've been treating them like victims but not treating them as equals.

James: Go with that.

Bilateral stimulation.

James: What did you get?

West: Minorities are people like me. All kinds, not uniformly good. Not victims, people. Then my mind went blank and I felt calm and had a hot sensation in my solar plexus. It felt good.

James: Go with that.

Bilateral stimulation.

James: What did you get?

West: It was a mix. I had both the powerful feeling in my belly and the fearful baby sensations in my lips, chin and arms. I recognised the belly feeling as my courage, my warrior self come through. I immediately rejected it. That's when I said, 'Oh no!' I have hated my warrior self, suppressed it. That's the imperialist, the bully, the criminal, the exploiter, the male chauvinist in me. I hate it. But it felt good. That was uncomfortable. The words came to me 'I have a right to defend myself.'

James: Go with that.

Bilateral stimulation.

James: What did you get?

West: I feel the warrior in me. The powerful courage in my belly. My strong arms. My feet firmly on the ground. It's a good sensation but my mind is uncomfortable with it. I am always talking about the importance of us rediscovering our wisdom, intuition and the spirit and community of our ancestors but I have rejected the warrior part because I am ashamed of it's past abuses.

James: Go with that.

Bilateral stimulation.

James: What did you get?

West: That's fascinating. I didn't expect that. I saw an ancient tribal scene in Africa, from our common ancestors. I felt totally comfortable as a member of the tribe. It was natural to be a warrior, totally natural to be part of a tribe, to fight other tribes for dominance and to enjoy the privileges that come with victory. Then it merged with postmodern me. I was allowing in members of the defeated tribes and they were very grateful to be there but deferential. I encouraged them to become members. I felt like we were extending our tribe to include others. I felt proud of that.

James: Well done. Let's take stock.

> *Positive cognitions: I forgive myself 7/7. I am forgiven N/A. I am safe 6/7. I am good 6/7. I am an agent for justice 6/7. I am one of the good ones N/A. I am putting bad history right N/A.*

> *Emotions: Shame 0/10. Guilt 0/10. Fear of retribution and revenge 2/10. Fear of loss of privilege 2/10. Anger 0/10.*

James: That is quite a change.

West: Seems like I got my warrior back.

James: Looks like you did. I'm delighted for you. Very well done. So, now invite Peter, Agatha and Patricia back together and see if they're willing to work together creatively or even to merge as one. Let's see how they respond to one another now. I'd like you to take turns to jump into the persona, the energy of each character in three different positions on the carpet here and we will invite them to collect with each other.

> *Agatha becomes choked up and tearful.*

Agatha: I'm sorry I hated you Patricia. What you said was beautiful and touching. I'm sorry that you've been afraid. I don't want to hurt you anymore. I think we could be friends.

> *Agatha physically turns in her chair — towards Peter.*

Agatha: I don't want you to carry that burden anymore. I've been using it to beat you with which I know isn't right because my past isn't spotless either. I'm not sure that I'm ready to forgive you yet but I'm ready to work with you on creating a better future. I think we need to do that together and I'm confident of your sincerity, I can imagine forgiving you then.

Peter: Patricia, I'm sorry I scapegoated you. I heard your fear and anger and all I could hear was the racism and oppression of the past so I shut you down. I used you as a dustbin for my own aggression, my own unresolved racism and for all of my guilt. I'm sorry for that. I acknowledge your fear of immigration, violation of your identity and I apologise for not allowing you to speak.

Peter: Sorry Agatha. I used you to offload my guilt. I patronised you and treated you in a racist way. I treated you as a child who needed me to rescue you. I didn't honour you own responsibility and choices. I was perpetuating your disempowerment by treating you as a victim and putting myself on a pedestal as your rescuer. I will treat you as an equal from now on.

> *With a real physical jump forward out of the chair, West leaps out of Peter and into Patricia. A huge smile comes across Patricia's face and she opens her arms to embrace Agatha.*

Patricia: I feel I love you as a sister, as part of my family. I'm sorry that I pushed you away because I was scared of you. I'd like to help me find a way to be open to the world and stay safe.

Patricia: Peter, I'm sorry I've hated you. You've been doing your best but the way did it hurt me and frightened me and I wasn't willing to accept all the blame that you wanted to put on me. I'm sorry that I've resisted your attempts to make things better. I'd like to do what he said, to find a way to make the world as fair as we can. I'd like every newborn baby, whatever colour they are, to have fresh start, a fair start in life. I need your help to feel safe and I need you to be more honest about human nature, to acknowledge your dark side and to be honest about the tribal and animal nature of all human beings as well as all the 'nice' stuff.

> *West sits down in his chair again, returning to Peter.*

Peter: It's a deal

> *He holds out his hand to Patricia.*

James: Thank you to all of the characters who were with us. West, can you stand in the middle now and check that the process is complete.

> *West jumps out of the chair and out of Peter, standing in the centre of the room, newly energised. He turns around slowly, acknowledging the gathered assembly of characters — nodding at them one by one until he has re-integrated the all.*

West: I feel peaceful, bigger, stronger, more powerful.

James: Well done, West. You've earned a good night's rest. Perhaps you could let me know when you're ready for next session. You may need a bit of time to think about what you've achieved today.

Actually it was me who needed time – to prepare for the up-coming GMC hearing. I decided not to tell West about it. I didn't want to add to his worries or distract from his therapy.

I was in no hurry to return to an empty house after the session, so I took a stroll along the river and treated myself to a pub meal.

———◆———

When I got home, Suki was in tears. She was sitting on the sofa under a duvet, wearing just a grey T-shirt and yellow knickers. There was a half-eaten box of chocolates and a bottle of Pino Grigio on the table,

'I'm so sorry James.'

'Sorry for what darling?'

She sobbed. I sat down beside her, holding her hand. She looked at me through her red, swollen eyes.

'I kissed Jake.'

I let go of her hand, standing up. I felt a horrible churning feeling in my stomach.

'I'm sorry. It was stupid. I felt so alone. I was angry with you,' she said. 'I am such a fool. Sorry.'

'What happened?'

'I was having a lovely time with the girls, out eating and drinking. Jake called to invite us to a house party. I went with Jessica and Sharon. We danced and I kissed him. I was flattered that he still fancied me. He tried to persuade me to go home with him but I said no. I thought of you. You're the best man I've ever known. I love you. I am tired of the endless push and pull. I realised I'm ready to open up and give you my love.

'Kissing an ex-boyfriend is a funny way of showing it, Suki.'

She looked at me lovingly, sitting cross legged in her underwear.

'I didn't have to tell you about what I did. I could have kept it a secret. But I wanted to tell you to get rid of it. To let it go. Come here darling.' She opened her arms to me and I knelt in front of her, kissing away the last of her tears.

THE GENERAL MEDICAL COUNCIL HEARING

'**D**r Hill, please take a seat.' Dr Foster, Chair of the Fitness to Practice Panel was sitting behind a large desk in a cavernous oak-panelled room. Heavily-framed pictures of illustrious doctors hung on the walls – Hippocrates, Joseph Lister, William Harvey, Edward Jenner. No psychiatrists. 'This is Dr Bobby Singh, a cardiologist from Birmingham and Theresa O'Connor, of the Patient's Society. Mrs Sevelame will be keeping the record of proceedings.'

'How do you do?' I said as I smiled and nodded at these people who had the power to end my medical practice.

Either side of me were sitting two barristers, one defence and one prosecution. 'We are here to consider evidence regarding certain allegations made against you and to give you the opportunity to speak for yourself. We have read the reports and will continue to take evidence from the witnesses. Given that West claims to be a public figure, I have excluded the media and members of the general public from this hearing. All of those present are professionals and all are bound to respect the patient's confidentiality.'

Behind me sat Dr Sugden, Dr Prasad, Dr Trenton, Seth, Jean, Phil and Ayesha. Suki mouthed, 'Good luck.' Most of them smiled at me. Dr Sugden was reading his notes.

The panel called the witnesses one by one and the barristers cross examined them.

'Dr Sugden,' said the Defence Barrister, 'you have persecuted Dr Hill for years and these charges are a thinly veiled attempt to remove someone who you perceive to be an obstacle to your change programme.'

'I wish that were true. I have done my best to support James over the years. I let him off recently with a verbal warning when I found out that he was abusing his authority by initiating a relationship with Dr Chen, a junior doctor.'

Dr Singh interrupted, 'Dr Chen will speak for herself.'

'Dr Hill is no doubt a sincere person,' said Dr Sugden, 'but he has crossed the line from maverick to unprofessional. He has deliberately kept the case of West secret from his colleagues. He has used bizarre and unethical treatments such as asking West to simulate having sexual intercourse with himself. He persisted with this and other non-evidence-based therapies when he should have been treating the patient with anti-psychotic medication. Notably, he encouraged the patient to speak to his inner voices, behaving as though they were real.'

'Has any harm come to the patient as a result?' asked Dr Singh.

'Yes, he came very close to killing himself.'

Seth, Ayesha, Phil and Jean each took the stand in turn, told the truth and defended me as best they could. The prosecution barrister took no prisoners. One by one, he ridiculed their professional integrity and dismissed them. Finally he called Dr Trenton, who was very smart and confident.

'What is West's diagnosis?' asked the Prosecution Barrister.

'Paranoid schizophrenia. He has delusions of grandeur that he is the consciousness of Western Civilization. He believes that he is 3000 years old and inhabits the mind of everyone in the West including the people in this room. He has a dissociated personality with many sub-characters many of whom go by the name of colours. He has poor self-esteem, low self-confidence and intense inner conflict leading to suicidal impulses.'

'What treatment does West need?'

'I was treating him with antipsychotics, antidepressants and sedatives. He was on a Section 3 but went absent without leave. The police failed to find him. He is at risk of suicide.'

'Dr Hill believes that West is the consciousness of Western Civilization and has been treating him as such. Is that a valid diagnosis and treatment?' asked the Prosecution Barrister.

'Absolutely not. While one must be respectful to a patient, one should never collude with a delusional system and certainly never indulge it and withhold medication,' said Dr Trenton.

Finally, I was called to speak.

The prosecution barrister asked, 'Dr Hill, why would you believe West's account of himself? The average person certainly wouldn't.'

'At first, I didn't believe him. It sounds ridiculous, doesn't it? The consciousness of Western Civilization. It's on a par with alien abductions, thinking you're Jesus and conspiracy theories. As I took the history, he was rational, fully orientated, emotionally responsive and the answers he gave were not at all consistent with a psychotic illness. I wondered if he was a fantasist or it may have been a prank. As I got to know him, I decided to act as if it were true. He was not at major risk, no harm to others and was willing to attend for appointments.'

'No risk? He was found drunk, having taken an overdose, about to jump into the Thames.'

'Yes, that's true but that can happen with any patient. It's a risk with anyone suffers from low self-esteem, suicidal impulses and dissociated subpersonalities.'

'Why did you not keep proper records of his care? Why did you not share his unusual case with your colleagues?'

'Because I believed West and because he insisted on maximum confidentiality. Because I knew I couldn't trust my medical colleagues to listen to the patient without prejudice.'

'Well, Dr Hill, your judgements were wrong. Mr West, a psychotic patient with a high suicide risk is now untreated in the community, at risk of suicide and neglect as a result of your misdiagnosis and charlatan treatments.'

'No, actually I am still treating West. He stayed with me for a couple of weeks …' There were gasps around the room.

'Quiet please,' said Dr Foster, 'Dr Hill please continue.'

'West chose to stay with me until he was detoxified from the cocktail of unnecessary drugs that Dr Trenton had prescribed him on the back of his misdiagnosis.'

The prosecution barrister couldn't believe his luck: 'You secretly took in a psychotic patient on a Section 3 who was absent without leave from hospital and being searched for by police. There can be no clearer admission of medical misconduct.'

The panel invited the barristers to sum up.

My defence barrister spoke: 'Dr Hill sincerely believes that he has made the correct diagnosis and provided the appropriate treatment. The issue here is a difference of professional opinion, not a breach of medical standards. As you have heard, Dr Hill is held in high esteem by those who work closest to him and many of those who have met West share Dr Hill's assessment.'

The prosecution barrister said, 'I regret to say that Dr Hill, a very compassionate and normally good doctor, has allowed himself to form an inappropriate relationship with this patient, failed to make a proper diagnosis and instead colluded with his psychotic delusions. Furthermore, he has spent months indulging and elaborating these delusions and fantasies with highly unconventional therapy sessions using techniques largely unknown or discredited by his psychiatrist colleagues. This included asking the patient to simulate copulation with himself, pretending to be Russia, talking to trees and encouraging the patient to speak with and elaborate the many voices in his head, even to stage arguments between the voices. He has allowed the patient to visit him at home twice and has entertained him in a coffee shop near his home. He failed to keep any proper written records. He did not write to the patient's GP. He did not appoint a key worker for the case. He kept the patient secret from his medical colleagues. He did not take the suicide risk seriously. He digitally recorded the sessions,'

'Hang on!' I said, standing up.

'Dr Hill, you have had your opportunity to speak. Please sit down,' said Dr Foster.

Mrs O'Connor interrupted, 'No, let him speak.'

'How do you know what went on in the sessions, since, as you say, there are no records? How do you know about the digital recordings? Those were my private property on my personal laptop. They were fully encrypted with a password which I have not told anyone.'

'Dr Sugden, would you like to explain this?' asked Dr Foster.

Dr Sugden had beads of sweat on his forehead. 'I can't explain it. I have acted on evidence from Dr Prasad.'

'Dr Prasad, how do you explain having access to Dr Hill's personal computer and encrypted sound recordings?' asked Mrs O'Connor.

Dr Prasad's eyes darted from left to right, his hands shaking. 'I acted on orders from the Chief Executive Dr Sugden. We were investigating serious breaches of Trust policy,' he replied. 'I borrowed Dr Hill's laptop from his room and copied the hard disk. Dr Sugden sent it to a company to examine the contents.'

'Thank you. This matter is well beyond the scope of the present hearing,' said Dr Foster. 'We will have to refer this to the police.'

The double doors at the back of the room opened loudly. West's voice boomed, 'There's one voice that you haven't yet heard in your inquiry.' There was a gasp around the room. The security staff went to restrain West. He held up his hands, commanding them firmly to 'Stand Down!' They promptly did so.

'Who are you?' asked Dr Foster.

'West, the consciousness of Western Civilization.'

'I am very sorry. We've been able to contact you until now. Please take the stand Mr West,' said Mrs O'Connor.

'Dr Foster, your favourite colour is green. You went on holiday to Tuscany last year. You lost your last tennis game to your friend Simon. You had two poached eggs for breakfast and a swig of Napoleon brandy before the hearing. Shall I go on?'

'I … I …I think that's quite enough,' he replied, his face draining of blood.

'Dr Singh, your parents got married in Liverpool where they met as junior obstetricians. You scored 35 runs in your cricket match last weekend. You went to Dulwich college. You're currently reading 'The Tipping Point' and you like Ocean Mist bubble bath.'

Dr Singh laughed nervously.

Theresa O'Connor knew she was up next. The poor woman looked positively terrified. 'Ms O'Connor,' said West, 'allow me to simply wish your daughter good luck in her Art School entrance exam this afternoon.' There was a look of relief on her face.

West turned and winked at me.

'Dr Foster,' said the prosecution barrister with outrage in his voice, 'it is unacceptable to allow a deluded patient to run amok in the court.'

'Ah, Michael,' said West, turning to face him. 'Dear old Michael enjoys the odd snort of cocaine at the sex parties he attends. He's wearing a lovely pair of silk stockings under his suit.'

The prosecution barrister turned as red as a beetroot and dropped into his chair.

West spoke quietly: 'Mrs Sevelame, would you mind passing the telephone over there to Dr Foster?' She did so without question or complaint. The room was still., and then suddenly the silence was broken by the phone ringing. Dr Foster answered.

'Hello. Who?' his mouth actually fell open. I had never seen that happen for real. 'Your Majesty. How can I …' Dr Foster looked at West with incredulity. 'Yes. Yes Ma'am. Thank you. Yes, I understand. Goodbye Ma'am.' Dr Foster put the phone down ever so slowly. He took off his glasses, also very slowly, and sat back in his chair, silent.

The phone rang again. Dr Foster didn't react – he was preoccupied with some thought. Dr Singh picked it up instead.

'Hello. Yes, Dr Singh here. Who is this?…. I'm sorry?' He looked straight at West with an expression of awe. 'Of course, Mr President. I understand, sir. Thank you. Good bye.' He put down the phone.

West addressed himself to the panel: 'I hope I now have your attention. I wish to say that James Hill is an excellent doctor. I have been around for quite some time – 3000 years now – and I have known healers of all kinds, doctors, nurses surgeons, practitioners of traditional medicine and even the odd shaman, and I chose this man as my psychiatrist because he is caring, respectful and highly skilled. He listened to me attentively and showed that he understood my special circumstances. His insights and questions were incisive. I thoroughly commend him to the panel.' West left the room in silence, leaving Dr Sugden and Dr Prasad looking terrified, like naughty schoolboys caught in the act of stealing.

With typically English understatement, Dr Foster closed the hearing: 'Dr Hill, thank you very much for coming. We will be in touch shortly to report the decision of the panel. I wish you a safe journey home.' Each member of the panel stood to shake my hand. Suki ran forward to hug me. 'Well done James, that was amazing. I am so proud of you.' I invited Suki, Phil, Jean, Seth and Joyce to the pub for lunch. I had a proposal for them.

HEALTHY BOUNDARIES AND IMMIGRATION

Over dinner at my house that evening, I raised my glass in a toast:

'Here's yo you, West. I can't thank you enough for your support at the GMC.'

'To West,' chimed in Suki.

'Don't mention it,' said West raising his glass. 'You've done me a great service and I am in your debt.' He seemed a very fatherly presence at the head of the table.

'I've been experimenting,' he continued. 'I imagined I could visit a much more advanced civilization in the future in a spaceship with a time machine. It was a lot of fun but when I tried to codify the rules, I still felt conflicted.

James: What happened?

West: I blasted off into space and we travelled for months and months until we reached the other planet. It was like a tropical island. We arrived beside a beautiful, still lake with a long wooden jetty. There was a tall man there, dressed in a suit seemingly made all of light, who received us, helping us to tie down the spaceship and disembark. He was wonderfully welcoming and friendly, guiding me around, introducing me to people on a sort of tour.

Suki: What were the people like?

West: They were racially mixed. There was no majority group. No one seemed to care about race. They had a strong identity and community spirit. I felt like a welcome visitor among a people who had immense self-confidence and pride in their way of life. I was an outsider, but an honoured one. They were never phased by anything – if some problem came up they always seemed confident that teamwork would overcome it.

James: Did that group cover the whole planet?

West: Its reach was certainly immense, but I did hear about other regions where things weren't so racially mixed up – highly traditional cultures where people were differentiated along racial line, like the places on Earth where I don't have much influence.

James: How did they manage the borders with those places?

West: They were open and allowed people to come and go, but they had very strong detection and intervention systems.

Suki: That sounds a bit scary. Detection of what?

West: Oh, there was nothing sinister about it. They were simply honest with them-selves about the people from those other regions. They never forgot that they were from a different culture with different values – that they were more likely to think in tribal and ethnocentric ways. They were very alert to the risks those people posed and were quick to detect signs of ethnocentric, tribal behaviour, always acting firmly and compassionately to discourage it.

In general the place felt very safe. Everybody was able to live freely and at their highest potential. They didn't tolerate the formation of any gangs or mafia and they were quick to remove any pockets of crime. They also had compassionate, effective so-cial systems, prepared to intervene in families and communities to correct delinquent behaviour at the first opportunity. They had strong boundaries as regards right and wrong, and thy were very comfortable with making judgements. They weren't afraid of enforcing those judgements either. It all felt very compassionate, loving and kind, not brutal or harsh. People seemed very happy.

James: I'm waiting for the *but*!

West: The *but* came when I returned to earth and tried to codify the rules for how I would implement that here.

James: What was the snag?

West: We're in a transition state. Some people have moved from the PURPLE ethno-centric and BLUE nationalistic stages into the ORANGE scientific, rational, business level of thinking. They value business, science, pragmatism and meritocracy. Others have shifted their consciousness beyond that to a GREEN world-centric, global identity. They see themselves as human and the old concepts of nationality, race, ethnicity, tribe and patriotism seem old-fashioned or harmful to them.

James: What's the problem? The majority of the people in the West are moving to-wards that future state you envisioned.

West: At least half the people still have strong attachments to PURPLE ethnic or BLUE na-tional identities and are resistant to faster transition to the GREEN thinking. They tend to be against immigration, more likely to be racist and to exclude those they perceive as outsiders.

James: Why is that an issue?

West: When large numbers of people who subscribe to ethnocentric ways of thinking come to me, they tend to continue that way of operating and this causes polarisation in the domestic population between domestic PURPLE and BLUE versus GREEN and ORANGE.

James: How do you mean?

West: When the ethnocentric part of the Western population receive large numbers of newcomers who exhibit a foreign tribal and nationalist identity, in other words patriotism for other places, loyalty to other cultures and beliefs, they perceive that as a threat and it can be a challenge to security, cohesion and democracy.

James: You mean like Patricia being fearful of Agatha's different loyalties, values and identity?

West: Exactly. Peter behaves differently towards the two sets of people with PURPLE-BLUE thinking. He treats the majority group, of which he is a part, aggressively, dismissing and suppressing Patricia's identity and values because that's the one from which he has emerged and to which he feels enlightened and superior. He treats Agatha's PURPLE-BLUE values as something to be celebrated and treated with huge sensitivity and reverence.

James: So Peter's racism is a recipe for resentment and conflict?

West: Patricia feels threatened and becomes hostile to both Agatha and Peter. Agatha feels a mix of entitlement and resentment, as a victim of Patricia's exclusion and there's basically a breakdown of relations. Peter is angry with Patricia and uses force to shut her up – essentially to make her comply with his beliefs.

James: Maybe that's OK if it gets good results in the long term. How will you manage the transition? When have you experienced race and identity working well already?

West: People use the term 'mixed-race' but we're all mixed-race already. Before the modern wave of mass migration, the British were a very cohesive, successful, patriotic group with clear values and identity. Yet, they were a mixed bunch racially. They're a mixture of the hunter-gatherers who walked there after the ice age before it was an island. They've absorbed waves of newcomers – Celts, Angles, Saxons, Irish, Normans, Vikings, Huguenots, Jews, refugees, travellers and traders from far and wide over the centuries. Genetic studies show that white Brits have some African and Arab genes, especially in Devon, Cornwall and Wales, which have a long maritime tradition.

James: What's your point?

West: A white British person can have blond hair and blue eyes, like you. They can have mousy brown hair and brown eyes. They can have pale skin and jet black hair with grey eyes. They can be ginger haired with green eyes. They can have olive-brown skin and brown eyes. Although you all look different, it never crosses your mind for a moment that you're anything other than British, an individual to be judged on their own merits.

James: So you see the whole world becoming like that?

West: Eventually, yes, it's happening already in some of my cities, although people will come to it at different rates according to their circumstances and experiences.

James: Keep going. This is positive stuff.

West: All human beings are of equal value, but all ideas, beliefs, values and faiths are fully open to debate, scrutiny and humour. Every new born baby should have a genuinely clean slate – free to develop its own potential, neither burdened by the prejudices of others nor by the excessive pull of group identity. Racism would be an absolute taboo with no discrimination, positive or negative. There would be a high level of security, and intolerance for crime, violence and intimidation. There would be an absolute taboo on anti-democratic activity, but otherwise true freedom of speech. No one would be permitted to impose their political or religious beliefs on anyone by force or manipulation. Systems would be in place to ensure fairness.

James: How would you manage immigration?

West: If we're confident and secure in our culture, institutions and identity then we can be open to immigration – new team members. Each town, city and country would be a dynamic, vibrant hub of human activity, each with its own self-confident identity. People would be as free as possible to move about, although with restrictions to enable security, stability and environmental wellbeing.

James: That sounds lovely but you can't sidestep the uncomfortable business of deciding who's a member and who's excluded.

West: The default would be open borders with freedom of travel.

James: Why not have that right now?

West: Because there's inequality in the world, different levels of development, quality of life, cultures and values. If we opened the borders, we'd be inundated.

James: Maybe that'd be a good thing? It'd stir up the economy, keep all the public services on their toes and it'd be a great way to bring opportunity to many people quickly.

West: Yes but it would cause a massive increase in crime, homelessness, poverty and alienation. Amidst the chaos and insecurity, many people would fall back to ethnocentric identity and conflict would undermine my liberal society.

James: If you believe in freedom and equality and maximum human potential, then why not open your borders?

West: The first duty of government is to protect the people.

James: Aren't you absolving responsibility for the rest of the world?

West: No, I have to strike a balance. All human beings have their humanity in common, and we all share the same home, the Earth. We're interconnected and interdependent so we so have responsibilities towards one another and that should naturally fall heaviest on the shoulders of the fittest and strongest. Humans are still, and probably will remain, territorial, tribal animals with strong attachments to their land, group and their own sovereignty. A basic rule of nature is that animals have the right and the duty to protect themselves, their home, family, food, water and territory from competitors. Maybe one day all humans will be Buddha-like beings but we have to deal with reality as it is.

James: How do you distinguish group members from outsiders?

West: The convention is that it's determined by birth. You inherit the rights of your family.

James: You realise that's a choice, a traditional choice but not a self-evident truth? Try speaking from different value systems.

YELLOW: The more interdependent we become, the more necessary it is for our collective survival that we think and act as a whole global civilization rather than separate countries.

PURPLE: Stick with the traditional nations, tribes, and ethnicities.

TURQUOISE: We're an emerging global tribe made up of many smaller tribes, all in the same boat.

RED: We're a patchwork of gangs, mafias and Empires. Race doesn't matter. It's about power, loyalty, hierarchy and allegiance.

BLUE: I want strict rules to distinguish insiders and outsiders according to codes and judgements on righteousness.

West: How does that look in practice?

BLUE: Australia has a rational, bureaucratic, law-based system.

ORANGE: Big companies need a free flow of skilled labour to meet its needs. People everywhere have the right to choose their own destiny, write their own script. I'm in favour of open borders.

GREEN: We are all one human community. We should have open borders to promote equality and fairness.

James: So your challenge is to integrate all that, pragmatically, across the territories you inhabit in order to achieve the best outcome. Let's try the future visioning technique again. Take a few minutes in your imaginary spaceship to the future.

West closes his eyes. After a while his brow begins to furrow.

West: I felt strong resistance this time.

James: Why?

West: It's easy to indulge an idealised fantasy in which everything is perfect and moral problems scarcely exist. But that's dishonest. Society is messy and complicated. A set of guiding principles is about all I can hope to achieve I think, and even that will take a lot of thought before it truly incorporates all the assumptions, aspirations and needs of my different value systems. It's up to democracy to handle the details.

There is momentary silence at the table.

James: Far from being disappointing, that's actually a truly great response. Are you willing to have a crack at this set of guiding principles?

Suki: Oh, come on. West is tired, I'm tired, and we've run out of wine.

West: Suki's right – we have run out of wine. I'm going to call a taxi, but I'll be back tomorrow. I promise.

———◆———

In the event, West hadn't shown up until nearly lunchtime so I drove out to see if I could find him at home. I realised that in order to reach his houseboat I had to park on an industrial estate and walk for half a mile down a tow path. I didn't mind – it was a lovely day, and the majestic River Thames was alive with bird life and boats.

I became more than a little concerned about West, though, when I knocked on the hatch of his little nineteenth-century river boat and received no answer from within. Thoughts of his last near suicide bid came to mind. What if he had undergone some kind of relapse? I was just beginning to wonder whether there was enough mobile reception to make a call to the police, when West came into view, marching purposefully along the tow path from the opposite direction.

He seemed to have been up all night, because he hadn't changed his clothes or shaved. He began talking loudly and excitedly when he was still thirty or forty feet away.

West: James, I can't decide about immigration.

James: Good Morning West. You made me jump!

West: Good morning and welcome. The problem is, I need to make decisions about how to handle identity and security within my nations first.

James: Well I agree. No point in building a castle on sand. What should the rules be regarding identity and tribalism?

> *West takes two deckchairs from the flat roof of his boat and plants them on the grassy bank. They sit.*

West: You can't legislate for the attachments of the heart. You can have a Dutch passport but not feel Dutch, think Dutch or act Dutch. In the current system, you can have a Dutch passport but be fully loyal, attached and identified with any number of foreign identities and there's no discipline about that. I can't impose artificial rules about how people should feel about themselves. That's against my principles as well as being impossible.

James: You can't control feelings. You can regulate behaviour.

West: I aim for a world in which all human beings are equal in value, free to speak, think, pray, live, work and move as they choose, while respecting the freedom and security of others. I envision a world where each new born child has the fullest opportunity to flourish and live to its highest potential according to its own free choice and responsibility, irrespective or its origins and initial circumstances.

James: That sounds fantastic.

West: Our world is in transition from a patchwork of parochial tribes and nations to a global consciousness. People are arriving at that global consciousness at different rates.

In the West, about half the population is still tribal, nationalist and the other half are global or individualist. In the rest of the world, the large majority have tribal ethnicities although that's changing fast. Regarding race and immigration, I've a responsibility to manage that transition safely, to avoid conflict, promote security and fairness and to be respectful of people's current identities.

James: What's your strategy?

West: Those who wish to come to live in the West must accept the values of the West, especially freedom and democracy. They may still feel attached to the identity of their place of origin but they must obey the rules of the West. Those who seek to colonise, undermine security or democracy or to impose a foreign identity, allegiance or religion are not welcome and must find an alternative home. There must be no discrimination according to race, religion, background or political views. Full effort must be made to eliminate racism in all its forms, in all groups equally. There must be no suppression of free speech, other than incitement to hatred and violence. Everyone should be open to full scrutiny, criticism and humour. Collusion with foreign enemies is forbidden.

James: Are you open to the possibility that people's identities will change over time?

West: Very much so. I fully expect that identities will change very fast. The only boundary I lay down is that the existing local people in any particular country have the right to their identity and culture and should not be subject to colonisation or denigration of their identity by the world-centric, globalist section of society.

James: What's your position on diversity?

West: I celebrate authentic diversity – the wonderful variety of human character, personality, ideas, behaviour, innovations, spiritual paths, purpose, passions, lifestyles, sexualities, personal choices, looks, humour, culture, ingenuity and creativity. Diversity by gender, race and looks is relatively superficial and will become less important in future.

James: What rules do you propose for immigration?

West: The default position is that human beings should be free to live and travel wherever they like so long as they act in accordance with the local rules and customs, so long as they respect the indigenous majority identity and culture, so long as they fully submit to the rules of democracy and the rule of law. Local populations have the right to include or exclude foreigners based upon their chosen criteria,. The criteria might include cultural compatibility and willingness to become a full member of that community. Local populations have the right to exclude those whom they believe to be acting as a group within a group, as a group loyal to some other entity, as a group that is acting in a supremacist way, as a group which is effectively colonising territory rather than joining in and becoming part of their new homeland. I will no longer give automatic group membership. Nationality is something to be earned over time through commitment, trust and loyalty. Newcomers must certainly not impose their culture, values or beliefs upon the people among whom they find themselves. Any attempts at colonisation, tribalism, or displays of loyalty to an external power are totally unacceptable. The receiving community has the responsibility to make newcomers feel welcome and included.

James: This is amazing stuff West. I don't know about you, but I need a coffee.

While West is scrabbling about in the galley of his boat, James takes in the beautiful scene: the water, the ducks and the passing boats. Airplanes pass noisily overhead from Heathrow — one every minute, arriving from all points around the globe. On the other side of the river there is a wedding reception in preparation at the Magna Carta Hotel — a big white marquee and scurrying waiters.

West emerges from the hatch, precariously climbing the steps with two mugs. He stops in his tracks when he sees James, whose eye are positively shining with some idea.

West: You look different. What's up?

James: West, why don't you rewrite the Magna Carta for the 21st Century?

West places the mugs on the roof of the boat, crosses his arms and thinks for a moment.

West: James. You are a genius. That is a fantastic idea. And you know the best bit? It's the 800th Anniversary of Magna Carta. Will you help?

James: Yes, certainly, I'd love to. But there's one problem. I'm ashamed to say I know very little about the first Magna Carta.

West: No problem — I was, after all, present in person.

James: Tell me about it.

West: King John had so mismanaged things that the Nobles and Clergy rose up against him and forced him to agree to a set of rules and agreements by which he would be bound. It was the first successful written document to set out the rights of a people and the responsibilities of the leader in the English Speaking World. It's the foundational document of democracy, freedom and human rights. It is still part of the law in all the countries using English Common Law: Britain, Ireland, America, India, Canada, South Africa, Australia, Pakistan, Bangladesh, Sri Lanka, Burma, New Zealand, Malaysia, Singapore, Nigeria, Ghana, Sierra Leone, Guyana, Uganda, Kenya, Malawi, Zambia, Botswana, Zimbabwe, Tanzania, Mauritius, New Guinea, Nepal, Honduras, Hong Kong, Jamaica, Trinidad and Tobago, Cyprus, Barbados, Cameroon, Namibia, Liberia, Sierra Leone and Israel.

James: You're showing off now! Imagine a modern document with an even grander purpose. It could envision future Civilization. You could start with the assumptions, your core beliefs, assertions and values. You could set out the rules, the rights and responsibilities. Then you could envision the ideal, a positive vision of where we are heading. It doesn't need to be set in stone. It can be a living document which captures the essence of Civilization against which leaders can be held to account and an inspiration.

West: When can we start?

James: Since we are so close here to the original site of the Magna Carta signing, let's have small ceremony. We could invite Suki, Joyce, Seth, Jean and Phil to join us for dinner on Thursday night at the hotel. On Friday morning we'll go out to the actual historic spot on the banks of the river, and you can announce your intentions. We'll fire questions at you and make you think on your feet. If you agree, I'd like to record it and use the transcript as a basis for the first draft of the new Magna Carta.

West: Fantastic, I love it. I'll book the rooms. Will you invite them? I am already excited about this.

ON THE BRINK OF COLLAPSE

We all drove over to Windsor – Suki, Phil, Joyce, Seth, Jean and I. It felt like a school trip. Lots of laughter, high spirits and jokes.

'Old Sugden has been suspended,' said Jean.

'Really?'

'When the police investigated Dr Prasad stealing your recordings, they stumbled upon some payments made to Dr Sugden from the developers who refurbished the Bernie Rosen Unit,' said Seth.

'No. Really?' I said.

Jen nodded gleefully. 'It turns out he's been taking backhanders for years.'

'I hope he likes prison food,' said Phil.

Seth put his arm round my shoulder. 'Do you plan to come back to the Trust when the GMC clears you, James?'

'I've been so busy with West, I haven't thought about it,' I said.

We pulled into the hotel car park. West had arranged the best rooms, overlooking the river. Suki immediately began unpacking and when I emerged from the bathroom after taking a shower I found her lying on the bed.

We met for drinks at 18:30 in the bar. West had arranged for us all to have a gin and tonic. He sent his apologies, saying that he'd join us for dinner at seven. Suki was wearing her stunning blue satin dress, showing off her curves. Joyce wore a sparkly beige dress with sequins. Jean, already on her second gin and tonic, was wearing her favourite green evening gown. Phil, Seth and I wore black tie. I explained the plan for the next day. Everyone was excited.

'About West,' said Joyce. 'Is he definitely in the clear now? No police looking for him or anything?'

'He's not on section any more,' I said. 'So he's a free agent.'

'It's 7 o'clock. Let's go in,' said Seth.

Suki took my hand and we led the group into the Great Charter Room. It was very grand, with pictures all around of Kings and Queens, parliaments, politicians and leaders.

'This is a bit posh for us!' said Jean.

We took out seats, awaiting West. The waiter poured us some fine claret.

While we were making conversation, a member of the hotel staff appeared and opened a set of double doors on one side of the room. Three men processed into the room in a line. Two of them had strange horn-like musical instruments raised and ready to play, and the third had an antiquated drum. They were dressed in elegant mediaeval costume with brightly-coloured doublets and feathers in their hats. They came in and stood to attention on one side. 'Please stand for Western Civilization,' said the master of ceremonies. The drum played a slow, steady roll and we stood up self-consciously. Suki giggled. All of us laughed. The three horn-like instruments struck up with a nasal sound that was loud and primitive – a glorious and rather noisy fanfare that announced West's arrival. We cheered and applauded as emerged in elegant mediaeval robes fit for a King. He was smiling ear to ear. I felt so proud of him. He took his seat at the head of the table and motioned for us to sit.

'James, Suki, Joyce, Jean, Seth and Phil, I am so grateful for the help and support you have given me. You have done me a remarkable service and I want to treat you to a magnificent feast.'

The double doors opened again, and in came a flock of waiters, each carrying a large platter. The musicians struck up with some quieter music and we ate and drank steadily for what seemed like hours. Course after course arrived, each more dainty and delicious than the last.

Eventually the master of ceremonies rang a bell. The music stopped and West stood. 'Friends, tomorrow you shall witness my statement of intent to rewrite the Magna Carta, the Great Charter, for the 21st Century. I would like to thank you all for helping me reach this proud moment. You have each shown me kindness and inspiration. You helped me through my lowest moments. Without your help, I would not be here at all. A very different world may have arisen. Specifically, I would like to thank Dr Hill, my friend James, who has courageously led me through a thorough and determined analysis, healing, challenge, therapy and integration process. You each risked your own career, indeed, your own freedom to help me, and for that, I thank you. Please charge your glasses and stand for a toast.

'Here's to the Future of Western Civilization!'

'The Future of Global Civilization!'

Phil started three cheers and then I felt it behoved me to give a toast in return. 'Here's to maximising human potential – becoming the very best that we can be!'

'Hooray!'

Not to be outdone, West came back with another: 'Here's to good will and friendship between myself and every other consciousness on earth!

'Hooray!'

'Here's to the Future of life!' called out Suki spontaneously.

'Hooray!'

The evening became steadily more riotous with toast and counter-toast, lively music and even an attempt at dancing. Sometime after midnight, I saw a member of hotel staff whisper discretely into West's ear. Calmly, he stood up, making his way round the table.

'James,' he said, 'the media have found out.'

'Found out what?' I replied, slurring my words only slightly. 'About tomorrow's ceremony? So what. Great in fact.'

'No James, not about tomorrow' He sounded a little impatient, and entirely sober. I put down my glass and focused. 'They found out that I'm seeing a psychiatrist. Some- one tipped them off. I'll have to deny it, so I can't be seen here with you. There'd be hell to pay. My reputation would be in tatters. Can you imagine what people would say — what they're probably already saying: *West the basket case. West is mad. West seeing a shrink*.'

I put a comforting hand on his and said nothing.

'Take this,' he said, producing a sleek black mobile phone from somewhere inside his medieval tunic. 'It's a secure line. Code 1215. Stay in touch. If anyone asks, you're here for an office night out, OK?'

I nodded drunkenly and West slipped out of the room. The musicians played on but the atmosphere became subdued. I quietly let the others know what had happened.

'Who knows we are here?' I asked the group.

'I told no one,' said Jean.

'Me neither,' said Seth.

I trusted Suki of course.

'Phil?'

Phil blushed. 'I'm sorry.'

'Sorry for what?'

'I was paid £30,000 for the story. I thought I'd lost my job over West. I was scared I'd have to sell my house,' he said.

'You selfish idiot,' said Jean. 'You greedy little man.'

He couldn't look me in the eye.

'Who knows?' I asked.

'The Sun.'

'The Sun? Well, hopefully they'll run it as a joke story. No one will take it seriously,' said Seth.

'James, I am sorry I let you down,' said Phil.

'Phil, you have let yourself down,' I said.

Phil got up to leave.

'Sit down Phil. The damage is done. You can help put it right. We will make a success out of this. I am going back to my room now. The rest of you carry on as normal but do not speak to anyone about anything. If anyone asks about West, say it was a joke and make light of it, OK?'

Back at the room, Suki fell fast asleep within five minutes — after a few years as a doctor most people had that skill of nodding off at a moment's notice. I lay awake for several hours with my mind buzzing, wondering how to turn the situation around.

———◆———

I woke at 5:30, and my mind was racing again within seconds. Suki beckoned me in for a kiss then rolled over, back to sleep.

I called room service for breakfast then put on the television quietly. I turned to the BBC News Channel. 'Dr James Hill, seen here with his girlfriend Dr Suki Chen, was recently up before the GMC having been accused of misdiagnosing a psychotic patient who claimed to be Western Civilization.' My mouth fell open.

Suki leapt out of bed. 'Oh my God, this is awful,' she said.

There were pictures of us leaving the GMC. 'The GMC have refused to confirm or deny whether the outcome of the hearing was influenced by a last minute political intervention. The bizarre allegations in 'The Sun' have already hit stock markets in Asia. The Nikkei has fallen by 5%, the Hang Seng by 6.7% and Sydney's ASX200 has tumbled by a record 11.2%. The British Prime Minister is reported to be in consultation with the US President over possible concerted action to avert a meltdown. Earlier we interviewed investor Mr George Soros on the implications of this story...'

Our breakfast arrived. Bacon and eggs with coffee, which I wolfed down rapidly.

I reached into my jacket pocket to find the secure phone West had given me. Carefully I typed in the numbers 1, 2, 1, 5. Had I misremembered in my drunkenness? No, it opened. 'Wow. This is incredible. Look!'

Suki read over my shoulder, 'Missed calls from The Chairman of the Federal Reserve, the CEO of Goldman Sachs, the Prime Minister of Canada, the Head of MI6, the Chair of the Joint Chiefs of Staff, Chancellor Merkel. My God.'

I flicked through the vast contacts list. It had the names of all the world's top leaders in every sphere. I looked for West's number.

'Try the one called "Me",' suggested Suki.

I tried "Me" and held the phone cautiously to my ear. It was ringing. On and on it rang, and eventually went to voicemail.

'Hi West,' I said after the bleep. 'It's James. If you can, put on the News. The news is out globally now. We've got to decide what to do.'

We turned to CNN. '...the South Korean President has put his forces on high alert after North Korea fired six missiles into the Sea of Japan. Japan has ordered a call up of its Naval Reserves. Meanwhile in Istanbul, crowds are forming this morning after President Erdogan ordered the closure of the nations TV channels late last night.'

Suki's phone rang. 'Dad, Hi ... Yes, I'm OK thanks ... Yes, James is my boyfriend ... I'm with him now ... No, we're not in danger. I don't think so. ... No, I can't come right now ... OK. I'll keep in touch ... I love you too.'

'James, do you think we could be in danger?'

'I don't honestly know, Suki. This is getting out of hand.'

The secure phone bleeped. It was a voicemail from West. 'Hi James, please stay put in the room. I am very busy as you can imagine. Use the room service. Charge it to my account. I will be in touch. Please do not speak to the media.'

Joyce, Seth and Jean joined us in our room.

Suki turned to Russia Today. 'Revelations that Western Civilization is on the brink of collapse have triggered a global uprising of anti-Western forces. This Good Friday morning, churches across the Philippines have been ordered to close for safety after suicide bombers killed dozens of worshippers in Santa Maria Cathedral. The US 7th Fleet has been placed on high alert in the region.'

We turned to Al Jazeera. 'At long last the global criminal syndicate which is the West has been exposed as a charade run by a madman in collaboration with the British Queen, the US President, the Bildeberg Club and the Council on Foreign Relations. The truth is out and the peoples of the world can now rise up and liberate themselves from this parasitic elite.' They cut to clips of blindfolded American and European hostages in Karachi being led off to trucks.

ABC News: 'The White House has dismissed the story as a prank by junior doctors in the UK. A spokesman said the President will give a security briefing tomorrow.'

There was a knock at the door. 'Room Service.' I opened the door.

A TV camera and bright lights were shoved right in my face.

'Carol Barwell, NBC News. Dr Hill, can you confirm that you have been carrying out psychotherapy on Western Civilization?'

'Dr Hill, John Majors, CNN. Please give us an interview.'

I tried to close the door but they were pushing against it. Suki jumped up and kicked the journalist hard in the shin. The door slammed shut. 'Well done,' I whispered.

'What shall we do?' asked Suki.

'Look at this,' said Seth. There was a swarm of journalists in the garden pointing cameras at our window.

'There's Phil with them! Judas!' said Joyce.

I called West but he didn't answer. I called Steve to ask him to let my family know I was fine and not to worry.

We could hear helicopters, trucks and police sirens. The noise faded back to quietness. The journalists were being moved from the grass by a line of police. There was a knock at the door. 'Ignore it James,' Suki said. Another knock, more insistent.

I looked though the spy hole. It was a man with close cropped brown hair and an ear piece. He seemed to be in military uniform. The journalists had gone. I spoke through the door. 'Who is it?'

'Sergeant Redwood, Household Cavalry Regiment, Sir.'

I opened the door.

'Sir, I have been instructed to take you and your group to a place of safety,' he said. He showed me his card. It didn't mean much to me, but the menacing rifle he was carrying spoke volumes.

'Instructed by whom?'

'Orders from on high sir, from the very top.' He looked at me, expecting me to know what that meant.

'All Right, thank you. It'll take 20 minutes to pack.'

'I'm sorry sir, you have five minutes.'

We followed him down the corridor, down the stairs and out onto a fire escape that led to a service area at the rear of the hotel. We climbed into a two waiting black Range Rover and left without delay. We were in a convoy with police motorcyclists front and back, and other Land Rovers with blacked out windows.

I could tell we were heading for Windsor, and I began to suspect the final destination. There was an Army roadblock at the entrance to the town, but we were waved straight through. On the High Street, the whole convoy took a sudden right turn up Castle Hill and sped in through the iron gates of the Castle.

'Pinch me' whispered Suki into my ear. 'I don't believe this is happening.'

I'd visited the castle as a tourist many years ago and on that occasion the place had seemed disappointingly like a toy fort with pretend soldiers. But now it was clearly the nerve centre of something very important. Combat-ready troops were positioned in sandbag bunkers and you could hear the crackle of radio messages. The police driver ushered us into the castle buildings and handed us over to a suited young woman with a clipboard. She didn't introduce herself, but told us to follow. We walked briskly through art-lined, red-carpeted corridors for what seemed like ten minutes but was probably only two. Men in in suits bustled past us and convened in groups here and there talking seriously. Eventually we were deposited in a drawing room and left to our own devices.

It was a comfortable little room with a view onto a walled garden. In appearance it was much like the living room of an ordinary house in the country. There was an open hearth and a mantelpiece. Magazines littered a coffee table. Horse and Hound. Country Life. The others, Joyce, Jean, Seth and Suki, collapsed onto sofas and armchairs – wide-eyed, silent and shaking their heads at one another. I knew exactly how they felt.

'Do you think we'll meet the Queen?' said Suki.

Before I could answer, the secure phone buzzed in my pocket. There was a text from West. 'You'll be safe there. Sit tight. I'll be in touch later, West.'

The phone rang while I was reading the message.

'Hello?'

'West?' said a man's voice.

'Dr James Hill speaking.'

'I am Stephen, the Prime Minister of Canada,' he said. 'I have been trying to get through to West but he is not answering. Can you ask him to call me when you speak to him please? It is rather urgent.'

'Yes,' I said, stunned, 'yes, Prime Minister, I shall.'

'Who was that?' asked Suki.

'The Prime Minister of Canada.'

———◆———

Three hours later, at 1:00PM, a young man in a morning coat served us several plateful of triangular sandwiches. A dove pecked at the window while we ate. Joyce thumbed through Country Life. We had been there four hours, and apart from short trips to an antiquated loo just along the corridor, we had been politely forbidden to leave. The hefty suited man outside the door would not even tell us why we were there or what to expect next.

Suki broke the silence eventually. She had been checking the news on her phone. 'Saudi Arabia has bombed Iranian nuclear sites and sunk six Iranian Naval ships in the Straights of Hormuz. The Israelis captured the Suez Canal overnight. Cairo is going wild. Martial law has been declared in Dubai. There's a piece about us in the South China Morning Post. Take a look.'

She passed me the phone. I read out loud just to hear the sound of my own voice again. 'Hong Kong born Dr Suki Chen has been linked to a conspiracy that sought to conceal West Civilization's serious mental health problems.'

'They've said awful things about my mother's family,' said Suki. 'They said they were executed as traitors. It's not a good sign. If the Communist Party senses West is going under, who knows where it'll lead. If you scroll down, you'll see they've started rounding up dissidents all over China. Chinese Marines have staged a practice assault on Hainan Island too.'

'Practice for what?' I asked.

'Taiwan. The PLA are massing troops in Fujian province and the airforce are redeploying their fighter jets in the south,' she said. 'Vietnam has landed some forces on the Spratly Islands. The Malaysians are furious. One of their frigates has sunk. They reckon it was a Chinese submarine.'

'It's just as well the markets are closed for Easter or they'd be falling through the floor,' I said.

'Markets are open elsewhere. The Dollar's at an all-time low against the Rouble, Renminbi and Riyal. The price of copper has collapsed. Gold has spiked 60% in Mumbai.'

'60%? West has got to sort this out before Monday.'

A man in tails with immaculately coiffed hair sidled through the door. 'Good afternoon, I trust you're all quite comfortable. They've given you tea I see. Good.'

Jean rose to her feet. 'When are we going to allowed out of here? My grandson David doesn't have anyone to pick him up from school.'

The man asked for David's school address. He made a note. 'He'll be taken care of. As for leaving the castle, West feels it would be best if you stayed here for the time-being – for your own protection.'

I had to agree with that.

'Well, we'd appreciate a bit of an update at least.' said Jean, sitting down.

'I apologise for the dearth of information, but things are moving very quickly, as you will appreciate. I can now tell you though, that Her Majesty has invited you to attend the Good Friday service in St George's Chapel this evening. That will be at 3:00 PM.'

'Church?' said Seth, mystified.

'The Queen?' said Jean, agog with excitement.

'Someone will be along to collect you in good time.'

'Thank you,' I said, and the courtier bowed his way out.

We spent the next couple of hours finishing the sandwiches and reading magazines. Suki curled up on one of the sofas and had a quick snooze.

The chapel was unexpectedly light-filled and colourful. I had expected it to be dark and heavy with history, but the intricately carved stone and bright rows of banners made it feel like a corner of heaven.

The Queen arrived shortly before 3PM – serene and, well, very much as she appears on television. Prince Philip caught Suki's eye as he walked past and gave her a warm smile. The service itself was short and dignified, consisting of little more than a reading of the story of the crucifixion. Since my experience of Church was limited, almost exclusively, to Christmas midnight mass with its noisy carols, uncomfortable seats and drunken late arrivals, I was surprised to find that this service calmed me and reassured me.

When we returned to the drawing room, West was standing looking out of the window. He was wearing an incredibly smart dark blue suit with a striking colourful tie. He looked confident and well rested, his eyes sparkling. 'Afternoon James. Afternoon all. I am so sorry to put you through this.'

'Are you going to go public, West?' I asked.

'Yes. It's sooner than I planned but the cat's out of the bag. Will you help me prepare?'

'Of course. You're ready to face the world.'

'I think so,' said West. 'It feels like such a long time ago that we first met. Thank you for all you've done, James.'

'That's my pleasure. It has been fascinating for me to get to know you and to witness your courage.'

'I've called a press conference this afternoon. Just like we planned at the site of the signing of the original Magna Carta. I've invited the world's media and leaders.'

'That's fantastic! What do we have to do to prepare you?'

'I'm feeling a bit of performance anxiety to be honest, which isn't necessarily a bad thing. But I'd like to ask you a few questions if I may. I think that's what I need right now.'

'Fire away.'

West: OK. First question. What's my diagnosis?

James: You're fit and healthy though there's plenty of room for improvement.' I said. 'Economically you're depressed. The seeds of the solutions are there if you choose to grow them. When I first met you, you had low self-esteem, low self-confidence and strong suicidal impulses. You were unconscious of your many different parts which were stuck in conflict and draining your energy. To thrive you need to draw together the best of all the parts. We've made progress with a few of your wounds but I think there are many more, so continue to be alert for those.

West: Any other recommendations?

James: Keep your attention as broad as possible to avoid groupthink. Keep asking questions with an open mind. Stay creative. Keep in mind your positive visualisations of the future. Remember that you're a living being, so be present and act like it. I think you're a fantastic success story.

West: Can you predict my future?

James: If you draw on your strengths, you'll thrive. You need to challenge many assumptions which you've held and change many of your behaviours and institutions. You will do this because you have to. It will be done by younger generations, less attached to the past. There will be ever-increasing interchange between you and the other civilizations. For the foreseeable future, the distinctions will remain but the boundaries will blur until you eventually merge into a global consciousness and civilization.

West: I'm more optimistic now. I've risen above the blocks, wounds and conflicts and I can see the way forward. I've learned to draw on my strengths. I feel more together.

James: Your high level of self-criticism is one of your greatest strengths relative to your competitors. It can go too far and become destructive. Balance criticism with appreciation, gratitude, optimism and positive vision of the future. Have the confidence and courage to lead, knowing that many of your parts will never thank you, respect you or show gratitude. You can't force your immature and wounded parts to grow up or to heal. Step into your most mature, most integrated and wise self and to lead from there.

West: Now that I've spread all round the world into so many different people, that's allowing me to let go of my historical and tribal baggage and get ready for global consciousness, aligning the whole human living system. That's exciting and scary, a huge responsibility. Who can help me?

James: The fact that you have so many different parts, ideas, values and people all around the world is a strength. Keep your bearings. Continually recalibrate your inner compass, update your map and lead with confidence. You have many different sources of wisdom, intelligence. You're going to be fine, West.

West: Here are some passes that'll get you through security. It's at 8PM on Runnymede Hill. You've got front row seats, so you'll be on hand if I need you.

They shake hands.

James: Good luck West! I'm proud of you.

West hugs each of them in turn, then leaves.

All afternoon there was a succession of calls to the secure phone from world leaders. Mostly they were calling because they couldn't get through to West. By now they all knew my name, and trusted me with advice, warnings and good luck messages for West.

My family left messages on my own mobile phone, but I was advised not to speak to them on an insecure line.

We were allowed a certain amount of freedom to wander – presumably West had arranged things with the security people – so we went out to get some fresh air in the private areas of the castle gardens. After twenty minutes we were rushed inside when a press helicopter breached the air cordon established by the RAF.

Instead, we used our freedom to wander the corridors of the castle until we found a room with a television. The crowds at the Vatican were three times the usual size this year. Fox News channel had a lively debate: 'Mad, bad or sad?' 60% of viewers thought West was mad and that I was a fraud. The newspapers were evenly split as to whether we were witnessing 'The Biggest Hoax in History' or 'The Western World on the Brink of Collapse'.

'Well, they'll find out soon enough,' said Suki. 'Come on, I need to get dressed up if we're going to be on TV in front of four billion people.' That put a lump in my throat. But there was no going back now.

When the courtier with the coiffed hair came back to the sitting room to collect us at 19.30, all five of us were standing ready in whatever smart clothes we had grabbed at the hotel. Suki looked stunning, of course. We set off through the castle, retracing the route we had taken that morning.

There were many more people milling around in the corridors. I recognised some journalists from TV.

'Look,' said Jean, pointing through a window to group standing on a manicured lawn. There's the United Nations Secretary General.'

'Who's that he's with?' asked Joyce.

'I don't believe it,' said Suki, 'that's Vladimir Putin.'

My stomach was churning. I'd been very comfortable treating West, but now I was badly out of my depth. Suki could tell I was becoming withdrawn and held my hand.

'You're going to be just fine, James.'

THE NEW MAGNA CARTA

en minutes after leaving the castle we arrived at the foot of Runnymede Hill. There were multiple security cordons manned by police and soldiers – searching bags and patting people down. A dozen outside broadcast vans sprouting aerials and satellite dishes were parked along the roadside. A river of people was flowing uphill to where a stage and VIP seating had been erected. Twilight was gathering, but the powerful TV lights threw the whole scene into sharp relief.

Flanked by firearms officers, we were ushered through security and up the hill to our seats in the front row.

'James!' exclaimed Suki. 'Look! There! It's the Pope with the Archbishop of Canterbury.'

We had a bit of a competition between the five of us then for the best celebrity spot. Jean claimed victory with Elton John and Madonna.

Someone sat down beside me. 'Hello James,' said a familiar voice.

'David. Good to meet you,' I said. It was David Cameron, the British Prime Minister. He shook my hand and reached across to Suki.

'I appreciate the work you've been doing. I've been aware of it for some time. Well done.'

'There's President Obama with Michelle and the girls,' said Joyce. The president was heading our way, waving and nodding at people left and right. He greeted Mr Cameron then turned to me.

'You must be Dr Hill.'

I stood up to shake his hand.

'How do you do? This is my fiancée, Suki Chen.'

He leaned forward to greet Suki with a hug. Michelle frowned briefly but then closed in for a hug with me. They sat down on the other side of Mr Cameron.

The VIP seats were almost full now, and, not surprisingly, Police helicopters were keeping careful watch overhead. Between us and the stage was a mass of ordinary people, divided, like the Red Sea, by a central aisle. They were sitting and standing – chatting excitedly. Some had deck chairs. Some even had picnics. Beyond that, right up against the stage, was the press corps, bristling with cameras and sound booms.

Two long lines of soldiers arrived. They were Grenadier Guards in their magnificent red tunics and giant black bearskin hats. They formed a guard all the way from the base of the hill, through the crowds of public, thought the media, besides the VIP stand and up to the stage.

A man in elegant Indian dress made his way across to say hello. He offered his hand, 'Narendra Modi.'

'James Hill, how do you do.'

'Who was he?' asked Seth.

'The Prime Minister of India,' said Angela Merkel, Chancellor of Germany from behind us. I turned around to greet her. It was weird — all these politicians seemed to know who we were.

The band of the Grenadier Guards marched up the hill though the gap to the Liberty Bell March.

'Listen, it's the Queen's Horses,' said Jean.

Sure enough, the Queen with Prince Philip arrived in a magnificent Golden Stage coach. Three trumpets announced their arrival with a fanfare. The TV crews turned en masse. They slowly made their way up through the cheering crowds of public, up to the Royal Box at the front of the VIP stand. When she took her seat, we stood and sang as the band played God Save the Queen. There was a festive, atmosphere. It was odd. The fear had passed.

I checked my watch. It was 20.05. Other people were beginning to doing likewise — looking restless.

'Where's West?' said Suki.

'I was just thinking the same thing.'

'Check the phone,' she said.

There were missed calls from West. I phoned him immediately and for the first time today he picked up.

'James, I am not sure I can go ahead with this,' he said.

'Where are you?'

'On the boat,' he replied.

I laughed nervously. 'Everyone is ready for you.'

David Cameron looked at me anxiously. 'Everything all right?'

'Absolutely fine. I'll be back shortly.'

I jogged down the hill, slipping and sliding in my smart shoes. How the hell was I going to get back to West's houseboat? I waved my pass at the security cordon and as I reached the road a hand grabbed my shoulder. It was Sergeant Redwood.

'This way, sir,' he said, and guided me to a white van with blacked-out windows. Excellent. At least I now had a lift. At Redwood's invitation, I climbed in through the rear door.

Inside, I found West sitting with his head in his hands. He was dressed in a beautifully tailored suit and his hair was freshly cut. He looked up balefully.

'West!' I said. 'Why on earth did you tell me you were on the boat?'

'That's where I'm heading. But these policemen insisted I saw you first.'

'What's the problem exactly?'

'I feel sick. My pulse is racing. My mouth is dry. I've got pins and needles in my hands.'

I put my arm round him. 'It's just performance anxiety — adrenaline, and you're breathing too fast.'

I pulled the van door shut and got West to rebreathe his air into a bag. Within two minutes, he was calmer.

'Performance anxiety is normal. All the greats get it — some of them every time they perform. Have you been to the toilet?'

He nodded.

'Imagine you can take all that fear in your belly and re-label it as courage. Remember all the great battles you've ever fought. Summon up the memory of how you felt when you showed maximum courage. Say to yourself, 'I am good enough. I am ready. I have prepared my whole life for this.'

He closed his eyes and sat in silence for perhaps a minute, then nodded and pushed open the van door.

'I want you to come with me,' he said as he climbed out. 'I want you at my side.'

Now I felt my own burst of performance anxiety. 'All right,' I said. 'But let me just dash in here first,' and I made my way to a nearby portable toilet.

A few minutes later we were approaching Runnymede hilltop. The sun had completely set now, and the powerful floodlighting lit the whole hillside.

'Act natural,' I urged, covering up my own fear. 'Like a walk in the park.'

Thunderous applause broke out from the crowd as we stepped into the circle of light — also a few boos. The media's cameras flashed blindingly as we stood together by the steps leading up to the stage. I could see West's eyes were filled with tears that I interpreted as pride rather than fear.

'You're ready for this,' I said. 'You've been preparing for thousands of years. I'm right behind you, all the way.' I made my way back to my seat. Suki smiled and placed a proud hand on my leg.

West mounted the stage with a confident bound and a tremendous cheer erupted from the audience. A small group of people disguised as members of the press corps unfurled a banner and shouted out: 'Rot in hell you war monger! Die you old racist!' but the cheers drowned them out and the photographers behind them made them take down the banner.

'Your Majesty, Presidents, Prime Ministers, Ladies, Gentlemen and Children, thank you all very much for coming. To the four billion of you viewing on television, thank you for watching. I am here to introduce myself to you in person. A few of you have met me before, but most of you only know of me as an idea or a feeling.'

'Tell us then. Who are you?' boomed a heckler's voice from the area of the protestors.

'I am West, the consciousness of Western Civilization, inhabiting billions of people all over the world, stretching back into history and out into the future. I'm a field, a consciousness, a set of evolving beliefs, evolving institutions, principles and values. I am part of the consciousness of all the human beings who have chosen to accept me. Every one of those people lives within me, and I live within them. Today you see me embodied in a human physical form.'

He stepped forward, opening his arms as if to embrace the crowd. Another huge cheer went up.

'On this very spot beside the River Thames, the Magna Carta was signed 800 years ago. Since then, Western Civilization has been by far the biggest driver of freedom, creativity, wealth, health, increasing living standards, opportunity and human potential in human history. The rights and freedoms that were granted to nobles and clergy here 800 years ago have since spread through the rest of the world – to all ages, genders, races, religions, rich and poor, an ever-expanding circle of freedom and rights.'

'I, West, invite you to join me in a grand undertaking – to rewrite the Magna Carta, creating a living document fit for the 21st Century. It will set out a vision for the future of our Civilization and codify its rules. By myself, I am nothing. I can only act through you. So I invite you all to join me in creating a living document – a Great Charter to inspire our generation and future generations to be the very best that we can be.'

A wave of applause, tentative at first, then more enthusiastic, spread through the audience, gathering power and conviction.

'And now, in the spirit of Magna Carta, it's only right that you have your chance to speak.'

A clamour of hand raising and yelling started in the press area. West was shading his eyes and peering out into the audience. I had a dreadful suspicion as to what was coming next.

'James, will you join me please,' he said.

My heart raced and my mouth went dry. What could I do, though? Messrs Cameron and Obama were clapping and encouraging me to go forward. I left my seat and joined West on stage. The lights were blinding. I couldn't see Suki anywhere.

'Allow me to introduce Dr James Hill, a psychiatrist who has been helping me to clarify my thinking and find my voice.'

I was embarrassed and proud simultaneously. I had never stood in front of such a vast number of people. The audience clapped politely.

'James, would you mind kicking off the question and answer session, and then open it up to the audience?'

'Certainly.' My voice croaked and sounded strange booming through the sound system. 'So, West, tell us, what are your strengths?'

He pondered for a moment. 'Openness, self-criticism, the media, democracy, embracing change, science, capitalism, authentic diversity, the rule of law, continuous learning, the Internet and military power.'

'And your weaknesses?'

'Excessive self-criticism, self-hatred and a suicidal streak. Unresolved shame and guilt for the past. Dehumanisation. Separation from nature. Vulnerability to shocks. Demographic weakness.'

'For what are you grateful?'

'The boldness of my people. I'm grateful for this planet with all its resources and life which enables me to thrive. I'm grateful for the opportunity to grow and to be the best I can. I'm grateful for the human being, this amazing conscious social animal.'

'What are you ashamed of?'

'I'm ashamed of the waste of human potential due to unemployment, inequality, low expectations, abuse, crime, racism, dysfunctional personalities, limiting beliefs, discrimination, corruption, bad values, poor leadership and victim mentality.'

'Are you ashamed of your past?'

The protestors started up again: 'Imperialist bastard! Racist bully!'

West politely waited for them to settle. 'Yes and No. No in that human beings alive today are responsible for their own actions and choices and can't be held responsible for the successes or failures of the past. But I do feel deeply sorry for the crimes and evil acts that I have committed. My strength is my ability to learn from the past, my ability to change my values. Feminism, anti-slavery, anti-racism, human rights, anti-imperialism and all the other movements for human progress are part of me too. I have learned and corrected myself. I will endeavour to continue doing so.

'Where are you heading?' I asked.

'Somewhere very exciting. It's a creative, emergent, evolutionary process. We will become a global Civilization, ever more integrated. When I get the hang of cheap, clean, abundant energy, human potential will flourish exponentially. We'll colonise space. We will tell our shared history of all humanity, our development together. We're going to correct the mistakes we've made and, unfortunately, make new ones.'

A chorus of voices started to call out questions. 'One question at a time,' I said. 'Please raise your hand if you have a question for West.' Hundreds of hands went up. 'The lady in the red dress with the blonde hair.'

'Why didn't you reveal yourself to us before?'

'Because I have only recently become conscious of myself. I didn't know I could speak like this.'

'Thank you. The man by the tree,' I said.

'Do you know God?'

'Yes but it's not a man in the sky. God is like me, like you, a consciousness, a feeling, a knowing within all of us, of which we can choose to be conscious. There are many ways of knowing and experiencing God, or not at all.'

'Are any of the religions true?' called out a young woman.

'We are all conscious beings and social animals in an interconnected living system. People differ widely on their spiritual and religious beliefs. They are free to think, feel and do whatever they like, so long as it doesn't infringe on the freedoms of others. God exists. This means different things to different people. For some it is the story of Jesus as told in the Bible and the other traditional religious stories. For others it means that life itself is sacred. For others, God is a human concept which others believe in which they do not. Our consciousness is life aware of itself. Life, the trees, the animals, the living system of which we are a part is sacred. For practical purposes, we should treat life as being sacred and respect every being as a being, though not necessarily their beliefs or behaviour.'

'Will you ban criticism of my religion?' asked a hawkish looking man.

'No. There must be freedom of religion and spiritual beliefs, and the freedom to believe nothing. Different people hold different things sacred. There has to be respect for the things which others hold sacred up to a certain point out of politeness but not in a way which inhibits other's freedoms, democracy and science. Religions are beliefs which must be open to scrutiny, debate and humour.'

'The gentleman by the fence.' We waited until a microphone was taken over to him. 'Are you going to sort out all our problems for us?'

'No, you are. I am a consciousness that lives in you all. I can only exist and act through you. By expressing myself here like this, I hope to encourage you all to start being more conscious of the role you each play in me. I hope that you will all choose to step up into your own highest potential and work together to be the best you can.'

'How are you feeling in yourself now?' asked Chancellor Merkel.

'Thank you for asking Angela. I'm tired, overwhelmed, excited all at once. I'm bigger, more diverse and more complex than ever. I inhabit more people from more places than ever before. I'm learning incredibly fast. I'm becoming more integrated and connected. I've got some massive challenges with the environment, resources, energy, migration and imbalance in the world economy. I'm confident that these things will turn out fine. I still have an extremely brutal inner critic and parts of me are wounded and self-hating. I'm trying to love and empower them and to heal the wounds to get all my energy aligned positively for the future. I'm very fortunate to have you as a friend and leader.'

She smiled, waving her hands to dismiss the compliment.

An Arab man with a French accent asked, 'Why are you so insecure, West?'

'My self-criticism has got out of hand, toxic and abusive. When I achieve something, I take it for granted and move on to the next thing. I tend to focus on the negative rather than showing gratitude for the huge successes that I've had. But look at it this way: I've had to adapt to a shift of power in the world because of decolonisation, globalisation, the rise of China and the rest. Many forces have dramatically changed my traditional identity, culture and values. The sexual revolution, mass migration, feminism, consumerism, television, terrorism, air travel and the Internet, to name but a few. These changes have been a challenge to my identity and values. Also, many of the other countries have caught up now and started taking on aspects of me, which challenges my original core countries.'

'What was your relationship with your dad like?' asked one of President Obama's girls, looking at her father with a mischievous smile.

'My memory is sketchy that far back, I'm afraid. I don't have a conscious relationship with my ancestors. I'd like to reconnect with them.'

'Why do you think you're so unique?' asked a young man with a Russian accent, dressed in a black polo neck sweater.

'I engage in an open-ended striving for freedom, learning, a thirst for new knowledge, new ideas and in openness to change and adaptation. Respect for the rights of the individual, freedom of thought, freedom of speech. The right to practise your religion while respecting the rights of others. The right for people to be who they choose to be. I've had the most dramatic effect on the world. There's been an explosion in population, technology, knowledge, trade and travel. Life expectancy at birth is twice what it was a century ago. Most people have clean water, abundant food, better shelter than ever. People have more freedom, property and personal rights than ever. I've brought together the world community into one global consciousness for the first time. My scientific and democratic systems are open-ended, adaptive, constructive and creative. No one else comes close.'

There were the inevitable boos and shouts: 'Bigot! Racist! Xenophobe! What about all your wars?'

A stout middle aged with an accent that may have been Israeli shouted from the front of the VIP seating: 'Why are you so gullible? Why do you let people walk all over you?'

'Ehud, Being open and accepting, is both a strength and weakness. On balance it's a strength because I trust myself, my values and institutions. So long as I stay fit, adaptive and have strong boundaries, I can be open to all comers because things will work out for the best. If you mean "gullible" in the sense of modern liberal naiveté to the darker side of human nature, tribal, territorial, religious, criminal, exploitative and selfish then, yes, that's a phase them much of me has been going through. The modern world with its education, freedom and opportunities has created some generations who don't have the experience of the other value systems. There's a naiveté that comes with the victim-rescuer dynamic. The solution is to ask incisive, empowering questions, transparency, democracy, freedom and learning. Learn from our mistakes and correct the imbalances.'

'Are you living according to your authentic values?' asked a tall Swedish man from just beyond the press corps.

'Jan, that's a tricky one to answer because I have so many different parts of me. Many of them have contradictory values and those values are in fast transition. You could ask particular individuals, organisations, companies and countries. 200 years ago most the West operated with imperialistic, power-driven leadership with a veneer of religion, bureaucracy and commerce. We've adapted into complex democracies, pluralistic, multicultural, multiracial, decolonized and globalised so, inevitably, we've got mixed values, different behaviours pulling in different directions, double standards and inconsistencies. I'm aware that it's easy to level the criticism of double standards and inauthenticity at me. No one is perfect. I have all the different value systems alive within me in their healthy and unhealthy forms. They're in a constant struggle to assert themselves differentially according to the situation.'

Jan got in quickly with a reply: 'What is your highest value?'

'My highest value is the maximum fulfilment of human potential, encompassing security, health, survival, freedom, order, justice, love, opportunity, fitness, creativity, high living standards and truth. Science, freedom, reason, democracy, individualism, law and capitalism have been the core drivers of human progress.'

'Could you be more modest?' asked a grey haired woman.

West smiled, nodding his head. 'Parts of me are modest and humble, parts are arrogant, cocky, and self-assured. Parts of me are deeply self-hating, self-critical, doubtful and uncertain. I'd like to be conscious, humble, modest and self-respecting, self-accepting and proud of my achievements.'

Someone with an Indian accent took up my theme: 'Why do you always assume that West is best?'

'For several hundred years, it has been largely true. Increasingly, that attitude will be less relevant because the others are catching up and are joining me. Anyone who's complacent or assumes their own superiority is putting themselves at risk. It in my interest to be as open to learning from others as possible. Where I fail to do that, I'd appreciate your reminder.'

'How can you garner peace and friendly relations with your brothers and sisters in the East and South?' asked President Goodluck Jonathan of Nigeria.

'Goodluck, we're going to merge ever more. I feel very close to Nigeria already – very much a part of the place, and I think that you are going to be a very dynamic and entrepreneurial part of me when you fully harness your people's creativity and potential and bring them security and justice. My countries should intend to remain dominant military powers, capable of defending themselves, their borders, property, resources and values. This will increasingly involve cyber security, information security, energy security and much more conscious approach to culture, values and relationships. Competition for resources should be on the basis of a free and open market although it's very important to make sure that poorer countries have proper access to resources that they need to survive and to make sure that no one country or group of countries exploit or gain access to exclusively to any particular set of resources. We could reduce tensions with Russia, North Korea and Iran by genuinely reassuring them that I'm not a threat to them and by moving into the consciousness of their people. However, we have to live in the world as it is, and while some are hostile to us, we must be properly defended.'

'Is mass immigration by members of a single religion a threat or an opportunity?' asked a tall white man with a Dutch accent and bleached blond hair.

'Geert, it's a fantastic opportunity, a challenge to my complacency, materialism and secular fundamentalism. It challenges my attitudes to sex, family, law, God, economics and life. It's helping me snap out of my cultural relativism and self-hatred. That's all positive. The West gives religious minorities a safe place in which to immerse in the modern world, the many voices, many challenges in a prosperous and pluralistic environment. What better catalyst for conscious evolution could there be? We're bringing humanity together. It's a bumpy ride but I'm confident of my values and open to learn. If we're creative, strong, compassionate and have clear boundaries, we will all end up stronger and better.'

'Do you feel guilty about imperialism?' asked a young woman with a nose stud and dyed red hair who was among the group of protestors.

'As an overall project, no, I don't feel guilty. Specific abuses and crimes like slavery and the genocide of some native peoples, yes, of course. Human beings have always spread themselves around, colonised, fought for control, sought to take the resources of others, systems competing for primacy and territory. They're still doing it. Because of my technical and economic superiority and because of the ingenuity, courage and energy of my people, I did it on a scale larger than anyone else ever before. The scale is different but the principle is the same. Others would do well to honestly examine their own history and present rather than projecting their negativity on me.

'What about the gap between rich and poor? How do you feel about that?' called out the young man sitting next to the last questioner. There was a sneer in his voice.

'Those who are successful, creative, well-organised, disciplined, work hard and those who take risks deserve to reap the rewards of their successes. However, people can suffer misfortune and events beyond their control. Children don't choose to be born into their families, time and place. By the time a child is 5, much of their character is laid down and they had little responsibility for that. They don't get to choose whether they have excellent, loving, encouraging, prosperous and skilful parents. So we need to make sure that we have systems in place to spread opportunity equally while having a safety net for those who, through misfortune, don't do as well as others. Healthcare should be provided equally for all people. Good education should be provided for all children. All people are entitled to live in freedom and security. The poor have to suffer the bad behaviour of those around them. I want us to end the poverty of love, opportunity, security, family, support, skills, discipline, community, spirit and imagination.'

I could see an elderly man sitting on a garden chair way off to one side. He didn't have his hand raised but I knew he had something to say. 'When are you going to grow up, West?' he asked.

'Good question. I'm pretty old in human terms – several thousand years – but parts of me are immature. My modern parts are still in their adolescence. My postmodern parts are still in their childhood, and my holistic, integral, global parts are still in infancy.

'Why are you here?' asked a girl, about ten years old.

'I don't know.'

She laughed, surprised at his honesty.

'Can we ignite a self-propagating group process to transform you?' A fellow psychiatrist perhaps, shouting out from somewhere in the midst of the crowd.

'I hope to do that by presenting myself today. I'd like to evolve a Magna Carta for the 21st Century together with you all. I will work on a first draft with Dr Hill and we will invite you all to help improve it to be the best it can be.'

An Australian woman in Buddhist robes shouted, 'Why can't you sit still?'

'I've always been restless and had a desire to travel, to try new things. I'm curious and love exploring. I would benefit from practicing mindfulness. You'll see more of that.'

'What do you most want to pass on to your children when you die?' asked a man with a boy sitting on his shoulders up near the front.

'A healthy, vibrant planet. A healthy, vibrant and resilient global Civilization, conscious, adaptive and learning, exploring the cosmos and consciousness.'

Spontaneous applause broke out across the crowd.

'The young man in the grey suit,' I said.

'Are you optimistic or realistic?'

'Optimistic, although I'm well aware of the many threats and risks. If I stick to my strengths and pull out all stops, I will thrive, survive and continue to push human potential way beyond its current level. I prefer to err on the side of optimism and enthusiasm because my history shows that human beings are capable of when they apply their imagination, energy and enthusiasm.'

'Can we choose our future?'

'We can influence the future. The future is emergent and depends on the behaviour of billions of people including everyone watching now.'

'Can you get rid of our awful political system please?'

'Democracy is the best form of government for a complex and well educated society like ours. However, it's messy and it's not a completed project. As society and technology evolves, so democracy needs to evolve to keep up with it. We should experiment to improve it. Democracy is like a garden. It needs to be continuously tended, otherwise it overgrows with weeds. There is a human tendency towards authoritarianism, corruption, complacency and groupthink which needs to be challenged. So democracy must be alive, vigorous, competitive with freedom of thought, argument, debate, constant vigilance for groupthink, authoritarianism, wishful thinking and other distortions of thinking. We must strive for maximum creativity to generate new ideas and to test them rigorously with science and reason. I want deep democracy that integrates the true diversity of human experience. Masculine and feminine, individual and group, authoritarian and libertarian, spiritual and secular. I want transpartisan, mature, integrating politics and wise leadership.'

'What are you doing to stop global warming?'

'By far the most important thing I can do is to put a massive global effort into discovering and operationalising clean, sustainable, cheap, abundant and secure energy. I'm not sure that I believe in global warming. Part of me does, part of me doesn't. It's not fully within my control because the rest of the world's population have taken on science, industry and technology and they're strongly motivated to develop themselves. They're less inclined to focus on the environment because they've other more immediate priorities. If global warming turns out to be real and as dramatic as some suggest, we will soon get some very direct feedback from nature to which will have no choice but to respond.'

Seth asked, 'West, what wounds do you need to heal?'

'First, I'd like to thank Seth for looking after me in hospital when I wasn't well. Please give him and the rest of the Bernie Rosen Unit a round of applause.' Seth blushed but beamed with a broad smile. 'Racism, patriarchy and feminism. We need to heal the wounds of abuse, trauma, poor parenting, violence and crime. We need to heal the wounds of low self-esteem, low confidence, lack of boundaries. We need to heal the wounds of past conflicts, imperialism and slavery. Above all, we need to heal the wound of our own dehumanisation.'

Some of those who had been booing earlier were now cheering.

'What threats do you need to address?' asked Mr Hagel, US Defense Secretary.

'Hi Chuck. A major risk is the United States being unwilling or unable to maintain and assert its full spectrum military dominance in the world. The last time one of my great Empires did that, the British, that led to two World Wars. I'd like to avoid a repeat of that if I can. I'm worried about the insecurity and unsustainability of my energy, resources, water and food supplies. Unhealthy diets and lifestyle. Integration of migrants and minorities. Terrorism. Destabilising balance of geopolitical power. Insufficient children to sustain our population, economy or services. Pandemics. Drug resistance. Loss of biodiversity. Bioterrorism. Cyberterrorism. Rising authoritarianism and the invasion of privacy. Religious fundamentalism. Unsustainable debt, unsustainable liabilities. Trade imbalance. Rising inequality. Reducing social mobility. Many more.

'Can I have total freedom now?'

'All humans must have the freedom to live their lives according to their own wishes. Freedom of thought, speech, movement, assembly, religion, sexuality, freedom to pursue a livelihood and trade and to live a lifestyle of their choice. Freedom requires us to accept a degree of conflict, chaos, uncertainty, diversity and disagreement. Therefore it has to be held within a safe container of law, boundaries and discipline; freedom under the law. You cannot violate the freedoms of others. For example, you cannot steal others' property. Your freedom of religion cannot allow you to impose that on someone who does not share you religion.'

'How can you handle the huge diversity of opinions within yourself?'

'I want a huge diversity of opinions and experience. Humanity is complex and the world is ever more complex. I want to integrate the best, most positive strands of all opinions with wise leadership, organisation and democracy.

'The lady there in the black top with the grey hair,' I said, pointing.

'What's your most painful experience?'

'Dehumanisation. Losing sight of our heart and spirit. The misuse of science, reason and capitalism have led to the loss of humanity. We've divided mind from body, head from heart, instinct from logic and masculine from feminine. I want to come back to life, after 10,000 years of development, to reconnect with human nature, to maximise human potential. I intend to bring Western Civilization back to life, placing consciousness, life, love, being and experience at its centre. It isn't an external object written on paper or in a box. It's a living thing. Human beings are part of nature. I am nature. We are natural. I'd like to make sure that we honour that in science, leadership, medicine.'

'What's the point of science if it has dehumanised us?'

'Scientific method, like democracy is an ideal which we are continuously evolving and adapting. Objectivity, rationality and reductionism must be integrated with life, consciousness, subjectivity, wisdom and intuition to enable us to get to a deeper lever of truth and to explore complex phenomena like the mind, economics, life and healing.'

'When are you going to drop your ego?'

'I don't think that we should. The ego is a necessary part of human nature. We need to have a drive to live, strive, compete, survive and thrive. It would be good if we were more conscious, wiser, less selfish, more aware of our connection with others, less concerned with status and materialism. This is a matter for individuals who will do that when they feel ready and when that's appropriate to their situation and stage of development. We should accept people as they are and deal with that rather than be frustrated that the world isn't the way we would like it to be.'

'How do you feel that while you do your best, you get so much criticism?'

'All leaders have to accept that. It's easy to sit on the sidelines, without responsibility, and criticise those with authority and responsibility. Some people do that in a constructive, empowering and helpful way. Others do it in a self-righteous, destructive, self-serving and abusive way. A wise leader needs some psychological armour and self-confidence. Often people criticise from a wounded place. It helps not to rub salt in their wounds or to respond with anger to their anger because that's not constructive.'

'What would the world be like without you?'

'If I never existed, human beings would still have developed science, democracy and capitalism. However they would have taken different forms, different assumptions and played out differently. The rate of progress would have been slower and taken longer. We're global now – all in the same boat. We sink or swim together.'

'What are your earliest memories?'

'I can faintly remember Ancient Greece, Rome and early pagan times. I can remember much of my Christian and mediaeval history. I don't have a conscious memory of my hundreds of thousands of years as hunter gatherers although I can get a sense of it by meeting the last few people still living at that level of existence. Biologically, we're still the same. We can get in touch with our instincts if we're willing.'

'Do you mind that you're held to a higher standard than the rest?'

'At times, it can be irritating but, I don't mind because I set those high standards myself and so I must expect others to hold me to them even when they don't themselves. That helps me to keep me on my toes, being the best I can be.'

'Science has created a spiritual void. Can you rediscover spirit?'

'Yes. Spirituality and some religions are growing fast within me. Christianity may yet rejuvenate itself. I've objectified things for the purpose of science while in the East there's still the concept of interconnection and the space between us. A long time ago my scientists realised that matter could be perceived as both waves and particles but the actual reality is probably well beyond our consciousness. Science is just getting started, there's lots more to come.'

'Why are you so violent?' asked a man with a 'Peace' T-shirt.

'I'm not more or less violent than other current cultures. If it appears more violent, it's because I'm larger, more spread out and have been the hegemonic power for several hundred years, and so naturally I'm the one with whom any challengers will seek to conflict. I'm also the one who maintains order. Even taking into account the Second

World War, First World War and other recent wars, the number of deaths as a percentage of population is less now than ever before. Human beings are safer and more peaceful now than they've ever been. Humans have a bias towards noticing negative events. The trend is towards ever greater peace.'

'Who hurt you?' said a Danish lady with long grey hair.

'In my early days, when I was smaller and weaker than my competitors, I was hurt by other powers. By far the majority of my suffering has come from within. It's best to focus upon the present and future, to forgive the past rather than nursing resentments and victim mentality.'

'You're dying. How shall we grieve for you?' said an American lady.

'Don't book the funeral just yet! I'm thriving more than ever. I'm evolving. I think you associate 'the West' with parts of me that you consider old or redundant, and you identify with parts of me that you consider novel and enlightened. It's all me. I'm adapting and changing, as ever.'

'Where did your joy and ecstasy go?'

'Life has become too serious, too formalised, too work-orientated and not as spontaneous and natural as it was when we lived a more simple life. We should reconnect with our humanity, align with human nature and the joy will return.'

'What has the enlightenment cost you?'

'Great question. The loss of our traditional culture of folktales, mysticism, community, connection to the land, intuition and spiritual beliefs. Peace of mind. God. Dehumanisation!'

'What are your goals?'

'To survive, spread and thrive. To be the very best I can, to maximise human potential, freedom, security and happiness.'

'Why be Western Civilization, not "global civilization"?'

'Human beings are the same the world over. If you want to address the challenges of life from healthcare to family to security, it no longer makes sense to look only at the national level because the same processes are going on much more widely. My consciousness has spread globally but there still are real differences in culture and life conditions around the world. If I did assume that I represented global civilization, I'd rightly be called arrogant and imperialistic.'

'What do you love about yourself?'

'I love learning, exploring, creating. I love being alive, spreading and growing. I love challenges and opportunities. I love this fantastic planet which is my home and I love humans, the most amazing social animal, conscious beings. Human beings are more able to live to their full potential and choose their own destiny than ever. I know that we can go far together and we're only at the start. Our limitation is our imagination, self-loathing, woundedness and victim mentality.'

'How do you feel about your loss of power?'

'I'm stronger than ever. You can find me in every country in the world and in most people in the world to some extent. Britain, France and America have lost relative power as a result of their own dramatic success in spreading me around the world. All the other people of the world now have the opportunity to grow their own potential, learn and empower themselves. Britain in 2015 no longer rules the world in a way that it did in 1870 and America no longer dominates the world like it did in 1960, but their people are better off than ever in most senses. I, Western Civilization, am more powerful than ever. Principally it's power by attraction. I spread because people choose me. Imperialism spread me by force, migration, trade, missionaries and learning. People liked me, learnt from me and adopted me as their own. Japan was defeated in a ferocious war but, after the war, they've chosen me and now a powerful part of me. The Chinese have chosen parts of me, the science, the capitalism, increasingly the rule of law and due process, and look how it has unleashed their potential.'

'What does the West need to do to survive and thrive?'

'I need to sort out my relationship with the planet. Sustainability is a matter of life and death. We need food, water, clean air, physical security, and an amazingly complex system to sustain our way of life. I must harness my technology and creativity to make sure that I can sustain myself with resources on this planet or to stretch out into the universe and find other resources. There are some serious risks from weapons of mass destruction. I need to attend to the wounds myself and I need to step up to use my strengths to help the marginalised and damaged parts of the world become happier, more stable integrated, less fearful. Help them reach their potential while having strong boundaries myself.'

'How can you become more adaptive?'

'Get every human access to the Internet, to get everyone connected and make all my knowledge, support and education available to everybody. Support for entrepreneurs, creators, visionaries. Be alert to wounds, suffering and pain and heal them. Have strong boundaries and discipline. Ensure fairness and justice. Have fun, keep an open mind, challenge groupthink. Evolve and experiment with democracy and capitalism. Make the justice system work quickly, fairly and to a high standard. Improve my diet and fitness. Practice mindfulness, gratitude and generosity. Practice forgiveness. Cut out all the limiting beliefs like zero-sum thinking, wishful thinking and victim mentality. Promote a culture of empowerment, coaching, love, support and challenge to help everyone fulfil their potential. Reconnect sex with life. Value children and old people. Make work fun.'

'How can you include all humans in your story – in your success?'

I'd love to do that. We must honour and cherish the different tribal stories, personal stories and family stories but we need a common, unifying human story. This is evolving fast through creativity and dialogue, through films, books, art and democracy.'

'What's your purpose?'

'My purpose is to survive and thrive because that's what living things do. My higher purpose is to maximise human potential, to enable human beings to thrive, to explore, to learn, grow and be the very best they can.'

'Why are you letting consumerism kill you?'

'It's an immature phase. See it in the context of one million years of evolution. We should put our energy into creative solutions rather than a blame game. We've become defined by objects and possessions. People will realise when they're out of balance and will seek a more meaningful, purposeful and spiritual existence. When emerging from poverty into modernity, they have the right to let their hair down for a while.'

'What do you say to the people who hate you and want you to die?'

'Invite them to sit down with me. I'd listen carefully as they released their anger and rage and help them heal the pain in their hearts. Where appropriate I would apologise and make amends. I'd like turn their anger into a powerful, constructive force for a better future.'

'Where we're fighting, what are we fighting for?'

'A mixture of motives. Security, control, resources, self-defence, self-preservation, to neutralise and minimise perceived threats. Living organisms need to protect themselves and I'm no different. Weakness invites attack. If you don't defend your boundaries, you get violated. Human beings are conscious, loving beings and competitive, territorial tribal animals. We must integrate all the parts as best we can. My greatest strength is attractiveness of my best parts, my highest ideals and most effective ideas. That's the best guarantor of my future.'

'How do we make our civilization so attractive that others choose to align with us, emulate us and synergise with us?'

'Be as successful as we can and inspire others to join us. We need healthy boundaries. We need to be open to allow in those who want to join us and become part of us. We need to respect that others may choose to be separate, choose to be different and allow them that space.'

'What's the minimum someone must believe to belong to the West?'

'Every human being, body and mind, is sacred and should be respected. Life is sacred. You must respect the freedom of the individual, the right of people to choose their beliefs, ideas, faith, family and relationships. You must respect their rights and properties of others. You must respect people's right to express themselves, to be who they choose to be. You must respect the right of others to engage in debate, discussion and politics. You treat others with a basic level of respect, not to cause harm to others, to respect the rights of others, not to kill others.'

'Where will you be in 30 years?'

'I will have sorted out my debt, balance of trade and unfunded liabilities. Capitalism will be humane, aligned with life and in service of the whole. Democracy will be deeper and wiser. Religions will have found a way to be authentically religious in a modern, pluralistic democracy. I will be comfortable with setting and enforcing my boundaries. The flow of immigrants will have dramatically slowed as the rest of the world becomes more prosperous and free. I'll be working hard to attract immigrants because I'll be feeling the pressure of supporting a large elderly population with a diminished young population. I'll be seeing the first signs of some fantastic new technologies, new sources of energy, and new space exploration which will lift the human spirit. The culture war of the past will have faded as those generations age into retirement and the younger, more optimistic, integrated and collaborative generations step into their adulthood. Medicine will be more holistic, focused on healthy lifestyle, health promotion and illness prevention. We will be eating healthy, natural food. We will have got past the gender wars and be much more comfortable with the strengths of the masculine and feminine, whatever forms those take. We will honour the family and the role of parenthood, balancing the needs of the family with the economy more effectively. We'll be seeing the benefits of experiments in justice, crime and punishment, finally getting some traction with rehabilitation and crime prevention. Victim mentality will be losing its dominant position and people will be more empowered and responsible. Education will look unrecognisable from its current top-down industrial model. It will be more diverse, online, creative and fun.'

'How can we accelerate your sustainable evolution?'

'Take responsibility for yourself, your family and community. Do your best to flourish, show leadership, creativity and live the best life you can. Contribute to democracy, creativity, entrepreneurship, care and love. Speak the truth, take responsibility for your thoughts, values and attitude. Generate a positive atmosphere. Ask challenging, empowering questions of others and yourself. See opportunities and grasp them. Integrate all your parts, heal your wounds and align with your purpose.'

A Canadian man called out from behind an armed policeman.

'Imagine you were given a magic wand and with it you could create Heaven on Earth. What would Heaven on Earth be for you?'

'Great question Martin! Human beings would know the power of that question and ask it frequently!'

An American man with grey hair called out, 'Who is going to own space?'

'Hi Buzz. When the last Magna Carta was written in 1215, no one knew the Americas existed and they barely knew where Africa, India and China were. Now we are familiar and interconnected with all of those. We don't know now what lies out there in space beyond the earth. I want to say at the outset that space and its contents are not the property of any individual, company or nation but are common to us all in service of the thriving of all life.'

'When can the rest of the world have compensation for imperialism?'

'They have had it many times over in gifts that keep giving. That question is old-fashioned, zero-sum thinking. There were transfers of wealth from colonies to colonisers, certainly. In the other direction went ideas, knowledge, technology, consciousness, resources, infrastructure, order, organisation and challenge. There were many examples of abuses and the dark side of human nature. Overall I've given the world infinitely more than I've taken from it. Where there's any legacy of past wrongdoing, I would like to heal that and do my best to support current and future potential of people the world over. I will no longer indulge victim mentality, hatred or scapegoating. I've been the most successful, most powerful civilization ever. I've been to more places than any other. So of course my flaws, limitations, mistakes and abuses are more visible and more known than those of others. Every human being, every culture, every country, every ethnicity and civilization should examine their own dark history and their own faults before blaming others. The Japanese, Chinese, Indians, Singaporeans, people of Hong Kong, Turks, Malaysians, Indonesians and the South Americans have become successful by empowering themselves, adapting, learning from me and drawing on their own strengths. Those who choose to languish in hatred, victimhood and resentment disempower themselves. I'm focused on maximising human potential.'

'How are you so good at turning a blind eye to the suffering of others?'

'Where I do that, I'm sorry. I think I'm more caring than ever. We're more aware of others suffering because of travel and communications. I would say that increasingly, human beings identify with a wider and wider circle of people. We used to identify with our family, clan or tribe. This is an ever-increasing circle. The first duty of every organism is to look after itself first, except for a mother looking after her children. The first duty of every family, tribe, nation, civilization is to look after itself. The West is more actively engaged in international development, education, security assistance, nation building than any one else.'

There were still hundreds of hands raised. West turned to me, 'James, I'm tired. That's enough. Can you wrap it up?'

I stepped forward. 'Your Majesty, distinguished guests, ladies and gentlemen, children, those watching at home, thank you all for your presence here today. I've had the privilege of getting to know West over the last nine months and I can promise you that we are in for a fascinating period now that he has stepped into full consciousness before you all.'

West stepped in again. 'I would like to thank the team who so ably supported James in his work over the last nine months. Please step up Suki, Joyce, Jean and Seth.'

After a lot of cheering and clapping by the crowd the others filed self-consciously onto the stage, blinking in the lights. The applause rolled on and on. While it did so, Suki yelled into my ear.

'The answer is yes.'

'Yes, what?' I shouted over the appreciative noise of the crowd.

'You introduced me to the US President as your fiancée. You forgot to pop the question first! The answer is yes.'

My heart gushed and I looked into her eyes to check that she wasn't joking. Her expression was calm and composed and infinitely loving. I held Suki close and kissed her passionately. The crowd erupted into applause and the press corps set off a fusillade of camera flashes.

'You can still get out of it if you have second thoughts tomorrow,' she yelled. 'Only a few thousand lip readers know.'

'No chance,' I laughed 'You're mine now.'

West seemed to know exactly what had occurred. He was gazing at us across the stage with exactly the same fathomless love that I had seen in Suki's face. What was the phrase he had used in his speech to the world? *You are within me and I am within you.* I had heard him say similar things before, but now, for the first time, I really felt I understood what he meant.

THE FUTURE OF WESTERN CIVILIZATION SERIES 1

The Future of Western Civilization Series 1 is a series of interviews by Dr Nicholas Beecroft with visionary leaders. It is available as paperbacks, ebooks and video. www.futureofwesterncivilization.com

Future of Western Civilization Series 1, Book 1
Introduction to the Series Dr Nicholas Beecroft interviewed by Melanie Mortiboys
British Patriotism *A Newcomer's Perspective-William Nkata Masembe*
The Next Big Shift *From Machine to Living System-Dr Nicholas Beecroft*
Global Simultaneous Policy Making *Bottom-Up Global Policy-John Bunzl*
The Future of Capitalism *Getting What We Really Want-Jon Freeman*
Transpartisan Politics *The Power of Integrating Diversity-Joseph McCormick*
Creating Heaven on Earth *Taking Small Steps in the Right Direction-Martin Rutte*
Bonds, Fields and Intentions *Culture Catches Up with Science-Lynne McTaggart*
Leadership with Integrity *How to be True to Yourself-Dr Mary Gentile*
Wisdom *Lost and Rediscovered-Professor Jim Garrison*
The Living Universe *Bringing Science, Finance and Society to Life-Dr Elisabet Sahtouris*
Organizational Democracy *10 Steps to Democratic Culture and Leadership-Traci Fenton*

Future of Western Civilization Series 1, Book 2
The West is Best *Insights from the PR Man to the Stars-Howard Bloom*
Evolutionary Enlightenment *Living from your Creative Impulse-Andrew Cohen*
Renaissance 2 *Catalyzing the Second Renaissance-Dr Robin Wood*
Positive Patriotism *The Evolving British-Chris Parish*
The Master Code *The Theory that Explains Everything-Dr Don Beck*

Future of Western Civilization Series 1, Book 3
Generational Cycles *Predicting the Future-Neil Howe*
Catalyzing Change *Engaging Emergence-Peggy Holman*
Successful Nations *Harnessing the Aspirations of the People-Richard Barrett*
Resurrecting Christianity *Rising to the Challenges of a Complex World-Bishop Michael Nazir-Ali*
German Identity & Patriotism *Healing the Wounds, Integrating the Shadow-Adrian Wagner*
Compassionate Healthcare *Re-humanising Medicine-Dr Robin Youngson*
New Money *The Evolution of Finance-Jordan MacLeod*

Future of Western Civilization Series 1, Book 4
Unleashing Human Potential *Alignment, Energetics and Connection-Soleira Green*
Wise Democracy *Discovering Solutions to Intractable Problems-Jim Rough*
Mindfulness *Applications for Leaders and Clinicians-Dr Nicholas Beecroft*
Evolutionary Leadership *Conscious Leadership in an Age of Transition-Peter Merry*
The Future of Europe *A View from Inside the European Union-Helen Titchen Beeth*
Ending the Culture War *A Devoted Conservative & Die-hard Liberal Make Friends-Phil Neisser & Jacob Hess*
Future of Western Civilization Progress Report Dr Nicholas Beecroft interviewed by Melanie Mortiboys

THE NEW MAGNA CARTA

A PSYCHIATRIST'S PRESCRIPTION FOR WESTERN CIVILIZATION

If you enjoyed *Analyze West*, please consider getting a copy of *The New Magna Carta: A Psychiatrist's Prescription for Western Civilization* (2015).

http://newmagnacarta.org

CONTACT & SOCIAL MEDIA

Thank you so much for reading *Analyze West*. Please do get in touch to share your comments. Join the mailing list to stay in touch.
www.analyzewest.com

www.futureofwesterncivilization.com
www.linkedin.com/pub/nicholas-beecroft/5/1b9/175
twitter.com/Future_of_West
www.facebook.com/groups/438696922812104/

WRITE A REVIEW

If you enjoyed *Analyze West*, please tell your friends, share it on social media and write some reviews. It'll help others decide whether to get a copy for themselves. If you found any errors, please contact me directly.

Best wishes,
Nicholas